W9-BBC-102

THE CONTEMPORARY SHAKESPEARE SERIES

VOLUME I

Hamlet
*
Julius Caesar
*
The Merchant of Venice
*
A Midsummer Night's Dream
*
Romeo and Juliet
*
The Tempest

Edited by A. L. Rowse

Modern Text with Introduction

UNIVERSITY PRESS OF AMERICA

University Press of America,™ Inc.

4720 Boston Way
Lanham, MD 20706

3 Henrietta Street
London WC2E 8LU England

Library of Congress Cataloging in Publication Data

Shakespeare, William, 1564-1616.
   The contemporary Shakespeare.

   Contents: v. 1. Hamlet. Julius Caesar. Merchant of
Venice. A midsummer night's dream. Romeo and Juliet.
The tempest.
   I. Rowse, A.L. (Alfred Leslie), 1903-
II. Title.
PR2754.R67   1984b   822.3'3   84-5105
ISBN 0-8191-3908-4

Hamlet

WHY A CONTEMPORARY SHAKESPEARE?

The starting point of my project was when I learned both from television and in education, that Shakespeare is being increasingly dropped in schools and colleges because of the difficulty of the language. In some cases, I gather, they are given just a synopsis of the play, then the teacher or professor embroiders from his notes.

This is deplorable. We do not want Shakespeare progressively dropped because of superfluous difficulties that can be removed, skilfully, conservatively, keeping to every line of the text. Nor must we look at the question statically, for this state of affairs will worsen as time goes on and we get further away from the language of 400 years ago—difficult enough in all conscience now.

We must begin by ridding our mind of prejudice, i.e. we must not pre-judge the matter. A friend of mine on New York radio said that he was 'appalled' at the very idea; but when he heard my exposition of what was proposed he found it reasonable and convincing.

Just remember, I do not need it myself: *I live in the Elizabethan age*, Shakespeare's time, and have done for years, and am familiar with its language, and his. But even for me there are still difficulties—still more for modern people, whom I am out to help.

Who, precisely?

Not only students at school and in college, but all readers of Shakespeare. Not only those, but all viewers of the plays, in the theatre, on radio and television—actors too, who increasingly find pronunciation of the words difficult, particularly obsolete ones—and there are many, besides the difficulty of accentuation.

The difficulties are naturally far greater for non-English-speaking peoples. We must remember that he is our greatest asset, and that other peoples use him a great deal in learning our language. There are no Iron Curtains for him—though, during Mao's Cultural Revolution in China, he was prohibited. Now that the ban has been lifted, I learn that the Chinese in thousands flock to his plays.

Now, a good deal that was grammatical four hundred years ago is positively ungrammatical today. We might begin by removing what is no longer good grammar.

For example: plural subjects with a verb in the singular:

'*Is* Bushy, Green and the earl of Wiltshire dead?' Any objection to replacing 'is' correctly by 'are'? Certainly not. I notice that some modern editions already correct—

These high wild hills and rough uneven ways
Draws out our miles and makes them wearisome

to 'draw' and 'make', quite sensibly. Then, why not go further and regularise this Elizabethan usage to modern, consistently throughout?

Similarly with archaic double negatives—'Nor shall you not think neither'—and double comparatives: 'this is more worser than before.' There are hundreds of instances of what is now just bad grammar to begin with.

There must be a few thousand instances of superfluous subjunctives to reduce to simplicity and sense. Today we use the subjunctive occasionally after 'if', when we say 'if it be'. But we mostly say today 'if it is'. Now Shakespeare has hundreds of subjunctives, not only after if, but after though, although, unless, lest, whether, until, till, etc.

I see no point whatever in retaining them. They only add superfluous trouble in learning English, when the great appeal of our language as a world-language is precisely that it has less grammar to learn than almost any. Russian is unbelievably complicated. Inflected languages—German is like Latin in this respect—are really rather backward; it has been a great recommendation that English has been more progressive in this respect in simplifying itself.

Now we can go further along this line: keep a few subjunctives, if you must, but reduce them to a minimum.

Let us come to the verb. It is a great recommendation to modern English that our verbs are comparatively simple to decline—unlike even French, for example. But in the Elizabethan age there was a great deal more of it, and some of it inconsistent in modern usage. Take Shakespeare's,

'Where is thy husband now? Where be thy brothers?'
Nothing is lost by rendering this as we should today:

Where is your husband now? Where are your brothers?

And so on.

The second and third person singular—all those shouldsts and wouldsts, wilts and shalts, haths and doths, have become completely obsolete. Here a vast simplification may be effected—with no loss as far as I can see, and with advantages from several points of view.

For example, 'st' at the end of a word is rather difficult to say, and more difficult even for us when it is succeeded by a word beginning with 'th'. Try saying, 'Why usurpedst thou this?' Foreigners have the greatest difficulty in pronouncing our 'th' anyway—many never succeed in getting it round their tongues. Many of these tongue-twisters even for us proliferate in Shakespeare, and I see no objection to getting rid of *superfluous* difficulties. Much easier for people to say, 'Why did you usurp this?'—the same number of syllables too.

This pre-supposes getting rid of almost all thous and thees and thines. I have no objection to keeping a few here and there, if needed for a rhyme—even then they are sometimes not necessary.

Some words in Shakespeare have changed their meaning into the exact opposite: we ought to remove that stumbling-block. When Hamlet says, 'By heaven, I'll make a ghost of him that *lets* me', he means *stops*; and we should replace it by stops, or holds me. Shakespeare regularly uses the word 'owe' where we should say own: the meaning has changed. Take a line like, 'Thou dost here usurp the name thou ow'st not': we should say, 'You do here usurp the name you own not', with the bonus of getting rid of two ugly 'sts'.

The word 'presently' in the Elizabethan age did not mean in a few minutes or so, but immediately—instantly has the same number of syllables. 'Prevent' then had its Latin meaning, to go before, or forestall. Shakespeare frequently uses the word 'still' for always or ever.

Let us take the case of many archaic forms of words, simple one-syllable words that can be replaced without the slightest difference to the scansion: 'sith' for since, 'wrack' for wreck, 'holp' for helped, 'writ' for wrote, 'brake' for broke, 'spake' for spoke, 'bare' for bore, etc.

These give no trouble, nor do a lot of other words that he uses: 'repeal' for recall, 'reproof' for disproof, 'decline' for incline. A few words do give more trouble. The linguistic scholar, C. T. Onions, notes that it is sometimes difficult to give the precise meaning Shakespeare attaches to the word 'conceit'; it usually means thought, or fancy, or concept. I do not know that it ever has our meaning; actually the word 'conceited' with him means ingenious or fantastic, as 'artificial' with Elizabethans meant artistic or ingenious.

There is a whole class of words that have completely gone out, of which moderns do not know the meaning. I find no harm in replacing the word 'coistrel' by rascal, which is what it means—actually it has much the same sound—or 'coil' by fuss; we find 'accite' for summon, 'indigest' for formless. Hamlet's word 'reechy', for the incestuous kisses of his mother and her brother-in-law, has gone out of use: the nearest word, I suppose, would be reeky, but filthy would be a suitable modern equivalent.

In many cases it is extraordinary how little one would need to change, how conservative one could be. Take Hamlet's famous soliloquy, 'To be or not to be.' I find only two words that moderns would not know the meaning of, and one of those we might guess:

> . . .When he himself might his *quietus* make
> With a bare bodkin? Who would *fardels* bear. . .

'Quietus' means put paid; Elizabethans wrote the Latin 'quietus est' at the bottom of a bill that was paid—when it was—to say that it was settled. So that you could replace 'quietus' by settlement, same number of syllables, though not the same accentuation; so I would prefer to use the word acquittance, which has both.

'Fardels' means burdens; I see no objection to rendering, 'Who would burdens bear'—same meaning, same number of syllables, same accent: quite simple. I expect all the ladies to know what a bodkin is: a long pin, or skewer.

Now let us take something really difficult—perhaps the most difficult passage to render in all Shakespeare. It is the virtuoso comic piece describing all the diseases that horseflesh is heir to, in *The Taming of the Shrew*. The horse is Petruchio's. President Reagan tells me that this is the one Shakespearean part that he played—and a very gallant one, too. In Britain last year we saw a fine performance of his on horseback in Windsor Park along-side of Queen Elizabeth II—very familiar ground to William Shakespeare and Queen Elizabeth I, as we know from *The Merry Wives of Windsor*.

Here is a headache for us: Petruchio's horse (not President Reagan's steed) was 'possessed with the glanders, and like to mose in the chine; troubled with the lampass, infected with the fashions, full of windgalls, sped with spavins, rayed with the yellows, past cure of the fives, stark spoiled with the staggers, begnawn with the bots; swayed in the back, and shoulder-shotten; near-legged before, and with a half-cheeked bit, and a headstall of sheep's leather', etc.

What on earth are we to make of that? No doubt it raised a laugh with Elizabethans, much more familiarly acquainted with horseflesh than we are; but I doubt if Hollywood was able to produce a nag for Reagan that qualified in all these respects.

Now, even without his horsemanship, we can clear one fence at the outset: 'mose in the chine'. Pages of superfluous commentary have been devoted to that word 'mose'. There was no such Elizabethan word: it was simply a printer's misprint for 'mourn', meaning dripping or running; so it suggests a running sore. You would need to consult the *Oxford English Dictionary*, compiled on historical lines, for some of the words, others like 'glanders' country folk know and we can guess.

So I would suggest a rendering something like this: 'possessed with glanders, and with a running sore in the back; troubled in the gums, and infected in the glands; full of galls in the fetlocks and swollen in the joints; yellow with jaundice, past cure of the strangles; stark spoiled with the staggers, and gnawed by worms; swayed in the back and shoulder put out; near-legged before, and with a half-cheeked bit and headgear of sheep's leather', etc. That at least makes it intelligible.

Oddly enough, one encounters the greatest difficulty with the least important words and phrases, Elizabethan expletives and malapropisms, or salutations like God 'ild you, Godden, for God shield you, Good-even, and so on. 'God's wounds' was Elizabeth I's favourite swearword; it appears frequently enough in Victorian novels as 'Zounds'— I have never heard anyone use it. The word 'Marry!', as in the phrase 'Marry come up!' has similarly gone out, though a very old gentleman at All Souls, Sir Charles Oman, had heard the phrase in the back-streets of Oxford just after the 1914-18 war. 'Whoreson' is frequent on the lips of coarse fellows in Shakespeare: the equivalent in Britain today would be bloody, in America (I suppose) s.o.b.

Relative pronouns, who and which: today we use who for persons, which for things. In Elizabethan times the two were hardly distinguished and were interchangeable. Provokingly Shakespeare used the personal relative 'who' more frequently for impersonal objects, rivers, buildings, towns; and then he no less frequently uses 'which' for persons. This calls out to be regularised for the modern reader.

Other usages are more confusing. The word 'cousin'

was used far more widely by the Elizabethans for their kin: it included nephews, for instance. Thus it is confusing in the English History plays to find a whole lot of nephews—like Richard III's, whom he had made away with in the Tower of London—referred to and addressed as cousins. That needs regularisation today, in the interests of historical accuracy and to get the relationship clear. The word 'niece' was sometimes used of a grandchild—in fact this is the word Shakespeare used in his will for his little grand-daughter Elizabeth, his eventual heiress who ended up as Lady Barnard, leaving money to her poor relations the Hathaways at Stratford. The Latin word *neptis*, from which niece comes also meant grandchild—Shakespeare's grammar-school education at Stratford was in Latin, and this shows you that he often thought of a word in terms of its Latin derivation.

Malapropisms, misuse of words, sometimes mistaking of meanings, are frequent with uneducated people, and sometimes not only with those. Shakespeare transcribed them from lower-class life to raise a laugh, more frequently than any writer for the purpose. They are an endearing feature of the talk of Mistress Quickly, hostess of the Boar's Inn in East Cheapside, and we have no difficulty in making out what she means. But in case some of us do, and for the benefit of non-native English speakers, I propose the correct word in brackets afterwards: 'You have brought her into such a canaries [quandary]. . .and she's as fartuous [virtuous] a civil, modest wife. . .'

Abbreviations: Shakespeare's text is starred—and in my view, marred—by innumerable abbreviations, which not only look ugly on the page but are sometimes difficult to pronounce. It is not easy to pronounce 'is't', or 'in't', or 'on't', and some others: if we cannot get rid of them altogether they should be drastically reduced. Similarly with 'i'th'', 'o'th'', with which the later plays are liberally bespattered, for in the or of the.

We also have a quite unnecessary spattering of apostrophes in practically all editions of the plays—''d' for the past participle, e.g. 'gather'd'. Surely it is much better to regularise the past participle 'ed', e.g. gathered; and when the last syllable is, far less frequently, to be pronounced, then accent it, gatherèd.

This leads into the technical question of scansion, where a practising poet is necessary to get the accents right, to help the reader, and still more the actor. Most people will hardly notice that, very often, the frequent ending of words in 'ion', like reputation, has to be pronounced with two syllables at the end. So I propose to accent this when necessary, e.g. reputatiòn. I have noticed the word 'ocean' as tri-syllabic, so I accent it, to help, oceàn. A number of words which to us are monosyllables were pronounced as two: hour, fire, tired; I sometimes accent or give them a dieresis, either hoùr or fïre. In New England speech words like prayèr, thëre, are apt to be pronounced as two syllables—closer to Elizabethan usage (as with words like gotten) than is modern speech in Britain.

What I notice in practically all editions of Shakespeare's plays is that the editors cannot be relied on to put the accents in the right places. One play edited by a well known Shakespearean editor had, I observed, a dozen accents placed over the wrong syllables. This is understandable, for these people don't write poetry and do not know how to scan. William Shakespeare knew all about scanning, and you need to be both familiar with Elizabethan usage and a practising traditional poet to be able to follow him.

His earlier verse was fairly regular in scansion, mostly iambic pentameter with a great deal of rhyme. As time went on he loosened out, until there are numerous irregular lines—this leaves us much freer in the matter of modernising. Our equivalents should be rhythmically as close as possible, but a strait-jacket need be no part of the equipment. A good Shakespearean scholar tells us, 'there is no necessity for Shakespeare's lines to scan absolutely. He thought of his verse as spoken rather than written and of his rhythmic units in terms of the voice rather than the page.'

There is nothing exclusive or mandatory about my project. We can all read Shakespeare in any edition we like—in the rebarbative olde Englishe spelling of the First Folio, if we wish. Any number of conventional academic editions exist, all weighed down with a burden of notes, many of them superfluous. I propose to make most of them unnecessary—only one occasionally at the foot of very few pages. Let the text be freed of superfluous difficulties, remove obstacles to let it speak for itself, while adhering conservatively to every line.

We really do not need any more editions of the Plays on conventional lines—more than enough of those exist already. But *A Contemporary Shakespeare* on these lines—both revolutionary and conservative—should be a help to everybody all round the world—though especially for younger people, increasingly with time moving away from the language of 400 years ago.

INTRODUCTION

amlet has the events of 1599–1601 much in mind, to which Shakespeare was close, when the play was written. These were tragic in themselves, when the Earl of Essex, the brightest luminary of the Court and the most popular—

The courtier's, soldier's, scholar's, eye, tongue, sword,
The expectancy and rose of the fair state—

was tottering to destruction. In 1599 Shakespeare had written into *Henry V* a salute to Essex, hopeful of his return from the war in Ireland in triumph, but it turned out a fiasco.

Southampton was with Essex in Ireland as Lieutenant-General of Horse, from which he was demoted by the Queen. Shakespeare's affiliation was with this group, in opposition to the Queen's chief minister, Lord Burghley—whose well-known characteristics are recognizably caricatured in Polonius, not only his position as chief minister, his intelligence system but personal features. It was safe to do so, for he had died in 1598.

Significantly, there are no forward references to the Hamlet theme as with other themes in some of Shakespeare's plays. The tragic events of the end of the Queen's reign brought it to the fore in his mind, as was his instinctive way. Dominant in people's minds was the

crucial question of the succession to the throne. The
Court was riven by the in-fighting between the two fac-
tions—something was indeed 'rotten in the state of
Denmark.'

Though the character of Hamlet grew from its conception in Shakespeare's mind, as is the way with creative writers, there are obvious touches of Essex. Dover
Wilson saw this, and thought of *Hamlet* as the most
topical of the Plays: it is in truth one of them. He sums
up well Hamlet's 'sense of frustration, of infirmity of
purpose, of character inhibited from meeting the demands of destiny, of the futility of life in general and
action in particular. His melancholy and his procrasti-
nation are all of a piece.' They are all of a piece with
Essex too, who was quite as psychotic as Hamlet. Dover
Wilson had reflected on the play to some point—unlike
most of its critics.

Everybody has to recognize Shakespeare's extended
treatment of the contemporary War of the Theatres,
between the Boys' Companies and the Men's, in Hamlet's discussion with the players. This in-fighting
dominated the theatrical situation in 1600–1, as that
around Essex did the political situation. Both are
clearly reflected in the play.

Prominent in men's minds in the war abroad was the
ding-dong struggle for the little patch of ground around
Ostend in just these years, immensely costly in lives:

> . . .to gain a little patch of ground
> That has in it no profit but the name . . .
> The imminent death of twenty thousand men . . .
> Go to their graves like beds, fight for a plot
> Whereon the numbers cannot try the cause.

This is exactly what most people were thinking at the
time: Shakespeare as usual was expressing the general

view. Indeed, a conformist, he did not go against it—
another reason for his popularity.

Many have felt that we are closer to him in this play
than any other—and, though it is too subtle a matter to
be put directly, some have seen it to have something
autobiographical about it. That is obviously true of all
that Shakespeare tells us about acting, his own profession:
he speaks not only from the actor's but the producer's
point of view. It is all most informative of contemporary conditions in the theatre: he makes it clear that
he stood for a more natural style of acting, against the
ranting and orating of earlier Elizabethan drama.

Moreover, the play is full of contemporary snatches
of phrase, songs, ballads and folklore—about ghosts, for
example. As an Elizabethan, William Shakespeare would
have believed in ghosts; an early tradition tells us that
he played the part of the Ghost here: it is a 'kingly part',
such as we are told he took in the plays. We learn that
he was a good actor, where Ben Jonson was better as an
instructor.

A Cambridge skit of the time, *The Return from Par-
nassus*, says that Shakespeare gave his junior a 'pill',
who was on the side of the Boys' against the Men's Companies, such as Shakespeare's, the Lord Chamberlain's.
This has never been identified, but to my mind it might
well occur in Hamlet's, 'O, it offends me to the soul to
hear a robustious periwig-pated fellow tear a passion to
tatters, to very rags, to split the ears of the groundlings.'
Certainly Ben Jonson was a robustious, passionate fellow. We now know that Shakespeare did not write his
plays for the groundlings, but for better-class audiences.
(See Ann Jenalee Cook's *The Privileged Playgoers of
Shakespeare's London*).

The Hamlet theme was perfectly familiar to
Shakespeare. There had been a play on the subject,

probably by Marlowe's companion, Thomas Kyd. He had written the most popular earlier revenge-play, *The Spanish Tragedy*—and *Hamlet* is a revenge-play, grandest of the *genre*. Shakespeare did not need to go all the way back to the remote 12th century Danish historian, Saxo Grammaticus, for the story. It was all there ready to hand in Belleforest's *Histoires Tragiques*. All Shakespeare had to do was to look it up for convenient details. That was his regular way, to look up a dramatic story to shape up what was in his mind at the moment—so that a great deal of recondite hunting for 'sources' is rather unnecessary. Dr. Jonson, greatest of Shakespeare critics—for he was on a level with the subject— saw how superfluous much of that was. And a good Shakespeare critic, Quiller Couch—for he was a creative writer as well as a critic—perceived that Shakespeare was often his own source and repeated a theme (as with that of Lucrece, appearing again later in *Cymbeline*).

For, of course, creative writers do not write largely out of other people's books, but out of, first, their own experience of life, its joys and griefs, hopes and fears; and secondly, out of their experience of what is going on around them at the time. This is why it is so important to know what *was* going on at the time *Hamlet* was written, to see it in contemporary terms.

Denmark, Elsinore in particular, was familiar ground to Elizabethan actors—several of their troupes had experience of playing there, and the greatest of contemporary song-writers, John Dowland, was employed at Court there for years. The play is indeed full of music. Nor is Shakespeare likely, when thinking of Ophelia's end, to have forgotten the Katherine Hamlet who was drowned in the Avon when he was a youth of sixteen— always observant, always registering everything—at Stratford.

With all these materials in his mind—the richest and most suggestive of the plays—Shakespeare proceeded to clothe them with all his experience of life and of the theatre and the power of his imagination, the richest and most powerful in the history of drama. Only think of all that is in it: the archetypal themes of brother-murder, and of a son's revulsion at his mother's faithlessness to his father; the searing bitterness of his treatment of Ophelia *because* he loves her but mistrusts whether she is not being used as a spy on him. In contrast we have the loyal and true friendship of Hamlet and Horatio. Against that is the treachery of courtiers like Rosencrantz and Guildenstern, the Court intelligence system of both Polonius and the King, the spying; and, for comic relief of the tension, the Court-foppery of an Osric.

The quip against 'equivocation' is directed against the Jesuit doctrine of casuistry, much in the public mind then, though more was to be made of it, after the shock of Gunpowder Plot, in *Macbeth*. Even theatre has a further reflection at the end, in the macabre scene in the graveyard when the skull of the famous clown, Yorick, is thrown up. This is thought to be a reminder of Tarleton, foremost of Elizabethan clowns, a great favourite with Queen and Court: 'Where are your gibes now? Your gambols, your songs, your flashes of merriment that were wont to set the table on a roar?' On top of that is the sheer excitement of madness—or feigned madness—always so effective on the stage—the psychotic brilliance of Hamlet's brain.

Altogether, its unexampled riches make this the most wonderful play ever written. It is also the work, in all literature, that most searches and expresses the griefs of the human heart. Never more so than in the character of Hamlet himself—all summed up in his touching phrase: 'You would not think how ill all's here about my heart.'

Everything that makes a great masterpiece is here present: characterisation, dramatic suspense and excitement, poetry—and the tension relieved by comic episodes, even the macabre scene in the graveyard towards the end. At every point we have Shakespeare's sharpest and most profound reflections on life. As against its dangers and treacheries, we have the true and faithful friendship between Hamlet and Horatio.

The variety and range in the characterisation is marvellously rich: the sepulchral dignity of Hamlet's father, the Ghost; the disingenuous smoothness, the politic cleverness of the King, Claudius, Hamlet's uncle, who has kingly qualities—except that he has murdered his brother, to gain the crown and his wife. Hamlet's mother, the Queen, is very convincing, in her femininity and inability to understand either what is going on around her or her brilliant, disturbed son. She thinks he is just mad; superficial and light of heart, she hardly conceives in what she has offended. Yet she has warmth of heart, loves her son and, woman-like, had hoped to see him married to his love, Ophelia.

Ophelia is one of the most touching of all Shakespeare's characters: innocence bitterly wounded by the tragic circumstances in which she is caught, unknowing Hamlet's tragedy driven to the edge of madness, while her own reason is overthrown by her father's killing and Hamlet's deranged treatment of her. There is more heartache here—it searches the very heart and reaches into the depths of everyone's compassion.

As for Hamlet—gifted, brilliant, with such promise, but *caught* in ineluctable tragedy—he is beyond all question.

We do not need to look further into sources for *Hamlet*, or to indulge in 'criticism' of it, the most critically discussed play in the world's literature. Rather, let it speak for itself.

CHARACTERS

HAMLET, Prince of Denmark.

CLAUDIUS, King of Denmark, Hamlet's uncle.

The GHOST of the late king, Hamlet's father.

GERTRUDE, the Queen, Hamlet's mother, now wife of Claudius.

POLONIUS, councillor of State.

LAERTES, Polonius's son.

OPHELIA, Polonius's daughter.

HORATIO, friend and confidant of Hamlet.

ROSENCRANTZ, } courtiers, former schoolfellows of
GUILDENSTERN, }   Hamlet.

FORTINBRAS, Prince of Norway.

VOLTEMAND, }   Danish councillors, ambassadors to
CORNELIUS, }   Norway.

MARCELLUS, }
BARNARDO, } members of the King's Guard.
FRANCISCO, }

OSRIC, caricature of a young courtier.

REYNALDO, a servant of Polonius.

Players, A Gentleman of the court, A Priest, A Grave-digger, A Sexton, A Captain in Fortinbras's army, English Ambassadors, Lords, Ladies, Soldiers, Messengers, and Attendants.

Act I

SCENE I
Elsinore. The Castle battlements.

Enter BARNARDO *and* FRANCISCO, *two Sentinels.*

BAR. Who's there?

FRAN. Nay, answer me. Stand and unfold yourself.

BAR. Long live the King!

FRAN. Barnardo?

BAR. He.

FRAN. You come most carefully upon your hour.

BAR. 'Tis now struck twelve. Get you to bed,
Francisco.

FRAN. For this relief much thanks. 'Tis bitter cold,
And I am sick at heart.

BAR. Have you had quiet guard?

FRAN. Not a mouse stirring.

BAR. Well, good night.
If you do meet Horatio and Marcellus,
The rivals of my watch, bid them make haste.

FRAN. I think I hear them.

Enter HORATIO *and* MARCELLUS.

                    Stand, ho! Who is there?

HOR. Friends to this ground.

MAR.   And liegemen to the Dane.

FRAN. Give you good night.

MAR. O, farewell honest soldier. Who has relieved
you?

FRAN.   Barnardo has my place. Give you good
    night.   *Exit.*

MAR.   Holla, Barnardo!

BAR.   Say, what, is Horatio there?

HOR.   A piece of him.

BAR.   Welcome, Horatio. Welcome, good Marcellus.

HOR.   What, has this thing appeared again tonight?

BAR.   I have seen nothing.

MAR.   Horatio says 'tis but our fantasy,
    And will not let belief take hold of him,
    Touching this dreaded sight twice seen of us.
    Therefore I have entreated him along
    With us to watch the minutes of this night,
    That if again this apparition comes,
    He may approve our eyes and speak to it.

HOR.   Tush, it will not appear.

BAR.   Sit down awhile,
    And let us once again assail your ears,
    That are so fortified against our story,
    What we have two nights seen.

HOR.   Well, sit we down.
    And let us hear Barnardo speak of this.

BAR.   Last night of all,
    When yon same star that's westward from the pole,
    Had made its course to illume that part of heaven
    Where now it burns, Marcellus and myself,
    The bell then beating one—

Enter GHOST.

MAR.   Peace, break off. Look where it comes again.

BAR.   In the same figure like the King that's dead.

MAR.   You are a scholar, speak to it, Horatio.

BAR.   Looks he not like the King? Mark it, Horatio.

HOR.   Most like. It harrows me with fear and wonder.

BAR.   It would be spoken to.

MAR.   Question it, Horatio.

HOR.   What are you that usurp this time of night,
Together with that fair and warlike form
In which the majesty of buried Denmark
Did sometime march? By heaven, I charge you
speak.

MAR.   It is offended.

BAR.   See, it stalks away.

HOR.   Stay, speak, speak, I charge you
speak.   *Exit Ghost.*

MAR.   'Tis gone and will not answer.

BAR.   How now, Horatio? You tremble and look pale.
Is not this something more than fantasy?
What think you of it?

HOR.   Before my God, I might not this believe
Without the sensible and true witness
Of my own eyes.

MAR.   Is it not like the King?

HOR.   As you are to yourself.
Such was the very armour he had on
When he the ambitious Norway combated.
So frowned he once, when in an angry parley
He smote the sledded Poles there on the ice.
It is strange.

MAR.   Thus twice before, and just at this dead hour,
With martial stalk has he gone by our watch.

HOR.   In what particular thought to work I know not,
But in the gross and scope of my opinion,
This bodes some strange eruption to our state.

MAR.   Good now; sit down, and tell me, he that
knows,
Why this same strict and most observant watch
So nightly toils the subject of the land,
And why such daily cast of brazen cannon

And foreign mart for implements of war;
Why such impress of shipwrights, whose sore task
Does not divide the Sunday from the week.
What might be toward that this sweaty haste
Does make the night joint-labourer with the day.
Who is it that can inform me?

HOR.   That can I.

At least the whisper goes so: our last King,
Whose image even but now appeared to us,
Was, as you know, by Fortinbras of Norway,
Thereto pricked on by a most emulate pride,
Dared to the combat. In which our valiant Hamlet
(For so this side of our known world esteemed him)
Did slay this Fortinbras: who, by a sealed compact
Well ratified by law and heraldry,
Did forfeit, with his life, all those his lands
Which he stood seized of to the conqueror.
Against which a moiety competent
Was gagèd by our King, which had returned
To the inheritance of Fortinbras,
Had he been vanquisher. By the same covenant
And carriage of the article designed,
His fell to Hamlet. Now, sir, young Fortinbras,
Of unimproved mettle, hot and full,
Has in the skirts of Norway here and here
Sharked up a list of lawless resolutes
For food and diet to some enterprise
That has a stomach in it. Which is no other,
As it does well appear unto our state,
But to recover of us, by strong hand
And terms compulsory, those foresaid lands
So by his father lost. And this, I take it,
Is the main motive of our preparations,
The source of this our watch, and the chief head
Of this post-haste and rummage in the land.

BAR.   I think it is no other but even so.
  Well may it sort that this portentous figure
  Comes armèd through our watch so like the King
  That was and is the question of these wars.
HOR.   A mote it is to trouble the mind's eye.
  In the most high and palmy state of Rome,
  A little ere the mightiest Julius fell,
  The graves stood tenantless and the sheeted dead
  Did squeak and gibber in the Roman streets;
  As stars with trains of fire and dews of blood,
  Disasters in the sun. And the moist star,
  Upon whose influence Neptune's empire stands,
  Was sick almost to doomsday with eclipse.
  And even the like precurse of feared events,
  As harbingers preceding still the fates
  And prologue to the omen coming on,
  Have heaven and earth together demonstrated
  Unto our climatures and countrymen.

Enter GHOST.

But soft, behold. Lo, where it comes again.
I'll cross it though it blasts me.
                                        Ghost spreads its arms.
                            Stay, illusion:
If you have any sound or use of voice,
Speak to me.
If there is any good thing to be done
That may to you do ease, and grace to me,
Speak to me.
If you are privy to your country's fate,
Which, happily, foreknowing may avoid,
O speak.
Or if you have uphoarded in your life
Extorted treasure in the womb of earth,

For which they say your spirits oft walk in death,
Speak of it, stay and speak.   *The cock crows.*
                              Stop it, Marcellus.
MAR. Shall I strike at it with my halberd now?
HOR. Do, if it will not stand.
BAR. 'Tis here.
HOR. 'Tis here.   *Exit Ghost.*
MAR. 'Tis gone.
We do it wrong, being so majestical,
To offer it the show of violence,
For it is as the air, invulnerable,
And our vain blows malicious mockery.
BAR. It was about to speak when the cock crew.
HOR. And then it started like a guilty thing
Upon a fearful summons. I have heard
The cock, that is the trumpet to the morn,
Does with his lofty and shrill-sounding throat
Awake the god of day. And at his warning,
Whether in sea or fire, in earth or air,
The extravagant and erring spirit hies
To his confine; and of the truth herein
This present object made probation.
MAR. It faded on the crowing of the cock.
Some say that ever when that season comes
Wherein our Saviour's birth is celebrated,
This bird of dawning sings then all night long;
And then, they say, no spirit dares stir abroad.
The nights are wholesome, then no planets strike,
No fairy stakes, nor witch has power to charm,
So hallowed and so gracious is that time.
HOR. So have I heard and do in part believe it.
But look, the morn in russet mantle clad
Walks o'er the dew of yon high eastward hill.
Break we our watch up, and by my advice
Let us impart what we have seen tonight
Unto young Hamlet; for upon my life

For they are actions that a man might play;
But I have that within which passes show,
These but the trappings and the suits of woe.
NG.   'Tis sweet and commendable in your nature,
   Hamlet,
To give these mourning duties to your father.
But you must know your father lost a father,
That father lost, lost his—and the survivor bound
In filial obligation for some term
To do obsequious sorrow. But to persèver
In obstinate condolement is a course
Of impious stubbornness, 'tis unmanly grief.
It shows a will most incorrect to heaven,
A heart unfortified, a mind impatient,
An understanding simple and unschooled.
For what we know must be, and is as common
As any the most vulgar thing to sense—
Why should we in our peevish opposition
Take it to heart? Fie, 'tis a fault to heaven,
A fault against the dead, a fault to nature,
To reason most absurd; whose common theme
Is death of fathers, and who still has cried
From the first corpse till he that died today,
'This must be so'. We pray you throw to earth
This unprevailing woe, and think of us
As of a father. For let the world take note
You are the most immediate to our throne,
And with no less nobility of love
Than that which dearest father bears his son
Do I impart toward you. For your intent
In going back to school in Wittenberg,
It is most retrograde to our desire,
And we beseech you bend you to remain
Here in the cheer and comfort of our eye,
Our chiefest courtier, nephew, and our son.

This spirit, dumb to us, will speak to him.
Do you consent we shall acquaint him with it
As needful in our loves, fitting our duty?
MAR.   Let's do it, I pray, and I this morning know
Where we shall find him most convenient.   *Exeunt.*

SCENE II
The Court.

Flourish. Enter Claudius KING *of Denmark,*
Gertrude the QUEEN, Councillors, POLONIUS, *his son*
LAERTES, HAMLET [*in black*].

KING.   Though yet of Hamlet our dear brother's death
   The memory is green, and that it us befitted
   To bear our hearts in grief, and our whole kingdom
   To be contracted in one brow of woe,
   Yet so far has discretion fought with nature
   That we with wisest sorrow think on him
   Together with remembrance of ourselves.
   Therefore our sometime sister, now our queen,
   The imperial jointress to this warlike state,
   Have we, as though with a defeated joy,
   With an auspicious and a dropping eye,
   With mirth in funeral and with dirge in marriage,
   In equal scale weighing delight and dole,
   Taken to wife. Nor have we herein barred
   Your better wisdoms, which have freely gone
   With this affair along. For all, our thanks.
   Now follows that you know young Fortinbras
   Holding a weak supposal of our worth,
   Or thinking by our late dear brother's death
   Our state to be disjointed out of frame,
   Colleagued with this dream of his advantage,
   He has not failed to pester us with message

Importing the surrender of those lands
Lost by his father, with all bonds of law,
To our most valiant brother. So much for him.
Now for ourself, and for this time of meeting,
Thus much the business is. We have written
To Norway, uncle of young Fortinbras—
Who, impotent, bedridden, scarcely hears
Of this his nephew's purpose—to suppress
His further gait herein, in that the levies,
The lists, and full proportions are all made
Out of his subjects. And we here dispatch
You, good Cornelius, and you, Voltemand,
For bearers of this greeting to old Norway,
Giving to you no further personal power
To business with the King more than the scope
Of these delated articles allow.
Farewell, and let your haste commend your duty.

COR. }
VOLT. }   In that, and all things, will we show our duty.

KING.   We doubt it nothing. Heartily farewell.
                    Exeunt Voltemand and Cornelius.
And now, Laertes, what's the news with you?
You told us of some suit: what is it, Laertes?
You cannot speak of reason to the Dane
And lose your voice. What would you beg, Laertes,
That shall not be my offer, not your asking?
The head is not more native to the heart,
The hand more instrumental to the mouth,
Than is the throne of Denmark to your father.
What would you have, Laertes?

LAER.   My dread lord,
Your leave and favour to return to France,
From whence—though willingly I came to Den-
   mark

To show my duty in your coronation—
Yet now I must confess, that duty done
My thoughts and wishes bend again tov
And bow them to your gracious leave ar

KING.   Have you your father's leave? Wh
   Polonius?

POL.   He has, my lord, wrung from me r
   leave
By laboursome petition, and at last
Upon his will I sealed my hard conser
I do beseech you give him leave to go.

KING   Take your fair hour, Laertes, time
And your best graces spend it at your
But now, my nephew Hamlet, and m

HAM.   A little more than kin, and less

KING.   How is it that the clouds still h

HAM.   Not so, my lord, I am too much

QUEEN.   Good Hamlet, cast your night
And let your eye look like a friend or
Do not for ever with your veilèd lids
Seek for your noble father in the dus
You know 'tis common: all that live
Passing through nature to eternity.

HAM.   Ay, madam, it is common.

QUEEN.   If it is,
Why seems it so particular with you

HAM.   Seems, madam? Nay, it is. I kn
'Tis not alone my inky cloak, good
Nor customary suits of solemn blac
Nor windy suspiration of forced bre
No, nor the fruitful river in the eye
Nor the dejected behavior of the vi
Together with all forms, moods, sh
That can denote me truly. These ir

To show my duty in your c
Yet now I must confess, th
My thoughts and wishes be
And bow them to your grac
KING. Have you your father'
     Polonius?
POL. He has, my lord, wrun
     leave
   By laboursome petition, a
   Upon his will I sealed my
   I do beseech you give him
KING Take your fair hour,
   And your best graces sper
   But now, my nephew Ha
HAM. A little more than k
KING. How is it that the c
HAM. Not so, my lord, I a
QUEEN. Good Hamlet, cas
   And let your eye look lil
   Do not for ever with yo
   Seek for your noble fath
   You know 'tis common
   Passing through nature
HAM. Ay, madam, it is c
QUEEN.
   Why seems it so partic
HAM. Seems, madam? N
   'Tis not alone my inky
   Nor customary suits o
   Nor windy suspiration
   No, nor the fruitful riv
   Nor the dejected beha
   Together with all forn
   That can denote me t

This spirit, dumb to us, will speak to him.
Do you consent we shall acquaint him with it
   As needful in our loves, fitting our duty?
MAR. Let's do it, I pray, and I this morning know
Where we shall find him most convenient. *Exeunt.*

SCENE II
The Court.

Flourish. Enter Claudius KING *of Denmark,*
Gertrude the QUEEN, *Councillors,* POLONIUS, *his son*
LAERTES, HAMLET [*in black*].

KING. Though yet of Hamlet our dear brother's death
   The memory is green, and that it us befitted
   To bear our hearts in grief, and our whole kingdom
   To be contracted in one brow of woe,
   Yet so far has discretion fought with nature
   That we with wisest sorrow think on him
   Together with remembrance of ourselves.
   Therefore our sometime sister, now our queen,
   The imperial jointress to this warlike state,
   Have we, as though with a defeated joy,
   With an auspicious and a dropping eye,
   With mirth in funeral and with dirge in marriage,
   In equal scale weighing delight and dole,
   Taken to wife. Nor have we herein barred
   Your better wisdoms, which have freely gone
   With this affair along. For all, our thanks.
   Now follows that you know young Fortinbras,
   Holding a weak supposal of our worth,
   Or thinking by our late dear brother's death
   Our state to be disjointed out of frame,
   Colleagued with this dream of his advantage,
   He has not failed to pester us with message

Importing the surrender
Lost by his father, with
To our most valiant bro
Now for ourself, and for
Thus much the busines
To Norway, uncle of yo
Who, impotent, bedrid
Of this his nephew's p
His further gait herein
The lists, and full proj
Out of his subjects. A
You, good Cornelius,
For bearers of this gre
Giving to you no furt
To business with the
Of these delated artic
Farewell, and let you

COR. ⎫
VOLT. ⎭ In that, and al

KING. We doubt it no

And now, Laertes, '
You told us of som
You cannot speak
And lose your voic
That shall not be
The head is not m
The hand more in
Than is the thron
What would you

LAER.
Your leave and fa
From whence—t
mark

For they are actions that a man might play;
But I have that within which passes show,
These but the trappings and the suits of woe.
KING. 'Tis sweet and commendable in your nature, Hamlet,
To give these mourning duties to your father.
But you must know your father lost a father,
That father lost, lost his—and the survivor bound
In filial obligation for some term
To do obsequious sorrow. But to persèver
In obstinate condolement is a course
Of impious stubbornness, 'tis unmanly grief.
It shows a will most incorrect to heaven,
A heart unfortified, a mind impatient,
An understanding simple and unschooled.
For what we know must be, and is as common
As any the most vulgar thing to sense—
Why should we in our peevish opposition
Take it to heart? Fie, 'tis a fault to heaven,
A fault against the dead, a fault to nature,
To reason most absurd; whose common theme
Is death of fathers, and who still has cried
From the first corpse till he that died today,
'This must be so'. We pray you throw to earth
This unprevailing woe, and think of us
As of a father. For let the world take note
You are the most immediate to our throne,
And with no less nobility of love
Than that which dearest father bears his son
Do I impart toward you. For your intent
In going back to school in Wittenberg,
It is most retrograde to our desire,
And we beseech you bend you to remain
Here in the cheer and comfort of our eye,
Our chiefest courtier, nephew, and our son.

QUEEN.   Let not your mother lose her prayers, Hamlet.
I pray you stay with us, go not to Wittenberg.
HAM.   I shall in all my best obey you, madam.
KING.   Why, 'tis a loving and a fair reply.
Be as ourself in Denmark. Madam, come.
This gentle and unforced accord of Hamlet
Sits smiling to my heart. In grace whereof
No jocund health that Denmark drinks today
But the great cannon to the clouds shall tell,
The King's carouse the heaven shall bruit again,
Re-speaking earthly thunder. Come away.
                    Flourish. Exeunt all but Hamlet.
HAM.   O that this too too solid flesh would melt,
Thaw and resolve itself into a dew,
Or that the Everlasting had not fixed
His canon against self-slaughter. O God! God!
How weary, stale, flat, and unprofitable
Seem to me all the uses of this world!
Fie on it, fie, 'tis an unweeded garden
That grows to seed; things rank and gross in nature
Possess it merely. That it should come to this!
But two months dead—nay, not so much, not two—
So excellent a king, that was to this
Hyperion to a satyr, so loving to my mother
That he might not permit the winds of heaven
Visit her face too roughly. Heaven and earth,
Must I remember? Why, she would hang on him
As if increase of appetite had grown
By what it fed on. And yet within a month—
Let me not think on it—Frailty, your name is
    woman—
A little month, before those shoes were old
With which she followed my poor father's body,
Like Niobe, all tears—why, she—
O God, a beast that wants discourse of reason

Would have mourned longer—married with my uncle,
My father's brother—but no more like my father
Than I to Hercules. Within a month,
Ere yet the salt of most unrighteous tears
Had left the flushing in her gallèd eyes,
She married—O most wicked speed! To post
With such dexterity to incestuous sheets!
It is not, and it cannot come to good.
But break, my heart, for I must hold my tongue.

Enter HORATIO, MARCELLUS, *and* BARNARDO.

HOR.   Hail to your lordship.
HAM.   I am glad to see you well.
  Horatio, or I do forget myself.
HOR.   The same, my lord, and your poor servant ever.
HAM.   Sir, my good friend, I'll change that name with
  you.
  And what make you from Wittenberg, Horatio?—
  Marcellus.
MAR.   My good lord.
HAM.   I am very glad to see you—[*To Barnardo*] Good
  even, sir.—
  But what in faith make you from Wittenberg?
HOR.   A truant disposition, good my lord.
HAM.   I would not hear your enemy say so,
  Nor shall you do my ear that violence
  To make it truster of your own report
  Against yourself. I know you are no truant.
  But what is your affair in Elsinore?
  We'll teach you to drink deep ere you depart.
HOR.   My lord, I came to see your father's funeral.
HAM.   I pray you do not mock me, fellow-student.
  I think it was to see my mother's wedding.
HOR.   Indeed, my lord, it followed hard upon.

HAM.   Thrift, thrift, Horatio. The funeral baked
    meats
  Did coldly furnish forth the marriage tables.
  Would I had met my dearest foe in heaven
  Ere ever I had seen that day, Horatio.
  My father—I think I see my father—
HOR.   Where, my lord?
HAM.   In my mind's eye, Horatio.
HOR.   I saw him once; he was a goodly king.
HAM.   He was a man, take him for all in all:
  I shall not look upon his like again.
HOR.   My lord, I think I saw him yesternight.
HAM.   Saw? Who?
HOR.   My lord, the king your father.
HAM.   The king my father?
HOR.   Season your admiration for a while
  With an attent ear till I may deliver
  Upon the witness of these gentlemen
  This marvel to you.
HAM.   For God's love let me hear!
HOR.   Two nights together had these gentlemen,
  Marcellus and Barnardo, on their watch
  In the dead waste and middle of the night
  Been thus encountered. A figure like your father
  Armed at point exactly, head to foot,
  Appears before them, and with solemn march
  Goes slow and stately by them. Thrice he walked
  By their oppressed and fear-surprisèd eyes
  Within his truncheon's length; while they, distilled
  Almost to jelly with the act of fear,
  Stand dumb and speak not to him. This to me
  In dreadful secrecy impart they did;
  And I with them the third night kept the watch,
  Where, as they had delivered, both in time,
  Form of the thing, each word made true and good,

The apparition comes. I knew your father;
These hands are not more like.

HAM.   But where was this?

MAR.   My lord, upon the platform where we watch.

HAM.   Did you not speak to it?

HOR.   My lord, I did,
But answer made it none. Yet once I thought
It lifted up its head and did address
Itself to motion like as it would speak.
But even then the morning cock crew loud,
And at the sound it shrunk in haste away
And vanished from our sight.

HAM.   'Tis very strange.

HOR.   As I do live, my honoured lord, 'tis true;
And we did think it written in our duty
To let you know of it.

HAM.   Indeed, sirs; but this troubles me.
Hold you the watch tonight?

ALL.   We do, my lord.

HAM.   Armed, say you?

ALL.   Armed, my lord.

HAM.   From top to toe?

ALL.   My lord, from head to foot.

HAM.   Then saw you not his face?

HOR.   O yes, my lord, he wore his helmet up.

HAM.   What looked he, frowningly?

HOR.   A countenance more in sorrow than in anger.

HAM.   Pale, or red?

HOR.   Nay, very pale.

HAM.   And fixed his eyes upon you?

HOR.   Most constantly.

HAM.   I would I had been there.

HOR.   It would have much amazed you.

HAM.   Very like.
  Stayed it long?

HOR.   While one with moderate haste might tell a
  hundred.

MAR.⎱
BAR.⎰ Longer, longer.

HOR.   Not when I saw it.

HAM.   His beard was grizzled, no?

HOR.   It was as I have seen it in his life,
  A sable silvered.

HAM.   I will watch tonight.
  Perchance it will walk again.

HOR.   I warrant it will.

HAM.   If it assumes my noble father's person,
  I'll speak to it though hell itself should gape
  And bid me hold my peace. I pray you all,
  If you have hitherto concealed this sight,
  Let it be tenable in your silence still,
  And whatsoever else shall hap tonight,
  Give it an understanding but no tongue.
  I will requite your loves. So fare you well.
  Upon the platform between eleven and twelve
  I'll visit you.

ALL.   Our duty to your honour.

HAM.   Your loves, as mine to you. Farewell.

                        Exeunt all but Hamlet.

My father's spirit—in arms! All is not well.
I fear some foul play. Would the night were come.
Till then sit still, my soul. Foul deeds will rise,
Though all the earth o'erwhelms them, to men's
  eyes.
                                Exit.

SCENE III
The Court.

Enter LAERTES *and* OPHELIA, *his sister.*

LAER.   My necessaries are embarked. Farewell.
And sister, as the winds give benefit
And convoy is assistant, do not sleep,
But let me hear from you.
OPH.   Do you doubt that?
LAER.   For Hamlet, and the trifling of his favour,
Hold it a fashion and a toy in blood,
A violet in the youth of primy nature,
Forward, not permanent, sweet, not lasting;
The perfume and suppliance of a minute,
No more.
OPH.   No more but so?
LAER.   Think it no more.
For nature crescent does not grow alone
In thighs and bulk, but as this temple waxes,
The inward service of the mind and soul
Grows wide with it. Perhaps he loves you now,
And now no soil nor evil does besmirch
The virture of his will. But you must fear,
His greatness weighed, his will is not his own.
For he himself is subject to his birth:
He may not, as unvalued persons do,
Carve for himself, for on his choice depends
The sanity and health of this whole state.
And therefore must his choice be circumscribed
Unto the voice and yielding of that body
Whereof he is the head. Then if he says he loves
    you,
It fits your wisdom so far to believe it
As he in his particular act and place
May give his saying deed: which is no further

Than the main voice of Denmark goes with it.
Then weigh what loss your honour may sustain
If with too credent ear you list his songs,
Or lose your heart, or your chaste treasure open
To his unmastered importunity.
Fear it, Ophelia, fear it, my dear sister,
And keep you in the rear of your affection
Out of the shot and danger of desire.
The chariest maid is prodigal enough
If she unmasks her beauty to the moon.
Virtue itself scapes not calumnious strokes.
The canker galls the infants of the spring
Too oft before their buttons are disclosed,
And in the morn and liquid dew of youth
Contagious blastments are most imminent.
Be wary then: best safety lies in fear.
Youth to itself rebels, though none else near.

OPH.   I shall the effect of this good lesson keep
As watchman to my heart. But good my brother,
Do not as some ungracious pastors do,
Show me the steep and thorny way to heaven,
While like a puffed and reckless libertine
Himself the primrose path of dalliance treads,
And heeds not his own word.

LAER.   O fear me not.
I stay too long.

Enter POLONIUS.

                              But here my father comes.
A double blessing is a double grace:
Occasion smiles upon a second leave.

POL.   Yet here, Laertes? Aboard, aboard for shame.
The wind sits in the shoulder of your sail,
And you are stayed for. There, my blessing with
you.

And these few precepts in your memory
Look you character. Give your thoughts no tongue,
Nor any unproportioned thought its act.
Be you familiar, but by no means vulgar;
Those friends you have, and their adoption tried,
Grapple them unto your soul with hoops of steel;
But do not dull your palm with entertainment
Of each new-hatched, unfledged gallant. Beware
Of entrance to a quarrel; but being in,
Bear it that the opposed may beware of you.
Give every man your ear, but few your voice;
Take each man's opinion, but reserve your
    judgment.
Costly your habit as your purse can buy,
But not expressed in fancy; rich, not gaudy;
For the apparel oft proclaims the man,
And they in France of the best rank and station,
Or of the most select and generous, chief in that.
Neither a borrower nor a lender be,
For loan oft loses both itself and friend,
And borrowing dulls the edge of husbandry.
This above all: to your own self be true,
And it must follow as the night the day
You can not then be false to any man.
Farewell, my blessing season this in you.

LAER.   Most humbly do I take my leave, my lord.

POL.   The time invests you; go, your servants tend.

LAER.   Farewell, Ophelia, and remember well
    What I have said to you.

OPH.   'Tis in my memory locked,
    And you yourself shall keep the key of it.

LAER.   Farewell.   *Exit.*

POL.   What is it, Ophelia, he has said to you?

OPH.   So please you, something touching the Lord
    Hamlet.

POL.   Indeed, well thought of.
    'Tis told me he has very oft of late

Given private time to you, and you yourself
Have of your audience been most free and
   bounteous.
If it is so—as so 'tis put on me,
And that in way of caution—I must tell you
You do not understand yourself so clearly
As it behoves my daughter and your honour.
What is between you? Give me up the truth.

OPH.   He has, my lord, of late made many tenders
Of his affection to me.

POL.   Affection? Pooh, you speak like a green girl,
Unsifted in such perilous circumstance.
Do you believe his tenders, as you call them?

OPH.   I do not know, my lord, what I should think.

POL.   Indeed, I will teach you. Think yourself a baby
That you have taken these tenders for true pay
Which are not sterling. Tender yourself more dearly
Or—not to crack the wind of the poor phrase,
Tendering it thus—you'll tender me a fool.

OPH.   My lord, he has importuned me with love
In honourable fashion.

POL.   Ay, fashion you may call it. Go to, go to.

OPH.   And has given countenance to his speech, my
   lord,
With almost all the holy vows of heaven.

POL.   Ay, snares to catch woodcocks. I do know,
When the blood burns, how prodigal the soul
Lends the tongue vows. These blazes, daughter,
Giving more light than heat, extinct in both
Even in their promise as it is a-making,
You must not take for fire. From this time
Be something scanter of your maiden presence;
Set your entreatments at a higher rate
Than a command to parley. For Lord Hamlet,
Believe so much in him that he is young,
And with a larger tether may he walk
Than may be given you. In short, Ophelia,

Do not believe his vows; for they are brokers
Not of that dye which their investments show,
But mere implorers of unholy suits,
Breathing like sanctified and pious bonds
The better to beguile. This is for all.
I would not, in plain terms, from this time forth
Have you so slander any moment's leisure
As to give words or talk with the Lord Hamlet.
Look to it, I charge you. Come your ways.

OPH.   I shall obey, my lord.   *Exeunt.*

SCENE IV
The Castle battlements.

Enter HAMLET, HORATIO, *and* MARCELLUS.

HAM.   The air bites shrewdly, it is very cold.
HOR.   It is a nipping and eager air.
HAM.   What hour now?
HOR.   I think it lacks of twelve.
MAR.   No, it has struck.
HOR.   Indeed? I heard it not.
   It then draws near the season
   Wherein the spirit held his wont to walk.

A flourish of trumpets, and two cannon shots go off.

   What does this mean, my lord?
HAM.   The King holds wake tonight and does carouse,
   Keeps wassail, and the swaggering upspring reels;
   And as he drains his draughts of Rhenish down,
   The kettle-drum and trumpet thus bray out
   The triumph of his pledge.

HOR.   Is it a custom?
HAM.   Indeed, it is.
   But to my mind, though I am native here
   And to the manner born, it is a custom
   More honoured in the breach than the observance.
   This heavy-headed revel east and west
   Makes us traduced and taxed of other nations—
   They call us drunkards, and with swinish phrase
   Soil our description. And indeed it takes
   From our achievements, though performed at height,
   The pith and marrow of our attribute.
   So, oft it chances in particular men
   That for some vicious mole of nature in them,
   As in their birth, wherein they are not guilty
   (Since nature cannot choose its origin),
   By their o'ergrowth of some complexiòn,
   Oft breaking down the bounds and forts of reason,
   Or by some habit, that too much o'erleavens
   The form of plausive manners—that these men,
   Carrying, I say, the stamp of one defect,
   Being Nature's livery or Fortune's star,
   Their virtues else, be they as pure as grace,
   As infinite as man may undergo,
   Shall in the general judgment take corruption
   From that particular fault. The dram of evil
   Does all the noble substance oft put out
   To its own scandal.

                   Enter GHOST.

HOR.   Look, my lord, it comes.
HAM.   Angels and ministers of grace defend us!
   Be you a spirit of health or goblin damned,
   Bring with you airs from heaven or blasts from hell,
   Be your intents wicked or charitable,

You come in such a questionable shape
That I will speak to you: I'll call you Hamlet,
King, father, royal Dane. O answer me.
Let me not burst in ignorance, but tell
Why your canònized bones, hearsed in death,
Have burst their cerements; why the sepulchre
Wherein we saw you quietly in-urned
Has opened its ponderous and marble jaws
To cast you up again. What may this mean,
That you, dead corpse, again in còmplete steel
Revisit thus the glimpses of the moon,
Making night hideous and we fools of nature
So horridly to shake our disposition
With thoughts beyond the reaches of our souls?
Say why is this? Wherefore? What should we do?

Ghost beckons.

HOR.   It beckons you to go away with it,
   As if it some impartment did desire
   To you alone.
MAR.   Look with what courteous action
   It waves you to a more removèd ground.
   But do not go with it.
HOR.   No; by no means.
HAM.   It will not speak. Then I will follow it.
HOR.   Do not, my lord.
HAM.   Why, what should be the fear?
   I do not set my life at a pin's fee,
   And for my soul, what can it do to that,
   Being a thing immortal as itself?
   It waves me forth again. I'll follow it.
HOR.   What if it tempts you toward the flood, my
      lord,
   Or to the dreadful summit of the cliff

That beetles o'er its base into the sea,
And there assume some other horrible form
Which might deprive your sovereignty of reason
And draw you into madness? Think of it.
The very place puts toys of desperation,
Without more motive, into every brain
That looks so many fathoms to the sea
And hears it roar beneath.

HAM.   It waves me still.
Go on, I'll follow you.

MAR.   You shall not go, my lord.

HAM.   Hold off your hands.

HOR.   Be ruled; you shall not go.

HAM.   My fate cries out
And makes each petty artery in this body
As hardy as the Nemean lion's nerve.
Still am I called. Unhand me, gentlemen.
By heaven, I'll make a ghost of him that stops me.
I say away.—Go on, I'll follow you.

                              Exeunt Ghost and Hamlet.

HOR.   He waxes desperate with imagination.

MAR.   Let's follow. 'Tis not fit thus to obey him.

HOR.   Follow after. To what issue will this come?

MAR.   Something is rotten in the state of Denmark.

HOR.   Heaven will direct it.

MAR.   Nay, let's follow him.   *Exeunt.*

SCENE V

Enter GHOST *and* HAMLET.

HAM.   Whither will you lead me? Speak, I'll go no
     further.

GHOST.   Mark me.

HAM.   I will.

GHOST.   My hour is almost come
  When I to sulphurous and tormenting flames
  Must render up myself.
HAM.   Alas, poor ghost.
GHOST.   Pity me not, but lend your serious hearing.
  To what I shall unfold.
HAM.   Speak, I am bound to hear.
GHOST.   So are you to revenge when you shall hear.
HAM.   What?
GHOST.   I am your father's spirit,
  Doomed for a certain term to walk the night,
  And for the day confined to fast in fires,
  Till the foul crimes done in my days of nature
  Are burnt and purged away. But that I am forbidden
  To tell the secrets of my prison-house,
  I could a tale unfold whose lightest word
  Would harrow up your soul, freeze your young
    blood,
  Make your two eyes like stars start from their
    spheres,
  Your knotted and combinèd locks to part,
  And each particular hair to stand on end
  Like quills upon the fretful porcupine.
  But this eternal secret must not be
  To ears of flesh and blood. List, list, O list!
  If you did ever your dear father love—
HAM.   O God!
GHOST.   Revenge his foul and most unnatural
  murder.
HAM.   Murder!
GHOST.   Murder most foul, as in the best it is,
  But this most foul, strange and unnatural.
HAM.   Haste me to know it, that I with wings as swift
  As meditation or the thoughts of love
  May sweep to my revenge.

GHOST.   I find you apt.
  And duller should you be than the fat weed
  That roots itself in ease on Lethe wharf,
  Would you not stir in this. Now, Hamlet, hear.
  'Tis given out that, sleeping in my orchard,
  A serpent stung me—so the whole ear of Denmark
  Is by a forgèd process of my death
  Rankly abused. But know, you noble youth,
  The serpent that did sting your father's life
  Now wears his crown.
HAM.   O my prophetic soul! My uncle!
GHOST.   Ay, that incestuous, that adulterous beast,
  With witchcraft of his wit, with traitorous gifts—
  O wicked wit, and gifts that have the power
  So to seduce!—won to his shameful lust
  The will of my most seeming-virtuous queen.
  O Hamlet, what a falling-off was there,
  From me, whose love was of that dignity
  That it went hand in hand even with the vow
  I made to her in marriage, and to decline
  Upon a wretch whose natural gifts were poor
  To those of mine!
  But virtue, as it never will be moved,
  Though lewdness courts it in a shape of heaven,
  So lust, though to a radiant angel linked,
  Will sate itself in a celestial bed
  And prey on garbage.
  But soft, I think I scent the morning air:
  Brief let me be. Sleeping within my orchard,
  My custom always of the afternoon,
  Upon my secure hour your uncle stole
  With juice of cursed hebenon in a vial,
  And in the porches of my ears did pour
  The leperous distilment. Whose effect
  Holds such an enmity with blood of man

That swift as quicksilver it courses through
The natural gates and alleys of the body.
And with a sudden vigour it does posset
And curd, like eager droppings into milk,
The thin and wholesome blood. So did it mine,
And a most instant tetter barked about,
Most lazar-like, with vile and loathsome crust
All my smooth body.
Thus was I, sleeping, by a brother's hand
Of life, of crown, of queen at once dispatched,
Cut off even in the blossoms of my sin,
Unconfessed, unready, unanointed,
No reckoning made, but sent to my account
With all my imperfections on my head.
O horrible! O horrible! most horrible!
If you have nature in you, bear it not;
Let not the royal bed of Denmark be
A couch for lustfulness and damnèd incest.
But howsoever you pursue this act,
Taint not your mind nor let your soul contrive
Against your mother aught. Leave her to heaven,
And to those thorns that in her bosom lodge
To prick and sting her. Fare you well at once:
The glow-worm shows the matin to be near,
Begins to pale its ineffectual fire.
Adieu, adieu, adieu. Remember me.   *Exit.*
HAM.   O all you host of heaven! O earth! What else?
And shall I couple hell? O fie! Hold, hold, my heart,
And you, my sinews, grow not instant old,
But bear me stiffly up. Remember you?
Ay, you poor ghost, while memory holds a seat
In this distracted globe. Remember you?
Yea, from the table of my memory
I'll wipe away all trivial vain recòrds,
All sayings of books, all forms, all pressures past

That youth and observation copied there,
And your commandment all alone shall live
Within the book and volume of my brain,
Unmixed with baser matter. Yes, by heaven!
O most pernicious woman!
O villain, villain, smiling damnèd villain!
My tables. Meet it is I set it down
That one may smile, and smile, and be a villain—
At least I am sure it may be so in Denmark.   *Writes.*
So, uncle, there you are. Now to my word.
It is 'Adieu, adieu, remember me.'
I have sworn it.

Enter HORATIO *and* MARCELLUS.

HOR. My lord, my lord.
MAR. Lord Hamlet.
HOR. Heavens secure him.
HAM. [*aside*] So be it.
MAR. Hello, ho, ho, my lord.
HAM. Hello, ho, ho, boy. Come, bird, come.
MAR. How is it, my noble lord?
HOR. What news, my Lord?
HAM. O, wonderful!
HOR. Good my lord, tell it.
HAM. No, you will reveal it.
HOR. Not I, my lord, by heaven.
MAR. Nor I, my lord.
HAM. How say you then, would heart of man once
       think it—
  But you'll be secret?
HOR. ⎫
MAR. ⎭ Ay, by heaven.
HAM. There's never a villain dwelling in all Denmark
  But he's an arrant knave.

HOR.   There needs no ghost, my lord, come from the
        grave
   To tell us this.
HAM.   Why, right, you are in the right.
   And so without more circumstance at all
   I hold it fit that we shake hands and part:
   You as your business and desire shall point you—
   For every man has business and desire,
   Such as it is—and for my own part,
   I will go pray.
HOR.   These are but wild and whirling words, my
        lord.
HAM.   I am sorry they offend you, heartily—
   Yes faith, heartily.
HOR.   There's no offence, my lord.
HAM.   Yes by Saint Patrick but there is, Horatio,
   And much offence too. Touching this vision here,
   It is an honest ghost, that let me tell you.
   For your desire to know what is between us,
   O'ermaster it as you may. And now, good friends,
   As you are friends, scholars, and soldiers,
   Give me one poor request.
HOR.   What is it my lord? We will.
HAM.   Never make known what you have seen
        tonight.
HOR.
MAR.   My lord, we will not.
HAM.   Nay, but swear it.
HOR.   In faith, my lord, not I.
MAR.   Nor I, my lord, in faith.
HAM.   Upon my sword.
MAR.   We have sworn, my lord, already.
HAM.   Indeed, upon my sword, indeed.
GHOST.   (*Beneath*) Swear.

HAM.   Ah ha, boy, say you so? Are you there, old
     fellow?
  Come on, you hear this fellow in the cellarage.
  Consent to swear.
HOR.   Propose the oath, my lord.
HAM.   Never to speak of this that you have seen.
  Swear by my sword.
GHOST.   Swear.
HAM.   Here and everywhere? Then we'll shift our
     ground.
  Come hither, gentlemen,
  And lay your hands again upon my sword.
  Swear by my sword
  Never to speak of this that you have heard.
GHOST.   Swear by his sword.   *They swear.*
HAM.   Well said, old mole. Can you work in the
     earth so fast?
  A worthy miner! Once more remove, good friends.
HOR.   O day and night, but this is wondrous strange.
HAM.   And therefore as a stranger give it welcome.
  There are more things in heaven and earth,
     Horatio,
  Than are dreamt of in your philosophy.
  But come,
  Here, as before, never, so help you mercy,
  How strange or odd soever I bear myself—
  As I perchance hereafter shall think meet
  To put an antic disposition on—
  That you, at such time seeing me, never shall,
  With arms akimbo thus, or this head-shake,
  Or by pronouncing of some doubtful phrase,
  As 'Well, we know', or 'We could then if we would',
  Or 'If we list to speak', or 'There are then if they
     might',

Or such ambiguous giving out, to note
That you know aught of me—this do swear,
So grace and mercy at your most need help you.
GHOST.   Swear   *They swear.*
HAM.   Rest, rest, perturbèd spirit. So gentlemen,
With all my love I do commend me to you;
And what so poor a man as Hamlet is
May do to express his love and friending to you,
God willing, shall not lack. Let us go in together.
And still your fingers on your lips, I pray.
The time is out of joint. O cursèd spite,
That ever I was born to set it right.
Nay, come, let us go together.   *Exeunt.*

Act II

SCENE I
The Court.

Enter POLONIUS *and* REYNALDO.

POL.   Give him this money and these notes, Reynaldo.
REY.   I will, my lord.
POL.   You shall do marvellous wisely, good Reynaldo,
Before you visit him, to make inquire
Of his behaviour.
REY.   My lord, I did intend it.
POL.   Indeed, well said, very well said. Look you, sir,

Inquire for me first what Danes are now in Paris,
And how, and who, what means, and where they
    lodge,
What company, at what expense. And finding
By this encompassment and drift of question
That they do know my son, come you more near
Than your particular demands will touch it.
Take you as though some distant knowledge of him,
As thus, 'I know his father, and his friends,
And in part him'—do you mark this, Reynaldo?
REY.   Ay, very well, my lord.
POL.   'And in part him. But', you may say, 'not well;
But if it is he I mean, he's very wild,
Addicted so and so'—and there put on him
What forgeries you please—well, none so rank
As may dishonour him—take heed of that—
But, sir, such wanton, wild, and usual slips
As are companions noted and most known
To youth and liberty.
REY.   As gaming, my lord?
POL.   Ay, or drinking, fencing, swearing,
Quarrelling, wenching—you may go so far.
REY.   My lord, that would dishonour him.
POL   'Faith no, as you may season it in the charge.
You must not put another scandal on him,
That he is open to incontinency—
That's not my meaning. Breathe his faults so
    quaintly
That they may seem the taints of liberty,
The flash and outbreak of a fiery mind,
A savageness in unreclaimèd blood,
Of general assault.
REY.   But, my good lord—
POL.   Wherefore should you do this?
REY.   Ay, my lord, I would know that.

POL.   For sure, sir, here's my drift,
   And I believe it is a trick of warrant.
   You laying these slight sullies on my son,
   As though a thing a little soiled in the working,
   Mark you,
   Your party in convèrse, him you would sound,
   Having ever seen in the prenominate crimes
   The youth you breathe of guilty, be assured
   He closes with you in this consequence:
   'Good sir', or so, or 'friend', or 'gentleman',
   According to the phrase or the addition
   Of man and country.
REY.   Very good, my lord.
POL.   And then, sir, does he this—he does—what was
      I about to say? By the mass, I was about to say
      something.
   Where did I leave?
REY.   At 'closes in the consequence'.
POL.   At 'closes in the consequence', ay, sure.
   He closes thus: 'I know the gentleman,
   I saw him yesterday', or 'the other day',
   Or then, or then, with such or such, 'and as you say,
   There was he gaming', 'o'ertaken in his cups',
   'There falling out at tennis', or perchance
   'I saw him enter such a house of sale'—
   To be sure, a brothel, or so forth.
   See you now,
   Your bait of falsehood takes this carp of truth.
   And thus do we of wisdom and of reach,
   With windlasses and with assays of bias,
   By indirections find directions out.
   So by my former lecture and advice
   Shall you my son. You have me, have you not?
REY.   My lord, I have.
POL.   Goodbye, fare you well.

REY. Good my lord.
POL. Observe his inclination in yourself.
REY. I shall, my lord.
POL.   And let him ply his music.
REY. Well, my lord.   *Exit.*

Enter OPHELIA.

POL. Farewell. How now, Ophelia, what's the
     matter?
OPH. O my lord, my lord, I have been so affrighted.
POL. With what, in the name of God?
OPH. My lord, as I was sewing in my closet,
     Lord Hamlet, with his doublet all unbraced,
     No hat upon his head, his stockings fouled,
     Ungartered and down-fallen to his ankle;
     Pale as his shirt, his knees knocking each other,
     And with a look so piteous in purport
     As if he had been loosed out of hell
     To speak of horrors, he comes before me.
POL. Mad for your love?
OPH.   My lord, I do not know,
     But truly I do fear it.
POL.   What said he?
OPH. He took me by the wrist and held me hard.
     Then goes he to the length of all his arm,
     And with his other hand thus o'er his brow
     He falls to such perusal of my face
     As he would draw it. Long stayed he so.
     At last, a little shaking of my arm,
     And thrice his head thus waving up and down,
     He raised a sigh so piteous and profound
     As it did seem to shatter all his bulk
     And end his being. That done, he lets me go,
     And with his head over his shoulder turned

He seemed to find his way without his eyes,
For out of doors he went without their helps,
And to the last bended their light on me.
POL.   Come, go with me, I will go seek the King.
This is the very ecstasy of love,
Whose violent property fordoes itself,
And leads the will to desperate undertakings
As oft as any passion under heaven
That does afflict our natures. I am sorry—
What, have you given him any hard words of late?
OPH.   No, my good lord, but as you did command,
I did repel his letters and denied
His access to me.
POL.   That has made him mad.
I am sorry that with better heed and judgment
I had not marked him. I feared he did but trifle
And meant to wreck you. But bless my suspicion!
By heaven, it is as proper to our age
To cast beyond ourselves in our opinions
As it is common for the younger sort
To lack discretion. Come, go we to the King.
This must be known, which, being kept close,
   might move
More grief to hide than hate to utter love.
Come.   *Exeunt.*

SCENE II

Flourish. Enter KING *and* QUEEN, ROSENCRANTZ *and*
GUILDENSTERN, *with* Attendants.

KING.   Welcome, dear Rosencrantz and Guildenstern.
Moreover that we much did long to see you,
The need we have to use you did provoke

Our hasty sending. Something have you heard
Of Hamlet's transformation—so I call it,
Since nor the exterior nor the inward man
Resembles that it was. What it should be,
More than his father's death, that thus has put him
So much from the understanding of himself
I cannot dream of. I entreat you both
That, being of so young days brought up with him,
And since so neighboured to his youth and conduct,
That you vouchsafe your rest here in our court
Some little time. So by your companies
To draw him on to pleasures and to gather,
So much as from occasion you may glean,
Whether aught to us unknown afflicts him thus
That, opened, lies within our remedy.

QUEEN.   Good gentlemen, he has much talked of you,
And sure I am, two men there are not living
To whom he more adheres. If it will please you
To show us so much gentry and good will
As to expend your time with us awhile
For the supply and profit of our hope,
Your visitation shall receive such thanks
As fits a king's remembrance.

ROS.   Both your Majesties
Might, by the sovereign power you have of us,
Put your dread pleasures more into command
Than to entreaty.

GUILD.   But we both obey,
And here give up ourselves in the full bent
To lay our service freely at your feet
To be commanded.

KING.   Thanks, Rosencrantz and gentle Guildenstern.

QUEEN.   Thanks, Guildenstern and gentle Rosencrantz.
And I beseech you instantly to visit
My too much changèd son. Go, some of you,

And bring these gentlemen where Hamlet is.
GUILD. Heavens make our presence and our practices
Pleasant and helpful to him.
QUEEN.   Ay, amen.
                    Exeunt Rosencrantz and Guildenstern.

                    Enter POLONIUS.

POL. The ambassadors from Norway, my good lord,
Are joyfully returned.
KING. You ever have been the father of good news.
POL. Have I, my lord? I assure my good lord
I hold my duty as I hold my soul,
Both to my God and to my gracious King.
And I do think—or else this brain of mine
Hunts not the trail of policy so sure
As it was used to do—that I have found
The very cause of Hamlet's lunacy.
KING. O speak of that: that do I long to hear.
POL. Give first admittance to the ambassadors.
My news shall be the fruit to that great feast.
KING. Yourself do grace to them and bring them in.
                                        Exit Polonius.
He tells me, my dear Gertrude, he has found
The head and source of all your son's distemper.
QUEEN. I suspect it is no other but the main,
His father's death and our o'er-hasty marriage.
KING. Well, we shall sift him.

        Enter POLONIUS, VOLTEMAND, and CORNELIUS.

                            Welcome, my good friends.
Say, Voltemand, what from our brother Norway?
VOLT. Most fair return of greetings and desires.
Upon our first, he sent out to suppress

His nephew's levies, which to him appeared
To be a preparation against the Poles.
But better looked into, he truly found
It was against your Highness. Whereat grieved
That so his sickness, age, and impotence   sick monkey
Were falsely used as pretence, sends out arrests
On Fortinbras. Which he, in brief, obeys,
Receives rebuke from Norway and, in fine,
Makes vow before his uncle never more
To give the assay of arms against your Majesty.
Whereon old Norway, overcome with joy,
Gives him three thousand crowns in annual fee
And his commission to employ those soldiers
So levied, as before, against the Poles;
With an entreaty, herein further shown,

                    [*Gives a paper.*]

That it might please you to give quiet pass
Through your dominions for this enterprise
On such regards of safety and allowance
As therein are set down.
KING.   It likes us well;
And at our more considered time we'll read,
Answer, and think upon this business.
Meantime, we thank you for your well-took labour.
Go to your rest, at night we'll feast together.
Most welcome home.
                    Exeunt Voltemand and Cornelius.
POL.   This business is well ended.
My lord and madam, to expostulate
What majesty should be, what duty is,
Why day is day, night night, and time is time,
Were nothing but to waste night, day, and time.
Therefore, since brevity is the soul of wit,

And tediousness the limbs and outward flourishes,
I will be brief. Your noble son is mad.
Mad call I it, for to define true madness,
What is it but to be nothing else but mad?
But let that go.

QUEEN.   More matter with less art.

POL.   Madam, I swear I use no art at all.
That he is mad 'tis true; 'tis true 'tis pity;
And pity 'tis 'tis true. A foolish figure—
But farewell it, for I will use no art.
Mad let us grant him then. And now remains
That we find out the cause of this effect,
Or rather say the cause of this defect,
For this effect defective comes by cause.
Thus it remains; and the remainder thus:
Consider,
I have a daughter—have while she is mine—
Who in her duty and obedience, mark,
Has given me this. Now gather and surmise.
(*Reads*) *To the celestial and my soul's idol, the most
beautified Ophelia*—That's an ill phrase, a vile
phrase, 'beautified' is a vile phrase. But you shall
hear—
these; in her excellent white bosom, these, &

QUEEN.   Came this from Hamlet to her?

POL.   Good madam, stay awhile, I will be faithful.
*Doubt you the stars are fire,
Doubt that the sun does move,
Doubt truth to be a liar,
But never doubt I love.*

*O dear Ophelia, I am ill at these numbers. I have
not art to reckon my groans. But that I love you
best, O most best, believe it. Adieu.*
*Yours evermore, most dear lady, while this
machine is to him,*   *Hamlet.*

This in obedience has my daughter shown me,
And, more above, have his solicitings,
As they fell out by time, by means, and place,
All given to my ear.

KING.   But how has she received his love?

POL.   What do you think of me?

KING.   As of a man faithful and honourable.

POL.   I would fain prove so. But what might you
    think,
When I had seen this hot love on the wing—
As I perceived it, I must tell you that,
Before my daughter told me—what might you
Or my dear Majesty your queen here think,
If I had played the desk or table-book,
Or given my heart a winking mute and dumb,
Or looked upon this love with idle sight—
What might you think? No, I went round to work,
And my young mistress thus I did bespeak:
'Lord Hamlet is a prince out of your star.
This must not be.' And then I prescripts gave her,
That she should lock herself from his resort,
Admit no messengers, receive no tokens.
Which done, she took the fruits of my advice,
And he, repelled—a short tale to make—
Fell into a sadness, then into a fast,
Thence to a watch, thence into a weakness,
Thence to a lightness and, by this declension,
Into the madness wherein now he raves
And all we mourn for.

KING.   Do you think 'tis this?

QUEEN.   It may be; very like.

POL.   Has there been such a time—I would fain
    know that—
That I have positively said ''Tis so',
When it proved otherwise?

KING.   Not that I know.

POL.   Take this from this if this is otherwise.

[*Points to his head and shoulder.*]

If circumstances lead me, I will find
Where truth is hid, though it were hid indeed
Within the centre.

KING.   How may we try it further?

POL.   You know sometimes he walks four hours
      together
Here in the lobby.

QUEEN.   So he does indeed.

POL.   At such a time I'll loose my daughter to him.
Be you and I behind an arras then,
Mark the encounter. If he loves her not,
And is not from his reason fallen thereon,
Let me be no assistant for a state,
But keep a farm and carters.

KING.   We will try it.

Enter HAMLET, *reading on a book.*

QUEEN.   But look where sadly the poor wretch comes
      reading.

POL.   Away, I do beseech you both, away.
I'll board him presently. O give me leave.

                  Exeunt King, Queen and Attendants
How does my good Lord Hamlet?

HAM.   Well, God-have-mercy.

POL.   Do you know me, my lord?

HAM.   Excellent well. You are a fishmonger.

POL.   Not I, my lord.

HAM.   Then I would you were so honest a man.

POL.   Honest, my lord?

HAM.   Ay sir. To be honest, as this world goes, is to
be one man picked out of ten thousand.

POL.   That's very true, my lord.

HAM.   For if the sun breeds maggots in a dead dog,
being a god kissing carrion—Have you a
daughter?

POL.   I have, my lord.

HAM.   Let her not walk in the sun. Conception is a
blessing, but as your daughter may conceive—
friend, look to it.

POL.   [aside] How say you by that? Still harping on
my daughter. Yet he knew me not at first; he said I
was a fishmonger. He is far gone. And truly in my
youth I suffered much extremity for love, very near
this. I'll speak to him again.—What do you read,
my lord?

HAM.   Words, words, words.

POL.   What is the matter, my lord?

HAM.   Between whom?

POL.   I mean the matter that you read, my lord.

HAM.   Slanders, sir. For the satirical rogue says here
that old men have gray beards, that their faces are
wrinkled, their eyes purging thick amber and plum-
tree gum, and that they have a plentiful lack of wit,
together with most weak hams—all which, sir,
though I most powerfully and potently believe, yet
I hold it not honesty to have it thus set down. For
yourself, sir, shall grow old as I am—if like a crab
you could go backward.

POL.   [aside] Though this is madness, yet there is
method in it.— Will you walk out of the air, my
lord?

HAM.   Into my grave?

POL.   Indeed, that's out of the air.—[aside] How pregnant sometimes his replies are—a happiness that

often madness hits on, which reason and sanity
could not so prosperously be delivered of. I will
leave him and suddenly contrive the means of
meeting between him and my daughter.—My lord,
I will take my leave of you.

HAM.   You cannot, sir, take from me anything that I
will not more willingly part with—except my life,
except my life, except my life.

POL.   Fare you well, my lord.

HAM.   These tedious old fools.

Enter ROSENCRANTZ *and* GUILDENSTERN.

POL.   You go to seek the Lord Hamlet. There he is.

ROS.   God save you, sir.   *Exit Polonius.*

GUILD.   My honoured lord.

ROS.   My most dear lord.

HAM.   My excellent good friends. How do you,
Guildenstern? Ah, Rosencrantz. Good lads, how do
you both?

ROS.   As the indifferent children of the earth.

GUILD.   Happy in that we are not over-happy: on Fortune's cap we are not the very button.

HAM.   Nor the soles of her shoe?

ROS.   Neither, my lord.

HAM.   Then you live about her waist, or in the
middle of her favours?

GUILD.   Faith, her privates we.

HAM.   In the secret parts of Fortune? O most true,
she is a strumpet. What news?

ROS.   None, my lord, but the world's grown honest.

HAM.   Then is doomsday near. But your news is not
true. Let me question more in particular. What
have you, my good friends, deserved at the hands of
Fortune that she sends you to prison hither?

GUILD.   Prison, my lord?

HAM.   Denmark's a prison.

ROS.   Then is the world one.

HAM.   A goodly one, in which there are many confines, wards, and dungeons, Denmark being of the
worst.

ROS.   We think not so, my lord.

HAM.   Why, then it is none to you; for there is
nothing either good or bad but thinking makes it
so. To me it is a prison.

ROS.   Why, then your ambition makes it one: it is
too narrow for your mind.

HAM.   O God, I could be bounded in a nutshell and
count myself a king of infinite space—were it not
that I have bad dreams.

GUILD.   Which dreams indeed are ambition; for the
very substance of the ambitious is merely the
shadow of a dream.

HAM.   A dream itself is but a shadow.

ROS.   Truly, and I hold ambition of so airy and light a
quality that it is but a shadow's shadow.

HAM.   Then are our beggars bodies, and our monarchs
and outstretched heroes the beggars' shadows. Shall
we to the court? For by my faith, I cannot reason.

ROS.
GUILD. } We'll wait upon you.

HAM.   No such matter. I will not sort you with the
rest of my servants; for, to speak to you like an
honest man, I am most dreadfully attended. But in
the beaten way of friendship, what make you at
Elsinore?

ROS.   To visit you, my lord, no other occasion.

HAM.   Beggar that I am, I am even poor in thanks,
but I thank you. And sure, dear friends, my thanks
are too dear a halfpenny. Were you not sent for? Is

it your own inclining? Is it a free visitation? Come,
come, deal justly with me. Come, come. Nay,
speak.

GUILD.   What should we say, my lord?

HAM.   Anything but to the purpose. You were sent
for, and there is a kind of confession in your looks,
which your modesties have not craft enough to
colour. I know the good King and Queen have sent
for you.

ROS.   To what end, my lord?

HAM.   That, you must teach me. But let me conjure you, by the rights of our fellowship, by the
consonancy of our youth, by the obligation of our
ever-preserved love, and by what more dear a better
proposer can charge you with, be even and direct
with me whether you were sent for or no.

ROS.   [aside to Guildenstern] What say you?

HAM.   Nay then, I have an eye on you. If you love
me, hold not off.

GUILD.   My lord, we were sent for.

HAM.   I will tell you why; so shall my anticipation
forestall your discovery, and your secrecy to the
King and Queen moult no feather. I have of late,
but wherefore I know not, lost all my mirth,
forgone all custom of exercises. And indeed it goes
so heavily with my disposition that this goodly
frame the earth seems to me a sterile promontory,
this most excellent canopy the air, look you, this
brave overhanging firmament, this majestical roof
fretted with golden fire—why, it appears nothing to
me but a foul and pestilent congregation of
vapours. What a piece of work is a man, how noble
in reason, how infinite in faculties, in form and
moving how express and admirable, in action how
like an angel, in apprehension how like a god: the

5th *distilled*
the best

beauty of the world, the paragon of animals—and
yet, to me, what is this quintessence of dust? Man
delights not me—nor woman either, though by
your smiling you seem to say so.

*man made
from dust*

ROS.   My lord, there was no such stuff in my
         thoughts.

HAM.   Why did you laugh then, when I said man
          delights not me?

ROS.   To think, my lord, if you delight not in man,
         what Lenten entertainment the players shall receive
         from you. We passed them on the way, and hither
         are they coming to offer you service.

HAM.   He that plays the king shall be welcome—his
          Majesty shall have tribute of me, the adventurous
          knight shall use his foil and shield; the lover shall
          not sigh gratis, the humorous man shall end his
          part in peace; the clown shall make those laugh
          whose lungs are tickled easily, and the lady shall
          say her mind freely—or the blank verse shall halt
          for it. What players are they?

ROS.   Even those you were wont to take such delight
         in, the tragedians of the city.

HAM.   How chances it they travel? Their residence,
          both in reputation and profit, was better both ways.

ROS.   I think their inhibition comes by the means of
         the late innovation.

HAM.   Do they hold the same estimation they did
          when I was in the city? Are they so followed?

ROS.   No, indeed are they not.

HAM.   How comes it? Do they grow rusty?

ROS.   Nay, their endeavour keeps in the wonted
         pace; but there is, sir, an eyrie of children, little
         hawks, that cry out on the top of controversy, and
         are most vehemently clapped for it. These are now
         the fashion, and so berattle the common stages—so

they call them—that many wearing rapiers are
afraid of goose-quills and dare scarce come thither.

HAM. What, are they children? Who maintains them?
How are they supported? Will they pursue the profession no longer than they can sing? Will they not
say afterwards, if they should grow themselves to
common players—as it is most likely if their means
are no better—their writers do them wrong to make
them exclaim against their own succession?

ROS. Faith, there has been much to do on both
sides; and the nation holds it no sin to spur them
to controversy. There was for a while no money bid
for argument unless the poet and the player went to
cuffs in the question.

HAM. Is it possible?

GUILD. O, there has been much throwing about of
brains.

HAM. Do the boys carry it away?

ROS. Ay, that they do, my lord, Hercules and his
load too.

HAM. It is not very strange; for my uncle is King of
Denmark, and those that would make mouths at
him while my father lived give twenty, forty, fifty,
a hundred ducats apiece for his picture in little.
God, there is something in this more than natural,
if philosophy could find it out.

A flourish of trumpets.

GUILD. There are the players.

HAM. Gentlemen, you are welcome to Elsinore. Your
hands. Come then, the appurtenance of welcome is
fashion and ceremony. Let me comply with you in
this garb—lest my manner to the players, which I
tell you must show fairly outwards, should more

appear like entertainment than yours. You are
welcome. But my uncle-father and aunt-mother are
deceived.

GUILD. In what, my lord?

HAM. I am but mad north-north-west. When the
wind is southerly, I know a hawk from a heron.

Enter POLONIUS.

POL. Well be with you, gentlemen.

HAM. Hark you, Guildenstern, and you too—at each
ear a hearer. That great baby you see there is not
yet out of his swaddling-clouts.

ROS. Happily he is the second time come to them,
for they say an old man is twice a child.

HAM. I will prophesy he comes to tell me of the
players. Mark it.—You say right, sir, a Monday
morning, 'twas then indeed.

POL. My lord, I have news to tell you.

HAM. My lord, I have news to tell you. When
Roscius was an actor in Rome—

POL. The actors are come hither, my lord.

HAM. Buzz, buzz.

POL. Upon my honour—

HAM. Then came each actor on his ass—

POL. The best actors in the world, either for tragedy,
comedy, history, pastoral; pastoral-comical,
historical-pastoral; tragical-historical, tragical-
comical-historical-pastoral; scene individable, or
poem unlimited. Seneca cannot be too heavy, nor
Plautus too light, for the law of writ and the
liberty. These are the only men.

HAM. O Jephthah, judge of Israel, what a treasure
had you!

POL. What a treasure had he, my lord?

HAM.   Why,
                 One fair daughter and no more,
                 Whom he lovèd passing well.

POL.   [*aside*] Still on my daughter.

HAM.   Am I not in the right, old Jephthah?

POL.   If you call me Jephthah, my lord, I have a
daughter that I love passing well.

HAM.   Nay, that follows not.

POL.   What follows then, my lord?

HAM.   Why,
                 As by lot God wot,
and then, you know,
                 It came to pass, as most like it was.
The first row of the pious chanson will show you
more, for look where my abridgement comes.

Enter the Players.

You are welcome, masters. Welcome, all. I am glad
to see you well.—Welcome, good friends.—O, old
friend, why, your face is valanced since I saw you
last. Come you to beard me in Denmark?— What,
my young lady and mistress! By our lady, your
ladyship is nearer to heaven than when I saw you
last by the altitude of a shoe-sole. Pray God your
voice, like a piece of uncurrent gold, be not cracked
within the ring.—Masters, you are all welcome.
We'll even to it like French falconers, fly at
anything we see. We'll have a speech straight.
Come, give us a taste of your quality. Come, a
passionate speech.

1ST PLAY.   What speech, my good lord?

HAM.   I heard you speak a speech once—but it was
never acted, or if it was, not above once—for the
play, I remember, pleased not the million, it was

caviare to the general. But it was, as I received
it—and others, whose judgments in such matters
cried in the top of mine—an excellent play, well
digested in the scenes, set down with as much
modesty as cunning. I remember one said there
were no salty bits in the lines to make the matter
savoury, nor any matter in the phrase that might
indict the author of affectation, but called it an
honest method, as wholesome as sweet, and by
very much more handsome than fine. One speech
in it I chiefly loved—it was Aeneas' tale to
Dido—and thereabout of it especially when he
speaks of Priam's slaughter. If it lives in your
memory, begin at this line—let me see, let me
see—
The rugged Pyrrhus, like the Hyrcanian beast—
'Tis not so. It begins with Pyrrhus—
The rugged Pyrrhus, he whose sable arms,
Black as his purpose, did the night resemble
When he lay couched in the ominous horse,
Has now this dread and black complexion smeared
With heraldry more dismal. Head to foot
Now is he total crimson, horridly tricked
With blood of fathers, mothers, daughters, sons,
Baked and impasted with the parching streets,
That lend a tyrannous and a damned light
To their lord's murder. Roasted in wrath and fire,
And thus o'ersized with coagulate gore,
With eyes like garnets red, the hellish Pyrrhus
Old grandsire Priam seeks.
So proceed you.
POL.   Before God, my lord, well spoken, with good
accent and good discretion.
1ST PLAY.   *Anon he finds him,*
Striking too short at Greeks. His antique sword,

Rebellious to his arm, lies where it falls,
Repugnant to command. Unequal matched,
Pyrrhus at Priam drives, in rage strikes wide;
But with the whiff and wind of his fell sword
The unnerved father falls. Then senseless Ilium,
Seeming to feel this blow, with flaming top
Stoops to his base, and with a hideous crash
Takes prisoner Pyrrhus' ear. For lo, his sword,
Which was declining on the milky head
Of reverend Priam, seemed in the air to stick;
So, as a painted tyrant, Pyrrhus stood,
And like a neutral to his will and matter,
Did nothing.
But as we often see against some storm
A silence in the heavens, the rack stand still,
The bold winds speechless, and the orb below
As hushed as death, anon the dreadful thunder
Does rend the region. So after Pyrrhus' pause
Aroused vengeance sets him new awork;
And never did the Cyclops' hammers fall
On Mars's armour, forged for proof eterne,
With less remorse than Pyrrhus' bleeding sword
Now falls on Priam.
Out, out, you strumpet Fortune! All you gods
In general synod take away her power,
Break all the spokes and pieces from her wheel,
And bowl the round hub down the hill of heaven
As low as to the fiends.

POL.   This is too long.

HAM.   It shall to the barber's with your beard.—Pray,
say on. He's for a jig or a tale of bawdry, or he
sleeps. Say on, come to Hecuba.

1ST PLAY.   But who—ah, woe!—had seen the
mobled[1] queen—

---

[1] Warwickshire dialect for 'muffled.'

HAM.   'The mobled queen.'

POL.   That's good.

1ST PLAY.   *Run barefoot up and down, threatening the*
   flames
   With blinding tears, a clout upon that head
   Where late the diadem stood and, for a robe,
   About her lank and all exhausted loins
   A blanket, in the alarm of fear caught up—
   Who this had seen, with tongue in venom steeped,
   Against Fortune's state would treason have
      pronounced.
   But if the gods themselves did see her then,
   When she saw Pyrrhus make malicious sport
   In mincing with his sword her husband's limbs,
   The instant burst of clamour that she made,
   Unless things mortal move them not at all,
   Would have made milk the burning eyes of heaven
   And passion in the gods.

POL.   Look whether he has not turned his colour and
   has tears in his eyes. Pray no more.

HAM.   'Tis well. I'll have you speak out the rest of
   this soon.—Good my lord, will you see the players
   well bestowed? Do you hear, let them be well used,
   for they are the abstract and brief chronicles of the
   time. After your death you were better have a bad
   epitaph than their ill report while you live.

POL.   My lord, I will use them according to their
   desert.

HAM.   God's bodkin, man, much better. Use every
   man after his desert, and who shall escape whip-
   ping? Use them after your own honour and dignity:
   the less they deserve, the more merit is in your
   bounty. Take them in.

POL.   Come, sirs.

HAM.   Follow him, friends. We'll hear a play
   tomorrow. [*To First Player*] Do you hear me, old

friend? Can you play *The Murder of Gonzago?*

1ST PLAY. Ay, my lord.

HAM. We'll have it tomorrow night. You could for a
need study a speech of some dozen or sixteen lines,
which I would set down and insert in it, could you
not?

1ST PLAY. Ay, my lord.

HAM. Very well. Follow that lord, and look you
mock him not.   *Exeunt Polonius and Players.*
[*To Rosencrantz and Guildenstern*] My good
friends, I'll leave you till night. You are welcome
to Elsinore.

ROS. Good my lord.
                 Exeunt Rosencrantz and Guildenstern.

HAM. Ay, so, Goodbye to you. Now I am alone.
O what a rogue and peasant slave am I!
Is it not monstrous that this player here,
But in a fiction, in a dream of passion,
Could force his soul so to his own concept
That from its working all his visage wanned,
Tears in his eyes, distraction in his aspect,
A broken voice, and his whole function suiting
With forms to his conception? And all for nothing!
For Hecuba!
What's Hecuba to him, or he to her,
That he should weep for her? What would he do
Had he the motive and the cue for passion
That I have? He would drown the stage with tears,
And cleave the general ear with horrid speech,
Make mad the guilty and appal the free,
Confound the ignorant, and amaze indeed
The very faculties of eyes and ears.
Yet I,
A dull and muddy-mettled rascal, mope
Like John-a-dreams, unpregnant of my cause,

And can say nothing—no, not for a king,
Upon whose property and most dear life
A damned defeat was made. Am I a coward?
Who calls me villain, breaks my pate across,
Plucks off my beard and blows it in my face,
Tweaks me by the nose, gives me the lie in the
   throat
As deep as to the lungs—who does me this?
Ha!
God, I should take it: for it cannot be
But I am pigeon-livered and lack gall
To make oppression bitter, or ere this
I should have fatted all the region kites
With this slave's offal. Bloody, bawdy villain!
Remorseless, treacherous, lecherous, kindless villain!
Why, what an ass am I! This is most brave,
That I, the son of a dear father murdered,
Prompted to my revenge by heaven and hell,
Must like a whore unpack my heart with words
And fall a-cursing like a very drab,
A scullion! Fie upon it! Foh!
About, my brains. Hum—I have heard
That guilty creatures sitting at a play
Have, by the very cunning of the scene,
Been struck so to the soul that instantly
They have proclaimed their malefactions.
For murder, though it has no tongue, will speak
With most miraculous organ. I'll have these players
Play something like the murder of my father
Before my uncle. I'll observe his looks;
I'll probe him to the quick. If he does blench,
I know my course. The spirit that I have seen
May be a devil, and the devil has power
To assume a pleasing shape; yea, and perhaps,
Out of my weakness and my melancholy,

As he is very potent with such spirits,
Abuses me to damn me. I'll have grounds
More relative than this. The play's the thing
Wherein I'll catch the conscience of the King. *Exit.*

Act III

SCENE 1
The Court.

Enter KING, QUEEN, POLONIUS, OPHELIA, ROSENCRANTZ,
GUILDENSTERN.

KING.   And can you by no drift of conference
   Get from him why he puts on this confusion,
   Grating so harshly all his days of quiet
   With turbulent and dangerous lunacy?
ROS.   He does confess he feels himself distracted,
   But from what cause he will by no means speak.
GUILD.   Nor do we find him forward to be sounded,
   But with a crafty madness keeps aloof
   When we would bring him on to some confession
   Of his true state.
QUEEN.   Did he receive you well?
ROS.   Most like a gentleman.
GUILD.   But with much forcing of his disposition.
ROS.   Niggard of question, but of our demands
   Most free in his reply.

QUEEN.   Did you assay him
  To any pastime?
ROS.   Madam, it so fell out that certain players
  We overtook on the way. Of these we told him,
  And there did seem in him a kind of joy
  To hear of it. They are here about the court,
  And, as I think, they have already order
  This night to play before him.
POL.   'Tis most true,
  And he beseeched me to entreat your Majesties
  To hear and see the matter.
KING.   With all my heart; and it does much content
    me
  To hear him so inclined.
  Good gentlemen, give him a further edge,
  And drive his purpose into these delights.
ROS.   We shall, my lord.

                    Exeunt Rosencrantz and Guildenstern.

KING.   Sweet Gertrude, leave us too,
  For we have closely sent for Hamlet hither
  That he, as though by accident, may here
  Affront Ophelia.
  Her father and myself, lawful espials,
  We'll so bestow ourselves that, seeing unseen,
  We may of their encounter frankly judge,
  And gather by him, as he does behave,
  If it is the affliction of his love or no
  That thus he suffers for.
QUEEN.   I shall obey you.
  And for your part, Ophelia, I do wish
  That your good beauties be the happy cause
  Of Hamlet's wildness. So shall I hope your virtues
  Will bring him to his wonted way again,
  To both your honours.

OPH.   Madam, I wish it may.
                                                Exit Queen.

POL.   Ophelia, walk you here.—Gracious, so please
       you,
    We will bestow ourselves.—Read on this book,
    That show of such an exercise may colour
    Your loneliness. We are oft to blame in this,
    'Tis too much proved, that with devotion's visage
    And pious action we do sugar over
    The devil himself.

KING.   [*aside*]   O it is too true.
    How smart a lash that speech does give my
       conscience.
    The harlot's cheek, beautied with plastering art,
    Is not more ugly to the thing that helps it
    Than is my deed to my most painted word.
    O heavy burden!

POL.   I hear him coming. Let's withdraw, my lord.
                                                Exeunt.

                    Enter HAMLET.

HAM.   To be, or not to be, that is the question:
    Whether 'tis nobler in the mind to suffer
    The slings and arrows of outrageous fortune,
    Or to take arms against a sea of troubles
    And by opposing end them. To die—to sleep,
    No more; and by a sleep to say we end
    The heart-ache and the thousand natural shocks
    That flesh is heir to: 'tis a consummation
    Devoutly to be wished. To die, to sleep;
    To sleep, perchance to dream—ay, there's the rub:
    For in that sleep of death what dreams may come,
    When we have shuffled off this mortal coil,
    Must give us pause. There's the respect

That makes calamity of so long life.
For who would bear the whips and scorns of time, *hamlets*
The oppressor's wrong, the proud man's contumely, *disciple*
The pangs of disprized love, the law's delay,   *of life*
sailing The insolence of office, and the spurns
in lines That patient merit of the unworthy takes,
When he himself might his acquittance make
dagger With a bare bodkin? Who would burdens bear,
To grunt and sweat under a weary life,
But that the dread of something after death,
The undiscovered country, from whose bourn
No traveller returns, puzzles the will,
And makes us rather bear those ills we have
Than fly to others that we know not of?
Thus conscience does make cowards of us all,
And thus the native hue of resolution
Is sicklied o'er with the pale cast of thought,
And enterprises of great pitch and moment
With this regard their currents turn awry
And lose the name of action. Soft you now,
The fair Ophelia! Nymph, in your orisons
Be all my sins remembered.
OPH.   Good my lord,
How does your honour for this many a day?
HAM.   I humbly thank you, well.
OPH.   My lord, I have remembrances of yours
That I have longed long to redeliver.
I pray you now receive them.
HAM.
                                    No, not I.
I never gave you aught.
OPH.   My honoured lord, you know right well you did,
And with them words of so sweet breath composed
As made the things more rich. Their perfume lost,
Take these again; for to the noble mind
Rich gifts wax poor when givers prove unkind.

There, my lord.

HAM.   Ha, ha! Are you honest?

OPH.   My lord?

HAM.   Are you fair?

OPH.   What means your lordship?

HAM.   That if you are honest and fair, your honesty should admit no discourse to your beauty.

OPH.   Could beauty, my lord, have better commerce than with honesty?

HAM.   Ay, truly, for the power of beauty will sooner transform honesty from what it is to a bawd than the force of honesty can translate beauty into its likeness. This was sometime a paradox, but now the time gives it proof. I did love you once.

OPH.   Indeed, my lord, you made me believe so.

HAM.   You should not have believed me; for virtue cannot so inoculate our old stock but we shall relish of it. I loved you not.

OPH.   I was the more deceived.

HAM.   Get you to a nunnery. Why, would you be a breeder of sinners? I am myself indifferent honest, but yet I could accuse me of such things that it were better my mother had not borne me. I am very proud, revengeful, ambitious, with more offences at my beck than I have thoughts to put them in, imagination to give them shape, or time to act them in. What should such fellows as I do crawling between earth and heaven? We are arrant knaves all, believe none of us. Go your ways to a nunnery. Where's your father?

OPH.   At home, my lord.

HAM.   Let the doors be shut upon him, that he may play the fool nowhere but in his own house. Farewell.

OPH.   O help him, you sweet heavens.

HAM.   If you do marry, I'll give you this plague for
   your dowry: be you as chaste as ice, as pure as
   snow, you shall not escape calumny. Get you to a
   nunnery, farewell. Or if you will needs marry,
   marry a fool; for wise men know well enough what
   monsters you make of them. To a nunnery, go—
   and quickly too. Farewell.

OPH.   Heavenly powers, restore him.

HAM.   I have heard of your paintings well enough.
   God has given you one face and you make
   yourselves another. You jig and amble, and you
   lisp, you nickname God's creatures, and make your
   wantonness your ignorance. Go to, I'll no more of
   it, it has made me mad. I say we will have no more
   marriage. Those that are married already—all but
   one—shall live; the rest shall keep as they are. To a
   nunnery, go.

                                                        Exit.

OPH.   O, what a noble mind is here o'erthrown!
   The courtier's, soldier's, scholar's, eye, tongue,
      sword,
   The expectancy and rose of the fair state,
   The glass of fashion and the mould of form,
   The observed of all observers, quite, quite down!
   And I, of ladies most deject and wretched,
   That sucked the honey of his musicked vows,
   Now see that noble and most sovereign reason
   Like sweet bells jangled out of tune and harsh,
   That unmatched form and feature of blown youth
   Blasted with very madness. O woe is me
   To have seen what I have seen, see what I see.

                  Enter KING *and* POLONIUS.

KING.   Love? His affections do not that way tend,

Nor what he spoke, though it lacked form a little,
Was not like madness. There's something in his soul
O'er which his melancholy sits on brood,
And I do fear the hatch and the disclose
Will be some danger. Which now to prevent,
I have in quick determinatiòn
Thus set it down: he shall with speed to England
For the demand of our neglected tribute.
Haply the seas and countries different,
With variable objects, shall expel
This something settled matter in his heart,
Whereon his brains still beating put him thus
From fashion of himself. What think you of it?
POL.   It shall do well. But yet do I believe
The origin and commencement of his grief
Sprung from neglected love. How now, Ophelia?
You need not tell us what Lord Hamlet said,
We heard it all. My lord, do as you please,
But if you hold it fit, after the play
Let his queen-mother all alone entreat him
To show his grief. Let her be round with him,
And I'll be placed, so please you, in the ear
Of all their conference. If she finds him not,
To England send him; or confine him where
Your wisdom best shall think.
KING.   It shall be so.
Madness in great ones must not unwatched go.

SCENE II

Enter HAMLET *and three* Players.

HAM.   Speak the speech, I pray you, as I pronounced it
to you, trippingly on the tongue; but if you mouth

it as many of your players do, I had as soon the
town-crier spoke my lines. And do not saw the air
too much with your hand, thus, but use all gently;
for in the very torrent, tempest and, as I may say,
whirlwind of your passion, you must acquire and
beget a temperance that may give it smoothness.
O, it offends me to the soul to hear a robustious
periwig-pated fellow tear a passion to tatters, to
very rags, to split the ears of the groundlings—who
for the most part are capable of nothing but
inexplicable dumb-shows and noise. I would have
such a fellow whipped for overdoing Termagant. It
out-Herods Herod. Pray you, avoid it.

1ST PLAY.   I warrant your honour.

HAM.   Be not too tame either, but let your own
discretion be your tutor. Suit the action to the
word, the word to the action, with this special
observance, that you overstep not the modesty of
nature. For anything so overdone is away from the
purpose of playing, whose end, both at the first and
now, was and is to hold as it were the mirror up to
nature; to show virtue its feature, scorn its own
image, and the very age and body of the time their
form and pressure. Now this overdone or come
tardily off, though it makes the unskilful laugh,
cannot but make the judicious grieve—the judgment
of whom one must in your allowance outweigh a
whole theatre of others. O, there are players that I
have seen play, and heard others praise, and that
highly—(not to speak it profanely) that—neither
having the accent of Christians, nor the gait of
Christian, pagan, nor man—have so strutted and
bellowed that I have thought some of Nature's
journeymen had made men, and not made them
well, they imitated humanity so abominably.

1ST PLAY.   I hope we have reformed that sufficiently
   with us.
HAM.   O reform it altogether. And let those that play
   your clowns speak no more than is set down for
   them. For there are of them that will themselves
   laugh, to set on some quantity of barren spectators
   to laugh too, though in the meantime some
   necessary question of the play is then to be considered. That's villainous, and shows a most pitiful
   ambition in the fool that uses it. Go make you
   ready.
                                        Exeunt Players.

Enter POLONIUS, ROSENCRANTZ, *and* GUILDENSTERN.

   How now, my lord? Will the King hear this piece of
      work?
POL.   And the Queen too, and that immediately.
HAM.   Bid the players make haste.   *Exit Polonius.*
   Will you two help to hasten them?
ROS.   Ay, my lord.
                        Exeunt Rosencrantz and Guildenstern.
HAM.   What ho, Horatio!

Enter HORATIO.

HOR.   Here, sweet lord, at your service.
HAM.   Horatio, you are even as just a man
   As ever my conversation coped with yet.
HOR.   O my dear lord.
HAM.   Nay, do not think I flatter,
   For what advancement may I hope from you
   That no revènue have but your good spirits
   To feed and clothe you? Why should the poor be
      flattered?

No, let the candied tongue lick absurd pomp,
And crook the pregnant hinges of the knee
Where thrift may follow fawning. Do you hear?
Since my dear soul was mistress of its choice,
And could of men distinguish its election,
It has sealed you for itself. For you have been
As one, in suffering all, that suffers nothing—
A man that Fortune's buffets and rewards
Have taken with equal thanks. And blest are those
Whose blood and judgment are so well commingled
That they are not a pipe for Fortune's finger
To sound what stop she pleases. Give me that man
That is not passion's slave, and I will wear him
In my heart's core, ay, in my heart of heart,
As I do you. Something too much of this.
There is a play tonight before the King:
One scene of it comes near the circumstance
Which I have told you of my father's death.
I pray you, when you see that act afoot,
Even with the very comment of your soul
Observe my uncle. If his occulted guilt
Does not itself unkennel in one speech,
It is a damnèd ghost that we have seen,
And my imaginations are as foul
As Vulcan's stithy. Give him heedful note;
For I my eyes will rivet to his face,
And after we will both our judgments join
In censure of his seeming.

HOR.   Well, my lord.
If he steals aught the while this play is playing
And escapes detecting, I will pay the theft.

                Trumpets *and* Kettle-drums within.

HAM.   They are coming to the play. I must be idle.

Get you a place.

Enter KING, QUEEN, POLONIUS, OPHELIA, ROSENCRANTZ,
GUILDENSTERN, *and other* Lords, *with the King's*
Guard *carrying torches.*

KING.   How fares our cousin Hamlet?

HAM.   Excellent, in faith, of the chameleon's dish. I
eat the air, promise-crammed. You cannot feed
capons so.

KING.   I have nothing with this answer, Hamlet.
These words are not mine.

HAM.   No, nor mine now.—[*To Polonius*] My lord,
you played once in the university, you say?

POL.   That did I, my lord, and was accounted a good
actor.

HAM.   What did you enact?

POL.   I did enact Julius Caesar. I was killed in the
Capitol. Brutus killed me.

HAM.   It was a brute part of him to kill so capital a
calf there. Are the players ready?

ROS.   Ay, my lord, they stay upon your patience.

QUEEN.   Come hither, my dear Hamlet, sit by me.

HAM.   No, good mother, here's metal more attractive.

POL.   [*aside to the King*] O ho! do you mark that?

HAM.   [*lying at Ophelia's feet*] Lady, shall I lie in
your lap?

OPH.   No, my lord.

HAM.   I mean, my head upon your lap.

OPH.   Ay, my lord.

HAM.   Do you think I meant bawdy matters?

OPH.   I think nothing, my lord.

HAM.   That's a fair thought to lie between maids'
legs.

OPH.   What is, my lord?

HAM.   Nothing.

OPH.   You are merry, my lord.

HAM.   Who, I?

OPH.   Ay, my lord.

HAM.   O God, your only jig-maker. What should a
man do but be merry? For look you how cheerfully
my mother looks and my father died within this
two hours.

OPH   Nay, 'tis twice two months, my lord.

HAM.   So long? Nay then, let the devil wear black, for
I'll have a suit of sables. O heavens, die two
months ago and not forgotten yet! Then there's
hope a great man's memory may outlive his life
half a year. But by our lady he must build churches
then, or else shall he suffer not thinking on, with
the hobby-horse, whose epitaph is 'For O, for O,
the hobby-horse is forgot'.

The trumpets sound. A dumb-show follows.

Enter a KING *and a* QUEEN *very lovingly, the Queen
embracing him and he her. She kneels, and makes
show of protestation unto him. He takes her up, and
declines his head upon her neck. He lies down upon a
bank of flowers. She, seeing him asleep, leaves him.
Anon comes in another* Man, *takes off his crown,
kisses it, pours poison in the sleeper's ears, and
leaves him. The* QUEEN *returns, finds the King dead,
makes passionate action. The* Poisoner *with some*
Three or Four *comes in again and seems to condole
with her. The dead body is carried away. The
Poisoner woos the Queen with gifts. She seems harsh
awhile, but in the end accepts his love.*

Exeunt.

OPH.   What means this, my lord?
HAM.   Sure, this is mischief afoot. It means mischief.
OPH.   Belike this show imports the argument of the
play.

Enter PROLOGUE.

HAM.   We shall know by this fellow. The players
cannot keep counsel: they will tell all.
OPH.   Will he tell us what this show meant?
HAM.   Ay, or any show that you will show him. Be
not you ashamed to show, he'll not shame to tell
you what it means.
OPH.   You are naught, you are naught. I'll mark the
play.
PROL.   *For us and for our tragedy,*
             Here stooping to your clemency,
             We beg your hearing patiently. [*Exit.*]
HAM.   Is this a prologue, or the posy of a ring?
OPH.   It is brief, my lord.
HAM.   As woman's love.

Enter the Player KING *and* QUEEN.

P. KING.   *Full thirty times has Phoebus' cart gone*
   round
Neptune's salt wash and Tellus' orbèd ground,
And thirty dozen moons with borrowed sheen
About the world have times twelve thirties been
Since love our hearts and Hymen did our hands
Unite commutual in most sacred bands.
P. QUEEN.   *So many journeys may the sun and moon*
Make us again count o'er ere love is done.
But woe is me, you are so sick of late,
So far from cheer and from your former state,

That I distrust you. Yet though I distrust,
Discomfort you, my lord, it nothing must;
For women's fear and love hold quantity,
In neither aught, or in extremity.
Now what my love is, proof has made you know,
And as my love is sized, my fear is so.
Where love is great, the littlest doubts are fear;
Where little fears grow great, great love grows
   there.

P. KING.   *Faith, I must leave you, love, and shortly*
   too:

My operant powers their functions leave to do;
And you shall live in this fair world behind,
Honoured, beloved; and haply one as kind
For husband shall you—

P. QUEEN.   *O confound the rest.*
Such love must needs be treason in my breast.
In second husband let me be accurst;
None wed the second but who killed the first.

HAM.   [aside] That's wormwood.

P. QUEEN.   *The instances that second marriage move*
Are base respects of thrift, but none of love.
A second time I kill my husband dead,
When second husband kisses me in bed.

P. KING.   *I do believe you think what now you*
   speak;

But what we do determine, oft we break.
Purpose is but the slave to memory,
Of violent birth but poor validity,
Which now, the fruit unripe, sticks on the tree,
But fall unshaken when they mellow be.
Most necessary 'tis that we forget
To pay ourselves what to ourselves is debt.
What to ourselves in passion we propose,
The passion ending, does the purpose lose.

The violence of either grief or joy
Their own enactments with themselves destroy.
Where joy most revels grief does most lament;
Grief joys, joy grieves, on slender accident.
This world is not for aye, and 'tis not strange
That even our loves should with our fortunes
   change,
For 'tis a question left us yet to prove,
Whether love leads fortune or else fortune love.
The great man down, you mark his favourite flies;
The poor advanced makes friends of enemies;
And hitherto does love on fortune tend:
For who not needs shall never lack a friend,
And who in want a hollow friend does try
Directly seasons him his enemy.
But orderly to end where I begun,
Our wills and fates do so contràry run
That our devices still are overthrown:
Our thoughts are ours, their ends none of our own.
So think you will no second husband wed,
But die your thoughts when your first lord is dead.

P. QUEEN.   *Nor earth to me give food, nor heaven*
   light,
Sport and repose lock from me day and night,
To desperation turn my trust and hope,
An anchor's cheer in prison be my scope,
Each opposite, that blanks the face of joy,
Meet what I would have well and it destroy,
Both here and hence pursue me lasting strife,
If, once a widow, ever I be a wife.

HAM.   If she should break it now!

P. KING.   *'Tis deeply sworn. Sweet, leave me here*
   awhile.
My spirits grow dull, and fain I would beguile
The tedious day with sleep.

P. QUEEN.   *Sleep rock your brain,*
  And never come mischance between us twain.

                                      Exit. He sleeps.

HAM.   Madam, how like you this play?

QUEEN.   The lady does protest too much, I think.

HAM.   O, but she will keep her word.

KING.   Have you heard the argument? Is there no
  offence in it?

HAM.   No, no, they do but jest—poison in jest. No
  offence in the world.

KING.   What do you call the play?

HAM.   *The Mousetrap*—surely, how metaphorically!
  This play is the image of a murder done in Vienna—
  Gonzago is the Duke's name, his wife Baptista—you
  shall see shortly. It is a knavish piece of work, but
  what of that? Your Majesty, and we that have free
  souls, it touches us not. Let the galled jade wince,
  our withers are unwrung.

                    Enter LUCIANUS.

  This is one Lucianus, nephew to the King.

OPH.   You are as good as a chorus, my lord.

HAM.   I could interpret between you and your love if I
  could see the puppets dallying.

OPH.   You are keen, my lord, you are keen.

HAM.   It would cost you a groaning to take off my
  edge.

OPH.   Still better, and worse.

HAM.   So you mis-take your husbands.—Begin,
  murderer. Leave your damnable faces and begin.
  Come, the croaking raven does bellow for revenge.

LUC.   *Thoughts black, hands apt, drugs fit, and time*
    agreeing,
  Confederate season, else no creature seeing,

You mixture rank, of midnight weeds collected,
With Hecate's ban thrice blasted, thrice infected,
Your natural magic and dire property
On wholesome life usurps immediately.

Pours the poison in his ears.

HAM.   He poisons him in the garden for his estate. His
name is Gonzago. The story is extant, and written in
very choice Italian. You shall see now how the
murderer gets the love of Gonzago's wife.

OPH.   The King rises.

HAM.   What, frighted with false fire?

QUEEN.   How fares my lord?

POL.   Give over the play.

KING.   Give me some light. Away.

ALL.   Lights, lights, lights.

Exeunt all but Hamlet and Horatio.

HAM.   Why, let the stricken deer go weep,
                 The hart ungallèd play;
            For some must watch while some must
                 sleep,
                 Thus runs the world away.
      Would not this, sir, and a forest of feathers, if the
      rest of my fortunes turn Turk with me, with
      Provincial slit roses on my shoes, get me a
      fellowship in a pack of players?

HOR.   Half a share.

HAM.   A whole one, I.
                 For you do know, O Damon dear,
                      This realm dismantled was
                 Of Jove himself, and now reigns here
                      A very, very—peacock.

HOR.   You might have rhymed.

HAM.   O good Horatio, I'll take the ghost's word for a

thousand pound. Did you perceive?

HOR.   Very well, my lord.

HAM.   Upon the talk of the poisoning?

HOR.   I did very well note him.

HAM.   Ah ha! Come, some music; come, the
recorders.

        For if the King likes not the comedy,

        Why then, belike he likes it not, perdie.

Come, some music.

Enter ROSENCRANTZ *and* GUILDENSTERN.

GUILD.   Good my lord, vouchsafe me a word with
you.

HAM.   Sir, a whole history.

GUILD.   The King, sir—

HAM.   Ay, sir, what of him?

GUILD.   Is in his retirement marvellous distempered.

HAM.   With drink, sir?

GUILD.   No, my lord, with choler.

HAM.   Your wisdom should show itself richer to
signify this to the doctor; for, for me to put him to
his purgation, would perhaps plunge him into more
choler.

GUILD.   Good my lord, put your discourse into some
frame, and start not so wildly from my affair.

HAM.   I am tame, sir. Pronounce.

GUILD.   The Queen your mother, in most great affliction of spirit, has sent me to you.

HAM.   You are welcome.

GUILD.   Nay, good my lord, this courtesy is not of the
right breed. If it shall please you to make me a
wholesome answer, I will do your mother's commandment; if not, your pardon and my return shall
be the end of my business.

HAM. Sir, I cannot.

ROS. What, my lord?

HAM. Make you a wholesome answer. My wit is
diseased. But sir, such answer as I can make, you
shall command—or rather, as you say, my mother.
Therefore no more, but to the matter. My mother,
you say—

ROS. Then thus she says: your behaviour has struck
her into amazement and wonder.

HAM. O wonderful son, that can so astonish a
mother! But is there no sequel at the heels of this
mother's astonishment? Impart.

ROS. She desires to speak with you in her closet ere
you go to bed.

HAM. We shall obey, were she ten times our mother.
Have you any further trade with us?

ROS. My lord, you once did love me.

HAM. And do still, by these pickers and stealers.

ROS. Good my lord, what is your cause of distemper?
You do surely bar the door upon your own liberty if
you deny your griefs to your friend.

HAM. Sir, I lack advancement.

ROS. How can that be, when you have the voice of
the King himself for your succession in Denmark?

HAM. Ay, sir, but while the grass grows—the proverb
is something musty.

Enter Players *with recorders.*

O, the recorders. Let me see one.—To withdraw
with you, why do you go about to recover the wind
of me, as if you would drive me into a trap?

GUILD. O my lord, if my duty is too bold, my love is
too unmannerly.

HAM. I do not well understand that. Will you play

upon this pipe?

GUILD. My lord, I cannot.

HAM. I pray you.

GUILD. Believe me, I cannot.

HAM. I do beseech you.

GUILD. I know no touch of it, my lord.

HAM. It is as easy as lying. Govern these vents with your fingers and thumb, give it breath with your mouth, and it will discourse most eloquent music. Look you, these are the stops.

GUILD. But these cannot I command to any utterance of harmony. I have not the skill.

HAM. Why, look you now, how unworthy a thing you make of me. You would play upon me, you would seem to know my stops, you would pluck out the heart of my mystery, you would sound me from my lowest note to the top of my compass. And there is much music, excellent voice, in this little organ, yet cannot you make it speak. God, do you think I am easier to be played on than a pipe? Call me what instrument you will, though you fret me, you cannot play upon me.

Enter POLONIUS.

God bless you, sir.

POL. My lord, the Queen would speak with you, and immediately.

HAM. Do you see yonder cloud that's almost in shape of a camel?

POL. By the mass and it is—like a camel indeed.

HAM. I think it is like a weasel.

POL. It is backed like a weasel.

HAM. Or like a whale.

POL. Very like a whale.

HAM.   Then I will come to my mother by and by.—
  [*Aside*] They fool me to the top of my bent.—I will
  come by and by.
POL.   I will say so.   *Exit.*
HAM.   'By and by' is easily said.—Leave me, friends.
                            [*Exeunt all but Hamlet.*]
'Tis now the very witching time of night,
When churchyards yawn and hell itself breathes out
Contagion to this world. Now could I drink hot
  blood,
And do such bitter business as the day
Would quake to look on. Soft, now to my mother.
O heart, lose not your nature. Let not ever
The soul of Nero enter this firm bosom;
Let me be cruel, not unnatural.
I will speak daggers to her, but use none.
My tongue and soul in this be hypocrites:
How in my words so ever she be rent,
To give them seals never my soul consent.   *Exit.*

SCENE III

Enter KING, ROSENCRANTZ, *and* GUILDENSTERN.

KING.   I like him not, nor stands it safe with us
  To let his madness range. Therefore prepare you.
  I your commission will forthwith dispatch,
  And he to England shall along with you.
  The terms of our estate may not endure
  Hazard so near us as does hourly grow
  Out of his brows.
GUILD.   We will ourselves provide.
  Most holy and religious fear it is
  To keep those many many bodies safe

That live and feed upon your Majesty.

ROS. The single and peculiar life is bound
With all the strength and armour of the mind
To keep itself from noyance; but much more
That spirit upon whose weal depend and rest
The lives of many. Decease of majesty
Dies not alone, but like a gulf does draw
What's near it with it. It is a massy wheel
Fixed on the summit of the highest mount,
To whose huge spokes ten thousand lesser things
Are mortised and adjoined, which when it falls,
Each small annexment, petty consequence,
Attends the boisterous ruin. Never alone
Did the King sigh, but with a general groan.

KING. Arm you, I pray you, to this speedy voyage,
For we will fetters put about this fear
Which now goes too free-footed.

ROS.   We will haste us.
        Exeunt Rosencrantz and Guildenstern.

        Enter POLONIUS.

POL. My lord, he's going to his mother's closet.
Behind the arras I'll convey myself
To hear the process. I'll warrant she'll tax him
  home,
And as you said—and wisely was it said—
'Tis meet that some more audience than a mother,
Since nature makes them partial, should overhear
The speech of vantage. Fare you well, my lord.
I'll call upon you ere you go to bed,
And tell you what I know.

KING.   Thanks, dear my lord.
               Exit Polonius.
O, my offence is rank, it smells to heaven;

It has the primal eldest curse upon it—
A brother's murder. Pray can I not,
Though inclination is as sharp as will,
My stronger guilt defeats my strong intent;
And, like a man to double business bound,
I stand in pause where I shall first begin,
And both neglect. What if this cursèd hand
Were thicker than itself with brother's blood,
Is there not rain enough in the sweet heavens
To wash it white as snow? Whereto serves mercy
But to confront the visage of offence?
And what's in prayer but this twofold force,
To be forestallèd ere we come to fall
Or pardoned being down? Then I'll look up.
My fault is past—but O, what form of prayer
Can serve my turn? 'Forgive me my foul murder?'
That cannot be, since I am still possessed
Of those effects for which I did the murder—
My crown, my own ambition, and my queen.
May one be pardoned and retain the offence?
In the corrupted currents of this world
Offence's gilded hand may shove by justice,
And oft 'tis seen the wicked prize itself
Buys out the law. But it is not so above:
There is no shuffling, there the action lies
In its true nature, and we ourselves compelled
Even to the teeth and forehead of our faults
To give in evidence. What then? What rests?
Try what repentance can. What can it not?
Yet what can it, when one cannot repent?
O wretched state, O bosom black as death,
O limèd soul, that struggling to be free
Are more engaged! Help angels—make assay.
Bow stubborn knees; and heart with strings of steel,
Be soft as sinews of the new-born babe.
All may be well.   *He kneels.*

Enter HAMLET.

HAM.   Now might I do it pat, now he is a-praying.
   And now I'll do it. And so he goes to heaven;
   And so am I revenged. That would be tested:
   A villain kills my father, and for that
   I, his sole son, do this same villain send
   To heaven.
   Why, this is hire and salary, not revenge.
   He took my father grossly, full of bread,
   With all his crimes broad blown, as flush as May;
   And how his audit stands who knows save heaven?
   But in our circumstance and course of thought
   'Tis heavy with him. And am I then revenged,
   To take him in the purging of his soul,
   When he is fit and seasoned for his passage?
   No.
   Up, sword, and know you a more horrid bent:
   When he is drunk asleep, or in his rage,
   Or in the incestuous pleasure of his bed,
   At game a-swearing, or about some act
   That has no relish of salvation in it,
   Then trip him, that his heels may kick at heaven
   And that his soul may be as damned and black
   As hell, whereto it goes. My mother stays.
   This physic but prolongs your sickly days.   *Exit.*
KING.   My words fly up, my thoughts remain below.
   Words without thoughts never to heaven go.   *Exit.*

SCENE IV

Enter QUEEN *and* POLONIUS.

POL.   He will come straight. Look you lay home to
   him,

Tell him his pranks have been too broad to bear
    with
And that your Grace has screened and stood between
Much heat and him. I'll silence me even here.
Pray you be round.
QUEEN.   I'll warrant you, fear me not.
Withdraw, I hear him coming.

> [*Polonius hides behind the arras.*]

Enter HAMLET.

HAM.   Now, mother, what's the matter?
QUEEN.   Hamlet, you have your father much offended.
HAM.   Mother, you have my father much offended.
QUEEN.   Come, come, you answer with an idle
    tongue.
HAM.   Go, go, you question with a wicked tongue.
QUEEN.   Why, how now, Hamlet?
HAM.   What's the matter now?
QUEEN.   Have you forgotten me?
HAM.   No, by the rood, not so.
  You are the Queen, your husband's brother's wife,
  And, would it were not so, you are my mother.
QUEEN.   Nay, then I'll set those to you that can speak.
HAM.   Come, come, and sit you down, you shall not
    budge.
  You go not till I set you up a glass
  Where you may see the inmost part of you.
QUEEN.   What will you do? You will not murder me?
  Help, ho!
POL.   (*behind the arras*] What ho! Help!
HAM.   How now? A rat? Dead for a ducat, dead.

> [*Thrusts his sword through the arras.*]

POL. [*behind*] O, I am slain.

QUEEN. O me, what have you done?

HAM.   Nay, I know not.
  Is it the King?

[*Lifts up the arras and discovers Polonius, dead.*]

QUEEN. O what a rash and bloody deed is this!

HAM. A bloody deed. Almost as bad, good mother,
  As kill a king and marry with his brother.

QUEEN. As kill a king?

HAM.   Ay, lady, it was my word.—
  You wretched, rash, intruding fool, farewell.
  I took you for your better. Take your fortune:
  You find to be too busy is some danger.—
  Leave wringing of your hands. Peace, sit you down,
  And let me wring your heart; for so I shall
  If it is made of penetrable stuff,
  If damned custom has not brazened it so,
  That it is proof and bulwark against sense.

QUEEN. What have I done that you dare wag your
    tongue
  In noise so rude against me?

HAM.   Such an act
  That blurs the grace and blush of modesty,
  Calls virtue hypocrite, takes off the rose
  From the fair forehead of an innocent love
  And sets a blister there, makes marriage vows
  As false as dicers' oaths. O, such a deed
  As from the body of contraction plucks
  The very soul, and sweet religion makes
  A rhapsody of words. Heaven's face does glow
  Over this solidity and compound mass
  With saddened visage, as against the doom;

Is thought-sick at the act.

QUEEN.   Ay me, what act
That roars so loud and thunders in the index?

HAM.   Look here upon this picture, and on this,
The counterfeit presentment of two brothers.
See what a grace was seated on this brow,
Hyperion's curls, the front of Jove himself,
An eye like Mars to threaten and command;
A station like the herald Mercury
New-lighted on a heaven-kissing hill—
A combination and a form indeed
Where every god did seem to set his seal
To give the world assurance of a man.
This was your husband. Look you now what
    follows.
Here is your husband, like a mildewed ear
Blasting his wholesome brother. Have you eyes?
Could you on this fair mountain leave to feed
And batten on this moor? Ha, have you eyes?
You cannot call it love; for at your age
The heyday in the blood is tame, is humble,
And waits upon the judgment, and what judgment
Would step from this to this? Sense sure you have,
Else would you not have motion; but sure that sense
Is apoplexed, for madness would not err
Nor sense to ecstasy was ever so thralled
But it reserved some quantity of choice
To serve in such a difference. What devil was it
That thus has cozened you at blindman's buff?
Eyes without feeling, feeling without sight,
Ears without hands or eyes, smelling without all,
Or but a sickly part of one true sense
Could not so mope. O shame, where is your blush?
Rebellious hell,
If you can mutiny in a matron's bones,

To flaming youth let virtue be as wax
And melt in its own fire; proclaim no shame
When the compulsive ardour gives the charge,
Since frost itself as actively does burn
And reason panders will.

QUEEN.   O Hamlet, speak no more.
You turn my eyes into my very soul,
And there I see such black and grainèd spots
As will not leave their tinct.

HAM.   Nay, but to live
In the rank sweat of a soiled, greasy bed,
Stewed in corruption, honeying and making love
Over the nasty sty!

QUEEN.   O speak to me no more.
These words like daggers enter in my ears.
No more, sweet Hamlet.

HAM.   A murderer and a villain,
A slave that is not twentieth part the tithe
Of your precèdent lord, a vice of kings,
A cutpurse of the empire and the rule,
That from a shelf the precious diadem stole
And put it in his pocket—

QUEEN.   No more.

HAM.   A king of shred and patches—

Enter GHOST.

Save me and hover over me with your wings,
You heavenly guards! What would your gracious
    figure?

QUEEN.   Alas, he's mad.

HAM.   Do you not come your tardy son to chide,
That, lapsed in time and passion, lets go by
The urgent acting of your dread command?
O say.

GHOST.   Do not forget. This visitation
  Is but to whet your almost blunted purpose.
  But look, amazement on your mother sits.
  O step between her and her fighting soul.
  Fancy in weakest bodies strongest works.
  Speak to her, Hamlet.

HAM.   How is it with you, lady?

QUEEN.   Alas, how is it with you,
  That you do bend your eye on vacancy,
  And with the incorporal air do hold discourse?
  Forth at your eyes your spirits wildly peep,
  And, as the sleeping soldiers in the alarm,
  Your bedded hair, like life in outgrowths dead,
  Starts up and stands on end. O gentle son,
  Upon the heat and flame of your distemper
  Sprinkle cool patience. Whereon do you look?

HAM.   On him, on him. Look you how pale he glares.
  His form and cause conjoined, preaching to stones,
  Would make them capable.—Do not look upon me,
  Lest with this piteous action you convert
  My stern effects. Then what I have to do
  Will want true colour—tears perchance for blood.

QUEEN.   To whom do you speak this?

HAM.   Do you see nothing there?

QUEEN.   Nothing at all; yet all that is I see.

HAM.   And did you nothing hear?

QUEEN.   No, nothing but ourselves.

HAM.   Why, look you there, look how it steals away.
  My father, in his habit as he lived!
  Look where he goes even now out at the portal.

                                        Exit Ghost.

QUEEN.   This is the very coinage of your brain.
  This bodiless creation madness itself
  Is very cunning in.

HAM.   My pulse as yours does temperately keep time,

And makes as healthful music. It is not madness
That I have uttered. Bring me to the test,
And I the matter will re-word, which madness
Would gambol from. Mother, for love of grace,
Lay not that flattering unction to your soul,
That not your trespass but my madness speaks.
It will but skin and film the ulcerous place,
While rank corruption, mining all within,
Infects unseen. Confess yourself to heaven,
Repent what's past, avoid what is to come;
And do not spread the compost on the weeds
To make them ranker. Forgive me this my virtue;
For in the fatness of these pursy times
Virtue itself of vice must pardon beg,
Yea, curb and woo for leave to do it good.
QUEEN.   O Hamlet, you have cleft my heart in twain.
HAM.   O throw away the worser part of it
And live the purer with the other half.
Good night. But go not to my uncle's bed.
Assume a virtue if you have it not.
That monster, custom, who all sense does eat
Of habits evil, is angel yet in this,
That to the use of actions fair and good
He likewise gives a frock or livery
That aptly is put on. Refrain tonight,
And that shall lend a kind of easiness
To the next abstinence, the next more easy.
For use almost can change the stamp of nature,
And either thwart the devil or throw him out
With wondrous potency. Once more, good night,
And when you are desirous to be blest,
I'll blessing beg of you. For this same lord
I do repent; but heaven has pleased it so,
To punish me with this and this with me,
That I must be their scourge and minister.

I will bestow him, and will answer well
The death I gave him. So, again, good night.
I must be cruel only to be kind.
This bad begins, and worse remains behind.
One word more, good lady.

QUEEN.   What shall I do?

HAM.   Not this by any means that I bid you do:
Let the bloat King tempt you again to bed,
Pinch wanton on your cheek, call you his mouse,
And let him, for a pair of reeky kisses,
Or paddling in your neck with his damned fingers,
Make you to ravel all this matter out
That I essentially am not in madness,
But mad in craft. 'Twere good you let him know,
For who that's but a queen, fair, sober, wise,
Would from a toad, from a bat, tom-cat,
Such dear concernings hide? Who would do so?
No, in despite of sense and secrecy,
Unpeg the basket on the house's top,
Let the birds fly, and like the famous ape,
To try conclusions, in the basket creep,
And break your own neck down.

QUEEN.   Be you assured, if words are made of breath,
And breath of life, I have no life to breathe
What you have said to me.

HAM.   I must to England, you know that?

QUEEN.   Alas,
I had forgotten. 'Tis so concluded on.

HAM.   The letters are sealed, and my two
    schoolfellows,
Whom I will trust as I will adders fanged—
They bear the mandate, they must sweep my way
And marshal me to knavery. Let it work;
For 'tis the sport to have the engineer
Hoist with his own petard; it shall go hard

But I will delve one yard below their mines
And blow them at the moon. O, 'tis most sweet
When in one line two crafts directly meet.
This man shall set me packing.
I'll lug the guts into the neighbour room.
Mother, good night indeed. This counsellor
Is now most still, most secret, and most grave,
Who was in life a foolish prating knave.
Come, sir, to draw toward an end with you.
Good night, mother.

Exit dragging in Polonius.

Act IV

SCENE I
The Court.

Enter KING, QUEEN, ROSENCRANTZ *and* GUILDENSTERN.

KING.   There's a matter in these sights, these
    profound heaves,
  You must translate. 'Tis fit we understand them
  Where is your son?
QUEEN.   Bestow this place on us a little while.
            [*Exeunt Rosencrantz and Guildenstern.*]
  Ah, my own lord, what have I seen tonight!
KING.   What, Gertrude, how does Hamlet?
QUEEN.   Mad as the sea and wind when both contend
  Which is the mightier. In his lawless fit,
  Behind the arras hearing something stir,

Whips out his rapier, cries 'A rat, a rat',
And in this brainish apprehension kills
The unseen good old man.

KING.   O heavy deed!
It had been so with us had we been there.
His liberty is full of threats to all—
To you yourself, to us, to everyone.
Alas, how shall this bloody deed be answered?
It will be laid to us, whose providence
Should have kept short, restrained, and out of haunt
This mad young man. But so much was our love,
We would not understand what was most fit,
But like the owner of a foul disease,
To keep it from divulging, let it feed
Even on the pith of life. Where has he gone?

QUEEN.   To draw apart the body he has killed,
Over whom—his very madness, like some ore
Among a mineral of metals base,
Shows itself pure—he weeps for what is done.

KING.   O Gertrude, come away.
The sun no sooner shall the mountains touch
But we will ship him hence; and this vile deed
We must with all our majesty and skill
Both countenance and excuse.—Ho, Guildenstern!

Enter ROSENCRANTZ *and* GUILDENSTERN.

Friends both, go join you with some further aid.
Hamlet in madness has Polonius slain,
And from his mother's closet has he dragged him.
Go seek him out—speak fair—and bring the body
Into the chapel. I pray you haste in this.

                    Exeunt Rosencrantz and Guildenstern.
Come, Gertrude, we'll call up our wisest friends,
And let them know both what we mean to do

And what's untimely done. So haply slander,
Whose whisper o'er the world's diameter,
As level as the cannon to its mark,
Transports its poisoned shot, may miss our name
And hit the woundless air. O come away,
My soul is full of discord and dismay.   *Exeunt.*

SCENE II

Enter HAMLET.

HAM.   Safely stowed.
  But soft, what noise? Who calls on Hamlet? O, here
  they come.

Enter ROSENCRANTZ and GUILDENSTERN.

ROS.   What have you done, my lord, with the dead
  body?
HAM.   Compounded it with dust, whereto it is kin.
ROS.   Tell us where it is, that we may take it thence
  and bear it to the chapel.
HAM.   Do not believe it.
ROS.   Believe what?
HAM.   That I can keep your counsel and not my own.
  Besides, to be demanded of a sponge—what replication should be made by the son of a king?
ROS.   Take you me for a sponge, my lord?
HAM.   Ay, sir, that soaks up the King's countenance,
  his rewards, his authorities. But such officers do
  the King best service in the end: he keeps them,
  like an ape, in the corner of his jaw—first mouthed,
  to be last swallowed. When he needs what you
  have gleaned, it is but squeezing you and, sponge,
  you shall be dry again.

ROS. I understand you not, my lord.

HAM. I am glad of it. A knavish speech sleeps in a
foolish ear.

ROS. My lord, you must tell us where the body is
and go with us to the King.

HAM. The body is with the King, but the King is not
with the body. The King is a thing—

GUILD. A thing, my lord?

HAM. Of nothing. Bring me to him. Hide fox, and all
after.   *Exeunt.*

SCENE III

Enter KING *and* Lords.

KING. I have sent to seek him and to find the body.
How dangerous is it that this man goes loose!
Yet must not we put the strong law on him:
He's loved of the distracted multitude,
Who like not in their judgment but their eyes;
And where 'tis so, the offender's scourge is weighed,
But never the offence. To bear all smooth and even,
This sudden sending him away must seem
Deliberate pause. Diseases desperate grown
By desperate appliance are relieved,
Or not at all.

Enter ROSENCRANTZ.

                        How now, what has befallen?

ROS. Where the dead body is bestowed, my lord,
We cannot get from him.

KING.   But where is he?

ROS. Without, my lord, guarded, to know your
pleasure.

KING.   Bring him before us.

ROS.   Ho! Bring in the lord.

Enter HAMLET *with* Guards.

KING.   Now, Hamlet, where's Polonius?

HAM.   At supper.

KING.   At supper? Where?

HAM.   Not where he eats, but where he is eaten. A
certain convocation of politic worms are even at
him. Your worm is your only emperor for diet: we
fat all creatures else to fat us, and we fat ourselves
for maggots. Your fat king and your lean beggar are
but variable service—two dishes, but to one table.
That's the end.

KING.   Alas, alas.

HAM.   A man may fish with the worm that has eaten
of a king, and eat of the fish that has fed of that
worm.

KING.   What do you mean by this?

HAM.   Nothing but to show you how a king may go a
progress through the guts of a beggar.

KING.   Where is Polonius?

HAM.   In heaven. Send thither to see. If your
messenger finds him not there, seek him in the
other place yourself. But if indeed you find him not
within this month, you shall nose him as you go
up the stairs into the lobby.

KING.   [*To some Attendants*] Go seek him there.

HAM.   He will stay till you come.

                                    [*Exeunt Attendants.*]

KING.   Hamlet, this deed, for your especial safety—
Which we do tender, as we dearly grieve
For that which you have done—must send you
      hence
With fiery quickness. Therefore prepare yourself.

The bark is ready, and the wind at help,
The associates attend. Everything is bent
For England.

HAM.   For England?

KING.   Ay, Hamlet.

HAM.   Good.

KING.   So is it, if you knew our purposes.

HAM.   I see a cherub that sees them. But come, for
England. Farewell, dear mother.

KING.   Your loving father, Hamlet.

HAM.   My mother. Father and mother are man and
wife, man and wife are one flesh; so my mother.
Come, for England.   *Exit.*

KING.   Follow him at foot. Tempt him with speed
   aboard,
Delay it not—I'll have him hence tonight.
Away, for everything is sealed and done
That else leans on the affair. Pray you make haste.
                                                        Exit.

And England, if my love you hold at aught—
As my great power thereof may give you sense,
Since yet your punishment looks raw and red
After the Danish sword, and your free awe
Pays homage to us—you may not coldly set
Our sovereign process. Which imports at full,
By letters congruing to that effect,
The instant death of Hamlet. Do it, England;
For like the hectic in my blood he rages,
And you must cure me. Till I know 'tis done,
However my haps, my joys were never begun. *Exit.*

SCENE IV

Enter FORTINBRAS *with his* Army.

FORT.   Go, captain, from me greet the Danish king.
  Tell him that by his licence Fortinbras
  Craves the conveyance of a promised march
  Over his kingdom. You know the rendezvous.
  If now his Majesty would aught with us,
  We shall express our duty in his eye;
  And let him know so.
CAP.   I will do it, my lord.
FORT.   Go softly on.   *Exeunt all but the Captain.*

Enter HAMLET, ROSENCRANTZ, GUILDENSTERN,
and Others.

HAM.   Good sir, whose powers are these?
CAP.   They are of Norway, sir.
HAM.   How purposed, sir, I pray you?
CAP.   Against some part of Poland.
HAM.   Who commands them, sir?
CAP.   The nephew to old Norway, Fortinbras.
HAM.   Goes it against the main of Poland, sir,
  Or for some frontier?
CAP.   Truly to speak, and with no addition,
  We go to gain a little patch of ground
  That has in it no profit but the name.
  To pay five ducats—five—I would not farm it;
  Nor will it yield to Norway or the Pole
  A ranker rate should it be sold in fee.
HAM.   Why, then the Poles now never will defend it.
CAP.   Yes, it is already garrisoned.

HAM. Two thousand souls and twenty thousand
ducats
Will not debate the question of this straw!
This is the abscess of much wealth and peace,
That inward breaks, and shows no cause without
Why the man dies. I humbly thank you, sir.
CAP. Goodbye, sir. `   [*Exit.*]
ROS.   Will it please you go, my lord?
HAM. I'll be with you straight. Go a little before.
                    [*Exeunt all but Hamlet.*]

How all occasions do inform against me,
And spur my dull revenge. What is a man
If his chief good and market of his time
Is but to sleep and feed? A beast, no more.
Sure he that made us with such large discourse,
Looking before and after, gave us not
That capability and godlike reason
To rust in us unused. Now whether it is
Bestial oblivion, or some craven scruple
Of thinking too precisely on the event—
A thought which, quartered, has but one part
wisdom
And ever three parts coward—I do not know
Why yet I live to say this thing is to do,
Since I have cause, and will, and strength, and
means
To do it. Examples gross as earth exhort me,
Witness this army of such mass and charge,
Led by a delicate and tender prince,
Whose spirit, with divine ambition puffed,
Makes mouths at the invisible event,
Exposing what is mortal and unsure
To all that fortune, death, and danger dare,
Even for an eggshell. Rightly to be great
Is not to stir without great argument,

surely God made me for something more

But greatly to find quarrel in a straw
When honour's at the stake. How stand I then,
That have a father killed, a mother stained,
Excitements of my reason and my blood,
And let all sleep; while to my shame I see
The imminent death of twenty thousand men
That, for a fantasy and trick of fame,
Go to their graves like beds, fight for a plot
Whereon the numbers cannot try the cause,
Which is not tomb enough and continent
To hide the slain? O, from this time forth
My thoughts be bloody or be nothing worth.   *Exit.*

SCENE V

Enter QUEEN, HORATIO, *and a* Gentleman.

QUEEN.   I will not speak with her.
GENT.   She is importunate,
  Indeed distract. Her mood will needs be pitied.
QUEEN.   What would she have?
GENT.   She speaks much of her father, says she hears
  There's tricks in the world, and hems, and beats
      her heart,
  Spurns enviously at straws, speaks things in doubt
  That carry but half sense. Her speech is nothing,
  Yet the unshaped use of it does move
  The hearers to collection. They aim at it,
  And botch the words up fit to their own thoughts:
  Which, as her winks and nods and gestures yield
      them,
  Indeed would make one think there might be
      thought,
  Though nothing sure, yet much unhappily.

HOR.   'Twere good she were spoken with, for she
   may strew
Dangerous conjectures in ill-breeding minds.
QUEEN.   Let her come in.   [*Exit Gentleman.*]
   [*Aside*] To my sick soul, as sin's true nature is,
   Each toy seems prologue to some great amiss.
   So full of artless apprehensive guilt—
   It spills itself in fearing to be spilt.

Enter OPHELIA.

OPH.   Where is the beauteous Majesty of Denmark?
QUEEN.   How now, Ophelia?
OPH.   (*sings*)   *How should I your true love know*
                      From another one?
                   By his cockle hat and staff
                   And his sandal [shoes]
QUEEN.   Alas, sweet lady, what imports this song?
OPH.   Say you? Nay, pray you mark.
   (*sings*)   *He is dead and gone, lady,*
                He is dead and gone,
               At his head a grass-green turf,
               At his heels a stone.

   O ho!
QUEEN.   Nay, but Ophelia—
OPH.   Pray you mark.
   [*sings*]   *White his shroud as the mountain snow—*

Enter KING.

QUEEN.   Alas, look here, my lord.
OPH.   (*sings*)   *Larded with sweet flowers*
                Which bewept to the grave did not go
                With true-love showers.
KING.   How do you, pretty lady?

OPH.   Well, God shield you. They say the owl was a
   baker's daughter. Lord, we know what we are, but
   know not what we may be. God be at your table.
KING.   Thinking upon her father.
OPH.   Pray let's have no words of this, but when they
   ask you what it means, say you this.
   (sings)   *Tomorrow is Saint Valentine's day,*
                  All in the morning betime,
               And I a maid at your window,
                  To be your Valentine.
            Then up he rose, and donned his clothes,
                  And opened the chamber door,
            Let in the maid that out a maid
                  Never departed more.
KING.   Pretty Ophelia—
OPH.   Indeed, without an oath, I'll make an end of it.
            Jesus and by Saint Charity,
               Alack and fie for shame,
            Young men will do it if they come to it—
               By Cock, they are to blame.
         Said she, 'Before you tumbled me,
               You promised me to wed.'
   He answers,
               'So would I have done, by yonder sun,
               If you had not come to my bed.'
KING.   How long has she been thus?
OPH.   I hope all will be well. We must be patient.
   But I cannot choose but weep to think they would
   lay him in the cold ground. My brother shall know
   of it. And so I thank you for your good counsel.
   Come, my coach. Good night, ladies, good night.
   Sweet ladies, good night, good night.   *Exit.*
KING.   Follow her close; give her good watch, I pray
      you.   [*Exit Horatio.*]
   O, this is the poison of deep grief: it springs

All from her father's death. And now behold—
O Gertrude, Gertrude,
When sorrows come, they come not single spies,
But in battalions. First, her father slain;
Next, your son gone, and he most violent author
Of his own just remove; the people muddied,
Thick and unwholesome in their thoughts and
    whispers
For good Polonius' death—and we have done simply
In hugger-mugger to inter him. Poor Ophelia
Divided from herself and her fair judgment,
Without which we are pictures, or mere beasts.
Last, and as much containing as all these,
Her brother is in secret come from France,
Feeds on this wonder, keeps himself in clouds,
And wants not buzzers to infect his ear
With pestilent speeches of his father's death.
Wherein necessity, of matter beggared,
Will nothing stick our person to arraign
In ear and ear. O my dear Gertrude, this,
Like to a murdering-piece, in many places
Gives me superfluous death.   *A noise within.*
                              Attend!
Where are my Switzers? Let them guard the door.

                Enter a Messenger.

    What is the matter?
MESS.   Save yourself, my lord.
    The ocean, overpeering of its bounds,
Eats not the flats with more impetuous haste
Than young Laertes, in a riotous head,
Overbears your officers. The rabble call him lord,
And, as the world were now but to begin,
Antiquity forgotten, custom not known—

The ratifiers and props of every word—
They cry, 'Choose we! Laertes shall be king.'
Caps, hands, and tongues applaud it to the clouds,
'Laertes shall be king, Laertes king.'
QUEEN. How cheerfully on the false trail they cry.
O, this is treason, you false Danish dogs.

A noise within.

KING. The doors are broken.

Enter LAERTES *with* Followers.

LAER. Where is this king?—Sirs, stand you all
without.
FOLLOWERS. No, let us in.
LAER.   I pray you give me leave.
FOLLOWERS. We will, we will.
LAER. I thank you. Keep the door. [*Exeunt Followers.*]
                              O you vile king,
Give me my father.
QUEEN.   Calmly, good Laertes.
LAER. That drop of blood that's calm proclaims me
bastard,
Cries cuckold to my father, brands the harlot
Even here between the chaste unsmirched brow
Of my true mother.
KING.   What is the cause,
Laertes,
That your rebellion looks so giant-like?—
Let him go, Gertrude. Do not fear our person.
There's such divinity does hedge a king
That treason can but peep to what it would,
Acts little of its will.—Tell me, Laertes,
Why you are thus incensed.—Let him go,
Gertrude.—
Speak, man.

LAER.   Where is my father?

KING.   Dead.

QUEEN.   But not by him.

KING.   Let him demand his fill.

LAER.   How came he dead? I'll not be juggled with.
To hell, allegiance! Vows to the blackest devil!
Conscience and grace, to the profoundest pit!
I dare damnation. To this point I stand,
That both the worlds I give to negligence,
Let come what comes, only I'll be revenged
Most thoroughly for my father.

KING.   Who shall stay you?

LAER.   My will, not all the world's.
And for my means, I'll husband them so well,
They shall go far with little.

KING.   Good Laertes,
If you desire to know the certainty
Of your father, is it written in your revenge
That, sweepstake, you will draw both friend and foe,
Winner and loser?

LAER.   None but his enemies.

KING.   Will you know them then?

LAER.   To his good friends thus wide I open my arms,
And, like the kind life-rendering pelican,
Repast them with my blood.

KING.   Why, now you speak
Like a good child and a true gentleman.
That I am guiltless of your father's death
And am most sensibly in grief for it,
It shall as level to your judgment appear
As day does to your eye.

Danes within.

                              Let her come in.

LAER.   How now, what noise is that?

Enter OPHELIA.

O heat, dry up my brains. Tears seven times salt
Burn out the sense and virtue of my eye.
By heaven, your madness shall be paid with weight
Till our scale turns the beam. O rose of May!
Dear maid—kind sister—sweet Ophelia—
O heavens, is it possible a young maid's wits
Should be as mortal as an old man's life?
Nature is fine in love, and where it is fine
It sends some precious instance of itself
After the thing it loves.

OPH. [*sings*] *They bore him bare-faced on the bier,*
                 And in his grave rained many a tear—
Fare you well, my dove.

LAER. Had you your wits and did persuade revenge,
It could not move thus.

OPH. You must sing *A-down, a-down,* and you *Call
him a-down-a.* O, how the wheel becomes it! It is
the false steward that stole his master's daughter.

LAER. This nothing's more than matter.

OPH. There's rosemary, that's for remembrance—
pray you, love, remember. And there are pansies,
that's for thoughts.

LAER. A document in madness: thoughts and
remembrance fitted.

OPH. There's fennel for you, and columbines.
There's rue for you. And here's some for me. We
may call it herb of grace on Sundays. You must
wear your rue with a difference. There's a daisy. I
would give you some violets, but they withered all
when my father died. They say he made a good
end.

[*sings*] *For bonny sweet Robin is all my joy.*

LAER. Thought and affliction, passion, hell itself
She turns to favour and to prettiness.

OPH.   (*sings*)   *And will he not come again?*
                     And will he not come again?
                        No, no, he is dead,
                          Go to your death-bed,
                     He never will come again.

                     His beard was as white as snow,
                     All flaxen was his poll.
                        He is gone, he is gone,
                        And we cast away moan.
                     God have mercy on his soul.
And of all Christian souls. God be with you.   *Exit.*

LAER.   Do you see this, O God?

KING.   Laertes, I must commune with your grief,
Or you deny me right. Go but apart,
Make choice of whom your wisest friends you will,
And they shall hear and judge between you and me.
If by direct or by collateral hand
They find us touched, we will our kingdom give,
Our crown, our life, and all that we call ours
To you in satisfaction. But if not,
Be you content to lend your patience to us,
And we shall jointly labour with your soul
To give it due content.

LAER.   Let this be so.
His means of death, his obscure funeral—
No trophy, sword, nor hatchment over his bones,
No noble rite, nor formal ostentation—
Cry to be heard, as though from heaven to earth,
That I must call it in question.

KING.   So you shall.
And where the offence is, let the great axe fall.
I pray you go with me.   *Exeunt.*

SCENE VI

Enter HORATIO *and a Servant.*

HOR.   What are they that would speak with me?
SERV.   Seafaring men, sir. They say they have letters
    for you.
HOR.   Let them come in.   [*Exit Servant.*]
  I do not know from what part of the world
  I should be greeted, if not from Lord Hamlet.

Enter Sailors.

1ST SAIL.   God bless you, sir.
HOR.   Let him bless you too.
1ST SAIL.   He shall, sir, and please him. There's a letter
  for you, sir. It came from the ambassador that was
  bound for England—if your name is Horatio, as I
  am let to know it is.
HOR.   (*reads the letter.*) *Horatio, when you shall have*
  overlooked this, give these fellows some means to
  the King. They have letters for him. Ere we were
  two days old at sea, a pirate of very warlike
  appointment gave us chase. Finding ourselves too
  slow of sail, we put on a compelled valour, and in
  the grapple I boarded them. On the instant they got
  clear of our ship, so I alone became their prisoner.
  They have dealt with me like thieves of mercy. But
  they knew what they did: I am to do a turn for
  them. Let the King have the letters I have sent, and
  repair you to me with as much speed as you would
  fly death. I have words to speak in your ear will
  make you dumb; yet are they much too light for

the core of the matter. These good fellows will
bring you where I am. Rosencrantz and Guilden-
stern hold their course for England; of them I have
much to tell you. Farewell.

> *He that you know yours,*
> > *Hamlet.*

Come, I will give you way for these your letters,
And do it the speedier that you may direct me
To him from whom you brought them.　　*Exeunt.*

SCENE VII

Enter KING *and* LAERTES.

KING.　Now must your conscience my acquittance
　　seal,
　　And you must put me in your heart for friend,
　　Since you have heard, and with a knowing ear,
　　That he who has your noble father slain
　　Pursued *my* life.

LAER.　　　　　　　It well appears. But tell me
　　Why you proceeded not against these feats,
　　So crimeful and so capital in nature,
　　As by your safety, wisdom, all things else
　　You mainly were stirred up.

KING.　　　　　　　O, for two special reasons,
　　Which may to you perhaps seem much unsinewed,
　　But yet to me they are strong. The Queen his
　　　mother
　　Lives almost by his looks, and for myself—
　　My virtue or my plague, be it either which—
　　She is so conjunctive to my life and soul
　　That, as the star moves not but in its sphere,
　　I could not but by her. The other motive
　　Why to a public count I might not go

Is the great love the general public bear him:
Who, dipping all his faults in their affection,
Work like the spring that turns yet wood to stone,
Convert his bonds to graces. So that my arrows,
Too slightly timbered for so loud a wind,
Would have reverted to my bow again,
But not where I had aimed them.

LAER.   And so have I a noble father lost,
A sister driven into desperate terms,
Whose worth, if praises may go back again,
Stood challenger on mount of all the age
For her perfections. But my revenge will come.

KING.   Break not your sleeps for that. You must not
   think
That we are made of stuff so flat and dull
That we can let our beard be shaken with danger,
And think it pastime. You shortly shall hear more.
I loved your father, and we love ourself,
And that, I hope, will teach you to imagine—

Enter Messenger.

MESS.   These to your Majesty, this to the Queen.
KING.   From Hamlet! Who brought them?
MESS.   Sailors, my lord, they say. I saw them not.
   They were given me by Claudio. He received them
   Of him that brought them.
KING.   Laertes, you shall hear them.—
   Leave us.   *Exit Messenger.*
[Reads] *High and mighty, you shall know I am set
naked on your kingdom. Tomorrow shall I beg
leave to see your kingly eyes, when I shall, first
asking your pardon, thereunto recount the occasion
of my sudden and more strange return.*
                                    Hamlet.

What should this mean? Are all the rest come
  back?
Or is it some abuse, and no such thing?

LAER.   Know you the hand?

KING.   It's Hamlet's character.
'Naked'—
And in a postscript here he says 'Alone'.
Can you advise me?

LAER.   I am lost in it, my lord. But let him come.
It warms the very sickness in my heart
That I shall live and tell him to his teeth,
'Thus die you'.

KING.   If it is so, Laertes—
As how should it be so, how otherwise?—
Will you be ruled by me?

LAER.   Ay, my lord,
So you will not overrule me to a peace.

KING.   To your own peace. If he has now returned,
As checking at his voyage, and that he means
No more to undertake it, I will work him
To an exploit, now ripe in my device,
Under which he shall not choose but fall.
And for his death no wind of blame shall breathe,
But even his mother shall uncharge the practice
And call it accident.

LAER.   My lord, I will be ruled,
The rather if you could devise it so
That I might be the organ.

KING.   It falls right.
You have been talked of since your travel much,
And that in Hamlet's hearing, for a quality
Wherein they say you shine. Your sum of parts

Did not together pluck such envy from him
As did that one, and that, in my regard,
Of the unworthiest sort.

LAER.   What part is that, my lord?

KING.   A very ribbon in the cap of youth—
Yet needful too, for youth no less becomes
The light and careless livery that it wears
Than settled age its sables and its weeds
Importing health and graveness. Two months since
Here was a gentleman of Normandy—
I have seen myself, and served against the French,
And they can well on horseback, but this gallant
Had witchcraft in it. He grew unto his seat,
And to such wondrous doing brought his horse
As had he been incorpsed and demi-natured
With the brave beast. So far he topped my thought
That I in forgery of shapes and tricks
Come short of what he did.

LAER.   A Norman was it?

KING.   A Norman.

LAER.   Upon my life, Lamond.

KING.   The very same.

LAER.   I know him well. He is the brooch indeed
And gem of all the nation.

KING.   He made confession of you,
And gave you such a masterly report
For art and exercise in your defence,
And for your rapier most especial,
That he cried out 'twould be a sight indeed
If one could match you. The swordsmen of their
    nation
He swore had neither motion, guard, nor eye,

If you opposed them. Sir, this report of his
Did Hamlet so envenom with his envy
That he could nothing do but wish and beg
Your sudden coming over to play with you.
Now out of this—

LAER.   What out of this, my lord?

KING.   Laertes, was your father dear to you?
Or are you like the painting of a sorrow,
A face without a heart?

LAER.   Why ask you this?

KING.   Not that I think you did not love your father,
But that I know love is begun by time,
And that I see, in passages of proof,
Time qualifies the spark and fire of it.
There lives within the very flame of love
A kind of wick or snuff that will abate it;
And nothing is at a like goodness still,
For goodness, growing to a pleurisy,
Dies in its own too-much. That we would do,
We should do when we would: for this 'would'
   changes
And has abatements and delays as many
As there are tongues, are hands, are accidents.
And then this 'should' is like a spendthrift sigh
That hurts by easing. But to the quick of the ulcer:
Hamlet comes back. What would you undertake
To show yourself in deed your father's son
More than in words?

LAER.   To cut his throat in the church.

KING.   No place indeed should murder sanctuarize;
Revenge should have no bounds. But good Laertes,
Will you do this, keep close within your chamber.
Hamlet, returned, shall know you are come home;
We'll put on those shall praise your excellence,

And set a double varnish on the fame
The Frenchman gave you, bring you in fine together,
And wager over your heads. He, being remiss,
Most generous, and free from all contriving,
Will not peruse the swords, so that with ease—
Or with a little shuffling—you may choose
A sword unbated, and in a pass of practice
Requite him for your father.

LAER.   I will do it.
And for that purpose, I'll anoint my sword.
I bought an unction of a mountebank
So mortal that but dip a knife in it,
Where it draws blood, no poultice yet so rare,
Collected from all simples that have virtue
Under the moon, can save the thing from death
That is but scratched with it. I'll touch my point
With this contagion, that if I gall him slightly,
It may be death.

KING.   Let's further think of this,
Weigh what convenience both of time and means
May fit us to our shape. If this should fail,
And that our drift looks through our bad
     performance,
'Twere better not essayed. Therefore this project
Should have a back or second that might hold
If this did blast in proof. Soft, let me see.
We'll make a solemn wager on your cunnings—
I have it!
When in your motion you are hot and dry—
As make your bouts more violent to that end—
And that he calls for drink, I'll have prepared him
A chalice for the purpose, whereon but sipping,
If he by chance escapes your venomed thrust,
Our purpose may hold there. But stay, what noise?

Enter QUEEN.

QUEEN.   One woe does tread upon another's heel,
  So fast they follow. Your sister's drowned, Laertes.
LAER.   Drowned? O, where?
QUEEN.   There is a willow grows askant the brook
  That shows its hoary leaves in the glassy stream.
  Therewith fantastic garlands did she make
  Of crow-flowers, nettles, daisies, and long purples,
  That liberal shepherds give a grosser name,
  But our cold maids do dead men's fingers call them.
  There on the pendent boughs her crownet weeds
  Clambering to hang, an envious sliver broke;
  When down her weedy trophies and herself
  Fell in the weeping brook. Her clothes spread wide,
  And mermaid-like awhile they bore her up,
  Which time she chanted snatches of old tunes,
  As one incapable of her own distress,
  Or like a creature native and indued
  Unto that element. But long it could not be
  Until her garments, heavy with their drink,
  Pulled the poor wretch from her melodious lay
  To muddy death.
LAER.   Alas, then she is drowned.
QUEEN.   Drowned, drowned.
LAER.   Too much of water have you, poor Ophelia,
  And therefore I forbid my tears. But yet
  It is our trick; nature its custom holds,
  Let shame say what it will. When these are gone,
  The woman will be out. Adieu, my lord,
  I have a speech of fire that fain would blaze
  But that this folly drowns it.   *Exit.*
KING.   Let's follow, Gertrude.
  How much I had to do to calm his rage.
  Now fear I this will give it start again.
  Therefore let's follow.   *Exeunt.*

Act V

SCENE I
A graveyard.

Enter Sexton and Grave-digger.

GRAVE. Is she to be buried in Christian burial, when she wilfully seeks her own salvation?

SEXT. I tell you she is, therefore make her grave straight. The coroner has sat on her and finds it Christian burial.

GRAVE. How can that be, unless she drowned herself in her own defence?

SEXT. Why, 'tis found so.

GRAVE. It must be *se offendendo*,[1] it cannot be else. For here lies the point: if I drown myself wittingly, it argues an act, and an act has three branches—it is to act, to do, to perform; argal,[2] she drowned herself wittingly.

SEXT. Nay, but hear you, Goodman Delver—

GRAVE. Give me leave. Here lies the water—good. Here stands the man—good. If the man goes to this water and drowns himself, it is, will he nill he, he goes; mark you that. But if the water comes to him and drowns him, he drowns not himself. Argal, he that is not guilty of his own death shortens not his own life.

SEXT. But is this law?

GRAVE. Ay, sure it is, coroner's quest law.

---

[1]Malapropism for *se defendendo*, in self-defence.
[2]Malapropism for *ergo*, therefore.

SEXT.   Will you have the truth of it? If this had not
   been a gentlewoman, she should have been buried
   out of Christian burial.

GRAVE.   Why, there you speak. And the more pity
   that great folk should have countenance in this
   world to drown or hang themselves more than their
   fellow Christians. Come, my spade. There are no
   ancient gentlemen but gardeners, ditchers, and
   gravemakers—they hold up Adam's profession.

He digs.

SEXT.   Was he a gentleman?

GRAVE.   He was the first that ever bore arms.

SEXT.   Why, he had none.

GRAVE.   What, you a heathen? How do you understand the Scripture? The Scripture says Adam
   digged. Could he dig without arms? I'll put another
   question to you. If you answer me not to the purpose, confess yourself—

SEXT.   Go to.

GRAVE.   What is he that builds stronger than either
   the mason, the shipwright, or the carpenter?

SEXT.   The gallows-maker, for that frame outlives a
   thousand tenants.

GRAVE.   I like your wit well in good faith, the gallows
   does well. But how does it well? It does well to
   those that do ill. Now, you do ill to say the gallows
   is built stronger than the church; argal, the gallows
   may do well to you. To it again, come.

SEXT.   Who builds stronger than a mason, a shipwright, or a carpenter?

GRAVE.   Ay, tell me that and unyoke.

SEXT.   Well, now I can tell.

GRAVE. To it.

SEXT. God, I cannot tell.

GRAVE. Cudgel your brains no more about it, for your dull ass will not mend his pace with beating. And when you are asked this question next, say 'A gravemaker'. The houses he makes last till dooms-day. Go, get you to Yaughan; fetch me a stoup of liquor.

Exit Sexton. The Grave-digger continues digging.

(Sings)   *In youth when I did love, did love,*
              I thought it was very sweet:
          To contract the time for my behove,
          O I thought there was nothing meet.

Enter HAMLET *and* HORATIO.

HAM. Has this fellow no feeling of his business he sings in grave-making?

HOR. Custom has made it in him a property of easiness.

HAM. 'Tis even so, the hand of little employment has the daintier sense.

GRAVE. *(sings)* *But age with his stealing steps*
                Has clawed me in his clutch,
            And has shipped me unto the land,
            As if I had never been such.
                        He throws up a skull.

HAM. That skull had a tongue in it, and could sing once. How the knave jowls it to the ground, as if it were Cain's jawbone that did the first murder. This might be the pate of a politician which this ass

now over-offices, one that would circumvent God,
might it not?

HOR.   It might, my lord.

HAM.   Or of a courtier, who could say, 'Good morrow, sweet lord. How do you, sweet lord?' This
might be my Lord Such-a-one, that praised my Lord
Such-a-one's horse when he meant to beg it, might
it not?

HOR.   Ay, my lord.

HAM.   Why, even so, and now my Lady Worm's,
chapless, and knocked about the block with a sexton's spade. Here's fine revolution had we the trick
to see it. Did these bones cost no more the
breeding but to play at bowls with them? Mine
ache to think of it.

GRAVE.   (sings)   *A pickaxe and a spade, a spade,*
                            For and a shrouding-sheet,
                     O a pit of clay for to be made
                            For such a guest is meet.

                                    [Throws up another skull.]

HAM.   There's another. Why, may not that be the
skull of a lawyer? Where are his quiddities now, his
quibbles, his cases, his tenures, and his tricks? Why
does he suffer this mad knave now to knock him
about the sconce with a dirty shovel, and will not
tell him of his action of battery? Hum, this fellow
might be in his time a great buyer of land, with his
statutes, his recognizances, his fines, his double
vouchers, his recoveries. Is this the fine of his fines
and the recovery of his recoveries, to have his fine
pate full of fine dirt? Will his vouchers vouch him
no more of his purchases, and double ones too,
than the length and breadth of a pair of indentures?
The very conveyances of his lands will scarcely lie
in this box, and must the inheritor himself have no
more, ha?

HOR.   Not a jot more, my lord.

HAM.   Is not parchment made of sheepskins?

HOR.   Ay, my lord, and of calveskins too.

HAM.   They are sheep and calves who seek out
assurance in that. I will speak to this
fellow.—Whose grave is this, man?

GRAVE.   Mine, sir.

[*Sings*]   *O a pit of clay for to be made—*

HAM.   I think it is yours indeed, for you lie in it.

GRAVE.   You lie out of it, sir, and therefore it is not
yours. For my part, I do not lie in it, yet it is mine.

HAM.   You do lie in it, to be in it and say it is yours.
It is for the dead, not for the quick: therefore you
lie.

GRAVE.   It is a quick lie, sir, it will away again from
me to you.

HAM.   What man do you dig it for?

GRAVE.   For no man, sir.

HAM.   What woman then?

GRAVE.   For none either.

HAM.   Who is to be buried in it?

GRAVE.   One that was a woman, sir; but rest her soul,
she's dead.

HAM.   How positive the knave is. We must speak by
the card or equivocation will undo us. By the Lord,
Horatio, these three years I have taken note of it, the
age is grown so finical that the toe of the peasant
comes so near the heel of the courtier he galls his
chilblain.—How long have you been grave-maker?

GRAVE.   Of all the days in the year I came to it that
day that our last King Hamlet overcame Fortinbras.

HAM.   How long is that since?

GRAVE.   Cannot you tell that? Every fool can tell that.
It was that very day that young Hamlet was
born—he that is mad and sent into England.

HAM.   Ay, to be sure. Why was he sent into England?

GRAVE. Why, because he was mad. He shall recover his wits there. Or if not, 'tis no great matter there.

HAM. Why?

GRAVE. It will not be seen in him there. There the men are as mad as he.

HAM. How came he mad?

GRAVE. Very strangely, they say.

HAM. How 'strangely'?

GRAVE. Faith, even with losing his wits.

HAM. Upon what ground?

GRAVE. Why, here in Denmark. I have been sexton here, man and boy, thirty years.

HAM. How long will a man lie in the earth ere he rots?

GRAVE. Faith, if he is not rotten before he dies—as we have many poxy corpses nowadays that will scarce hold the laying in—he will last you some eight year or nine year. A tanner will last you nine year.

HAM. Why he more than another?

GRAVE. Why, sir, his hide is so tanned with his trade that he will keep out water a great while, and your water is a sore decayer of your dead body. Here's a skull now that has lain in the earth three and twenty years.

HAM. Whose was it?

GRAVE. A mad fellow's it was. Whose do you think it was?

HAM. Nay, I know not.

GRAVE. A pestilence on him for a mad rogue! He poured a flagon of Rhenish on my head once. This same skull, sir, was Yorick's skull, the King's jester.

HAM. This?   [Takes up the skull.]

GRAVE. Even that.

HAM.   Alas, poor Yorick. I knew him, Horatio, a
fellow of infinite jest, of most excellent fancy. He
has borne me on his back a thousand times, and
now—how abhorred in my imagination it is. My
gorge rises at it. Here hung those lips that I have
kissed I know not how oft. Where are your gibes
now, your gambols, your songs, your flashes of
merriment, that were wont to set the table on a
roar? Not one now to mock your own grinning?
Quite chap-fallen? Now get you to my lady's
chamber and tell her, let her paint an inch thick, to
this complexion she must come. Make her laugh at
that.—Pray, Horatio, tell me one thing.

HOR.   What's that, my lord?

HAM.   Do you think Alexander looked of this fashion
in the earth?

HOR.   Even so.

HAM.   And smelt so? Pah!   *[Puts down the skull.]*

HOR.   Even so, my lord.

HAM.   To what base uses we may return, Horatio!
Why, may not imagination trace the noble dust of
Alexander till he finds it stopping a bung-hole?

HOR.   It is to consider too curiously to consider so.

HAM.   No, faith, not a jot, but to follow him thither
with modesty enough, and likelihood to lead it.
Alexander died, Alexander was buried, Alexander
returns to dust, the dust is earth, of earth we make
loam. And why of that loam whereto he was con-
verted might they not stop a beer-barrel?
Imperious Caesar, dead and turned to clay,
Might stop a hole to keep the wind away.
O that that earth which kept the world in awe
Should patch a wall to expel the winter's flaw,
                                        [storm].

But soft, but soft awhile. Here come the King,
The Queen, the courtiers.

Enter KING, QUEEN, LAERTES, Priest *and* Attendants
bearing OPHELIA'S *coffin*

                                Who is this they follow?
And with such maimed rites? This does betoken
The corpse they follow did with desperate hand
Fordo its own life. It was of some estate.
Couch we awhile and mark.

LAER.   What ceremony else?

HAM.   That is Laertes, a very noble youth. Mark.

LAER.   What ceremony else?

PRIEST.   Her obsequies have been as far enlarged
   As we have warranty. Her death was doubtful;
   And but that great command o'ersways the order,
   She should in ground unsanctified have lodged
   Till the last trumpet: for charitable prayers
   Shards, flints, and pebbles should be thrown on
     her.
   Yet here she is allowed her virgin wreaths,
   Her maiden strewments, and the bringing home
   Of bell and burial.

LAER.   Must there no more be done?

PRIEST.   No more be done.
   We should profane the service of the dead
   To sing sage requiem and such rest to her
   As to peace-parted souls.

LAER.   Lay her in the earth,
   And from her fair and unpolluted flesh
   May violets spring. I tell you, churlish priest,
   A ministering angel shall my sister be
   When you lie howling.

HAM.   What, the fair Ophelia!

QUEEN.   [*scattering flowers*] Sweets to the sweet.
  Farewell.
  I hoped you should have been my Hamlet's wife:
  I thought your bride-bed to have decked, sweet
    maid,
  And not have strewed your grave.
LAER.   O, treble woe
  Fall ten times treble on that cursèd head
  Whose wicked deed your most ingenious sense
  Deprived you of.—Hold off the earth awhile,
  Till I have caught her once more in my arms.
                           Leaps in the grave.
  Now pile your dust upon the quick and dead,
  Till of this flat a mountain you have made
  To overtop old Pelion or the skyish head
  Of blue Olympus.
HAM.   What is he whose grief
  Bears such an emphasis, whose phrase of sorrow
  Conjures the wandering stars and makes them
    stand
  Like wonder-wounded hearers? This is I,
  Hamlet the Dane.
LAER.   [*grappling with him*] The devil take your soul!
HAM.   You pray not well.
  I pray you take your fingers from my throat,
  For though I am not splenitive and rash,
  Yet have I in me something dangerous,
  Which let your wisdom fear. Hold off your hand.
KING.   Pluck them asunder.
QUEEN.   Hamlet! Hamlet!
ALL.   Gentlemen!
HOR.   Good my lord, be quiet.
HAM.   Why, I will fight with him upon this theme
  Until my eyelids will no longer wag.
QUEEN.   O my son, what theme?

HAM.   I loved Ophelia. Forty thousand brothers
   Could not with all their quantity of love
   Make up my sum. What will you do for her?
KING.   O, he is mad, Laertes.
QUEEN.   For love of God forbear him.
HAM.   God's wounds, show me what you'd do.
   Would weep, would fight, would fast, would tear
     yourself,
   Would drink up acid, eat a crocodile?
   I'll do it. Do you come here to whine,
   To outface me with leaping in her grave?
   Be buried quick with her, and so will I.
   And if you prate of mountains, let them throw
   Millions of acres on us, till our ground,
   Singeing his pate against the burning zone,
   Make Ossa like a wart. Nay, if you'll mouth,
   I'll rant as well as you.
QUEEN.   This is mere madness,
   And thus awhile the fit will work on him.
   Anon, as patient as the female dove
   When then her golden couplets are disclosed,
   His silence will sit drooping.
HAM.   Hear you, sir,
   What is the reason that you use me thus?
   I loved you ever. But it is no matter.
   Let Hercules himself do what he may,
   The cat will mew, and dog will have his day.
                      Exit.
KING.   I pray you, good Horatio, wait upon him.
                   Exit Horatio.
   [*To Laertes*] Strengthen your patience in our last
     night's speech:
   We'll put the matter to the present push.—
   Good Gertrude, set some watch over your son.
   This grave shall have a living monument.

An hour of quiet shortly shall we see;
Till then in patience let our proceeding be. *Exeunt.*

SCENE II
The Court.

Enter HAMLET *and* HORATIO.

HAM.   So much for this, sir. Now shall you see the
    other.
    You do remember all the circumstance?
HOR.   Remember it, my lord!
HAM.   Sir, in my heart there was a kind of fighting
    That would not let me sleep. I thought I lay
    Worse than the mutineers in shackles. Rashly—
    And praised be rashness for it: let us know
    Our indiscretion sometimes serves us well
    When our deep plots do pall; and that should teach
    us
    There's a divinity that shapes our ends,
    Rough-hew them how we will—
HOR.   That is most certain.
HAM.   Up from my cabin,
    My sea-gown scarfed about me, in the dark
    Groped I to find out them, had my desire,
    Fingered their packet, and in fine withdrew
    To my own room again; making so bold,
    My fears forgetting manners, to unseal
    Their grand commission. Where I found, Horatio—
    Ah, royal knavery!—an exact command,
    Larded with many several sorts of reasons
    Importing Denmark's health, and England's too,
    With ho! such bogeys and goblins in my life,

That on perusal of it, no leisure bated,
No, not to stay the grinding of the axe,
My head should be struck off.

HOR.   Is it possible?

HAM.   Here's the commission, read it at more leisure.
But will you hear now how I did proceed?

HOR.   I beseech you.

HAM.   Being thus benetted round with villainies—
Ere I could make a prologue to my brains,
They had begun the play—I sat me down,
Devised a new commission, wrote it fair—
I once did hold it, as our statesmen do,
A baseness to write fair, and laboured much
How to forget that learning—but, sir, now
It did me yeoman's service. Will you know
The effect of what I wrote?

HOR.   Ay, good my lord.

HAM.   An earnest conjuration from the King,
As England was his faithful tributary,
As love between them like the palm might flourish,
As peace should still her wheaten garland wear
And stand a comma between their amities,
And many such-like as'es of great charge—
That on the view and knowing of these contents,
Without debatement further more or less,
He should those bearers put to sudden death,
Not shriving-time allowed.

HOR.   How was this sealed?

HAM.   Why, even in that was heaven ordinant.
I had my father's signet in my purse,
Which was the model of the Danish seal,
Folded the writ up in the form of the other,
Subscribed it, gave it the impression, placed it safely,
The changeling never known. Now the next day
Was our sea-fight, and what to this was sequent
You know already.

HOR.   So Guildenstern and Rosencrantz go to it.

HAM.   Why, man, they did make love to this
        employment.
    They are not near my conscience, their defeat
    Does by their own insinuation grow.
    It is dangerous when the baser nature comes
    Between the pass and fierce incensèd points
    Of mighty opposites.

HOR.   Why, what a king is this!

HAM.   Does it not, think you oblige me now—
    He that has killed my king and whored my mother,
    Popped in between the election and my hopes,
    Thrown out his angle for my very life
    And with such cozenage—is it not perfect conscience
    To quit him with this arm? And is it not to be
        damned
    To let this canker of our nature come
    In further evil?

HOR.   It must be shortly known to him from England
    What is the issue of the business there.

HAM.   It will be short. The interim is mine.
    And a man's life is no more than to say 'one'.
    But I am very sorry, good Horatio,
    That to Laertes I forgot myself;
    For by the image of my cause I see
    The portraiture of his. I'll court his favours.
    But sure the bravery of his grief did put me
    Into a towering passion.

HOR.   Peace, who comes here?

Enter OSRIC, *a Courtier.*

OSR.   Your Lordship is right welcome back to Den-
    mark.

HAM.   I humbly thank you, sir.—Do you know this
    waterfly?

HOR.   No, my good lord.

HAM.   Your state is the more gracious, for it is a vice
to know him. He has much land and fertile. Let a
beast be lord of beasts and his crib shall stand at
the king's mess. 'Tis a churl, but, as I say, spacious
in the possession of dirt.

OSR.   Sweet lord, if your lordship were at leisure, I
should impart a thing to you from his Majesty.

HAM.   I will receive it, sir, with all diligence of spirit.
Your bonnet to its right use: it is for the head.

OSR.   I thank your lordship, it is very hot.

HAM.   No, believe me, it is very cold, the wind is
northerly.

OSR.   It is moderately cold, my lord, indeed.

HAM.   But yet I think it is very sultry and hot for my
constitution.

OSR.   Exceedingly, my lord, it is very sultry—as it
were—I cannot tell how. My lord, his Majesty bade
me signify to you that he has laid a great wager on
your head. Sir, this is the matter—

HAM.   [*moves him to put on his hat*] I beseech you
remember—

OSR.   Nay, good my lord, for my ease, in good faith.
Sir, here is newly come to court Laertes—believe
me, an absolute gentleman, full of most excellent
qualities, of very soft society and great showing.
Indeed, to speak feelingly of him, he is the card or
calendar of gentry; for you shall find in him the
continent of what part a gentleman would see.

HAM.   Sir, his definement suffers no perdition in you,
though I know to divide him inventorially would
dizzy the arithmetic of memory, and yet diverge
neither, in respect of his quick sail. But, in the
verity of extolment, I take him to be a soul of great
article and his infusion of such dearth and rareness
as, to make true diction of him, his semblable is

his mirror and who else would trace him his
umbrage, nothing more.

OSR.   Your lordship speaks most infallibly of him.

HAM.   The concernancy, sir? Why do we wrap the
gentleman in our rawer breath?

OSR.   Sir?

HOR.   Is it not possible to understand in another
tongue? You will to it, sir, really.

HAM.   What imports the nomination of this
gentleman?

OSR.   Of Laertes?

HOR.   His purse is empty already, all his golden
words are spent.

HAM.   Of him, sir.

OSR.   I know you are not ignorant—

HAM.   I would you did, sir. Yet in faith if you did, it
would not much commend me. Well sir?

OSR.   You are not ignorant of what excellence Laertes
is—

HAM.   I dare not confess that, lest I should compare
with him in excellence; but to know a man well
is to know himself.

OSR.   I mean, sir, for his weapon; but in the
imputation laid on him, by them in his service,
he's unfellowed.

HAM.   What's his weapon?

OSR.   Rapier and dagger.

HAM.   That's two of his weapons. But well.

OSR.   The King, sir, has wagered with him six Barbary
horses, against which he has impawned, as I take
it, six French rapiers and poniards, with their
assigns, as girdle, hanger, and so. Three of the
carriages, in faith, are very dear to fancy, very
responsive to the hilts, most delicate carriages, and
of very liberal design.

HAM.   What call you the carriages?

HOR.   I knew you must be edified by the margin ere
you had done.

HOR.   The carriages, sir, are the hangers.

HAM.   The phrase would be more german to the
matter if we could carry a cannon by our sides—I
would it might be hangers till then. But on. Six
Barbary horses against six French swords, their
assigns, and three liberal-designed carriages—that's
the French bet against the Danish. Why is this—
impawned, as you call it?

OSR.   The King, sir, has laid, sir, that in a dozen
passes between yourself and him he shall not
exceed you three hits; he has laid on twelve for
nine. And it would come to immediate trial if your
lordship would vouchsafe the answer.

HAM.   How if I answer no?

OSR.   I mean, my lord, the opposition of your person
in trial.

HAM.   Sir, I will walk here in the hall. If it pleases
his Majesty, it is the breathing time of day with
me. Let the weapons be brought, the gentleman
willing, and the King hold his purpose, I will win
for him if I can; if not, I will gain nothing but my
shame and the odd hits.

OSR.   Shall I deliver you so?

HAM.   To this effect, sir, after what flourish your
nature will.

OSR.   I commend my duty to your lordship.

HAM.   Yours.   *Exit Osric.*
He does well to commend it himself, there are no
tongues else for his turn.

HOR.   This lapwing runs away with the shell on his
head.

HAM.   He did compliment his dug before he sucked it.
Thus has he—and many more of the same bevy

that I know the drossy age dotes on—only got the tune of the time, and out of an habit of encounter, a kind of yeasty collection, which carries them through and through the most refined and winnowed opinions. And do but blow them to their trial, the bubbles are out.

Enter a Lord.

LORD.   My lord, his Majesty commended to you by young Osric, who brings back to him that you attend him in the hall. He sends to know if your pleasure holds to play with Laertes or that you will take longer time.

HAM.   I am constant to my purposes, they follow the King's pleasure. If his fitness speaks, mine is ready. Now or whensoever, provided I am so able as now.

LORD.   The King and Queen and all are coming down.

HAM.   In happy time.

LORD.   The Queen desires you to use some gentle entertainment to Laertes before you fall to play.

HAM.   She well instructs me.   [*Exit Lord.*]

HOR.   You will lose, my lord.

HAM.   I do not think so. Since he went into France, I have been in continual practice. I shall win at the odds. You would not think how ill all's here about my heart; but it is no matter.

HOR.   Nay, good my lord.

HAM.   It is but foolery, but it is such a kind of misgiving as would perhaps trouble a woman.

HOR.   If your mind dislikes anything, obey it. I will forestall their repair hither and say you are not fit.

HAM.   Not a whit. We defy augury. There is special providence in the fall of a sparrow. If it is now, 'tis not to come; if it is not to come, it will be now; if

it is not now, yet it will come. The readiness is all.
Since no man, of aught he leaves, knows aught,
what is it to leave betimes? Let be.

A table prepared. Trumpets, Drums, *and* Officers
with cushions. Enter KING, QUEEN, LAERTES,
OSRIC, LORDS, *and* Attendants.

KING.   Come, Hamlet, come, and take this hand
from me.

[Puts Laertes' hand into Hamlet's.]

HAM.   Give me your pardon, sir. I have done you
wrong;
But pardon it as you are a gentleman.
This presence knows, and you must needs have
heard,
How I am punished with a sore distraction.
What I have done
That might your nature, honour, and exception
Roughly awake, I here proclaim was madness.
Was it Hamlet wronged Laertes? Never Hamlet.
If Hamlet from himself is taken away
And when he's not himself does wrong Laertes,
Then Hamlet does it not, Hamlet denies it.
Who does it then? His madness. If it is so,
Hamlet is of the faction that is wronged;
His madness is poor Hamlet's enemy.
Sir, in this audience,
Let my disclaiming from a purposed evil
Free me so far in your most generous thoughts
That I have shot my arrow over the house
And hurt my brother.

LAER.   I am satisfied in nature,
Whose motive in this case should stir me most

To my revenge. But in my terms of honour
I stand aloof, and will no reconcilement
Till, by some elder masters of known honour,
I have a voice and precedent of peace
To keep my name ungored. But till that time
I do receive your offered love like love
And will not wrong it.

HAM.   I embrace it freely,
And will this brothers' wager frankly play.—
Give us the weapons.

LAER.   Come, one for me.

HAM.   I'll be your weapon, Laertes. In my ignorance
Your skill shall like a star in the darkest night
Stick fiery off indeed.

LAER.   You mock me, sir.

HAM.   No, by this hand.

KING.   Give them the weapons, young Osric. Nephew
   Hamlet,
You know the wager?

HAM.   Very well, my lord.
Your Grace has laid the odds on the weaker side.

KING.   I do not fear it. I have seen you both,
But since he is bettered, we have therefore odds.

LAER.   This is too heavy. Let me see another.

HAM.   This likes me well. These swords have all a
   length?

OSR.   Ay, my good lord.   *They prepare to play.*

               Enter Servants *with wine.*

KING.   Set the stoups of wine upon that table.
If Hamlet gives the first or second hit,
Or quit in answer of the third exchange,
Let all the battlements their ordnance fire.
The King shall drink to Hamlet's better breath,
And in the cup a pearl then shall he throw

Richer than that which four successive kings
In Denmark's crown have worn.—Give me the
   cups—
And let the kettle to the trumpet speak,
The trumpet to the cannoneer without,
The cannons to the heavens, the heaven to earth,
'Now the King drinks to Hamlet.' Come, begin.
And you, the judges, bear a wary eye.

HAM. Come on, sir.
LAER. Come, my lord.   *They play.*
HAM. One.
LAER. No.
HAM. Judgment.
OSR. A hit, a very palpable hit.
LAER. Well, again.
KING. Stay, give me drink. Hamlet this pearl is yours.
  Here's to your health.
           Drums; trumpets, and shot goes off.
           Give him the cup.
HAM. I'll play this bout first. Set it by awhile.
  Come.   *They play again.*
  Another hit. What say you?
LAER. I do confess it.
KING. Our son shall win.
QUEEN.   He's fat and scant of breath.
  Here, Hamlet, take my napkin, rub your brows.
  The Queen carouses to your fortune, Hamlet.
HAM. Good madam.
KING. Gertrude, do not drink.
QUEEN. I will, my lord, I pray you pardon me.
         She drinks, offers the cup to Hamlet.
KING. [*aside*] It is the poisoned cup. It is too late.
HAM. I dare not drink yet, madam—by and by.
QUEEN. Come, let me wipe your face.
LAER. My lord, I'll hit him now.
KING.   I do not think it.

LAER. [*aside*] And yet it is almost against my
    conscience.
HAM. Come for the third, Laertes. You do but dally.
  I pray you pass with your best violence.
  I am afraid you make a wanton of me.
LAER. Say you so? Come on.
OSR. Nothing either way.
LAER. Have at you now. *Laertes wounds Hamlet; then*
                in scuffling, they change rapiers.
KING. Part them; they are incensed.
HAM. Nay, come again.   *He wounds Laertes. The*
                                    Queen falls.
OSR. Look to the Queen there, ho!
HOR. They bleed on both sides. How is it my lord?
OSR. How is it, Laertes?
LAER. Why, as a woodcock to my own snare, Osric.
  I am justly killed with my own treachery.
HAM. How does the Queen?
KING.   She swoons to see them bleed.
QUEEN. No, no, the drink, the drink! O my dear
    Hamlet!
  The drink, the drink! I am poisoned.   *Dies.*
HAM. O villainy! Ho! Let the door be locked.
  Treachery! Seek it out.
LAER. It is here, Hamlet. Hamlet, you are slain.
  No medicine in the world can do you good;
  In you there is not half an hour's life.
  The treacherous instrument is in your hand,
  Unbuttoned and envenomed. The foul practice
  Has turned itself on me. Lo, here I lie,
  Never to rise again. Your mother's poisoned.
  I can no more. The King—the King's to blame.
HAM. The point envenomed too! Then, venom, to
    your work.
                                    Stabs the King.

ALL. Treason! treason!

KING.   O yet defend me, friends. I am but hurt.

HAM.   Here, you incestuous, murderous, damned
     Dane,
   Drink off this potion. Is your pearl here now?
   Follow my mother.   *King dies.*

LAER.   He is justly served.
   It is a poison tempered by himself.
   Exchange forgiveness with me, noble Hamlet.
   Mine and my father's death come not upon you,
   Nor yours on me.

HAM.   Heaven make you free of it. I follow you.
   I am dead, Horatio. Wretched Queen, adieu.
   You that look pale and tremble at this chance,
   That are but mutes or audience to this act,
   Had I but time—as this fierce sergeant, Death,
   Is strict in his arrest—O, I could tell you—
   But let it be. Horatio, I am dead,
   You live. Report me and my cause aright
   To the unsatisfied.

HOR.   Never believe it.
   I am more an antique Roman than a Dane.
   Here's yet some liquor left.

HAM.   As you are a man
   Give me the cup. Let go, by Heaven I'll have it.
   O God, Horatio, what a wonderful name,
   Things standing thus unknown, shall I leave behind
     me.
   If you did ever hold me in your heart,
   Absent you from felicity awhile,
   And in this harsh world draw your breath in pain
   To tell my story.   *A march afar off and shot within.*
               What warlike noise is this?

Enter OSRIC.

OSR.   Young Fortinbras, with conquest come from
       Poland,
   To the ambassadors of England gives
   This warlike volley.
HAM.   O, I die, Horatio.
   The potent poison quite o'ercomes my spirit.
   I cannot live to hear the news from England,
   But I do prophesy the election lights
   On Fortinbras. He has my dying voice.
   So tell him, with the occurrents more and less
   Which have solicited—the rest is silence.   *Dies.*
HOR.   Now cracks a noble heart. Good night, sweet
       prince,
   And flights of angels sing you to your rest.
                                      [*March within.*]
   Why does the drum come hither?

           Enter FORTINBRAS, *the English* Ambassadors,
               and Soldiers *with drum and colours.*

FORT.   Where is this sight?
HOR.   What is it you would see?
   If aught of woe or wonder, cease your search.
FORT.   This sight cries out no quarter. O proud Death,
   What feast is toward in your eternal cell,
   That you so many princes at a shot
   So bloodily have struck?
1ST AMBASS.   The sight is dismal;
   And our affairs from England come too late.
   The ears are senseless that should give us hearing

To tell him his commandment is fulfilled,
That Rosencrantz and Guildenstern are dead.
Where should we have our thanks?

HOR.   Not from his mouth,
Had it the ability of life to thank you.
He never gave commandment for their death.
But since, so straight upon this bloody question,
You from the Polish wars and you from England
Are here arrived, give order that these bodies
High on a stage be placèd to the view,
And let me speak to the yet unknowing world
How these things came about. So shall you hear
Of carnal, bloody, and unnatural acts.
Of accidental judgments, chance slaughters,
Of deaths put on by cunning and forced cause,
And, in this upshot, purposes mistaken
Fallen on the inventors' heads. All this can I
Truly deliver.

FOR.   Let us haste to hear it,
And call the noblest to the audience.
For me, with sorrow I embrace my fortune.
I have some rights of memory in this kingdom,
Which now to claim my vantage do invite me.

HOR.   Of that I shall have also cause to speak,
And from his mouth whose voice will draw on
    more.
But let this same be immediately performed
Even while men's minds are wild, lest more
    mischance
On plots and errors happen.

FORT.   Let four captains
Bear Hamlet like a soldier to the stage,
For he was likely, had he been put on,

To have proved most royal. And for his passage,
The soldier's music and the rite of war
Speak loudly for him.
Take up the bodies. Such a sight as this
Becomes the field, but here shows much amiss.
Go, bid the soldiers shoot.

           Exeunt marching, bearing off the bodies.

Julius Caesar

INTRODUCTION

Julius Caesar is, along with *Coriolanus*, the most classic of Shakespeare's plays and of a noble perfection. Nothing distracts from its direct and chaste impact—no sub-plot, no deviation, little in the way of humour, except for his usual portrayal of the fickleness and foolery, the credulity and changeability, of the mob. The citizens—the 'plebeians', the First Folio reads—play a character-part in the action, as indeed they did in the actual history of Rome.

The memory of Rome, and especially the personality of Caesar, were very present to Shakespeare's mind, from grammar-school days. As Professor C.J. Sisson says, 'in this respect he was of his age, which was deeply concerned and moved by Roman history . . . Caesar himself bestrode the imagination of Shakespeare—as of others—like a colossus, and haunted him throughout his writing days.'

For his material he had Sir Thomas North's translation of Plutarch's *Lives* ready to hand—'much of which he was able to absorb direct into his play, turning noble prose into nobler verse. This ample material is compressed and selected with skill and great judgment.' This was his way from the first; and if we follow his plays chronologically, as we should, we see how rapidly

157

this completely professional man of the theatre developed this skill; we can watch his developing mastery until it became second nature with him, as easy as a glove.

Many evidences attest the abiding popularity of the play, the crowds that flocked to it, and

> how the audience

Were ravished! with what wonder they went thence!

A young Swiss tourist, Thomas Platter, was one such who recorded an early performance at the Globe on 21 September 1599. 'After dinner, about 2 o'clock, I went with my companions across the water [across the Thames to the Southwark side], and in the straw-thatched house saw the tragedy of Julius Caesar excellently performed by some fifteen persons.' The play calls for a larger cast, but as usual some parts could be doubled.

The date is precisely 1599. Before finishing *Henry V* Shakespeare already had his next play in mind, as we sometimes see with his forward-planning mind. *Henry V* has a well known tribute to Essex, hopefully describing a comparable welcome from the London populace on his return from Ireland. Here again, in the opening scene, another reference occurs in the description of the crowd that would climb up to walls and battlements, windows and chimney pots—Elizabethan London, not Rome—to see Pompey pass; and now the fickle mob were abasing themselves before Caesar. This is as things are in human affairs—no one knew better than Shakespeare.

In one sense the play offers a portrait of human changeability, not only the variability and chances of fortune—also a favourite theme, as with Elizabethans in general. For the crux is reached in the splendid crowd

scene in the Forum (Act III Scene II), in which Brutus puts his case, in reasoned prose, to the citizens, who are then over-persuaded and worked up to fury by Mark Antony's appeal to their emotions, in rhetorical verse: 'Friends, Romans, countrymen!' etc. How well Shakespeare knew the politician's arts—always a pejorative term with him, as usually in his time.

He keeps the dramatic balance admirably, accentuating some of the defects of the marvellous man Caesar was, to bring him down to scale; on the other hand, he idealises Brutus to level things up, who was in historic fact not such a noble character as is made out. After all, he was a political assassin—whom Caesar had always treated with favour and affection. Hence the poignancy of Caesar's last despairing cry, which has rung down the ages: 'Et tu, Brute!'—you, above all, Brutus.

Brutus was not only an idealist, but an idealogue, who did what he did for that much abused, and no less confused, concept Liberty: liberty of the people—and we are shown what use they made of it, as in all revolutions. 'Burn! Fire! Kill! Slay! Let not a traitor live!'—this is William Shakespeare speaking.

Like most idealists, Brutus has bad judgment. He gives Antony the opportunity to sway the mob against himself and his fellow conspirators—against Cassius' better judgment. Again, before Philippi he urged on an immediate battle in unfavourable circumstances, when Cassius' more experienced judgment was against it. The quarrel that then takes place between these two makes another strong scene, humanly touching: just the sort of split that comes about in politics between collaborators in such events. Brutus is a stoic, who keeps a stiff upper lip at the news of his wife's death; Cassius is more human and shows his grief. Like such liberal idealists, Brutus is also conceited, morally smug:

> For I am armed so strong in honesty—

that threats pass him by as the idle wind.

One cannot altogether regret that he got his come-uppance at Philippi, nor altogether subscribe to the famous line, 'This was the noblest Roman of them all.' Shakespeare did him more than justice, for the benefit of his play, probably against his private opinion.

Something of his own age is yet present in this most Roman play. The press of suitors around Caesar, pre-senting their petitions, airing their grievances, is drawn from Elizabethan life: it was regular at the Queen's appearances, and one recalls her minister, Lord Burghley, taking refuge in the country at Theobalds from the press of suitors at Court. The conspirators are muffled up in their cloaks, as we see them portrayed in Gunpowder Plot engravings; they are dressed in con-temporary doublets, not togas. The regular term for a conspiracy was a 'knot'—

> So often shall the knot of us be called
> The men that gave their country liberty.

(In fact they gave Rome civil war for a generation.)

As always we have several references to his own pro-fession. When Caesar was offered the crown, 'if the rag-tag people did not clap him and hiss him, according as he pleased and displeased them, as they use to do the players in the theatre . . . ' Brutus enforces upon the con-spirators that they do not give away the game by their looks,

> But bear it as our Roman actors do.

At Caesar's death they were all to act their part, bathing their hands in his blood, self-consciously as on a stage:

> How many ages hence
> Shall this lofty scene be acted over,
> In states unborn, and accents yet unknown!

This has a further personal reference: it shows that the dramatist had been reading his fellow-writer, Samuel Daniel's fine poem *Musophilus*, with its famous passage:

> And who in time knows whither we may vent
> The treasure of our tongue, to what strange shores
> This gain of our best glory shall be sent,
> To enrich unknowing nations with our stores?
> What worlds in the yet unformèd Occident
> May come refined with the accents that are ours?

The text of this play presents few difficulties. We may note that occasionally short lines occur. Shakespeare varied the stress in such a word as 'conster', for construe, according to the demand of the scansion. This edition therefore aids the reader by showing where the accent should fall, as also simplifying punctuation. What point is there in retaining Elizabethan forms like 'whiles' for while; 'ha'' for have; 'disgest' for digest? etc. These and other archaisms have been eliminated.

CHARACTERS

JULIUS CAESAR
CALPHURNIA, his wife

MARCUS BRUTUS
CAIUS CASSIUS
CASCA
TREBONIUS
DECIUS BRUTUS } conspirators against Caesar
METELLUS CIMBER
CINNA
CAIUS LIGARIUS

OCTAVIUS CAESAR
MARK ANTONY } triumvirs after Caesar's death
LEPIDUS

CICERO
PUBLIUS } Senators
POPILIUS LENA

FLAVIUS } Tribunes of the People
MARULLUS

LUCILIUS
MESSALA
YOUNG CATO
VOLUMNIUS
TITINIUS } followers of Brutus and Cassius
VARRO
CLITUS
CLAUDIUS
DARDANIUS

PORTIA, Marcus Brutus's wife
ARTEMIDORUS, a Sophist
CINNA, a poet
PINDARUS, a servant of Cassius
LUCIUS ⎱ servants of Brutus
STRATO ⎰

A Soothsayer, a Poet, a Cobbler, a Carpenter, a Servant of Caesar, a Servant of Antony, a Servant of Octavius, the Ghost of Caesar, Senators, Soldiers, Plebeians, Attendants and others

Act I

SCENE I
Rome. A public place.

Enter FLAVIUS, MARULLUS, *and citizens*

FLAVIUS

    Hence! home, you idle creatures, get you home:
    Is this a holiday? What, know you not,
    Being mechanical, you ought not walk
    Upon a labouring day without the sign
    Of your profession? Speak, what trade are you?

CARPENTER   Why, sir, a carpenter.

MARULLUS

    Where is your leather apron, and your rule?
    What do you with your best apparel on?
    You, sir, what trade are you?

COBBLER   Truly, sir, in respect of a fine workman, I
am but, as you would say, a cobbler.

MARULLUS   But what trade are you? Answer me
directly.

COBBLER   A trade, sir, that I hope I may use with a
safe conscience; which is indeed, sir, a mender of
bad soles.

FLAVIUS

    What trade, you knave? You naughty knave, what
    trade?

COBBLER   Nay, I beseech you, sir, be not out with
me: yet if you be out, sir, I can mend you.

MARULLUS

    What mean you by that? Mend me, you saucy
    fellow?

165

COBBLER   Why, sir, cobble you.

FLAVIUS   You are a cobbler, are you?

COBBLER   Truly, sir, all that I live by is with the awl:
I meddle with no tradesman's matters, nor
women's matters, but with all. I am, indeed, sir, a
surgeon to old shoes: when they are in great danger,
I recover them. As proper men as ever trod upon
cowhide have gone upon my handiwork.

FLAVIUS
But wherefore are you not in your shop today?
Why do you lead these men about the streets?

COBBLER   Truly, sir, to wear out their shoes to get
myself into more work. But indeed, sir, we make
holiday to see Caesar, and to rejoice in his triumph.

MARULLUS
Wherefore rejoice? What conquest brings he home?
What tributaries follow him to Rome,
To grace in captive bonds his chariot wheels?
You blocks, you stones, you worse than senseless
    things!
O you hard hearts, you cruel men of Rome,
Knew you not Pompey? Many a time and oft
Have you climbed up to walls and battlements,
To towers and windows, yea, to chimney-tops,
Your infants in your arms, and there have sat
The livelong day, with patient expectation,
To see great Pompey pass the streets of Rome.
And when you saw his chariot but appear,
Have you not made an universal shout,
That Tiber trembled underneath her banks
To hear the replication of your sounds
Made in her concave shores?
And do you now put on your best attire?
And do you now cull out a holiday?
And do you now strew flowèrs in his way,
That comes in triumph over Pompey's blood?

Be gone!
Run to your houses, fall upon your knees,
Pray to the gods to intermit the plague
That needs must light on this ingratitude.

FLAVIUS

Go, go, good countrymen, and for this fault
Assemble all the poor men of your sort;
Draw them to Tiber banks, and weep your tears
Into the channel, till the lowest stream
Does kiss the most exalted shores of all.

Exeunt citizens

See whether their basest mettle is not moved:
They vanish tongue-tied in their guiltiness.
Go you down that way towards the Capitol;
This way will I. Disrobe the images,
If you do find them decked with ceremonies.

MARULLUS   May we do so?
You know it is the feast of Lupercal.

FLAVIUS

It is no matter; let no images
Be hung with Caesar's trophies. I'll about,
And drive away the vulgar from the streets;
So do you too, where you perceive them thick.
These growing feathers plucked from Caesar's wing
Will make him fly an ordinary pitch,
Who else would soar above the view of men,
And keep us all in servile fearfulness.   *Exeunt*

SCENE II
The same.

Enter CAESAR; ANTONY, *stripped for the course;*
CALPHURNIA, PORTIA, DECIUS, CICERO, BRUTUS,
CASSIUS, CASCA, *a* Soothsayer, *and citizens; after*
them MARULLUS *and* FLAVIUS

CAESAR
  Calphurnia.
CASCA   Peace, ho! Caesar speaks.
CAESAR   Calphurnia.
CALPHURNIA   Here, my lord.
CAESAR
  Stand you directly in Antonius' way
  When he does run his course. Antonius.
ANTONY   Caesar, my lord?
CAESAR
  Forget not, in your speed, Antonius,
  To touch Calphurnia; for our elders say,
  The barren, touchèd in this holy chase,
  Shake off their sterile curse.
ANTONY   I shall remember:
  When Caesar says, 'Do this', it is performed.
CAESAR
  Set on, and leave no ceremony out.
SOOTHSAYER   Caesar!
CAESAR   Ha! Who calls?
CASCA
  Bid every noise be still; peace yet again!
CAESAR
  Who is it in the press that calls on me?
  I hear a tongue shriller than all the music
  Cry 'Caesar!' Speak. Caesar is turned to hear.
SOOTHSAYER
  Beware the ides of March.
CAESAR   What man is that?
BRUTUS
  A soothsayer bids you beware the ides of March.
CAESAR
  Set him before me; let me see his face.
CASSIUS
  Fellow, come from the throng; look upon Caesar.

CAESAR
    What say you to me now? Speak once again.
SOOTHSAYER   Beware the ides of March.
CAESAR
    He is a dreamer. Let us leave him. Pass.

                                    Sennet. Exeunt

                                conspirators
                BRUTUS *and* CASSIUS *remain*

CASSIUS
    Will you go see the order of the course?
BRUTUS   Not I.
CASSIUS   I pray you, do.
BRUTUS
    I am not gamesome: I do lack some part
    Of that quick spirit that is in Antony.
    Let me not hinder, Cassius, your desires;
    I'll leave you.
CASSIUS
    Brutus, I do observe you now of late:
    I have not from your eyes that gentleness
    And show of love as I was wont to have.
    You bear too stubborn and too strange a hand
    Over your friend that loves you.
BRUTUS   Cassius,
    Be not deceived: if I have veiled my look,
    I turn the trouble of my countenance
    Merely upon myself. Vexèd I am
    Of late with passions of some difference,
    Conceptions only proper to myself,
    Which give some soil, perhaps, to my behaviour.
    But let not therefore my good friends be
        grieved—
    Among which number, Cassius, be you one—
    Nor cònstrue any further my neglect,

Than that poor Brutus, with himself at war,
Forgets the shows of love to other men.

CASSIUS

Then, Brutus, I have much mistaken your passion,
By means whereof this breast of mine has buried
Thoughts of great value, worthy cogitations.
Tell me, good Brutus, can you see your face?

BRUTUS

No, Cassius; for the eye sees not itself
But by reflection, by some other things.

CASSIUS   'Tis just;
And it is very much lamented, Brutus,
That you have no such mirrors as will turn
Your hidden worthiness into your eye,
That you might see your shadow. I have heard,
Where many of the best respect in Rome,
Except immortal Caesar, speaking of Brutus,
And groaning underneath this age's yoke,
Have wished that noble Brutus had his eyes.

BRUTUS

Into what dangers would you lead me, Cassius,
That you would have me seek into myself
For that which is not in me?

CASSIUS

Therefore, good Brutus, be prepared to hear;
And since you know you cannot see yourself
So well as by reflection, I, your glass,
Will modestly discover to yourself
That of yourself which you yet know not of.
Be not suspicious of me, gentle Brutus:
Were I a common laugher, or did use
To stale with ordinary oaths my love
To every new protester; if you know
That I do fawn on men and hug them hard,
And after scandal them; or if you know

That I profess myself in banqueting
To all the rout, then hold me dangerous.

Flourish and shout

BRUTUS

What means this shouting? I do fear the people
Choose Caesar for their king.

CASSIUS   Ay, do you fear it?
Then must I think you would not have it so.

BRUTUS

I would not, Cassius; yet I love him well.
But wherefore do you hold me here so long?
What is it that you would impart to me?
If it is aught toward the general good,
Set honour in one eye, and death in the other,
And I will look on both impartially.
For let the gods so speed me as I love
The name of honour more than I fear death.

CASSIUS

I know that virtue to be in you, Brutus,
As well as I do know your outward aspect.
Well, honour is the subject of my story.
I cannot tell what you and other men
Think of this life; but for my single self,
I had as soon not be as live to be
In awe of such a thing as I myself.
I was born free as Caesar, so were you;
We both have fed as well, and we can both
Endure the winter's cold as well as he.
For once, upon a raw and gusty day,
The troubled Tiber chafing with her shores,
Caesar said to me, 'Dare you, Cassius, now
Leap in with me into this angry flood,
And swim to yonder point? Upon the word,

Accoutered as I was, I plungèd in
And bade him follow; so indeed he did.
The torrent roared, and we did buffet it
With lusty sinews, throwing it aside
And stemming it with hearts of controversy.
But ere we could arrive the point proposed,
Caesar cried, 'Help me, Cassius, or I sink!'
I, as Aeneas, our great ancestor,
Did from the flames of Troy upon his shoulder
The old Anchises bear, so from the waves of Tiber
Did I the tirèd Caesar. And this man
Is now become a god, and Cassius is
A wretched creature, and must bend his body
If Caesar carelessly but nods on him.
He had a fever when he was in Spain,
And when the fit was on him, I did mark
How he did shake; 'tis true, this god did shake.
His coward lips did from their colour fly,
And that same eye whose bend does awe the world
Did lose its lustre; I did hear him groan.
Ay, and that tongue of his, that bade the Romans
Mark him and write his speeches in their books,
'Alas!' it cried, 'Give me some drink, Titinius',
As a sick girl. Ye gods, it does amaze me
A man of such a feeble temper should
So get the start of the majestic world,
And bear the palm alone.

Shout. Flourish

BRUTUS   Another general shout?
  I do believe that these applauses are
  For some new honours that are heaped on Caesar.
CASSIUS
  Why, man, he does bestride the narrow world
  Like a Colossus, and we petty men

Walk under his huge legs, and peep about
To find ourselves dishonourable graves.
Men at some time are masters of their fates;
The fault, dear Brutus, is not in our stars,
But in ourselves, that we are underlings.
Brutus and Caesar. What should be in that 'Caesar'?
Why should that name be sounded more than yours?
Write them together, yours is as fair a name;
Sound them, it does become the mouth as well;
Weigh them, it is as heavy; conjure with them,
'Brutus' will start a spirit as soon as 'Caesar.'
Now in the names of all the gods at once,
Upon what meat does this our Caesar feed,
That he is grown so great? Age, you are shamed!
Rome, you have lost the breed of noble bloods!
When went there by an age, since the great flood,
But it was famed with more than with one man?
When could they say, till now, that talked of Rome,
That her wide walls encompassed but one man?
Now is it Rome indeed, and room enough,
When there is in it but one only man.
O, you and I have heard our fathers say,
There was a Brutus once that would have brooked
The eternal devil to keep his state in Rome
As easily as a king.

BRUTUS

That you do love me, I am nothing doubtful;
What you would work me to, I have some aim:
How I have thought of this, and of these times,
I shall recount hereafter. For this present,
I would not—so with love I might entreat you—
Be any further moved. What you have said
I will consider; what you have to say
I will with patience hear, and find a time
Both meet to hear and answer such high things.
Till then, my noble friend, chew upon this:

Brutus had rather be a villager
Than to repute himself a son of Rome
Under these hard conditions as this time
Is likely to lay upon us.

CASSIUS   I am glad
That my weak words have struck but thus much
        show
Of fire from Brutus.

Enter CAESAR *and his train*

BRUTUS
The games are done and Caesar is returning.

CASSIUS
As they pass by, pluck Casca by the sleeve,
And he will, after his sour fashion, tell you
What has proceeded worthy note today.

BRUTUS
I will do so. But look you, Cassius,
The angry spot does glow on Caesar's brow,
And all the rest look like a chidden train.
Calphurnia's cheek is pale, and Cicero
Looks with such ferret and such fiery eyes
As we have seen him in the Capitol
Being crossed in conference by some senators.

CASSIUS
Casca will tell us what the matter is.

CAESAR   Antonius.

ANTONY   Caesar?

CAESAR
Let me have men about me that are fat,
Sleek-headed men, and such as sleep of nights.
Yon Cassius has a lean and hungry look;
He thinks too much: such men are dangerous.

ANTONY

   Fear him not, Caesar; he is not dangerous;
   He is a noble Roman, and well given.

CAESAR

   Would he were fatter! But I fear him not;
   Yet if my name were liable to fear,
   I do not know the man I should avoid
   So soon as that spare Cassius. He reads much,
   He is a great observer, and he looks
   Quite through the deeds of men. He loves no plays,
   As you do, Antony; he hears no music;
   Seldom he smiles, and smiles in such a sort
   As if he mocked himself, and scorned his spirit
   That could be moved to smile at anything.
   Such men as he are never at heart's ease
   While they behold a greater than themselves,
   And therefore are they very dangerous.
   I rather tell you what is to be feared
   Than what I fear; for always I am Caesar.
   Come on my right hand, for this ear is deaf,
   And tell me truly what you think of him.

               Sennet. Exeunt Caesar and his train

CASCA

   You pulled me by the cloak; would you speak with
     me?

BRUTUS

   Ay, Casca, tell us what has chanced today
   That Caesar looks so sad.

CASCA   Why, you were with him, were you not?

BRUTUS

   I should not then ask Casca what had chanced.

CASCA   Why, there was a crown offered him; and,
   being offered him, he put it by with the back of his
   hand, thus; and then the people fell a-shouting.

BRUTUS   What was the second noise for?

CASCA   Why, for that too.

CASSIUS   They shouted thrice: what was the last cry for?

CASCA   Why, for that too.

BRUTUS   Was the crown offered him thrice?

CASCA   Ay, indeed, was it, and he put it by thrice, every time gentler than the other; and at every putting-by my honest neighbours shouted.

CASSIUS   Who offered him the crown?

CASCA   Why, Antony.

BRUTUS   Tell us the manner of it, gentle Casca.

CASCA   I can as well be hanged as tell the manner of it; it was mere foolery; I did mark it. I saw Mark Antony offer him a crown; yet it was not a crown either, it was one of these coronets; and, as I told you, he put it by once; but for all that, to my thinking, he would fain have had it. Then he offered it to him again; then he put it by again; but to my thinking, he was very loth to lay his fingers off it. And then he offered it the third time; he put it the third time by; and still as he refused it, the rabblement hooted, and clapped their chapped hands, and threw up their sweaty night-caps, and uttered such a deal of stinking breath because Caesar refused the crown, that it had almost choked Caesar; for he swooned, and fell down at it. And for my own part, I durst not laugh, for fear of opening my lips and receiving the bad air.

CASSIUS

But soft, I pray you; what, did Caesar swoon?

CASCA   He fell down in the market-place, and foamed at mouth, and was speechless.

BRUTUS   It is very likely he has the falling sickness.

CASSIUS
  No, Caesar has it not; but you, and I,
  And honest Casca, we have the falling sickness.

CASCA   I know not what you mean by that, but I am
  sure Caesar fell down. If the rag-tag people did not
  clap him and hiss him, according as he pleased and
  displeased them, as they use to do the players in
  the theatre, I am no true man.

BRUTUS
  What said he when he came unto himself?

CASCA   Sure, before he fell down, when he perceived
  the common herd was glad he refused the crown,
  he plucked open his doublet, and offered them his
  throat to cut. If I had been a man of any
  occupation, if I would not have taken him at a
  word, I would I might go to hell among the rogues.
  And so he fell. When he came to himself again, he
  said, if he had done or said anything amiss, he
  desired their worships to think it was his infirmity.
  Three or four wenches, where I stood, cried, 'Alas,
  good soul!' and forgave him with all their hearts.
  But there's no heed to be taken of them; if Caesar
  had stabbed their mothers, they would have done
  no less.

BRUTUS
  And after that, he came thus sad away?

CASCA   Ay.

CASSIUS   Did Cicero say anything?

CASCA   Ay, he spoke Greek.

CASSIUS   To what effect?

CASCA   Nay, if I tell you that, I'll never look you in
  the face again. But those that understood him
  smiled at one another, and shook their heads; but
  for my own part, it was Greek to me. I could tell

you more news too: Marullus and Flavius, for
pulling scarfs off Caesar's images, are put to
silence. Fare you well. There was more foolery yet,
if I could remember it.

CASSIUS   Will you sup with me tonight, Casca?

CASCA   No, I am promised forth.

CASSIUS   Will you dine with me tomorrow?

CASCA   Ay, if I am alive, and your mind holds, and
your dinner worth the eating.

CASSIUS   Good; I will expect you.

CASCA   Do so. Farewell, both.   *Exit*

BRUTUS

What a blunt fellow is this grown to be!
He was quick mettle when he went to school.

CASSIUS

So is he now in execution
Of any bold or noble enterprise,
However he puts on this tardy form.
This rudeness is a sauce to his good wit,
Which gives men stomach to digest his words
With better appetite.

BRUTUS

And so it is. For this time I will leave you.
Tomorrow, if you please to speak with me,
I will come home to you; or if you will,
Come home to me, and I will wait for you.

CASSIUS

I will do so: till then, think of the world.

Exit Brutus

Well, Brutus, you are noble; yet I see
Your honourable metal may be wrought
From that it is disposed: therefore it is meet
That noble minds keep ever with their likes;
For who so firm that cannot be seduced?
Caesar does bear me hard, but he loves Brutus.

If I were Brutus now, and he were Cassius,
He should not humour me. I will this night,
In several hands, in at his windows throw—
As if they came from several citizens—
Writings, all tending to the great opinion
That Rome holds of his name; wherein obscurely
Caesar's ambition shall be glancèd at.
And after this, let Caesar seat him sure,
For we will shake him, or worse days endure.   *Exit*

SCENE III
The same.

Thunder and lightning
Enter CASCA *and* CICERO, *meeting*

CICERO
Good even, Casca: brought you Caesar home?
Why are you breathless? and why stare you so?
CASCA
Are not you moved, when all the sway of earth
Shakes like a thing unfirm? O Cicero,
I have seen tempests, when the scolding winds
Have rived the knotty oaks, and I have seen
The ambitious ocean swell and rage and foam,
To be exalted with the threatening clouds;
But never till tonight, never till now,
Did I go through a tempest dropping fire.
Either there is a civil strife in heaven,
Or else the world, too saucy with the gods,
Incenses them to send destructiòn.
CICERO
Why, saw you something more wonderful?

CASCA

A common slave—you know him well by sight—
Held up his left hand, which did flame and burn
Like twenty torches joined; and yet his hand,
Not sensible of fire, remained unscorched.
Besides—I have not since put up my sword—
Against the Capitol I met a lion,
Which glazed upon me, and went surly by,
Without annoying me. And there were drawn
Upon a heap a hundred ghastly women,
Transformèd with their fear, who swore they saw
Men, all in fire, walk up and down the streets.
And yesterday the bird of night did sit,
Even at noon-day, upon the market-place,
Hooting and shrieking. When these prodigies
Do so conjointly meet, let not men say,
'These are their reasons, they are natural';
For I believe, they are portentous things
Unto the climate that they point upon.

CICERO

Indeed, it is a strange-disposèd time:
But men may cònstrue things after their fashion,
Clean from the purpose of the things themselves.
Comes Caesar to the Capitol tomorrow?

CASCA

He does; for he did bid Antonius
Send word to you he would be there tomorrow.

CICERO

Good night then, Casca: this disturbèd sky
Is not to walk in.

CASCA   Farewell, Cicero.   *Exit Cicero*

Enter CASSIUS

CASSIUS

Who's there?

CASCA   A Roman.

CASSIUS   Casca, by your voice.

CASCA
Your ear is good. Cassius, what night is this!

CASSIUS
A very pleasing night to honest men.

CASCA
Who ever knew the heavens menace so?

CASSIUS
Those that have known the earth so full of faults.
For my part, I have walked about the streets,
Submitting me unto the perilous night,
And, thus embracèd, Casca, as you see,
Have bared my bosom to the thunder-stone.
And when the cross blue lightning seemed to open
The breast of heaven, I did present myself
Even in the aim and very flash of it.

CASCA
But wherefore did you so much tempt the heavens?
It is the part of men to fear and tremble
When the most mighty gods by tokens send
Such dreadful heralds to astonish us.

CASSIUS
You are dull, Casca, and those sparks of life
That should be in a Roman you do want,
Or else you use not. You look pale, and gaze,
And put on fear, and cast yourself in wonder,
To see the strange impatience of the heavens.
But if you would consider the true cause
Why all these fires, why all these gliding ghosts,
Why birds and beasts from quality and kind,
Why old men, fools, and children calculate,
Why all these things change from their ordinance,
Their natures, and pre-formèd faculties,
To monstrous quality, why, you shall find
That heaven has infused them with these spirits

To make them instruments of fear and warning
Unto some monstrous state.
Now could I, Casca, name to you a man
Most like this dreadful night,   *Ceasar*
That thunders, lightens, opens graves, and roars
As does the lion in the Capitol;
A man no mightier than yourself, or me,
In person or action, yet prodigious grown,
And fearful, as these strange eruptions are.

CASCA
It is Caesar that you mean; is it not, Cassius?

CASSIUS
Let it be who it is: for Romans now
Have strength and limbs like their ancestors;
But woe the while! our fathers' minds are dead,
And we are governed with our mothers' spirits:
Our yoke and sufferance show us womanish.

CASCA
Indeed, they say the senators tomorrow
Mean to establish Caesar as a king;
And he shall wear his crown by sea and land,
In every place save here in Italy.

CASSIUS
I know where I will wear this dagger then:
Cassius from bondage will deliver Cassius.
Therein, ye gods, you make the weak most strong;
Therein, ye gods, you tyrants do defeat.
Nor stony tower, nor walls of beaten brass,
Nor airless dungeon, nor strong links of iron,
Can be retentive to the strength of spirit;
But life, being weary of these worldly bars,
Never lacks power to dismiss itself.
If I know this, know all the world besides,
That part of tyranny that I do bear
I can shake off at pleasure.

Thunder still

CASCA   So can I;
 So every bondman in his own hand bears
 The power to cancel his captivity.

CASSIUS
 And why should Caesar be a tyrant then?
 Poor man! I know he would not be a wolf,
 But that he sees the Romans are but sheep.
 He were no lion, were not Romans hinds.
 Those that with haste will make a mighty fire
 Begin it with weak straws. What trash is Rome,
 What rubbish, and what offal, when it serves
 For the base matter to illuminate
 So vile a thing as Caesar! But, O grief,
 Where have you led me? I perhaps speak this
 Before a willing bondman; then I know
 My answer must be made. But I am armed,
 And dangers are to me indifferent.

CASCA
 You speak to Casca, and to such a man
 That is no sneering tell-tale. Hold, my hand;
 Form faction for redress of all these griefs,
 And I will set this foot of mine as far
 As who goes farthest.

CASSIUS   There's a bargain made.
 Now know you, Casca, I have moved already
 Certain of the noblest-minded Romans
 To undergo with me an enterprise
 Of honourable-dangerous consequence.
 And I do know, by this they stay for me
 In Pompey's Porch: for now, this fearful night,
 There is no stir or walking in the streets;
 And the complexion of the element
 In look is like the work we have in hand,
 Most bloody, fiery, and most terrible.

Enter CINNA

CASCA

Stand close awhile, for here comes one in haste.

CASSIUS

'Tis Cinna; I do know him by his gait;
He is a friend. Cinna, where haste you so?

CINNA

To find you out. Who's that? Metellus Cimber?

CASSIUS

No, it is Casca, one incorporate
To our attempts. Am I not stayed for, Cinna?

CINNA

I am glad of it. What a fearful night is this!
Two or three of us have seen strange sights.

CASSIUS

Am I not stayed for? Tell me.

CINNA   Yes, you are.

O Cassius, if you could
But win the noble Brutus to our party—

CASSIUS

Be you content. Good Cinna, take this paper,
And see you lay it in the praetor's chair,
Where Brutus may but find it; and throw this
In at his window; set this up with wax
Upon old Brutus' statue. All this done,
Repair to Pompey's Porch, where you shall find us.
Are Decius Brutus and Trebonius there?

CINNA

All but Metellus Cimber; and he's gone
To seek you at your house. Well, I will hie,
And so bestow these papers as you bade me.

CASSIUS

That done, repair to Pompey's Theatre.   *Exit Cinna*
Come, Casca, you and I will yet ere day

See Brutus at his house: three parts of him
Are ours already, and the man entire
Upon the next encounter yields him ours.

CASCA

O, he sits high in all the people's hearts;
And that which would appear offence in us,
His countenance, like richest alchemy,
Will change to virtue and to worthiness.

CASSIUS

Him and his worth and our great need of him
You have right well conceived. Let us go,
For it is after midnight, and ere day
We will awake him, and be sure of him.   *Exeunt*

Act II

SCENE I
Brutus' house.

Enter BRUTUS *in his orchard*

BRUTUS   What, Lucius, ho!
I cannot, by the progress of the stars,
Give guess how near to day. Lucius, I say!
I would it were my fault to sleep so soundly.
When, Lucius, when? Awake, I say! What, Lucius!

Enter LUCIUS

LUCIUS   Called you, my lord?
BRUTUS

Get me a taper in my study, Lucius;
When it is lighted, come and call me here.
LUCIUS   I will, my lord.   *Exit*
BRUTUS

It must be by his death; and for my part,
I know no personal cause to spurn at him,
But for the general.—He would be crowned.
How that might change his nature, there's the
    question.
It is the bright day that brings forth the adder,
And that craves wary walking. Crown him that,
And then, I grant, we put a sting in him
That at his will he may do danger with.
The abuse of greatness is when it disjoins
Mercy from power; and, to speak truth of Caesar,
I have not known when his affections swayed
More than his reason. But it is a common proof,
That lowliness is young ambition's ladder,
Whereto the climber-upward turns his face;
But when he once attains the upmost round,
He then unto the ladder turns his back,
Looks in the clouds, scorning the base degrees
By which he did ascend. So Caesar may;
Then, lest he may, prevent. And, since the quarrel
Will bear no colour for the thing he is,
Fashion it thus: that what he is, augmented,
Would run to these and these extremities;
And therefore think him as a serpent's egg,
Which, hatched, would, as its kind, grow
    mischievous,
And kill him in the shell.

                    Enter LUCIUS

LUCIUS
  The taper burns now in your closet, sir.
  Searching the window for a flint, I found
  This paper, thus sealed up; and I am sure
  It did not lie there when I went to bed.

He gives him the letter

BRUTUS
  Get you to bed again, it is not day.
  Is not tomorrow, boy, the ides of March?
LUCIUS   I know not, sir.
BRUTUS
  Look in the calendar and bring me word.
LUCIUS   I will, sir.   *Exit*
BRUTUS
  The exhalations, whizzing in the air,
  Give so much light that I may read by them.

He opens the letter and reads

Brutus, you sleep: awake, and see yourself.
Shall Rome, etc. Speak, strike, redress.
  'Brutus, you sleep: awake.'
  Such instigations have been often dropped
  Where I have taken them up.
  'Shall Rome, etc.' Thus must I piece it out:
  Shall Rome stand under one man's awe? What,
      Rome?
  My ancestors did from the streets of Rome
  The Tarquin drive, when he was called a king.
  'Speak, strike, redress.' Am I entreated
  To speak and strike? O Rome, I make you promise,
  If the redress will follow, you receive
  Your full petition at the hand of Brutus.

Enter LUCIUS

LUCIUS
  Sir, March is wasted fifteen days.

Knock within

BRUTUS
  'Tis good. Go to the gate; somebody knocks.

                                          Exit Lucius

  Since Cassius first did whet me against Caesar,
  I have not slept.
  Between the acting of a dreadful thing
  And the first motion, all the interim is
  Like a phantasm or a hideous dream:
  The genius and the mortal instruments
  Are then in council; and the state of man,
  Like to a little kingdom, suffers then
  The nature of an insurrection.

Enter LUCIUS

LUCIUS
  Sir, it is your brother Cassius at the door,
  Who does desire to see you.
BRUTUS   Is he alone?
LUCIUS
  No, sir, there are more with him.
BRUTUS   Do you know them?
LUCIUS
  No, sir, their hats are plucked about their ears,
  And half their faces buried in their cloaks,
  That by no means I may discover them
  By any mark of looks.

BRUTUS   Let them enter.   *Exit Lucius*
  They are the faction. O conspiracy,
  Shame you to show your dangerous brow by night,
  When evils are most free? O then, by day
  Where will you find a cavern dark enough
  To mask your monstrous visage? Seek none, conspiracy;
  Hide it in smiles and affability:
  For if you put your native semblance on,
  Not Erebus itself were dim enough
  To hide you from prevention.

Enter the conspirators: CASSIUS, CASCA, DECIUS, CINNA,
    METELLUS, *and* TREBONIUS

CASSIUS
  I think we are too bold upon your rest.
  Good morrow, Brutus; do we trouble you?
BRUTUS
  I have been up this hour, awake all night.
  Know I these men that come along with you?
CASSIUS
  Yes, every man of them; and no man here
  But honours you; and every one does wish
  You had but that opinion of yourself
  Which every noble Roman bears of you.
  This is Trebonius.
BRUTUS   He is welcome hither.
CASSIUS
  This, Decius Brutus.
BRUTUS   He is welcome too.
CASSIUS
  This, Casca; this, Cinna; and this, Metellus Cimber.
BRUTUS   They are all welcome.

What watchful cares do interpose themselves
Betwixt your eyes and night?

CASSIUS   Shall I entreat a word?

They whisper apart

DECIUS
Here lies the east; does not the day break here?

CASCA   No.

CINNA
O pardon, sir, it does; and yon grey lines
That fret the clouds are messengers of day.

CASCA
You shall confess that you are both deceived:
Here, as I point my sword, the sun arises,
Which is a great way growing on the south,
Weighting the youthful season of the year.
Some two months hence, up higher toward the north
It first presents its fire; and the high east
Stands, as the Capitol, directly here.

BRUTUS
Give me your hands all over, one by one.

CASSIUS
And let us swear our resolution.

BRUTUS
No, not an oath. If not the face of men,
The sufferance of our souls, the time's abuse—
If these are motives weak, break off betimes,
And every man hence to his idle bed;
So let high-sighted tyranny range on
Till each man drops by lottery. But if these,
As I am sure they do, bear fire enough
To kindle cowards and to steel with valour
The melting spirits of women, then, countrymen,
What need we any spur but our own cause

To prick us to redress? What other bond
Than secret Romans that have spoken the word,
And will not palter? And what other oath
Than honesty to honesty engaged
That this shall be, or we will fall for it?
Swear priests and cowards and deceitful men,
Old feeble carrions, and such suffering souls
That welcome wrongs; unto bad causes swear
Such creatures as men doubt. But do not stain
The even virtue of our enterprise,
Nor the insuppressive mettle of our spirits,
To think that our cause or our performance
Did need an oath. When every drop of blood
That every Roman bears, and nobly bears,
Is guilty of a separate bastardy,
If he does break the smallest particle
Of any promise that has passed from him.

CASSIUS

But what of Cicero? Shall we sound him?
I think he will stand very strong with us.

CASCA

Let us not leave him out.

CINNA   No. By no means.

METELLUS

O, let us have him, for his silver hairs
Will purchase us a good opiniòn
And buy men's voices to commend our deeds.
It shall be said his judgement ruled our hands;
Our youths and wildness shall no whit appear,
But all be buried in his gravity.

BRUTUS

O, name him not; let us not close with him,
For he will never follow anything
That other men begin.

CASSIUS   Then leave him out.

CASCA   Indeed he is not fit.

DECIUS

Shall no man else be touched but only Caesar?

CASSIUS

Decius, well urged. I think it is not meet
Mark Antony, so well beloved of Caesar,
Should outlive Caesar. We shall find of him
A shrewd contriver; and you know his means,
If he improves them, may well stretch so far
As to annoy us all; which to prevent,
Let Antony and Caesar fall together.

BRUTUS

Our course will seem too bloody, Caius Cassius,
To cut the head off and then hack the limbs,
Like wrath in death, and envy afterwards;
For Antony is but a limb of Caesar.
Let us be sacrificers, but not butchers, Caius.
We all stand up against the spirit of Caesar,
And in the spirit of men there is no blood.
O, that we then could come by Caesar's spirit,
And not dismember Caesar! But, alas,
Caesar must bleed for it. And, gentle friends,
Let's kill him boldly, but not wrathfully;
Let's carve him as a dish fit for the gods,
Not hew him as a carcass fit for hounds.
And let our hearts, as subtle masters do,
Stir up their servants to an act of rage,
And after seem to chide them. This shall make
Our purpose necessary, and not envious;
Which so appearing to the common eyes,
We shall be called purgers, not murderers.
And for Mark Antony, think not of him;
For he can do no more than Caesar's arm
When Caesar's head is off.

CASSIUS   Yet I fear him;
    For in the ingrafted love he bears to Caesar—
BRUTUS
    Alas, good Cassius, do not think of him.
    If he loves Caesar, all that he can do
    Is to himself: take thought, and die for Caesar.
    And that were much he should; for he is given
    To sports, to wildness, and much company.
TREBONIUS
    There is no fear in him; let him not die;
    For he will live, and laugh at this hereafter.

A clock strikes

BRUTUS
    Peace, count the clock.
CASSIUS   The clock strikes three.
TREBONIUS
    'Tis time to part.
CASSIUS   But it is doubtful yet
    Whether Caesar will come forth today or no;
    For he is superstitious grown of late,
    Quite from the main opinion he held once
    Of fantasy, of dreams, and ceremonies.
    It may be these apparent prodigies,
    The unaccustomed terror of this night,
    And the persuasion of his augurers
    May hold him from the Capitol today.
DECIUS
    Never fear that. If he is so resolved,
    I can oversway him; for he loves to hear
    That unicorns may be betrayed with trees,
    And bears with glasses, elephants with holes,
    Lions with toils, and men with flatterers.

But when I tell him he hates flatterers,
He says he does, being then most flattered.
Let me work;
For I can give his humour the true bent,
And I will bring him to the Capitol.

CASSIUS
Nay, we will all of us be there to fetch him.

BRUTUS
By the eighth hour; is that the uttermost?

CINNA
Be that the uttermost, and fail not then.

METELLUS
Caius Ligarius mislikes Caesar much,
Who rated him for speaking well of Pompey;
I wonder none of you have thought of him.

BRUTUS
Now, good Metellus, go along by him;
He loves me well, and I have given him reasons.
Send him but hither, and I'll fashion him.

CASSIUS
The morning comes upon us; we leave you, Brutus.
And, friends, disperse yourselves; but all remember
What you have said, and show yourselves true
  Romans.

BRUTUS
Good gentlemen, look fresh and merrily;
Let not our looks put on our purposes,
But bear it as our Roman actors do,
With untired spirits and formal constancy.
And so good morrow to you every one.

Exeunt the conspirators

BRUTUS *remains*

Boy! Lucius! Fast asleep? It is no matter.
Enjoy the honey-heavy dew of slumber;

You have no figures and no fantasies,
Which busy care draws in the brains of men;
Therefore you sleep so sound.

Enter PORTIA

PORTIA   Brutus, my lord.

BRUTUS
Portia! What mean you? Wherefore rise you now?
It is not for your health thus to commit
Your weak condition to the raw cold morning.

PORTIA
Nor for yours either. You have ungently, Brutus,
Stolen from my bed; and yesternight at supper
You suddenly arose and walked about,
Musing and sighing, with your arms across;
And when I asked you what the matter was,
You stared upon me with ungentle looks.
I urged you further; then you scratched your head,
And too impatiently stamped with your foot;
Yet I insisted, yet you answered not,
But with an angry wafting of your hand
Gave sign for me to leave you. So I did,
Fearing to strengthen that impatiènce
Which seemed too much enkindled, and with that
Hoping it was but an effect of humour,
Which sometimes has its hour with every man.
It will not let you eat, nor talk, nor sleep;
And could it work so much upon your shape,
As it has much prevailed on your condition,
I should not know you Brutus. Dear my lord,
Make me acquainted with your cause of grief.

BRUTUS
I am not well in health, and that is all.

PORTIA
  Brutus is wise, and were he not in health,
  He would embrace the means to come by it.
BRUTUS
  Why, so I do. Good Portia, go to bed.
PORTIA
  Is Brutus sick? And is it physical
  To walk unbracèd and suck up the humours
  Of the dank morning? What, is Brutus sick?
  And will he steal out of his wholesome bed
  To dare the vile contagion of the night,
  And tempt the rheumy and unpurgèd air,
  To add unto his sickness? No, my Brutus;
  You have some sick offence within your mind,
  Which, by the right and virtue of my place,
  I ought to know of. And, upon my knees,
  I charm you, by my once commended beauty,
  By all your vows of love, and that great vow
  Which did incorporate and make us one,
  That you unfold to me, your self, your half,
  Why you are heavy, and what men tonight
  Have had resort to you. For here have been
  Some six or seven, who did hide their faces
  Even from darkness.
BRUTUS   Kneel not, gentle Portia.
PORTIA
  I should not need, if you were gentle Brutus.
  Within the bond of marriage, tell me, Brutus,
  Is it excepted I should know no secrets
  That appertain to you? Am I your self
  But, as it were, in sort or limitation,
  To keep with you at meals, comfort your bed,
  And talk to you sometimes? Dwell I but in the
     suburbs
  Of your good pleasure? If it is no more,
  Portia is Brutus' harlot, not his wife.

BRUTUS

   You are my true and honourable wife,
   As dear to me as are the ruddy drops
   That visit my sad heart.

PORTIA

   If this were true, then should I know this secret.
   I grant I am a woman; nevertheless
   A woman that Lord Brutus took to wife.
   I grant I am a woman; nevertheless
   A woman well reputed, Cato's daughter.
   Think you I am no stronger than my sex,
   Being so fathered, and so husbanded?
   Tell me your counsels, I will not disclose them.
   I have made strong proof of my constancy,
   Giving myself a voluntary wound
   Here, in the thigh; can I bear that with patience,
   And not my husband's secrets?

BRUTUS
                          O ye gods,
   Render me worthy of this noble wife!

Knocking

   Hark, hark! one knocks. Portia, go in awhile;
   And by and by your bosom shall partake
   The secrets of my heart.
   All my engagements I will construe to you,
   All the character of my sad brows.
   Leave me with haste.
                         Exit Portia

Enter LUCIUS *and* LIGARIUS

                    Lucius, who is that knocks?

LUCIUS

   Here is a sick man that would speak with you.

BRUTUS

   Caius Ligarius, that Metellus spoke of.
   Boy, stand aside. Caius Ligarius, how?

LIGARIUS

　　Pardon good morrow from a feeble tongue.

BRUTUS

　　O, what a time have you chosen, brave Caius,
　　To wear a kerchief! Would you were not sick!

LIGARIUS

　　I am not sick if Brutus has in hand
　　Any exploit worthy the name of honour.

BRUTUS

　　Such an exploit have I in hand, Ligarius,
　　Had you a healthful ear to hear of it.

LIGARIUS

　　By all the gods that Romans bow before,
　　I here discard my sickness.

He throws off the kerchief

　　　　　　　　　　　　　　　　　　　Soul of Rome!
　　Brave son, derived from honourable loins!
　　You, like an exorcist, have conjured up
　　My mortifièd spirit. Now bid me run,
　　And I will strive with things impossible,
　　Yea, get the better of them. What's to do?

BRUTUS

　　A piece of work that will make sick men whole.

LIGARIUS

　　But are not some whole that we must make sick?

BRUTUS

　　That must we also. What it is, my Caius,
　　I shall unfold to you, as we are going
　　To whom it must be done.

LIGARIUS

　　　　　　　　　　　　　　　　　Set on your foot,
　　And with a heart new-fired I follow you,
　　To do I know not what; but it suffices
　　That Brutus leads me on.

Thunder

BRUTUS   Follow me then.   *Exeunt*

SCENE II
Caesar's house.

Thunder and lightning
Enter JULIUS CAESAR *in his night-gown*

CAESAR
  Nor heaven nor earth have been at peace tonight;
  Thrice has Calphurnia in her sleep cried out,
  'Help, ho! They murder Caesar!' Who is within?

Enter a Servant

SERVANT   My lord?
CAESAR
  Go bid the priests do present sacrifice,
  And bring me their opinions of the outcome.
SERVANT   I will, my lord.   *Exit*

Enter CALPHURNIA

CALPHURNIA
  What mean you, Caesar? Think you to walk forth?
  You shall not stir out of your house today.
CAESAR
  Caesar shall forth. The things that threatened me
  Never looked but on my back; when they shall
    see
  The face of Caesar, they are vanishèd.

CALPHURNIA
Caesar, I never stood on ceremonies,
Yet now they frighten me. There is one within,
Besides the things that we have heard and seen,
Recounts most horrid sights seen by the watch.
A lioness has whelpèd in the streets,
And graves have yawned and yielded up their dead.
Fierce fiery warriors fought upon the clouds
In ranks and squadrons and right form of war,
Which drizzled blood upon the Capitol.
The noise of battle hurtled in the air,
Horses did neigh, and dying men did groan,
And ghosts did shriek and squeal about the streets.
O Caesar, these things are beyond all use,
And I do fear them.

CAESAR   What can be avoided
Whose end is purposed by the mighty gods?
Yet Caesar shall go forth; for these predictions
Are to the world in general as to Caesar.

CALPHURNIA
When beggars die, there are no comets seen;
The heavens themselves blaze forth the death of
    princes.

CAESAR
Cowards die many time before their deaths;
The valiant never taste of death but once.
Of all the wonders that I yet have heard,
It seems to me most strange that men should fear,
Seeing that death, a necessary end,
Will come when it will come.

Enter a Servant

What say the augurers?

SERVANT
 They would not have you to stir forth today.
 Plucking the entrails of an offering forth,
 They could not find a heart within the beast.
CAESAR
 The gods do this in shame of cowardice:
 Caesar should be a beast without a heart
 If he should stay at home today for fear.
 No, Caesar shall not. Danger knows full well
 That Caesar is more dangerous than he.
 We were two lions littered in one day,
 And I the elder and more terrible;
 And Caesar shall go forth.
CALPHURNIA   Alas, my lord,
 Your wisdom is consumed in confidence.
 Do not go forth today: call it my fear
 That keeps you in the house, and not your own.
 We'll send Mark Antony to the Senate House,
 And he shall say you are not well today.
 Let me upon my knee prevail in this.
CAESAR
 Mark Antony shall say I am not well,
 And for your humour I will stay at home.

      Enter DECIUS

 Here's Decius Brutus; he shall tell them so.
DECIUS
 Caesar, all hail! Good morrow, worthy Caesar;
 I come to fetch you to the Senate House.
CAESAR
 And you are come in very happy time
 To bear my greeting to the senators,
 And tell them that I will not come today:

Cannot, is false; and that I dare not, falser;
I will not come today. Tell them so, Decius.

CALPHURNIA
    Say he is sick.

CAESAR   Shall Caesar send a lie?
Have I in conquest stretched my arm so far,
To be afraid to tell greybeards the truth?
Decius, go tell them Caesar will not come.

DECIUS
    Most mighty Caesar, let me know some cause,
    Lest I be laughed at when I tell them so.

CAESAR
    The cause is in my will: I will not come;
    That is enough to satisfy the Senate.
    But for your private satisfaction,
    Because I love you, I will let you know:
    Calphurnia here, my wife, stays me at home.
    She dreamt tonight she saw my statue,
    Which, like a fountain with a hundred spouts,
    Did run pure blood; and many lusty Romans
    Came smiling, and did bathe their hands in it.
    And these does she apply for warnings and portents
    And evils imminent; and on her knee
    Has begged that I will stay at home today.

DECIUS
    This dream is all amiss interpreted;
    It was a vision fair and fortunate.
    Your statue spouting blood in many pipes,
    In which so many smiling Romans bathed,
    Signifies that from you great Rome shall suck
    Reviving blood, and that great men shall press
    For tinctures, stains, relics, and recognition.
    This by Calphurnia's dream is signified.

CAESAR
    And this way have you well expounded it.

DECIUS
  I have, when you have heard what I can say:
  And know it now. The Senate have concluded
  To give this day a crown to mighty Caesar.
  If you shall send them word you will not come,
  Their minds may change. Besides, it were a mock
  Apt to be rendered, for some one to say,
  'Break up the Senate till another time,
  When Caesar's wife shall meet with better dreams.'
  If Caesar hides himself, shall they not whisper,
  'Lo, Caesar is afraid'?
  Pardon me, Caesar, for my dear dear love
  To your proceeding bids me tell you this,
  And reason to my love is dependable.
CAESAR
  How foolish do your fears seem now, Calphurnia!
  I am ashamèd I did yield to them.
  Give me my robe, for I will go.

        Enter BRUTUS, LIGARIUS, METELLUS, CASCA,
           TREBONIUS, CINNA, *and* PUBLIUS

  And look where Publius is come to fetch me.
PUBLIUS
  Good morrow, Caesar.
CAESAR   Welcome, Publius.
  What, Brutus, are you stirred so early too?
  Good morrow, Casca. Caius Ligarius,
  Caesar was never so much your enemy
  As that same ague which has made you lean.
  What is it o'clock?
BRUTUS   Caesar, it has struck eight.
CAESAR
  I thank you for your pains and courtesy.

Enter ANTONY

See! Antony, that revels long of nights,
Is notwithstanding up. Good morrow, Antony.
ANTONY
So to most noble Caesar.
CAESAR   Bid them prepare within.
I am to blame to be thus waited for.
Now, Cinna; now Metellus; what, Trebonius;
I have an hoür's talk in store for you;
Remember that you call on me today;
Be near me, that I may remember you.
TREBONIUS
Caesar, I will. *(Aside)* And so near will I be
That your best friends shall wish I had been
further.
CAESAR
Good friends, go in, and taste some wine with me;
And we, like friends, will straightway go together.
BRUTUS   *(aside)*
That every like is not the same, O Caesar,
The heart of Brutus yearns to think upon.   *Exeunt*

SCENE III
Before Caesar's house.

Enter ARTEMIDORUS *reading a paper*

ARTEMIDORUS   *Caesar, beware of Brutus; take heed of
Cassius; come not near Casca; have an eye to
Cinna, trust not Trebonius, mark well Metellus
Cimber; Decius Brutus loves you not; you have
wronged Caius Ligarius. There is but one mind in
all these men, and it is bent against Caesar. If you*

are not immortal, look about you: security gives
way to conspiracy. The mighty gods defend you!
                    Your lover,

                              Artemidorus.

Here will I stand till Caesar passes along,
And as a suitor will I give him this.
My heart laments that virtue cannot live
Out of the teeth of emulatiòn.
If you read this, O Caesar, you may live;
If not, the Fates with traitors do contrive.

                                                    Exit

SCENE IV
Before Brutus' house.

Enter PORTIA *and* LUCIUS

PORTIA

  I pray you, boy, run to the Senate House.
  Stay not to answer me, but get you gone.
  Why do you stay?

LUCIUS   To know my errand, madam.

PORTIA

  I would have had you there and here again
  Ere I can tell you what you should do there.
  O constancy, be strong upon my side;
  Set a huge mountain between my heart and tongue!
  I have a man's mind, but a woman's might.
  How hard it is for women to keep counsel!
  Are you here yet?

LUCIUS   Madam, what should I do?

  Run to the Capitol and nothing else?
  And so return to you, and nothing else?

PORTIA

    Yes, bring me word, boy, if your lord looks well,
    For he went sickly forth; and take good note
    What Caesar does, what suitors press to him.
    Hark, boy, what noise is that?

LUCIUS

    I hear none, madam.

PORTIA   Pray, listen well.

    I heard a bustling rumour like a fray,
    And the wind brings it from the Capitol.

LUCIUS   Truth, madam, I hear nothing.

Enter the Soothsayer

PORTIA

    Come hither fellow. Which way have you been?

SOOTHSAYER   At my own house, good lady.

PORTIA

    What is it o'clock?

SOOTHSAYER   About the ninth hour, lady.

PORTIA

    Is Caesar yet gone to the Capitol?

SOOTHSAYER

    Madam, not yet; I go to take my stand,
    To see him pass on to the capital.

PORTIA

    You have some suit to Caesar, have you not?

SOOTHSAYER

    That I have, lady, if it will please Caesar
    To be so good to Caesar as to hear me:
    I shall beseech him to befriend himself.

PORTIA

    Why, know you any harm intended towards him?

SOOTHSAYER

    None that I know will be, much that I fear may
      chance.

Good morrow to you. Here the street is narrow;
The throng that follows Caesar at the heels,
Of senators, of praetors, common suitors,
Will crowd a feeble man almost to death;
I'll get me a place more void, and there
Speak to great Caesar as he comes along.   *Exit*

PORTIA
I must go in. Ay me, how weak a thing
The heart of woman is! O Brutus,
The heavens speed you in your enterprise!
(*Aside*) Sure, the boy heard me. (*To Lucius*) Brutus
     has a suit
That Caesar will not grant. (*Aside*) O, I grow faint.
Run, Lucius, and commend me to my lord;
Say I am merry; come to me again,
And bring me word what he does say to you.

                                             Exeunt

Act III

SCENE I
Before the Capitol.

Flourish
Enter CAESAR, BRUTUS, CASSIUS, CASCA, DECIUS,
METELLUS, TREBONIUS, CINNA, ANTONY, LEPIDUS,
POPILIUS, ARTEMIDORUS, PUBLIUS,
and the Soothsayer

CAESAR   (*to the Soothsayer*) The ides of March are
     come.

SOOTHSAYER   Ay, Caesar, but not gone.

ARTEMIDORUS   Hail, Caesar! Read this schedule.

DECIUS
Trebonius does desire you to o'er-read,
At your best leisure, this his humble suit.

ARTEMIDORUS
O Caesar, read mine first; for mine's a suit
That touches Caesar nearer. Read it, great Caesar.

CAESAR
What touches us ourself shall be last served.

ARTEMIDORUS
Delay not, Caesar. Read it instantly.

CAESAR
What, is the fellow mad?

PUBLIUS   Fellow, give place.

CASSIUS
What, urge you your petitions in the street?
Come to the Capitol.

CAESAR *enters the Capitol, the rest following*

POPILIUS
I wish your enterprise today may thrive.

CASSIUS
What enterprise, Popilius?

POPILIUS   Fare you well.

He goes to speak to CAESAR

BRUTUS   What said Popilius Lena?

CASSIUS
He wished today our enterprise might thrive.
I fear our purpose is discoverèd.

BRUTUS
Look how he makes to Caesar: mark him.

CASSIUS

   Casca, be sudden, for we fear prevention.
   Brutus, what shall be done? If this is known,
   Cassius or Caesar never shall turn back,
   For I will slay myself.

BRUTUS   Cassius, be constant:

   Popilius Lena speaks not of our purposes;
   For look, he smiles, and Caesar does not change.

CASSIUS

   Trebonius knows his time; for look you, Brutus,
   He draws Mark Antony out of the way.

                 Exeunt Antony and Trebonius

DECIUS

   Where is Metellus Cimber? Let him go,
   And presently prefer his suit to Caesar.

BRUTUS

   He is addressed. Press near and second him.

CINNA

   Casca, you are the first that rears your hand.

CAESAR

   Are we all ready? What is now amiss
   That Caesar and his senate must redress?

METELLUS (*kneeling*)

   Most high, most mighty, and omnipotent Caesar,
   Metellus Cimber throws before your seat
   An humble heart—

CAESAR   I must forestall you, Cimber;

   These couchings, and these lowly courtesies
   Might fire the blood of ordinary men,
   And turn pre-ordinance and first decree
   Into the law of children. Be not a fool,
   To think that Caesar bears such rebel blood
   That will be thawed from the true quality
   With that which melts fools—I mean sweet words,
   Low-crookèd curtsies and base spaniel fawning.

Your brother by decree is banishèd:
If you do bend and pray and fawn for him,
I spurn you like a cur out of my way.
Know, Caesar does not wrong, nor without cause
Will he be satisfied.

METELLUS

Is there no voice more worthy than my own,
To sound more sweetly in great Caesar's ear
For the recalling of my banished brother?

BRUTUS

I kiss your hand, but not in flattery, Caesar,
Desiring you that Publius Cimber may
Have an immediate freedom of recall.

CAESAR   What, Brutus?

CASSIUS   [*kneeling*]   Pardon, Caesar; Caesar, pardon;
As low as to your foot does Cassius fall,
To beg enfranchisement for Publius Cimber.

CAESAR

I could be well moved, if I were as you:
If I could pray to move, prayers would move me;
But I am constant as the northern star,
Of whose true-fixed and resting quality
There is no fellow in the firmament.
The skies are painted with unnumbered sparks,
They are all fire, and every one does shine;
But there's but one in all does hold its place.
So in the world: 'tis furnished well with men,
And men are flesh and blood, and sensitive.
Yet in the number I do know but one
That unassailable holds on his rank,
Unshaked of motion. And that I am he,
Let me a little show it, even in this:
That I was constant Cimber should be banished,
And constant do remain to keep him so.

CINNA

   O Caesar—

CAESAR   Hence! Will you lift up Olympus?

DECIUS

   Great Caesar—

CAESAR   Does not Brutus kneel in vain?

CASCA   Speak hands for me!

They stab CAESAR

CAESAR

   Et tu, Brute!—then fall Caesar!   *He dies*

CINNA

   Liberty! Freedom! Tyranny is dead!

   Run hence, proclaim, cry it about the streets.

CASSIUS

   Some to the common pulpits, and cry out,

   'Liberty, freedom, and enfranchisement!'

BRUTUS

   People and senators, be not affrighted.

   Fly not; stand still; ambition's debt is paid.

CASCA

   Go to the pulpit, Brutus.

DECIUS   And Cassius too.

BRUTUS   Where's Publius?

CINNA

   Here, quite confounded with this mutiny.

METELLUS

   Stand fast together, lest some friend of Caesar's

   Should chance—

BRUTUS

   Talk not of standing. Publius, good cheer;

   There is no harm intended to your person,

   Nor to any Roman else. So tell them, Publius.

CASSIUS
   And leave us, Publius, lest now the people,
   Rushing on us, should do your age some mischief.

BRUTUS
   Do so; and let no man pay for this deed
   But we the doers.

Enter TREBONIUS

CASSIUS
   Where is Antony?

TREBONIUS   Fled to his house amazed.
   Men, wives, and children stare, cry out, and run,
   As it were doomsday.

BRUTUS   Fates, we will know your pleasures.
   That we shall die, we know; 'tis but the time
   And drawing days out, that men set store by.

CASCA
   Why, he that cuts off twenty years of life
   Cuts off so many years of fearing death.

BRUTUS
   Grant that, and then is death a benefit:
   So are we Caesar's friends, that have abridged
   His time of fearing death. Stoop, Romans, stoop,
   And let us bathe our hands in Caesar's blood
   Up to the elbows, and besmear our swords.
   Then walk we forth, even to the market-place,
   And waving our red weapons over our heads,
   Let's all cry, 'Peace, freedom, and liberty!'

CASSIUS
   Stoop then, and wash. How many ages hence
   Shall this lofty scene be acted over,
   In states unborn, and accents yet unknown!

BRUTUS
   How many times shall Caesar bleed in sport,
   That now on Pompey's basis lies along,
   No worthier than the dust!

[handwritten margin note: ritual not murder to them]

CASSIUS   So oft as that shall be,
  So often shall the knot of us be called
  The men that gave their country liberty.
DECIUS
  What, shall we forth?
CASSIUS   Ay, every man away.
  Brutus shall lead, and we will grace his heels
  With the boldest and best hearts of Rome. *superlative*

Enter a Servant

BRUTUS
  Soft, who comes here? A friend of Antony's.
SERVANT   *(kneeling)*
  Thus, Brutus, did my master bid me kneel;
  Thus did Mark Antony bid me fall down;
  And, being prostrate, thus he bade me say:
  Brutus is noble, wise, valiant, and honest;
  Caesar was mighty, bold, royal, and loving:
  Say I love Brutus, and I honour him;
  Say I feared Caesar, honoured him, and loved him.
  If Brutus will permit that Antony
  May safely come to him, and be resolved
  How Caesar has deserved to lie in death,
  Mark Antony shall not love Caesar dead
  So well as Brutus living; but will follow
  The fortunes and affairs of noble Brutus
  Thorough the hazards of this untrodden state,
  With all true faith. So says my master Antony.
BRUTUS
  Your master is a wise and valiant Roman;
  I never thought him worse.
  Tell him, if he will come unto this place,
  He shall be satisfied; and, by my honour,
  Depart untouched.
SERVANT   I'll fetch him presently.

Exit Servant

BRUTUS
  I know that we shall have him well to friend.
CASSIUS
  I wish we may: but yet have I a mind
  That fears him much; and my misgiving ever
  Falls shrewdly to the purpose.

Enter ANTONY

BRUTUS
  But here comes Antony. Welcome, Mark Antony.
ANTONY
  O mighty Caesar! Do you lie so low?
  Are all your conquests, glories, triumphs, spoils
  Shrunk to this little measure? Fare you well.
  I know not, gentlemen, what you intend,
  Who else must be let blood, who else is rank.
  If I myself, there is no hour so fit
  As Caesar's death's hour; and no instrument
  Of half that worth as those your swords, made rich
  With the most noble blood of all this world.
  I do beseech you, if you bear me ill will,
  Now, while your purpled hands do reek and smoke,
  Fulfil your pleasure. Live a thousand years,
  I shall not find myself so apt to die;
  No place will please me so, no means of death,
  As here by Caesar, and by you cut off,
  The choice and master spirits of this age.
BRUTUS
  O Antony, beg not your death of us.
  Though now we must appear bloody and cruel,
  As by our hands and this our present act
  You see we do; yet see you but our hands
  And this the bleeding business they have done.
  Our hearts you see not; they are pitiful;

manipulation

And pity to the general wrong of Rome—
As fire drives out fire, so pity, pity—
Has done this deed on Caesar. For your part,
To you our swords have leaden points, Mark
   Antony;
Our arms in strength of malice, and our hearts
Of brothers' temper, do receive you in
With all kind love, good thoughts, and reverence.

CASSIUS
Your voice shall be as strong as any man's
In the disposing of new dignities.

BRUTUS
Only be patient till we have appeased
The multitude, beside themselves with fear,
And then we will deliver you the cause
Why I, that did love Caesar when I struck him,
Have thus proceeded.

ANTONY   I doubt not of your wisdom.
Let each man render me his bloody hand.
First, Marcus Brutus, will I shake with you;
Next, Caius Cassius, do I take your hand;
Now, Decius Brutus, yours; now yours, Metellus;
Yours, Cinna; and, my valiant Casca, yours;
Though last, not least in love, yours, good
   Trebonius.
Gentlemen all—alas, what shall I say?
My credit now stands on such slippery ground,
That one of two bad ways you must conceive me,
Either a coward, or a flatterer.
That I did love you, Caesar, O, 'tis true!
If then your spirit looks upon us now,
Shall it not grieve you dearer than your death,
To see your Antony making his peace,
Shaking the bloody fingers of your foes,
Most noble, in the presence of your corpse?

Had I as many eyes as you have wounds,
Weeping as fast as they stream forth your blood,
It would become me better than to close
In terms of friendship with your enemies.
Pardon me, Julius! Here were you bayed, brave hart;
Here did you fall; and here your hunters stand,
Signed in your spoil, and crimsoned in your life
    blood.
O world, you were the forest to this hart;
And this indeed, O world, the heart of you.
How like a deer, struck by many princes,
Do you here lie!

CASSIUS
    Mark Antony—

ANTONY   Pardon me, Caius Cassius;
    The enemies of Caesar shall say this;
    Then, in a friend, it is cold modesty.

CASSIUS
    I blame you not for praising Caesar so;
    But what compact mean you to have with us?
    Will you be pricked in number of our friends,
    Or shall we on, and not depend on you?

ANTONY
    Therefore I took your hands, but was indeed
    Swayed from the point by looking down on Caesar.
    Friends am I with you all, and love you all,
    Upon this hope, that you shall give me reasons
    Why, and wherein, Caesar was dangerous.

BRUTUS
    Or else were this a savage spectacle.
    Our reasons are so full of good regard,
    That were you, Antony, the son of Caesar,
    You should be satisfied.

ANTONY   That's all I seek,
    And am moreover suitor that I may
    Produce his body to the market-place,

And in the pulpit, as becomes a friend,
Speak in the order of his funeral.

BRUTUS

You shall, Mark Antony.

CASSIUS   Brutus, a word with you.
(*Aside to Brutus*) You know not what you do; do
    not consent
That Antony speaks in his funeral.
Know you how much the people may be moved
By that which he will utter?

BRUTUS   (*aside to Cassius*)   By your pardon:
I will myself into the pulpit first,
And show the reason of our Caesar's death.
What Antony shall speak, I will protest
He speaks by leave and by permission;
And that we are contented Caesar shall
Have all true rites and lawful ceremonies,
It shall advantage more than do us wrong.

CASSIUS   (*aside to Brutus*)
I know not what may fall; I like it not.

BRUTUS

Mark Antony, here take you Caesar's body.
You shall not in your funeral speech blame us,
But speak all good you can devise of Caesar,
And say you do it by our permission.
Else shall you not have any hand at all
About his funeral. And you shall speak
In the same pulpit whereto I am going,
After my speech is ended.

ANTONY   Be it so;
I do desire no more.

BRUTUS

Prepare the body, then, and follow us.   *Exeunt*

ANTONY *remains*

ANTONY
    O, pardon me, you bleeding piece of earth,
    That I am meek and gentle with these butchers.
    You are the ruins of the noblest man
    That ever livèd in the tide of times.
    Woe to the hand that shed this costly blood!
    Over your wounds now do I prophesy—
    Which like dumb mouths open their ruby lips,
    To beg the voice and utterance of my tongue—
    A curse shall light upon the limbs of men;
    Domestic fury and fierce civil strife
    Shall cumber all the parts of Italy.
    Blood and destruction shall be so in use,
    And dreadful objects so familiàr,
    That mothers shall but smile when they behold
    Their infants quartered with the hands of war,
    All pity choked with custom of fierce deeds.
    And Caesar's spirit, ranging for revenge,
    With Ate by his side, come hot from hell,
    Shall in these confines with a monarch's voice
    Cry havoc and let slip the dogs of war—
    That this foul deed shall smell above the earth
    With carrion men, groaning for burial.

                    Enter OCTAVIUS'S Servant

    You serve Octavius Caesar, do you not?
SERVANT   I do, Mark Antony.
ANTONY
    Caesar did write for him to come to Rome.
SERVANT
    He did receive his letters, and is coming,
    And bid me say to you by word of mouth—
    O Caesar!

ANTONY
  Your heart is big; get you apart and weep.
  Passion, I see, is catching, for my eyes,
  Seeing those beads of sorrow stand in yours,
  Began to water. Is your master coming?
SERVANT
  He lies tonight within seven leagues of Rome.
ANTONY
  Post back with speed, and tell him what has
    chanced.
  Here is a mourning Rome, a dangerous Rome,
  No Rome of safety for Octavius yet.
  Hie hence, and tell him so. Yet stay awhile;
  You shall not back till I have borne this corpse
  Into the market-place. There shall I try,
  In my oration, how the people take
  The cruel issue of these bloody men.
  According to which, then you shall discourse
  To young Octavius of the state of things.
  Lend me your hand.   *Exeunt*

SCENE II
The Forum

Enter BRUTUS *and* CASSIUS, *with the citizens.*

CITIZENS We will be satisfied; let us be satisfied.
BRUTUS
  Then follow me, and give me audience, friends.
  Cassius, go you into the other street,
  And part the numbers.
  Those that will hear me speak, let them stay here;

Those that will follow Cassius, go with him;
And public reasons shall be renderèd
Of Caesar's death.

FIRST CITIZEN   I will hear Brutus speak.

SECOND CITIZEN
I will hear Cassius, and compare their reasons,
When separately we hear them renderèd.

Exit CASSIUS, *with some of the citizens*

THIRD CITIZEN
The noble Brutus is ascended. Silence!

BRUTUS   Be patient till the last.
Romans, countrymen, and lovers, hear me for my
cause, and be silent, that you may hear. Believe me
for my honour, and have respect to my honour,
that you may believe. Judge me in your wisdom,
and awake your senses, that you may the better
judge. If there are any in this assembly, any dear
friend of Caesar's, to him I say that Brutus' love to
Caesar was no less than his. If then that friend
demands why Brutus rose against Caesar, this is
my answer: not that I loved Caesar less, but that I
loved Rome more. Had you rather Caesar were
living, and die all slaves, than that Caesar were
dead, to live all free men? As Caesar loved me, I
weep for him; as he was fortunate, I rejoice at it; as
he was valiant, I honour him; but, as he was
ambitious, I slew him. There are tears for his love;
joy for his fortune; honour for his valour; and death
for his ambition. Who is here so base that would be
a bondman? If any, speak; for him have I offended.
Who is here so rude that would not be a Roman? If
any, speak; for him have I offended. Who is here so
vile that will not love his country? If any, speak;
for him have I offended. I pause for a reply.

ALL   None, Brutus, none.

BRUTUS   Then none have I offended. I have done no
more to Caesar than you shall do to Brutus. The
question of his death is enrolled in the Capitol; his
glory not extenuated, wherein he was worthy; nor
his offences enforced, for which he suffered death.

Enter MARK ANTONY *and others, with* CAESAR'S *body*

Here comes his body, mourned by Mark Antony,
who, though he had no hand in his death, shall
receive the benefit of his dying, a place in the
commonwealth, as which of you shall not? With
this I depart, that, as I slew my best lover for the
good of Rome, I have the same dagger for myself,
when it shall please my country to need my death.

ALL   Live, Brutus! live! live!

FIRST CITIZEN

Bring him with triumph home unto his house.

SECOND CITIZEN

Give him a statue with his ancestors.

THIRD CITIZEN

Let him be Caesar.

FOURTH CITIZEN   Caesar's better parts
Shall be crowned in Brutus.

FIRST CITIZEN

We'll bring him to his house with shouts and
clamours.

BRUTUS

My countrymen—

SECOND CITIZEN   Peace! Silence! Brutus speaks.

FIRST CITIZEN   Peace, ho!

BRUTUS

Good countrymen, let me depart alone,
And, for my sake, stay here with Antony.
Do grace to Caesar's corpse, and grace his speech

Tending to Caesar's glories, which Mark Antony,
By our permission, is allowed to make.
I do entreat you, not a man depart,
Save I alone, till Antony has spoken.

FIRST CITIZEN
Stay, ho! and let us hear Mark Antony.

THIRD CITIZEN
Let him go up into the public chair;
We'll hear him. Noble Antony, go up.

ANTONY
For Brutus' sake, I am beholden to you.

FOURTH CITIZEN
What does he say of Brutus?

THIRD CITIZEN   He says, for Brutus' sake
He finds himself beholden to us all.

FOURTH CITIZEN
'Twere best he speaks no harm of Brutus here!

FIRST CITIZEN
This Caesar was a tyrant.

THIRD CITIZEN   Nay, that's certain.
We are blest that Rome is rid of him.

SECOND CITIZEN
Peace! let us hear what Antony can say.

ANTONY
You gentle Romans—

SECOND CITIZEN   Peace, ho! let us hear him.

ANTONY
Friends, Romans, countrymen, lend me your ears;
I come to bury Caesar, not to praise him.
The evil that men do lives after them,
The good is oft interrèd with their bones;
So let it be with Caesar. The noble Brutus
Has told you Caesar was ambitious.
If it were so, it was a grievous fault,
And grievously has Caesar answered it.

Here, under leave of Brutus and the rest—
For Brutus is an honourable man;
So are they all, all honourable men—
Come I to speak in Caesar's funeral.
He was my friend, faithful and just to me;
But Brutus says he was ambitious,
And Brutus is an honourable man.
He has brought many captives home to Rome,
Whose ransoms did the general coffers fill:
Did this in Caesar seem ambitious?
When the poor have cried, Caesar has wept;
Ambition should be made of sterner stuff:
Yet Brutus says he was ambitious,
And Brutus is an honourable man.
You all did see that on the Lupercal
I thrice presented him a kingly crown,
Which he did thrice refuse. Was this ambition?
Yet Brutus says he was ambitious,
And sure he is an honourable man.
I speak not to disprove what Brutus spoke,
But here I am to speak what I do know.
You all did love him once, not without cause;
What cause withholds you then to mourn for him?
O judgement! You are fled to brutish beasts,
And men have lost their reason. Bear with me;
My heart is in the coffin there with Caesar,
And I must pause till it comes back to me.

FIRST CITIZEN
I think there is much reason in his sayings.

SECOND CITIZEN
If you consider rightly of the matter,
Caesar has had a great wrong.

THIRD CITIZEN   Has he, masters?
I fear there will a worse come in his place.

FOURTH CITIZEN
  Marked you his words? He would not take the crown;
  Therefore 'tis certain he was not ambitious.
FIRST CITIZEN
  If it is found so, some will pay dear for it.
SECOND CITIZEN
  Poor soul! His eyes are red as fire with weeping.
THIRD CITIZEN
  There's not a nobler man in Rome than Antony.
FOURTH CITIZEN
  Now mark him; he begins again to speak.
ANTONY
  But yesterday the word of Caesar might
  Have stood against the world; now lies he there,
  And none so poor to do him reverence.
  O masters! If I were disposed to stir
  Your hearts and minds to mutiny and rage,
  I should do Brutus wrong, and Cassius wrong,
  Who, you all know, are honourable men.
  I will not do them wrong; I rather choose
  To wrong the dead, to wrong myself and you,
  Than I will wrong such honourable men.
  But here's a parchment with the seal of Caesar;
  I found it in his closet; it is his will.
  Let but the commons hear this testament—
  Which, pardon me, I do not mean to read—
  And they would go and kiss dead Caesar's wounds,
  And dip their napkins in his sacred blood,
  Yea, beg a hair of him for memory,
  And, dying, mention it within their wills,
  Bequeathing it as a rich legacy
  Unto their issue.
FOURTH CITIZEN
  We'll hear the will. Read it, Mark Antony.
ALL
  The will, the will! We will hear Caesar's will!

ANTONY

Have patience, gentle friends; I must not read it.
It is not meet you know how Caesar loved you.
You are not wood, you are not stones, but men;
And being men, hearing the will of Caesar,
It will inflame you, it will make you mad.
'Tis good you know not that you are his heirs;
For if you should, O, what would come of it?

FOURTH CITIZEN

Read the will! We'll hear it, Antony!
You shall read us the will, Caesar's will!

ANTONY

Will you be patient? Will you stay awhile?
I have overshot myself to tell you of it.
I fear I wrong the honourable men
Whose daggers have stabbed Caesar; I do fear it.

FOURTH CITIZEN   They were traitors. Honourable men!

ALL   The will! The testament!

SECOND CITIZEN   They were villains, murderers! The
will! Read the will!

ANTONY

You will compel me then to read the will?
Then make a ring about the corpse of Caesar,
And let me show you him that made the will.
Shall I descend? And will you give me leave?

ALL   Come down.

ANTONY *comes down from the pulpit*

SECOND CITIZEN   Descend.

THIRD CITIZEN   You shall have leave.

FOURTH CITIZEN   A ring! Stand round.

FIRST CITIZEN

Stand from the hearse! Stand from the body!

SECOND CITIZEN

Room for Antony, most noble Antony!

ANTONY
  Nay, press not so upon me; stand far off.
ALL   Stand back! Room! Bear back!
ANTONY
  If you have tears, prepare to shed them now.
  You all do know this mantle. I remember
  The first time ever Caesar put it on;
  It was on a summer's evening in his tent,
  That day he overcame the Nervii.
  Look, in this place ran Cassius' dagger through;
  See what a rent the envious Casca made;
  Through this, the well-belovèd Brutus stabbed,
  And as he plucked his cursèd steel away,
  Mark how the blood of Caesar followed it,
  As rushing out of doors, to be resolved
  If Brutus so unkindly knocked or no;
  For Brutus, as you know, was Caesar's angel.
  Judge, O you gods, how dearly Caesar loved him!
  This was far the unkindest cut of all;
  For when the noble Caesar saw him stab,
  Ingratitude, more strong than traitor's arms,
  Quite vanquished him. Then burst his mighty heart;
  And in his mantle muffling up his face,
  Even at the base of Pompey's statue,
  Which all the while ran blood, great Caesar fell.
  O, what a fall was there, my countrymen!
  Then I, and you, and all of us fell down,
  While bloody treason flourished over us.
  O, now you weep, and I perceive you feel
  The dint of pity. These are gracious drops.
  Kind souls, what weep you when you but behold
  Our Caesar's vesture wounded? Look you here,
  Here is himself, marred, as you see, with traitors.

              ANTONY *plucks off the mantle*

FIRST CITIZEN   O piteous spectacle!

SECOND CITIZEN   O noble Caesar!

THIRD CITIZEN   O woeful day!

FOURTH CITIZEN   O traitors! villains!

FIRST CITIZEN   O most bloody sight!

SECOND CITIZEN   We will be revenged.

ALL   Revenge! About! Seek! Burn! Fire! Kill! Slay! Let
not a traitor live.

ANTONY   Stay, countrymen.

FIRST CITIZEN   Peace there! Hear the noble Antony!

SECOND CITIZEN   We'll hear him, we'll follow him,
we'll die for him.

ANTONY

Good friends, sweet friends, let me not stir you up
To such a sudden flood of mutiny.
They that have done this deed are honourable.
What private griefs they have, alas, I know not,
That made them do it. They are wise and
honourable,
And will, no doubt, with reasons answer you.
I come not, friends, to steal away your hearts;
I am no orator, as Brutus is,
But, as you know me all, a plain blunt man,
That love my friend; and that they know full well
That gave me public leave to speak of him.
For I have neither wit, nor words, nor worth,
Action, nor utterance, nor the power of speech
To stir men's blood; I only speak right on.
I tell you that which you yourselves do know,
Show you sweet Caesar's wounds, poor dumb
mouths,
And bid them speak for me. But were I Brutus,
And Brutus Antony, there were an Antony
Would ruffle up your spirits, and put a tongue
In every wound of Caesar that should move
The stones of Rome to rise and mutiny.

ALL
  We'll mutiny.
FIRST CITIZEN   We'll burn the house of Brutus.
THIRD CITIZEN
  Away then! Come, seek the conspirators.
ANTONY
  Yet hear me, countrymen; yet hear me speak.
ALL   Peace, ho! Hear Antony, most noble Antony!
ANTONY
  Why, friends, you go to do you know not what.
  Wherein has Caesar thus deserved your loves?
  Alas, you know not! I must tell you then:
  You have forgotten the will I told you of.
ALL
  Most true. The will! Let's stay and hear the will.
ANTONY
  Here is the will, and under Caesar's seal.
  To every Roman citizen he gives,
  To each individual man, seventy-five pence.
SECOND CITIZEN
  Most noble Caesar! We'll revenge his death.
THIRD CITIZEN   O royal Caesar!
ANTONY   Hear me with patience.
ALL   Peace, ho!
ANTONY
  Moreover, he has left you all his walks,
  His private arbours, and new-planted orchards,
  On this side Tiber; he has left them you,
  And to your heirs for ever: common pleasures,
  To walk abroad and recreate yourselves.
  Here was a Caesar! When comes such another?
FIRST CITIZEN
  Never, never! Come, away, away!
  We'll burn his body in the holy place,
  And with the brands fire the traitors' houses.
  Take up the body.

SECOND CITIZEN   Go fetch fire.
THIRD CITIZEN   Pluck down benches.
FOURTH CITIZEN   Pluck down forms, windows,
    anything.

Exeunt Citizens with the body

ANTONY
    Now let it work. Mischief, you are afoot,
    Take you what course you will.

Enter SERVANT

                                    How now, fellow?

SERVANT
    Sir, Octavius has already come to Rome.
ANTONY   Where is he?
SERVANT
    He and Lepidus are at Caesar's house.
ANTONY
    And thither will I straight to visit him.
    He comes upon a wish. Fortune is merry,
    And in this mood will give us anything.
SERVANT
    I heard him say Brutus and Cassius
    Did ride like madmen through the gates of Rome.
ANTONY
    Perhaps they had some notice of the people,
    How I had moved them. Bring me to Octavius.

                                    Exeunt

SCENE III
The same.

Enter CINNA THE POET, *and after him the* Citizens

CINNA

  I dreamt tonight that I did feast with Caesar,
  And things unluckily charge my fantasy;
  I have no will to wander forth of doors,
  Yet something leads me forth.

The Citizens *surround him*

FIRST CITIZEN   What is your name?
SECOND CITIZEN   Whither are you going?
THIRD CITIZEN   Where do you dwell?
FOURTH CITIZEN   Are you a married man or a bachelor?
SECOND CITIZEN   Answer every man directly.
FIRST CITIZEN   Ay, and briefly.
FOURTH CITIZEN   Ay, and wisely.
THIRD CITIZEN   Ay, and truly, you were best.
CINNA   What is my name? Whither am I going?
  Where do I dwell? Am I a married man or a
  bachelor? Then to answer every man directly and
  briefly, wisely and truly; wisely I say, I am a
  bachelor.
SECOND CITIZEN   That's as much as to say they are
  fools that marry. You'll bear me a bang for that, I
  fear. Proceed, directly.
CINNA   Directly, I am going to Caesar's funeral.
FIRST CITIZEN   As a friend or an enemy?
CINNA   As a friend.
SECOND CITIZEN   That matter is answered directly.
FOURTH CITIZEN   For your dwelling, briefly.
CINNA   Briefly, I dwell by the Capitol.
THIRD CITIZEN   Your name, sir, truly.
CINNA   Truly, my name is Cinna.
FIRST CITIZEN   Tear him to pieces! He's a conspirator.
CINNA   I am Cinna the poet, I am Cinna the poet.
FOURTH CITIZEN   Tear him for his bad verses, tear him
  for his bad verses!

CINNA   I am not Cinna the conspirator.
FOURTH CITIZEN   It is no matter, his name is Cinna;
  pluck but his name out of his heart, and turn him
  going.
THIRD CITIZEN   Tear him, tear him!

They attack CINNA

Come, brands, ho, firebrands! To Brutus', to
Cassius'; burn all! Some to Decius' house, and
some to Casca's; some to Ligarius'. Away, go!
                    Exeunt all the Citizens with Cinna's body

Act IV

SCENE I
Antony's house.

Enter ANTONY, OCTAVIUS, *and* LEPIDUS

ANTONY
  These many then shall die; their names are pricked.
OCTAVIUS
  Your brother too must die; consent you, Lepidus?
LEPIDUS
  I do consent.
OCTAVIUS   Prick him down, Antony.
LEPIDUS
  Upon condition Publius shall not live,
  Who is your sister's son, Mark Antony.

ANTONY
   He shall not live. Look, with a spot I damn him.
   But, Lepidus, go you to Caesar's house;
   Fetch the will hither, and we shall determine
   How to cut off some charge in legacies.

LEPIDUS   What, shall I find you here?

OCTAVIUS   Either here or at the Capitol.   *Exit Lepidus*

ANTONY
   This is a slight unmeritable man,
   Meet to be sent on errands. Is it fit,
   The three-fold world divided, he should stand
   One of the three to share it?

OCTAVIUS   So you thought him,
   And took his voice who should be pricked to die
   In our black sentence and proscriptiòn.

ANTONY
   Octavius, I have seen more days than you;
   And though we lay these honours on this man,
   To ease ourselves of divers slanderous loads,
   He shall but bear them as the ass bears gold,
   To groan and sweat under the business,
   Either led or driven, as we point the way.
   And having brought our treasure where we will,
   Then take we down his load, and turn him off,
   Like to the empty ass, to shake his ears
   And graze in commons.

OCTAVIUS   You may do your will;
   But he's a tried and valiant soldier.

ANTONY
   So is my horse, Octavius, and for that
   I do appoint him store of provender.
   It is a creature that I teach to fight,
   To wind, to stop, to run directly on,
   His corporal motion governed by my spirit.
   And, in some taste, is Lepidus but so:

He must be taught, and trained, and bid go forth:
A barren-spirited fellow; one that feeds
On objects, arts, and imitatiòns,
Which, out of use and staled by other men,
Inspire his fashion. Do not talk of him
But as a property. And now, Octavius,
Listen to great things. Brutus and Cassius
Are levying forces; we must straight make head.
Therefore let our alliance be combined,
Our best friends made, our means stretched;
And let us presently go sit in council,
How covert matters may be best disclosed,
And open perils surest answerèd.

OCTAVIUS
Let us do so; for we are at the stake,
And bayed about with many enemies;
And some that smile have in their hearts, I fear,
Millions of mischiefs.   *Exeunt*

SCENE II
Before Brutus' tent, near Sardis.

Drum
Enter BRUTUS, LUCILIUS, LUCIUS, *and the army.*
TITINIUS *and* PINDARUS *meet them*

BRUTUS   Stand, ho!
LUCILIUS   Give the word, ho! and stand!
BRUTUS
What now, Lucilius, is Cassius near?
LUCILIUS
He is at hand, and Pindarus is come
To do you salutation from his master.

BRUTUS
   He greets me well. Your master, Pindarus,
   In his own change, or by ill officers,
   Has given me some worthy cause to wish
   Things done undone; but if he is at hand
   I shall be satisfied.
PINDARUS   I do not doubt
   But that my noble master will appear
   Such as he is, worthy of respect and honour.
BRUTUS
   He is not doubted. A word, Lucilius;

         BRUTUS *and* LUCILIUS *draw apart*

   How he received you, let me be resolved.
LUCILIUS
   With courtesy and with respect enough,
   But not with such familiar instances,
   Nor with such free and friendly conference,
   As he has used of old.
BRUTUS   You have described
   A hot friend cooling. Ever note, Lucilius,
   When love begins to sicken and decay,
   It uses an enforcèd ceremony.
   There are no tricks in plain and simple faith;
   But hollow men, like horses hot at hand,
   Make gallant show and promise of their mettle;

         Low march within

   But when they should endure the bloody spur,
   They lower their crests, and like deceitful jades
   Sink in the trial. Comes his army on?

LUCILIUS
   They mean this night in Sardis to be quartered;
   The greater part, the horse in general,
   Have come with Cassius.

Enter CASSIUS *and soldiers*

                    Hark! he has arrived.
  March gently on to meet him.
CASSIUS   Stand, ho!
BRUTUS   Stand, ho! Speak the word along.
FIRST SOLDIER   Stand!
SECOND SOLDIER   Stand!
THIRD SOLDIER   Stand!
CASSIUS
   Most noble brother, you have done me wrong.
BRUTUS
   Judge me, you gods; wrong I my enemies?
   And if not so, how should I wrong a brother?
CASSIUS
   Brutus, this sober form of yours hides wrongs;
   And when you do them—
BRUTUS
                   Cassius, be content.
  Speak your griefs softly; I do know you well.
  Before the eyes of both our armies here,
  Which should perceive nothing but love from us,
  Let us not wrangle. Bid them move away;
  Then in my tent, Cassius, enlarge your griefs,
  And I will give you audience.
CASSIUS   Pindarus,
  Bid our commanders lead their charges off
  A little from this ground.

BRUTUS

    Lucius, do you the like, and let no man
    Come to our tent till we have done our conference.
    Lucilius and Titinius guard our door.

               Exeunt all except Brutus and Cassius

SCENE III
The same.

CASSIUS

    That you have wronged me does appear in this:
    You have condemned and noted Lucius Pella
    For taking bribes here of the Sardians;
    Wherein my letter, praying on his side,
    Because I knew the man, was slighted off.

BRUTUS

    You wronged yourself to write in such a case.

CASSIUS

    In such a time as this it is not meet
    That every nice offence should bear its comment.

BRUTUS

    Let me tell you, Cassius, you yourself
    Are much condemned to have an itching palm,
    To sell and bid your offices for gold
    To undeservers.

CASSIUS   I an itching palm!

    You know that you are Brutus that speaks this,
    Or, by the gods, this speech were else your last.

BRUTUS

    The name of Cassius honours this corruption,
    And chastisement does therefore hide its head.

CASSIUS   Chastisement!

BRUTUS

    Remember March, the ides of March remember.
    Did not great Julius bleed for justice' sake?

What villain touched his body, that did stab,
And not for justice? What, shall one of us,
That struck the foremost man of all this world
But for supporting robbers, shall we now
Contaminate our fingers with base bribes,
And sell the mighty space of our large honours
For so much trash as may be graspèd thus?
I had rather be a dog, and bay at the moon,
Than such a Roman.

CASSIUS   Brutus, bait not me;
I'll not endure it. You forget yourself,
To hedge me in. I am a soldier, I,
Older in practice, abler than yourself
To make conditions.

BRUTUS   Go to! You are not, Cassius.

CASSIUS   I am.

BRUTUS   I say you are not.

CASSIUS

Urge me no more, I shall forget myself;
Have mind upon your health; tempt me no further.

BRUTUS   Away, slight man!

CASSIUS

Is it possible?

BRUTUS   Hear me, for I will speak.
Must I give way and room to your rash choler?
Shall I be frighted when a madman stares?

CASSIUS

O ye gods, ye gods! Must I endure all this?

BRUTUS

All this? Ay, more: fret till your proud heart breaks;
Go show your slaves how choleric you are,
And make your bondmen tremble. Must I budge?
Must I respect you? Must I stand and crouch
Under your testy humour? By the gods,
You shall digest the venom of your spleen,
Though it should split you; for, from this day forth,

I'll use you for my mirth, yea, for my laughter,
When you are waspish.

CASSIUS   Is it come to this?

BRUTUS

You say you are a better soldier:
Let it appear so; make your vaunting true,
And it shall please me well. For my own part,
I shall be glad to learn of noble men.

CASSIUS

You wrong me every way; you wrong me, Brutus.
I said an elder soldier, not a better;
Did I say better?

BRUTUS   If you did, I care not.

CASSIUS

When Caesar lived, he durst not thus have moved
   me.

BRUTUS

Peace, peace! You durst not so have tempted him.

CASSIUS   I durst not?

BRUTUS   No.

CASSIUS

What, durst not tempt him?

BRUTUS   For your life you durst not.

CASSIUS

Do not presume too much upon my love;
I may do that I shall be sorry for.

BRUTUS

You have done that you should be sorry for.
There is no terror, Cassius, in your threats;
For I am armed so strong in honesty
That they pass by me as the idle wind,
Which I respect not. I did send to you
For certain sums of gold, which you denied me;
For I can raise no money by vile means.
By heaven, I had rather coin my heart,

And drop my blood for pennies, than to wring
From the hard hands of peasants their vile trash
By any indirection. I did send
To you for gold to pay my legions.
Which you denied me; was that done like Cassius?
Should I have answered Caius Cassius so?
When Marcus Brutus grows so covetous,
To lock such rascal counters from his friends,
Be ready, gods, with all your thunderbolts,
Dash him to pieces!

CASSIUS   I denied you not.

BRUTUS
You did.

CASSIUS   I did not. He was but a fool
That brought my answer. Brutus has cleft my heart;
A friend should bear his friend's infirmities;
But Brutus makes mine greater than they are.

BRUTUS
I do not, till you practise them on me.

CASSIUS
You love me not.

BRUTUS   I do not like your faults.

CASSIUS
A friendly eye could never see such faults.

BRUTUS
A flatterer's would not, though they do appear
As huge as high Olympus.

CASSIUS
Come, Antony, and young Octavius, come,
Revenge yourselves alone on Cassius,
For Cassius is aweary of the world;
Hated by one he loves; braved by his brother;
Checked like a bondman; all his faults observed,
Set in a notebook, learned, and conned by rote,
To cast into my teeth. O, I could weep

My spirit from my eyes! There is my dagger,
And here my naked breast; within, a heart
Dearer than Pluto's mine, richer than gold:
If you are a Roman, take it forth.
I, that denied you gold, will give my heart:
Strike, as you did at Caesar; for I know,
When you did hate him worst, you loved him better
Than ever you loved Cassius.

BRUTUS   Sheathe your dagger.
Be angry when you will, it shall have scope;
Do what you will, dishonour shall be humour.
O Cassius, you are yokèd with a lamb
That carries anger as the flint bears fire,
Who, much enforcèd, shows a hasty spark,
And straight is cold again.

CASSIUS   Has Cassius lived
To be but mirth and laughter to his Brutus,
When grief and blood ill-tempered anger him?

BRUTUS
When I spoke that, I was ill-tempered too.

CASSIUS
Do you confess so much? Give me your hand.

BRUTUS
And my heart too.

CASSIUS   O Brutus!

BRUTUS   What's the matter?

CASSIUS
Have not you love enough to bear with me,
When that rash humour which my mother gave me
Makes me forgetful?

BRUTUS   Yes, Cassius; and from henceforth,
When you are over-earnest with your Brutus,
He'll think your mother chides, and leave you so.

Enter a Poet *followed by* LUCIUS; TITINIUS *and*
LUCILIUS *attempting to restrain him*

POET

   Let me go in to see the Generals.

   There is some grudge between them; 'tis not meet

   They be alone.

LUCILIUS   You shall not come to them.

POET   Nothing but death shall stay me.

CASSIUS   How now? What's the matter?

POET

   For shame, you Generals! What do you mean?

   Love, and be friends, as two such men should be;

   For I have seen more years, I'm sure, than ye.

CASSIUS

   Ha, ha! How vilely does this cynic rhyme!

BRUTUS

   Get you hence, sir! Saucy fellow, hence!

CASSIUS

   Bear with him, Brutus; it is his fashion.

BRUTUS

   I'll know his humour, when he knows his time.

   What should the wars do with these jigging fools?

   Companion, hence!

CASSIUS   Away, away, be gone!   *Exit Poet*

BRUTUS

   Lucilius and Titinius, bid the commanders

   Prepare to lodge their companies tonight.

CASSIUS

   And come yourselves, and bring Messala with you

   Immediately to us.   *Exeunt Lucilius and Titinius*

BRUTUS   Lucius, a bowl of wine.   *Exit Lucius*

CASSIUS

   I did not think you could have been so angry.

BRUTUS

   O Cassius, I am sick of many griefs.

CASSIUS

   Of your philosophy you make no use,

   If you give place to accidental evils.

BRUTUS
   No man bears sorrow better. Portia is dead.
CASSIUS   Ha? Portia?
BRUTUS   She is dead.
CASSIUS
   How escaped I killing, when I crossed you so?
   O insupportable and touching loss!
   Upon what sickness?
BRUTUS   Impatient of my absence,
   And grief that young Octavius with Mark Antony
   Have made themselves so strong; for with her death
   That tidings came. With this she fell distract,
   And, her attendants absent, swallowed fire.
CASSIUS
   And died so?
BRUTUS   Even so.
CASSIUS   O ye immortal gods!

Enter Boy (LUCIUS) *with wine and tapers*

BRUTUS
   Speak no more of her. Give me a bowl of wine.
   In this I bury all unkindness, Cassius.

He drinks

CASSIUS
   My heart is thirsty for that noble pledge.
   Fill, Lucius, till the wine o'erswell the cup;
   I cannot drink too much of Brutus' love.
                      Exit Lucius

CASSIUS *drinks*
Enter TITINIUS *and* MESSALA

BRUTUS

Come in, Titinius. Welcome, good Messala.
Now sit we close about this taper here,
And call in question our necessities.

CASSIUS

Portia, are you gone?

BRUTUS   No more, I pray you.
Messala, I have here receivèd letters,
That young Octavius and Mark Antony
Come down upon us with a mighty army,
Bending their expedition toward Philippi.

MESSALA

Myself have letters of the self-same tenor.

BRUTUS   With what addition?

MESSALA

That by proscription and bills of outlawry
Octavius, Antony, and Lepidus
Have put to death a hundred senators.

BRUTUS

Therein our letters do not well agree.
Mine speak of seventy senators that died
By their proscriptions, Cicero being one.

CASSIUS

Cicero one?

MESSALA   Cicero is dead,
And by that order of proscriptiòn.
Had you your letters from your wife, my lord?

BRUTUS   No, Messala.

MESSALA

And nothing in your letters written of her?

BRUTUS

Nothing, Messala.

MESSALA   That, I think, is strange.

BRUTUS

Why ask you? Hear you aught of her in yours?

MESSALA　　No, my lord.

BRUTUS

Now, as you are a Roman, tell me true.

MESSALA

Then like a Roman bear the truth I tell;
For certain she is dead, and by strange manner.

BRUTUS

Why, farewell, Portia. We must die, Messala.
With meditating that she must die once,
I have the patience to endure it now.

MESSALA

Even so great men great losses should endure.

CASSIUS

I have as much of this in art as you,
But yet my nature could not bear it so.

BRUTUS

Well, to our work alive. What do you think
Of marching to Philippi presently?

CASSIUS

I do not think it good.

BRUTUS　　　　　　　　　Your reason?

CASSIUS　　　　　　　　　　　　　　　　This it is:

It is better that the enemy seek us;
So shall he waste his means, weary his soldiers,
Doing himself offence; while we, lying still,
Are full of rest, defence, and nimbleness.

BRUTUS

Good reasons must of force give place to better.
The people between Philippi and this ground
Do stand but in a forced affectiòn;
For they have grudged us contributiòn.
The enemy, marching along by them,
By them shall make a fuller number up,
Come on refreshed, new-added, and encouraged;
From which advantage shall we cut him off,

If at Philippi we do face him there,
These people at our back.

CASSIUS   Hear me, good brother—

BRUTUS
Under your pardon. You must note beside
That we have tried the utmost of our friends,
Our legions are brim-full, our cause is ripe.
The enemy increases every day;
We, at the height, are ready to decline.
There is a tide in the affairs of men,
Which, taken at the flood, leads on to fortune;
Omitted, all the voyage of their life,
Is bound in shallows and in miseries.
On such a full sea are we now afloat,
And we must take the current when it serves,
Or lose our ventures.

CASSIUS   Then, with your will, go on;
We'll along ourselves, and meet them at Philippi.

BRUTUS
The deep of night is crept upon our talk,
And nature must obey necessity,
Which we will nurse now with a little rest.
There is no more to say?

CASSIUS   No more. Good night.
Early tomorrow will we rise, and hence.

BRUTUS
Lucius!

Enter LUCIUS

My gown.   *Exit Lucius*
Farewell, good Messala.

Good night, Titinius. Noble, noble Cassius,
Good night, and good repose.

CASSIUS   O my dear brother,
  This was an ill beginning of the night;
  Never come such division between our souls!
  Let it not, Brutus.

Enter LUCIUS, *with the gown*

BRUTUS   Everything is well.
CASSIUS
  Good night, my lord.
BRUTUS   Good night, good brother.
TITINIUS *and* MESSALA
  Good night, Lord Brutus.
BRUTUS   Farewell, every one.
          Exeunt Cassius, Titinius, and Messala
  Give me the gown. Where is your instrument?
LUCIUS
  Here in the tent.
BRUTUS   What, you speak drowsily?
  Poor knave, I blame you not; you are overdone.
  Call Claudius and some others of my men;
  I'll have them sleep on cushions in my tent.
LUCIUS   Varro and Claudius!

Enter VARRO *and* CLAUDIUS

VARRO   Calls my lord?
BRUTUS
  I pray you, sir, lie in my tent and sleep;
  It may be I shall raise you by and by
  On business to my brother Cassius.
VARRO
  So please you, we will stand and watch your
    pleasure.
BRUTUS
  I will not have it so; lie down, good sirs.
  It may be I shall otherwise bethink me.

VARRO *and* CLAUDIUS *lie down*

Look, Lucius, here's the book I sought for so;
I put it in the pocket of my gown.
LUCIUS
I was sure your lordship did not give it me.
BRUTUS
Bear with me, good boy, I am much forgetful.
Can you hold up your heavy eyes awhile,
And touch your instrument a strain or two?
LUCIUS
Ay, my lord, if it pleases.
BRUTUS   It does, my boy.
I trouble you too much, but you are willing.
LUCIUS   It is my duty, sir.
BRUTUS
I should not urge your duty past your might;
I know young bloods look for a time of rest.
LUCIUS   I have slept, my lord, already.
BRUTUS
It was well done, and you shall sleep again;
I will not hold you long. If I do live,
I will be good to you.

Music, and a song
LUCIUS *falls asleep*

This is a sleepy tune; O murderous slumber,
Lay you your leaden mace upon my boy,
That plays you music? Gentle knave, good night;
I will not do you so much wrong to wake you.
If you do nod, you break your instrument;
I'll take it from you; and, good boy, good night.
Let me see, let me see; is not the leaf turned down
Where I left reading? Here it is, I think.

He sits and reads

Enter the GHOST OF CAESAR

How ill this taper burns! Ha! Who comes here?
I think it is the weakness of my eyes
That shapes this monstrous apparitìon.
It comes upon me. Are you any thing?
Are you some god, some angel, or some devil,
That makes my blood cold, and my hair to stare?
Speak to me what you are.

GHOST
Your evil spirit, Brutus.

BRUTUS   Why come you?

GHOST
To tell you you shall see me at Philippi.

BRUTUS   Well; then I shall see you again?

GHOST   Ay, at Philippi.

BRUTUS
Why, I will see you at Philippi then.   *Exit Ghost*
Now I have taken heart, you vanish.
Ill spirit, I would hold more talk with you.
Boy! Lucius! Varro! Claudius! Sirs, awake!
Claudius!

LUCIUS   The strings, my lord, are false.

BRUTUS
He thinks he still is at his instrument.
Lucius, awake!

LUCIUS   My Lord?

BRUTUS
Did you dream, Lucius, that you so cried out?

LUCIUS
My lord, I do not know that I did cry.

BRUTUS
Yes, that you did. Did you see anything?

LUCIUS   Nothing, my lord.

BRUTUS
  Sleep again, Lucius. Claudius, man!'
  Fellow you, awake!
VARRO   My lord?
CLAUDIUS   My lord?
BRUTUS
  Why did you so cry out, sirs, in your sleep?
VARRO *and* CLAUDIUS
  Did we, my lord?
BRUTUS   Ay; saw you anything?
VARRO
  No, my lord, I saw nothing.
CLAUDIUS   Nor I, my lord.
BRUTUS
  Go and commend me to my brother Cassius.
  Bid him set on his forces betimes before,
  And we will follow.
VARRO *and* CLAUDIUS   It shall be done, my lord.

                                          Exeunt

Act V

SCENE I
A plain near Philippi.

Enter OCTAVIUS, ANTONY, *and their army*

OCTAVIUS
  Now, Antony, our hopes are answerèd:
  You said the enemy would not come down,

But keep the hills and upper regions.
It proves not so; their forces are at hand;
They mean to warn us at Philippi here,
Answering before we do demand of them.

ANTONY
Tut, I am in their bosoms, and I know
Wherefore they do it. They could be content
To visit other places, and come down
With fearful bravery, thinking by this face,
To fasten in our thoughts that they have courage;
But it is not so.

Enter a Messenger

MESSENGER   Prepare you, Generals;
The enemy comes on in gallant show.
Their bloody sign of battle is hung out,
And something to be done immediately.

ANTONY
Octavius, lead your army softly on
Upon the left hand of the even field.

OCTAVIUS
Upon the right hand I. Keep you the left.

ANTONY
Why do you cross me in this emergency?

OCTAVIUS
I do not cross you; but I will do so.

March
Drum
Enter BRUTUS, CASSIUS, *and their army*; LUCILIUS,
TITINIUS, MESSALA, *and others*

BRUTUS   They stand, and would have parley.
CASSIUS
Stand fast, Titinius; we must out and talk.

OCTAVIUS
  Mark Antony, shall we give sign of battle?
ANTONY
  No, Caesar, we will answer on their charge.
  Make forth; the Generals would have some words.
OCTAVIUS   Stir not until the signal.
BRUTUS
  Words before blows: is it so, countrymen?
OCTAVIUS
  Not that we love words better, as you do.
BRUTUS
  Good words are better than bad strokes, Octavius.
ANTONY
  In your bad strokes, Brutus, you give good words;
  Witness the hole you made in Caesar's heart,
  Crying, 'Long live! Hail, Caesar!'
CASSIUS   Antony,
  The posture of your blows is yet unknown;
  But for your words, they rob the Hybla bees,
  And leave them honeyless.
ANTONY   Not stingless too.
BRUTUS   O yes, and soundless too;
  For you have stolen their buzzing, Antony,
  And very wisely threat before you sting.
ANTONY
  Villains! You did not so, when your vile daggers
  Hacked one another in the sides of Caesar.
  You showed your teeth like apes, and fawned like
      hounds,
  And bowed like bondmen, kissing Caesar's feet;
  While damnèd Casca, like a cur, behind
  Struck Caesar on the neck. O you flatterers!
CASSIUS
  Flatterers? Now, Brutus, thank yourself:
  This tongue had not offended so today,
  If Cassius might have ruled.

OCTAVIUS

Come, come, the cause. If arguing make us sweat,
The proof of it will turn to redder drops.
Look,
I draw a sword against conspirators.
When think you that the sword goes up again?
Never till Caesar's three and thirty wounds
Are well avenged; or till another Caesar
Has added slaughter to the sword of traitors.

BRUTUS

Caesar, you can not die by traitors' hands,
Unless you bring them with you.

OCTAVIUS   So I hope.

I was not born to die on Brutus' sword.

BRUTUS

O, if you were the noblest of your strain,
Young man, you could not die more honourable.

CASSIUS

A peevish schoolboy, worthless of such honour,
Joined with a masquer and a reveller.

ANTONY

Old Cassius, still!

OCTAVIUS   Come, Antony; away!

Defiance, traitors, hurl we in your teeth.
If you dare fight today, come to the field;
If not, when you have stomachs.

                        Exeunt Octavius, Antony, and army

CASSIUS

Why now, blow wind, swell billow, and swim bark!
The storm is up, and all is on the hazard.

BRUTUS

Ho, Lucilius, hark, a word with you.

LUCILIUS   My lord?

LUCILIUS *stands forth, and talks with* BRUTUS *apart*

CASSIUS
  Messala.
MESSALA   What says my General?

MESSALA *stands forth*

CASSIUS   Messala,
  This is my birthday; this very day
  Was Cassius born. Give me your hand, Messala:
  Be you my witness that against my will—
  As Pompey was—am I compelled to set
  Upon one battle all our liberties.
  You know that I held Epicurus strong,
  And his opinion; now I change my mind,
  And partly credit things that do portend.
  Coming from Sardis, on our former ensign
  Two mighty eagles fell, and there they perched,
  Gorging and feeding from our soldiers' hands,
  Who to Philippi here accompanied us.
  This morning are they fled away and gone,
  And in their steads do ravens, crows, and kites
  Fly over our heads and downward look on us,
  As if we were sickly prey. Their shadows seem
  A canopy most fatal, under which
  Our army lies, ready to give up the ghost.
MESSALA
  Believe not so.
CASSIUS   I but believe it partly,
  For I am fresh of spirit, and resolved
  To meet all perils very constantly.
BRUTUS
  Even so, Lucilius.

BRUTUS *rejoins* CASSIUS

CASSIUS   Now, most noble Brutus,
　The gods today stand friendly, that we may,
　Lovers in peace, lead on our days to age!
　But since the affairs of men rest ever uncertain,
　Let's reason with the worst that may befall.
　If we do lose this battle, then is this
　The very last time we shall speak together;
　What are you then determinèd to do?

BRUTUS
　Even by the rule of that philosophy
　By which I did blame Cato for the death
　Which he did give himself—I know not how,
　But I do find it cowardly and vile,
　For fear of what might fall, so to forestall
　The time of life—arming myself with patience
　To stay the providence of some high powers
　That govern us below.

CASSIUS   Then, if we lose this battle,
　You are contented to be led in triumph
　Through the streets of Rome?

BRUTUS
　No, Cassius, no; think not, you noble Roman,
　That ever Brutus will go bound to Rome;
　He bears too great a mind. But this same day
　Must end that work the ides of March began;
　And whether we shall meet again I know not.
　Therefore our everlasting farewell take:
　For ever, and for ever, farewell, Cassius.
　If we do meet again, why, we shall smile;
　If not, why then this parting was well made.

CASSIUS
　For ever, and for ever, farewell, Brutus.
　If we do meet again, we'll smile indeed;
　If not, 'tis true this parting was well made.

BRUTUS

Why then, lead on. O, that a man might know
The end of this day's business ere it comes!
But it suffices that the day will end,
And then the end is known. Come, ho! Away!

Exeunt

SCENE II
The same

Alarum
Enter BRUTUS *and* MESSALA

BRUTUS

Ride, ride, Messala, ride, and give these bills
Unto the legions on the other side.

Loud alarum

Let them set on at once; for I perceive
But cold demeanour in Octavius' wing,
And sudden push gives them the overthrow.
Ride, ride, Messala; let them all come down.

Exeunt

SCENE III
The same.

Alarums
Enter CASSIUS *and* TITINIUS

CASSIUS

O, look, Titinius, look, the villains fly.
Myself have to my own turned enemy:

This ensign here of mine was turning back;
I slew the coward, and did take it from him.
TITINIUS
O Cassius, Brutus gave the word too early,
Who, having some advantage on Octavius,
Took it too eagerly; his soldiers fell to spoil,
While we by Antony are all enclosed.

Enter PINDARUS

PINDARUS
Fly further off, my lord, fly further off!
Mark Antony is in your tents, my lord.
Fly therefore, noble Cassius, fly far off!
CASSIUS
This hill is far enough. Look, look, Titinius!
Are those my tents where I perceive the fire?
TITINIUS
They are, my lord.
CASSIUS   Titinius, if you love me,
Mount you my horse, and hide your spurs in him,
Till he has brought you up to yonder troops
And here again, that I may rest assured
Whether yon troops are friend or enemy.
TITINIUS
I will be here again, even with a thought.   *Exit*
CASSIUS
Go, Pindarus, get higher on that hill;
My sight was ever thick. Regard Titinius,
And tell me what you note about the field.

PINDARUS *ascends*

This day I breathèd first. Time is come round,
And where I did begin, there shall I end.

My life has run its compass. (*To Pindarus*) Fellow,
  what news?
PINDARUS   (*above*) O my lord!
CASSIUS   What news?
PINDARUS

Titinius is enclosèd round about
With horsemen, that make to him on the spur,
Yet he spurs on. Now they are almost on him.
Now, Titinius! Now some light. O, he lights too!
He's taken!

Shout

                    And hark! They shout for joy.
CASSIUS   Come down; behold no more.
  O, coward that I am, to live so long,
  To see my best friend taken before my face!

Enter PINDARUS *from above*

Come hither, fellow.
In Parthia did I take you prisoner;
And then I swore you, saving of your life,
That whatsoever I did bid you do,
You should attempt it. Come now, keep your oath;
Now be a freeman; and with this good sword,
That ran through Caesar's bowels, search this
  bosom.
Stand not to answer. Here, take you the hilts,
And when my face is covered, as 'tis now,
Guide you the sword.—Caesar, you are revenged,
Even with the sword that killed you.   *He dies*
PINDARUS
  So, I am free; yet would not so have been,
  Durst I have done my will. O Cassius!
  Far from this country Pindarus shall run,
  Where never Roman shall take note of him.   *Exit*

Enter TITINIUS *and* MESSALA

MESSALA

   It is but change, Titinius; for Octavius
   Is overthrown by noble Brutus' power,
   As Cassius' legions are by Antony.

TITINIUS

   These tidings will well comfort Cassius.

MESSALA

   Where did you leave him?

TITINIUS   All disconsolate,
   With Pindarus his bondman, on this hill.

MESSALA

   Is not that he that lies upon the ground?

TITINIUS

   He lies not like the living. O my heart!

MESSALA

   Is not that he?

TITINIUS   No, this was he, Messala,
   But Cassius is no more. O setting sun,
   As in your red rays you do sink to night,
   So in his red blood Cassius' day is set.
   The sun of Rome is set. Our day is gone;
   Clouds, dews, and dangers come; our deeds are done.
   Mistrust of my fortune has done this deed.

MESSALA

   Mistrust of good fortune has done this deed.
   O hateful Error, Melancholy's child,
   Why do you show to the apt thoughts of men
   The things that are not? O Error, soon conceived,
   You never come unto a happy birth,
   But kill the mother that engendered you.

TITINIUS

   What, Pindarus! Where are you, Pindarus?

MESSALA
    Seek him, Titinius, while I go to meet
    The noble Brutus, thrusting this report
    Into his ears. I may say 'thrusting' it;
    For piercing steel and darts envenomèd
    Shall be as welcome to the ears of Brutus
    As tidings of this sight.
TITINIUS   Hie you, Messala,
    And I will seek for Pindarus the while. *Exit Messala*
    Why did you send me forth, brave Cassius?
    Did I not meet your friends, and did not they
    Put on my brows this wreath of victory,
    And bid me give it you? Did you not hear their
      shouts?
    Alas, you have misconstruèd everything!
    But hold you, take this garland on your brow;
    Your Brutus bid me give it you, and I
    Will do his bidding. Brutus, come apace,
    And see how I regarded Caius Cassius.
    By your leave, gods. This is a Roman's part;
    Come, Cassius' sword, and find Titinius' heart.
                             He dies

Alarum
Enter BRUTUS, MESSALA, YOUNG CATO, STRATO,
VOLUMNIUS, LABEO, FLAVIUS, *and* LUCILIUS

BRUTUS
    Where, where, Messala, does his body lie?
MESSALA
    Lo, yonder, and Titinius mourning it.
BRUTUS
    Titinius' face is upward.

CATO   He is slain.

BRUTUS
  O Julius Caesar, you are mighty yet!
  Your spirit walks abroad, and turns our swords
  In our own proper entrails.

Low alarums

CATO   Brave Titinius,
  Look where he has not crowned dead Cassius.

BRUTUS
  Are yet two Romans living such as these?
  The last of all the Romans, fare you well!
  It is impossible that ever Rome
  Should breed your fellow. Friends, I owe more tears
  To this dead man than you shall see me pay.
  I shall find time, Cassius, I shall find time.
  Come therefore, and to Thasos send his body.
  His funeral shall not be in our camp,
  Lest it discomforts us. Lucilius, come;
  And come, young Cato; let us to the field.
  Labeo and Flavius, set our forces on.
  'Tis three o'clock; and, Romans, yet ere night
  We shall try fortune in a second fight.   *Exeunt*

SCENE IV
The same.

Alarum
Enter BRUTUS, MESSALA, YOUNG CATO,
LUCILIUS, *and* FLAVIUS

BRUTUS
  Yet countrymen, O, yet hold up your heads!
        Exit, followed by Messala and Flavius

CATO
>   What bastard does not? Who will go with me?
>   I will proclaim my name about the field.
>   I am the son of Marcus Cato, ho!

Enter soldiers, and fight

LUCILIUS
>   And I am Brutus, Marcus Brutus, I!
>   Brutus, my country's friend; know me for Brutus!
>   *Young Cato is slain*
>   O young and noble Cato, are you down?
>   Why, now you die as bravely as Titinius,
>   And may be honoured, being Cato's son.

FIRST SOLDIER
>   Yield, or you die.

LUCILIUS   Only I yield to die.
>   There is so much that you will kill me straight:
>   Kill Brutus, and be honoured in his death.

FIRST SOLDIER   We must not. A noble prisoner!

Enter ANTONY

SECOND SOLDIER
>   Room, ho! Tell Antony, Brutus is taken.

FIRST SOLDIER
>   I'll tell the news. Here comes the General.
>   Brutus is taken, Brutus is taken, my lord.

ANTONY   Where is he?

LUCILIUS
>   Safe, Antony; Brutus is safe enough.
>   I dare assure you that no enemy
>   Shall ever take alive the noble Brutus.
>   The gods defend him from so great a shame!
>   When you do find him, or alive or dead,
>   He will be found like Brutus, like himself.

ANTONY
 This is not Brutus, friend; but, I assure you,
 A prize no less in worth. Keep this man safe;
 Give him all kindness. I had rather have
 Such men my friends than enemies. Go on,
 And see whether Brutus is alive or dead;
 And bring us word unto Octavius' tent
 How every thing has chanced.   *Exeunt*

SCENE V
The same.

Enter BRUTUS, DARDANIUS, CLITUS,
STRATO, *and* VOLUMNIUS

BRUTUS
 Come, poor remains of friends, rest on this rock.
CLITUS
 Statilius showed the torch-light; but, my lord,
 He came not back; he is taken or slain.
BRUTUS
 Sit you down, Clitus. Slaying is the word;
 It is a deed in fashion. Hark you, Clitus.

He whispers

CLITUS
 What, I, my lord? No, not for all the world.
BRUTUS
 Peace then. No words.
CLITUS   I'll rather kill myself.
BRUTUS
 Hark you, Dardanius.

He whispers   *she*

DARDANIUS   Shall I do such a deed?
CLITUS   O Dardanius!
DARDANIUS   O Clitus!
CLITUS
   What ill request did Brutus make to you?
DARDANIUS
   To kill him, Clitus. Look, he meditates.
CLITUS
   Now is that noble vessel full of grief,
   That it runs over even at his eyes.
BRUTUS
   Come hither, good Volumnius; list a word.
VOLUMNIUS
   What says my lord?
BRUTUS   Why, this, Volumnius:
   The ghost of Caesar has appeared to me
   Two several times by night: at Sardis once,
   And this last night, here in Philippi fields.
   I know my hour is come.
VOLUMNIUS   Not so, my lord.
BRUTUS
   Nay, I am sure it is, Volumnius.
   You see the world, Volumnius, how it goes:
   Our enemies have beat us to the pit.

Low alarums

   It is more worthy to leap in ourselves
   Than tarry till they push us. Good Volumnius,
   You know that we two went to school together;
   Even for that our love of old, I pray you
   Hold you my sword-hilts while I run on it.

VOLUMNIUS
That's not an office for a friend, my lord.

Alarum still

CLITUS
Fly, fly, my lord, there is no tarrying here.
BRUTUS
Farewell to you; and you; and you, Volumnius.
Strato, you have been all this while asleep;
Farewell to you too, Strato. Countrymen,
My heart does joy that yet in life
I found no man but he was true to me.
I shall have glory by this losing day,
More than Octavius and Mark Antony
By this vile conquest shall attain unto.
So fare you well at once; for Brutus' tongue
Has almost ended its life-history.
Night hangs upon my eyes; my bones would rest,
That have but laboured to attain this hour.

Alarum
Cry within, 'Fly, fly, fly!'

CLITUS
Fly, my lord, fly!
BRUTUS   Hence! I will follow.
Exeunt Clitus, Dardanius, and Volumnius
I pray, Strato, stay you by your lord.
You are a fellow of good respect;
Your life has had some touch of honour in it.
Hold then my sword, and turn away your face,
While I do run upon it. Will you, Strato?
STRATO
Give me your hand first. Fare you well, my lord.

BRUTUS

Farewell, good Strato.—Caesar, now be still;
I killed not you with half so good a will.   *He dies*

Alarum
Retreat
Enter ANTONY, OCTAVIUS, MESSALA, LUCILIUS,
and the army

OCTAVIUS   What man is that?

MESSALA

My master's man. Strato, where is your master?

STRATO

Free from the bondage you are in, Messala.
The conquerors can but make a fire of him;
For Brutus only overcame himself,
And no man else has honour by his death.

LUCILIUS

So Brutus should be found. I thank you, Brutus,
That you have proved Lucilius' saying true.

OCTAVIUS

All that served Brutus, I will entertain them.
Fellow, will you bestow your time with me?

STRATO

Ay, if Messala will prefer me to you.

OCTAVIUS   Do so, good Messala.

MESSALA   How died my master, Strato?

STRATO

I held the sword, and he did run on it.

MESSALA

Octavius, then take him to follow you,
That did the latest service to my master.

ANTONY

This was the noblest Roman of them all.
All the conspirators save only he

Did that they did in envy of great Caesar;
He only, in a general honest thought
And common good to all, made one of them.
His life was gentle, and the elements
So mixed in him, that Nature might stand up
And say to all the world, 'This was a man!'

OCTAVIUS

According to his virtue let us use him,
With all respect and rites of burial.
Within my tent his bones tonight shall lie,
Most like a soldier, ordered honourably.
So call the field to rest, and let's away,
To part the glories of this happy day.   *Exeunt all*

The Merchant of Venice

INTRODUCTION

No play of Shakespeare is more important to see in the perspective of the time than *The Merchant of Venice*. For it deals with the distasteful subject of anti-Semitism in that age. Paradoxically, tragically, that makes it all the more modern because that popular phenomenon has become even more important with its appalling consequences in our own disgraceful time.

For the play we must see this theme in Elizabethan terms. The populace regarded the Jew partly in a comic light—so Shylock, the outstanding character, is partly comic. To us he is more tragic, and the play has that serious element in it, an infusion of iron to stiffen it; and modern sympathies are more likely to be with Shylock than contemporary ones were.

Once more the dramatist was taking up a subject with box-office appeal—as so often as to appear almost regular with him. Two years before, in 1594, a great sensation had been made in London by the case and trial of Dr. Lopez, the Queen's Jewish physician, accused of being paid by Spain to poison her. He was an intelligence agent, who had incurred the enmity of Essex, who pursued him to the death. The Queen did not believe him guilty; but, as in Russia today, since he could not prove his innocence, he was held guilty.

The Admiral's Company cashed in by reviving Marlowe's play, *The Jew of Malta*, which was given some fifteen performances later that year. The newly formed Lord Chamberlain's Company was, as usual, out to go one better—which it did. *The Merchant* is a better play, the treatment of Shylock in revealing contrast with that of Marlowe's Barabas, who is just a comic villain belaboured for the delight of the groundlings.

Shylock is a human being, and one's (modern) sympathies are with him. He has been badly treated by the merchant, Antonio—who appears rather a weak figure to give title to the play: it is simply the bond that he gives for his friend Bassanio that provides the starting point and motive of the action. Shylock is the real character, as that intelligent appreciator of Shakespeare, Charles I, noted in his copy of the works. 'Has not a Jew eyes? Has not a Jew hands, organs, dimensions, senses, affections, passions? Fed with the same food, hurt with the same weapons, subject to the same diseases, healed by the same means, warmed and cooled by the same winter and summer, as a Christian is?'

This is very different from Marlowe: one sees Shakespeare's superiority. Shylock has been ill-treated, spat upon; Antonio has disparaged his credit: Shylock not only wants his revenge but has a motive for wanting Antonio out of the way—'for were he out of Venice I can make what merchandise I will.' Better dramatically—nor is it funny to us that Shylock's daughter is abducted from him, even for love, and both he and she made to turn Christian. That is merely Elizabethan.

The pound of flesh exacted by the bond—which gives the fair Portia the chance to display her legal virtuosity and make her famous speeches (so beloved by the Victorians)—is ancient folklore; and, as Sisson tells us, the plot is made up of elements 'common to many old and re-told stories.' Discussion of sources 'has led scholarship into a maze of innumerable possibilities.' Unprofitable as this is, we need only notice that the main plot and the Casket story are both Italian, and note the Italian colouring and ambience of the play.

For we are not far away from Shakespeare's intense affair with Emilia Bassano in 1592–3. Professor Roger Prior thinks that the Bassanos were Jewish,[1] as Florio certainly was, and that this would give Shakespeare a much more intimate concern with and insight into, the subject, the combined Italian-Jewish theme, than has been realised.

For the rest, we agree with Sisson that the play 'rests more upon English realities than is commonly thought. Antonio is readily recognisable as an Elizabethan Englishman, in days when a Lord Mayor of London could be bankrupted by the wreck of ventures at sea.' Indeed, the opening scene, where the merchants are discussing their ventures,

> Plucking the grass to know where sits the wind
> —(a countryman's image, by the way, not a
> townsman's)—
> Peering in maps for ports and piers and roads,

reminds one forcibly of Thames-side scenes in Simon Forman's Case Books and the anxious inquiries of London merchants who were his clients. So too with Shylock: 'with him the whole picture of Jewish thought, family life, religion, communal and racial feeling, emerges for the first time in England', and Sisson regards the creation of Shylock as, above all, 'surprising'. Shakespeare may have had a closer observation

---

[1] cf his article, 'Shakespeare, the Bassanos, and *The Merchant*', *Jewish Chronicle Literary Supplement*, 12 June 1981.

post than we know, in the Bassanos; though we need attach no importance to the closeness of the name
Bassanio, we might remark that the Elizabethans pronounced the name, and often spelt it, Bassany.

Several personal touches bring the dramatist before
us, his tastes and associations, links with his other
writings. The reference to 'those crispèd snaky golden
locks', false hair, 'often known

> To be the dowry of a second head,
> The skull that bred them in the sepulchre,

virtually repeats the words of Sonnet 68. Background
and dating present no difficulty. We have the theatre in
Antonio's image of the world as

> A stage where every man must play a part,
> And mine a sad one,

while his friend Gratiano will play that of a clown. At
the same time Shakespeare's regular observation of
monuments appears:

> Why should a man whose blood is warm within
> Sit, like his grandsire cut in alabaster?

The observant dramatist would have had oppor-
tunities of hearing the Queen, an accomplished actor
herself, speak, and the reaction of the audience:

> As, after some oration fairly spoken
> By a belovèd prince, there does appear
> Among the buzzing pleasèd multitude,
> Where every something being blent together
> Turns to a wild of nothing, save of joy.

The play reflects a recent experience, the capture of
Cadiz in the summer of 1596, when the galleon St.
Andrew ran aground:

> my wealthy 'Andrew' docked in sand,
> Vailing [doffing] her high top lower than her ribs.

When being brought up-Channel she nearly ran aground again. Antonio's ship is reported wrecked on the Goodwin Sands. The date of the play would be the winter of 1596.

We have an earlier reflection from Stratford days in:

> In my schooldays, when I had lost one shaft
> I shot one fellow of the self-same flight
> The self-same way, with more advisèd watch
> To find the other forth, and by adventuring both
> I oft found both.

The archery-butts were by the bridge, between it and the modern Theatre, where now his statue stands—not a long step down from the old home in Henley Street. Everything in the earlier works shows his youthful addiction to out-of-doors sports. Does the following reflect a more recent experience?—

> All things that are
> Are with more spirit chasèd than enjoyed.

Old habits still remained in the countryside, as we have other evidences from the documents of the time:

> she does stray about
> By holy crosses where she kneels and prays.

The innumerable references throughout the plays, regularly to priests and holy-water, adjurations by our Lady and by the mass, bespeak the continuance of medieval England, especially in folklore and popular speech, into the Elizabethan age. Do we not detect the characteristic superior note in the posy inscribed on a ring, 'Love me, and leave me not'—

> For all the world like a cutler's poetry
> Upon a knife.

A constant note heard throughout his work, often in closely similar words, occurs with this:

> What many men desire: that 'many' may be meant
> By the fool multitude that choose by show,
> Not learning more than the fond [foolish] eye does
>   teach,
> Which pries not to the interior.

The comparison of Portia's locks to the golden fleece is commonplace enough, but its association with Colchos echoes Marlowe's description of Southampton's in *Hero and Leander*.

The play is filled with music, the last Act drenched in it, with a whole speech—a characteristic *inventio*, like Portia's on Mercy—in praise of it: a famous tribute,

> The man that has no music in himself,
> And is not moved with concord of sweet sounds,

is strongly condemned. No doubt this represents the writer's own view. Shakespeare became the most musical of all the dramatists—but was this reinforced by a recent musical experience?

The language of the play offers little difficulty, even in modernising archaic usages. One of them is more common in Shakespeare than with any other writer: the constant confusion of the personal relative 'who' for impersonal 'which'. Indeed it often seems that he will use the impersonal 'which' for human beings, and, when referring to animals or inanimate objects, use 'who'. Perverse to a modern mind, it has been regularised in accordance with modern usage.

Malapropisms—confusions of words, as with lower-class people like Launcelot Gobbo—afford traditional fun on the stage. It seems that Shakespeare began it.

CHARACTERS

THE DUKE OF VENICE
THE PRINCE OF MOROCCO ⎱ suitors of Portia
THE PRINCE OF ARRAGAN ⎰
ANTONIO, a merchant of Venice
BASSANIO, his friend
PORTIA, the Lady of Belmont
SHYLOCK, a Jew of Venice
GRATIANO ⎱
SALERIO ⎰ friends of Antonio and Bassanio
SOLANIO
LORENZO, in love with Jessica
NERISSA, Portia's waiting-woman
JESSICA, daughter of Shylock
TUBAL, a Jew of Venice, Shylock's friend
LEONARDO, servant of Bassanio
BALTHASAR ⎱ servants of Portia
STEPHANO ⎰

LAUNCELOT GOBBO, servant of Shylock
OLD GOBBO, father of Launcelot.

Magnificoes of Venice, Officers of the Court of Justice, Gaoler, Servants, and other Attendants

Act I

SCENE I
Venice. A street.

Enter ANTONIO, SALERIO, *and* SOLANIO

ANTONIO.
In truth I know not why I am so sad.
It wearies me, you say it wearies you;
But how I caught it, found it, or came by it,
What stuff it is made of, whereof it is born,
I am to learn.
And such a want-wit sadness makes of me
That I have much ado to know myself.
SALERIO
Your mind is tossing on the oceàn,
There where your argosies with portly sail,
Like signors and rich burghers on the flood,
Or as it were the pageants of the sea,
Do overpeer the petty traffickers
That curtsy to them, do them reverence,
As they fly by them with their woven wings.
SOLANIO
Believe me, sir, had I such venture forth,
The better part of my affections would
Be with my hopes abroad. I should be still
Plucking the grass to know where sits the wind,
Peering in maps for ports and piers and roads,
And every object that might make me fear
Misfortune to my ventures, out of doubt
Would make me sad.

277

SALERIO.   My wind cooling my broth
   Would blow me to an ague when I thought
   What harm a wind too great might do at sea.
   I should not see the sandy hour-glass run
   But I should think of shallows and of flats,
   And see my wealthy 'Andrew' docked in sand,
   Doffing her high-top lower than her ribs
   To kiss her burial. Should I go to church
   And see the holy edifice of stone
   And not bethink me straight of dangerous rocks,
   Which touching but my gentle vessel's side
   Would scatter all her spices on the stream,
   Enrobe the roaring waters with my silks—
   And in a word, but even now worth this,
   And now worth nothing? Shall I have the thought
   To think on this, and shall I lack the thought
   That such a thing bechanced would make me sad?
   But tell not me; I know Antonio
   Is sad to think upon his merchandise.

ANTONIO
   Believe me, no. I thank my fortune for it
   My ventures are not in one vessel trusted,
   Nor to one place; nor is my whole estate
   Upon the fortune of this present year.
   Therefore my merchandise makes me not sad.

SOLANIO
   Why then you are in love.

ANTONIO   Fie, fie!

SOLANIO
   Not in love either? Then let us say you are sad
   Because you are not merry; it were as easy
   For you to laugh and leap, and say you are merry
   Because you are not sad. Now by two-headed Janus,
   Nature has framed strange fellows in her time:
   Some that will evermore peep through their eyes
   And laugh like parrots at a bagpiper,

And others of such vinegar aspèct
That they'll not show their teeth in way of smile,
Though Nestor swears the jest is laughable.

Enter BASSANIO, LORENZO, *and* GRATIANO

Here come Bassanio your most noble kinsman,
Gratiano, and Lorenzo. Fare ye well;
We leave you now with better company.
SALERIO
I would have stayed till I had made you merry,
If worthier friends had not invited me.
ANTONIO
Your worth is very dear in my regard.
I take it your own business calls on you,
And you embrace the occasion to depart.
SALERIO
Good morrow, my good lords.
BASSANIO
Good signors both, when shall we laugh? Say, when?
You grow exceeding strange. Must it be so?
SALERIO
We'll make our leisures to attend on yours.
                    Exeunt Salerio and Solanio
LORENZO
My Lord Bassanio, since you have found Antonio,
We two will leave you; but at dinner-time
I pray you have in mind where we must meet.
BASSANIO.
I will not fail you.
GRATIANO
You look not well, Signor Antonio.
You have too much regard now for the world;
They lose it that do buy it with much care.
Believe me, you are marvellously changed.

ANTONIO

   I hold the world but as the world, Gratiano,
   A stage where every man must play a part,
   And mine a sad one.

GRATIANO   Let me play the fool;
   With mirth and laughter let old wrinkles come,
   And let my liver rather heat with wine
   Than my heart cool with mortifying groans.
   Why should a man whose blood is warm within
   Sit, like his grandsire cut in alabaster?
   Sleep when he wakes? And creep into the jaundice
   By being peevish? I tell you what, Antonio,
   I love you, it is my love that speaks:
   There are a sort of men whose visages
   Do cream and mantle like a standing pond,
   And do a wilful stillness entertain
   With purpose to be dressed in an opinion
   Of wisdom, gravity, and profound thought—
   As who should say, 'I am Sir Oracle,
   And when I open my lips, let no dog bark.'
   O my Antonio, I do know of these
   That therefore only are reputed wise
   For saying nothing; when I am very sure
   If they should speak, would almost damn those ears,
   Which hearing them would call their brothers fools.
   I'll tell you more of this another time.
   But fish not with this melancholy bait
   For this fool gudgeon, this opiniòn.
   Come, good Lorenzo. Fare ye well awhile;
   I'll end my exhortation after dinner.

LORENZO

   Well, we will leave you then till dinner-time.
   I must be one of these same dumb wise men,
   For Gratiano never lets me speak.

GRATIANO
  Well, keep me company but two years more,
  You shall not know the sound of your own tongue.

ANTONIO
  Fare you well; I'll grow a talker for this time.

GRATIANO
  Thanks in faith; for silence is only commendable
  In a calf's tongue dried and a maid not vendible.

                    Exeunt Gratiano and Lorenzo

ANTONIO   Is that anything now?

BASSANIO   Gratiano speaks an infinite deal of nothing,
  more than any man in all Venice. His reasons are
  as two grains of wheat hidden in two bushels of
  chaff: you shall seek all day ere you find them, and
  when you have them they are not worth the search.

ANTONIO
  Well, tell me now what lady is the same
  To whom you swore a secret pilgrimage,
  That you today promised to tell me of.

BASSANIO
  It is not unknown to you, Antonio,
  How much I have disabled my estate
  By something showing a more swelling style
  Than my faint means would grant continuance.
  Nor do I now make moan to be abridged
  From such a noble rate. But my chief care
  Is to come fairly off from the great debts
  Wherein my time, something too prodigal,
  Has left me engaged. To you, Antonio,
  I owe the most in money and in love,
  And from your love I have a warranty
  To unburden all my plots and purposes
  How to get clear of all the debts I owe.

ANTONIO

   I pray you, good Bassanio, let me know it,
   And if it stands as you yourself ever do,
   Within the eye of honour, be assured
   My purse, my person, my extremest means
   Lie all unlocked to your occasìons.

BASSANIO

   In my schooldays, when I had lost one shaft,
   I shot his fellow of the self-same flight
   The self-same way, with more advisèd watch,
   To find the other forth; and by adventuring both
   I oft found both. I urge this childhood proof
   Because what follows is pure innocence.
   I owe you much, and like a wilful youth,
   That which I owe is lost; but if you please
   To shoot another arrow that same way
   Which you did shoot the first, I do not doubt,
   As I will watch the aim, either to find both
   Or bring your latter hazard back again
   And thankfully rest debtor for the first.

ANTONIO

   You know me well, and herein spend but time
   To wind about my love with circumstance;
   And out of doubt you do me now more wrong
   In making question of my uttermost
   Than if you had made waste of all I have.
   Then do but say to me what I should do
   That in your knowledge may by me be done,
   And I am ready for it. Therefore speak.

BASSANIO

   In Belmont is a lady richly left,
   And she is fair and, fairer than that word,
   Of wondrous virtues. Sometimes from her eyes
   I did receive fair speechless messages.
   Her name is Portia, nothing undervalued

To Cato's daughter, Brutus' Portia.
Nor is the wide world ignorant of her worth,
For the four winds blow in from every coast
Renownèd suitors, and her sunny locks
Hang on her temples like a golden fleece,
Which makes her seat of Belmont Colchos' strand,
And many Jasons come in quest of her.
O my Antonio, had I but the means
To hold a rival place with one of them,
I have a mind presages me such thrift
That I should questionless be fortunate.

ANTONIO
You know that all my fortunes are at sea,
Neither have I money, nor commodity
To raise a present sum. Therefore go forth;
Try what my credit can in Venice do—
That shall be stretched even to the uttermost
To furnish you to Belmont, to fair Portia.
Go immediately inquire, and so will I,
Where money is; and I no question make
To have it of my trust or for my sake.   *Exeunt*

SCENE II
Belmont. Portia's house.

Enter PORTIA *with her waiting-woman*, NERISSA

PORTIA   By my faith, Nerissa, my little body is
aweary of this great world.

NERISSA   You would be, sweet madam, if your
miseries were in the same abundance as your good
fortunes are; and yet for aught I see, they are as
sick that surfeit with too much as they that starve
with nothing. It is no mean happiness, therefore, to

be seated in the mean; superfluity comes sooner by white hairs, but competency lives longer.

PORTIA   Good sentences, and well pronounced.

NERISSA   They would be better if well followed.

PORTIA   If to do were as easy as to know what were good to do, chapels had been churches, and poor men's cottages princes' palaces. It is a good divine that follows his own instructions. I can easier teach twenty what were good to be done than to be one of the twenty to follow my own teaching. The brain may devise laws for the blood, but a hot temper leaps over a cold decree, such a hare is madness the youth to skip over the meshes of good counsel, the cripple. But this reasoning is not in the fashion to choose me a husband. O me, the word 'choose'! I may neither choose whom I would nor refuse whom I dislike; so is the will of a living daughter curbed by the will of a dead father. Is it not hard, Nerissa, that I cannot choose one, nor refuse one?

NERISSA   Your father was ever virtuous, and holy men at their death have good inspirations. Therefore the lottery that he has devised in these three chests of gold, silver, and lead, whereof who chooses his meaning chooses you, will no doubt never be chosen by any rightly but one whom you shall rightly love. But what warmth is there in your affection towards any of these princely suitors that are already come?

PORTIA   I pray you overname them, and as you name them I will describe them, and according to my description level at my affection.

NERISSA   First, there is the Neapolitan prince.

PORTIA   Ay, that's a colt indeed, for he does nothing but talk of his horse, and he makes it a great appropriation to his own good parts that he can shoe him himself. I am much afraid my lady his mother played false with a smith.

NERISSA   Then is there the Count Palatine.

PORTIA   He does nothing but frown, as who should say, 'If you will not have me, choose.' He hears merry tales and smiles not. I fear he will prove the weeping philosopher when he grows old, being so full of unmannerly sadness in his youth. I had rather be married to a death's-head with a bone in his mouth than to either of these. God defend me from these two!

NERISSA   How say you by the French lord, Monsieur Le Bon?

PORTIA   God made him and therefore let him pass for a man. In truth, I know it is a sin to be a mocker, but he—why he has a horse better than the Neapolitan's, a better bad habit of frowning than the Count Palatine; he is every man in no man. If a throstle sings, he falls straight a-capering; he will fence with his own shadow. If I should marry him, I should marry twenty husbands. If he would despise me, I would forgive him, for if he loves me to madness, I shall never requite him.

NERISSA   What say you then to Falconbridge, the young baron of England?

PORTIA   You know I say nothing to him, for he understands not me, nor I him. He has neither Latin, French, nor Italian, and you will come into the court and swear that I have a poor pennyworth in the English. He is a proper man's picture, but alas, who can converse with a dumb-show? How oddly he is suited! I think he bought his doublet in Italy, his round hose in France, his bonnet in Germany, and his behaviour everywhere.

NERISSA   What think you of the Scottish lord, his
neighbour?

PORTIA   That he has a neighbourly charity in him, for
he borrowed a box of the ear of the Englishman and
swore he would pay him again when he was able. I
think the Frenchman became his surety and sealed
under for another.

NERISSA   How like you the young German, the Duke
of Saxony's nephew?

PORTIA   Very vilely in the morning when he is sober
and most vilely in the afternoon when he is drunk.
When he is best he is a little worse than a man,
and when he is worst he is little better than a
beast. If the worst fall that ever fell, I hope I shall
make shift to go without him.

NERISSA   If he should offer to choose, and choose the
right casket, you should refuse to perform your
father's will if you should refuse to accept him.

PORTIA   Therefore, for fear of the worst, I pray you set
a deep glass of Rhenish wine on the contrary
casket, for if the devil be within and that
temptation without, I know he will choose it. I
will do anything, Nerissa, ere I will be married to a
sponge.

NERISSA   You need not fear, lady, the having any of
these lords. They have acquainted me with their
determination: which is indeed to return to their
home and to trouble you with no more suit, unless
you may be won by some other sort than your
father's imposition, depending on the caskets.

PORTIA   If I live to be as old as Sibylla, I will die as
chaste as Diana unless I am obtained by the
manner of my father's will. I am glad this parcel of
wooers are so reasonable, for there is not one
among them but I dote on his very absence, and I
pray God grant them a fair departure.

NERISSA Do you not remember, lady, in your father's
time, a Venetian, a scholar and a soldier, that came
hither in company of the Marquis of Montferrat?

PORTIA Yes, yes, it was Bassanio, as I think, so was
he called.

NERISSA True, madam. He, of all the men that ever
my foolish eyes looked upon, was the best
deserving a fair lady.

PORTIA I remember him well, and I remember him
worthy of your praise.

Enter a Servingman

How now, what news?

SERVINGMAN The four strangers seek for you, madam,
to take their leave, and there is a forerunner come
from a fifth, the Prince of Morocco, who brings
word the Prince his master will be here tonight.

PORTIA If I could bid the fifth welcome with so good
heart as I can bid the other four farewell, I should
be glad of his approach. If he has the condition of a
saint and the complexion of a devil, I had rather he
should shrive me than wive me. Come, Nerissa.
Fellow, go before. While we shut the gate upon one
wooer, another knocks at the door.   *Exeunt*

SCENE 3
Venice. A street.

Enter BASSANIO *with* SHYLOCK.

SHYLOCK Three thousand ducats, well.
BASSANIO Ay, sir, for three months.
SHYLOCK For three months, well.

BASSANIO   For which, as I told you, Antonio shall be bound.

SHYLOCK   Antonio shall become bound, well.

BASSANIO   May you assist me? Will you pleasure me? Shall I know your answer?

SHYLOCK   Three thousand ducats for three months, and Antonio bound.

BASSANIO   Your answer to that.

SHYLOCK   Antonio is a good man.

BASSANIO   Have you heard any imputation to the contrary?

SHYLOCK   Ho no, no, no, no! My meaning in saying he is a good man is to have you understand me that he is sufficient. Yet his means are in supposition. He has an argosy bound to Tripoli, another to the Indies; I understand, moreover, upon the Rialto, he has a third at Mexico, a fourth for England, and other ventures he has squandered abroad. But ships are but boards, sailors but men; there are land rats and water rats, water thieves and land thieves, I mean pirates; and then there is the peril of waters, winds, and rocks. The man is, notwithstanding, sufficient. Three thousand ducats; I think I may take his bond.

BASSANIO   Be assured you may.

SHYLOCK   I will be assured I may; and that I may be assured, I will bethink me. May I speak with Antonio?

BASSANIO   If it pleases you to dine with us.

SHYLOCK   Yes, to smell pork, to eat of the habitation which your prophet the Nazarite conjured the devil into. I will buy with you, sell with you, talk with you, walk with you, and so following; but I will not eat with you, drink with you, nor pray with you. What news on the Rialto? Who is he comes here?

Enter ANTONIO

BASSANIO

  This is Signor Antonio.

SHYLOCK (*aside*)

  How like a fawning tax-collector he looks.
  I hate him for he is a Christian;
  But more, for that in low simplicity
  He lends out money gratis and brings down
  The rate of usury here with us in Venice.
  If I can catch him once upon the hip,
  I will feed fat the ancient grudge I bear him.
  He hates our sacred nation and he rails
  Even there where the merchants most do
    congregate
  On me, my bargains, and my well-won thrift,
  Which he calls interest. Cursèd be my tribe
  If I forgive him.

BASSANIO   Shylock, do you hear?

SHYLOCK

  I am debating of my present store,
  And by the near guess of my memory
  I cannot instantly raise up the gross
  Of full three thousand ducats. What of that?
  Tubal, a wealthy Hebrew of my tribe,
  Will furnish me. But soft, how many months
  Do you desire? (*To Antonio*) Rest you fair, good
    signor!
  Your worship was the last man in our mouths.

ANTONIO

  Shylock, albeit I neither lend nor borrow
  By taking nor by giving of excess,
  Yet to supply the ripe wants of my friend,
  I'll break a custom. (*To Bassanio*) Is he yet informed
  How much you would?

SHYLOCK   Ay, ay, three thousand ducats.

ANTONIO

And for three months.

SHYLOCK

I had forgotten—three months, you told me so.
Well then, your bond. And let me see; but hear you,
I thought you said you neither lend nor borrow
Upon advantage.

ANTONIO　　　　　　　　I do never use it.

SHYLOCK

When Jacob grazed his uncle Laban's sheep—
This Jacob from our holy Abram was,
As his wise mother wrought in his behalf,
The third possessor; ay, he was the third—

ANTONIO

And what of him? Did he take interest?

SHYLOCK

No, not take interest, not as you would say
Directly interest. Mark what Jacob did:
When Laban and himself were compromised
That all the young lambs which were streaked and
　　pied
Should fall as Jacob's hire, the ewes in heat,
In end of autumn turnèd to the rams.
And when the work of generation was
Between these woolly breeders in the act,
The skilful shepherd peelèd certain wands;
And in the doing of the deed of kind
He stuck them up before the fulsome ewes.
Who then conceiving, did in breeding time
Drop parti-coloured lambs, and those were Jacob's.
This was a way to thrive, and he was blest,
And thrift is blessing if men steal it not.

ANTONIO

This was a venture, sir, that Jacob served for,
A thing not in his power to bring to pass,

But swayed and fashioned by the hand of heaven.
Was this inserted to make interest good?
Or are your gold and silver ewes and rams?

SHYLOCK

I cannot tell, I make it breed as fast.
But note me, signor—

ANTONIO   Mark you this, Bassanio,
The devil can cite Scripture for his purpose.
An evil soul producing holy witness
Is like a villain with a smiling cheek,
A goodly apple rotten at the heart.
O what a goodly outside falsehood has!

SHYLOCK

Three thousand ducats, it is a good round sum.
Three months from twelve, then let me see, the
    rate . . .

ANTONIO

Well, Shylock, shall we be beholding to you?

SHYLOCK

Signor Antonio, many a time and oft
In the Rialto you have rated me
About my moneys and my usuries.
Ever have I borne it with a patient shrug,
For sufferance is the badge of all our tribe.
You call me misbeliever, cut-throat dog,
And spit upon my Jewish uniform,
And all for use of that which is my own.
Well then, it now appears you need my help.
Go to then. You come to me and you say,
'Shylock, we would have money,' you say so,
You, that did void your spit upon my beard
And foot me as you spurn a stranger cur
Over your threshold, money is your suit—
What should I say to you? Should I not say,
'Has a dog money? Is it possible

A cur can lend three thousand ducats?' Or
Shall I bend low, and in a bondman's key,
With bated breath and whispering humbleness,
Say this:
'Fair sir, you spat on me on Wednesday last,
You spurned me such a day, another time
You called me dog, and for these courtesies
I'll lend you thus much money.'

ANTONIO
I am as likely to call you so again,
To spit on you again, to spurn you too.
If you will lend this money, lend it not
As to your friends; for when did friendship take
A breed of barren metal of his friend?
But lend it rather to your enemy,
Who if he breaks, you may with better face
Exact the penalty.

SHYLOCK   Why look you, how you storm!
I would be friends with you and have your love,
Forget the shames that you have stained me with,
Supply your present wants, and take no farthing
Of interest for my money, and you'll not hear me.
This is kind I offer.

BASSANIO
This were kindness.

SHYLOCK   This kindness will I show.
Go with me to a notary, seal me there
Your single bond and, in a merry sport,
If you repay me not on such a day,
In such a place, such sum or sums as are
Expressed in the condition, let the forfeit
Be nominated for equal pound
Of your fair flesh, to be cut off and taken
In what part of your body pleases me.

ANTONIO
   Content, in faith. I'll seal to such a bond
   And say there is much kindness in the Jew.
BASSANIO
   You shall not seal to such a bond for me;
   I'll rather dwell in my necessity.
ANTONIO
   Why fear not, man; I will not forfeit it.
   Within these two months—that's a month before
   This bond expires—I do expect return
   Of thrice times the value of this bond.
SHYLOCK
   O father Abram, what these Christians are,
   Whose own hard dealings teaches them suspect
   The thoughts of others! Pray you tell me this:
   If he should break his day, what should I gain
   By the exaction of the forfeiture?
   A pound of man's flesh taken from a man
   Is not so estimable, profitable either,
   As flesh of muttons, beefs, or goats. I say
   To buy his favour I extend this friendship.
   If he will take it, so; if not, adieu.
   And for my love I pray you wrong me not.
ANTONIO
   Yes, Shylock, I will seal unto this bond.
SHYLOCK
   Then meet me forthwith at the notary's;
   Give him direction for this merry bond,
   And I will go and purse the ducats straight,
   See to my house, left in the fearful guard
   Of an unthrifty knave, and presently
   I'll be with you.
ANTONIO   Hie you, gentle Jew.
   The Hebrew will turn Christian; he grows kind.

BASSANIO
  I like not fair terms and a villain's mind.
ANTONIO
  Come on. In this there can be no dismay;
  My ships come home a month before the day.

                                            Exeunt

Act II

SCENE I
Belmont. Portia's house.

Flourish of cornets. Enter the PRINCE OF MOROCCO, *and
three or four followers, with* PORTIA, NERISSA,
and their train.

MOROCCO
  Mislike me not for my complexiòn,
  The shadowed livery of the burnished sun,
  To whom I am neighbour and near bred.
  Bring me the fairest creature northward born,
  Where Phoebus' fire scarce thaws the icicles,
  And let us make incision for your love
  To prove whose blood is reddest, his or mine.
  I tell you, lady, this aspèct of mine
  Frightens the valiant. By my love I swear,
  The best-regarded virgins of our clime
  Have loved it too. I would not change this hue,
  Except to steal your thoughts, my gentle queen.

PORTIA
   In terms of choice I am not solely led
   By nice direction of a maiden's eyes.
   Besides, the lottery of my destiny
   Bars me the right of voluntary choosing.
   But if my father had not scanted me,
   And hedged me by his will to yield myself
   His wife who wins me by that means I told you,
   Yourself, renownèd Prince, then stood as fair
   As any comer I have looked on yet
   For my affection.
MOROCCO   Even for that I thank you.
   Therefore I pray you lead me to the caskets
   To try my fortune. By this scimitar
   That slew the Sophy and a Persian prince
   That won three fields of Sultan Solyman,
   I would outstare the sternest eyes that look,
   Outbrave the heart most daring on the earth,
   Pluck the young sucking cubs from the she-bear,
   Yea, mock the lion when he roars for prey,
   To win you, lady. But alas the while,
   If Hercules and Lichas play at dice
   Which is the better man, the greater throw
   May turn by fortune from the weaker hand.
   So is Alcides beaten by his page,
   And so may I, blind Fortune leading me,
   Miss that which one unworthier may attain,
   And die with grieving.
PORTIA   You must take your chance,
   And either not attempt to choose at all
   Or swear before you choose, if you choose wrong
   Never to speak to lady afterward
   In way of marriage. Therefore be advised.
MOROCCO
   Nor will I. Come, bring me unto my chance.

PORTIA
  First, forward to the temple; after dinner
  Your hazard shall be made.
MOROCCO   Good fortune then,
  To make me blest or cursèd among men!
                        Flourish of cornets. Exeunt

SCENE II
A street.

Enter LAUNCELOT GOBBO, *alone*

LAUNCELOT   Certainly my conscience will serve me to
  run from this Jew my master. The fiend is at my
  elbow and tempts me, saying to me, 'Gobbo,
  Launcelot Gobbo, good Launcelot,' or 'Good
  Gobbo,' or 'Good Launcelot Gobbo, use your legs,
  take the start, run away.' My conscience says, 'No,
  take heed, honest Launcelot, take heed, honest
  Gobbo,' or as aforesaid, 'Honest Launcelot Gobbo,
  do not run, scorn running with your heels.' Well,
  the most courageous fiend bids me pack. 'Off!' says
  the fiend; 'Away!' says the fiend. 'For the heavens,
  rouse up a brave mind,' says the fiend, 'and run.'
  Well, my conscience hanging about the neck of my
  heart says very wisely to me, 'My honest friend
  Launcelot', being an honest man's son or rather an
  honest woman's son, for indeed my father did
  something smack, something grow to, he had a
  kind of taste—well, my conscience says,
  'Launcelot, budge not.' 'Budge,' says the fiend.
  'Budge not,' says my conscience. 'Conscience,' say
  I, 'you counsel well.' 'Fiend,' say I, 'you counsel
  well.' To be ruled by my conscience, I should stay

with the Jew my master who, God bless the mark, is a kind of devil; and to run away from the Jew, I should be ruled by the fiend, who, saving your reverence, is the devil himself. Certainly the Jew is the very devil incarnate; and in my conscience, my conscience is but a kind of hard conscience to offer to counsel me to stay with the Jew. The fiend gives the more friendly counsel. I will run, fiend; my heels are at your commandment; I will run.

Enter OLD GOBBO *with a basket*

GOBBO   Master young man, you I pray you, which is the way to Master Jew's?

LAUNCELOT   *(aside)* O heavens, this is my true-begotten father who, being more than sand-blind, high-gravel-blind, knows me not. I will try confusions [conclusions] with him.

GOBBO   Master young gentleman, I pray you which is the way to Master Jew's?

LAUNCELOT   Turn up on your right hand at the next turning, but at the next turning of all, on your left, sure, at the very next turning turn of no hand, but turn down indirectly to the Jew's house.

GOBBO.   By God's saints, it will be a hard way to hit! Can you tell me whether one Launcelot that dwells with him, dwells with him or no?

LAUNCELOT   Talk you of young Master Launcelot? *(aside)* Mark me now, now will I raise the waters.— Talk you of young Master Launcelot?

GOBBO   No master, sir, but a poor man's son. His father, though I say it, is an honest exceeding poor man and, God be thanked, well to live.

LAUNCELOT   Well, let his father be what he will, we talk of young Master Launcelot.

GOBBO   Your worship's friend, and Launcelot, sir.

LAUNCELOT   But I pray you, therefore old man,
therefore I beseech you, talk you of young Master
Launcelot.

GOBBO   Of Launcelot, if it please your mastership.

LAUNCELOT   Therefore, Master Launcelot. Talk not of
Master Launcelot, father, for the young gentleman,
according to Fates and Destinies and such odd
sayings, the Sisters Three and such branches of
learning, is indeed deceased, or as you would say in
plain terms, gone to heaven.

GOBBO   Indeed, God forbid! The boy was the very
staff of my age, my very prop.

LAUNCELOT   Do I look like a cudgel or a hovel-post,
a staff or a prop? Do you know me, father?

GOBBO   Alas the day, I know you not, young
gentleman! But I pray you tell me, is my boy, God
rest his soul, alive or dead?

LAUNCELOT   Do you not know me, father?

GOBBO   Alas, sir, I am sand-blind! I know you not.

LAUNCELOT   Nay, indeed if you had your eyes you
might fail of knowing me; it is a wise father that
knows his own child. Well, old man, I will tell you
news of your son. (*He kneels*) Give me your
blessing. Truth will come to light; murder cannot
be hidden long—a man's son may, but in the end
truth will out.

GOBBO   Pray you, sir, stand up. I am sure you are not
Launcelot my boy.

LAUNCELOT   Pray you let's have no more fooling about
it, but give me your blessing. I am Launcelot, your
boy that was, your son that is, your child that shall
be.

GOBBO   I cannot think you are my son.

LAUNCELOT   I know not what I shall think of that;
but I am Launcelot, the Jew's man, and I am sure
Margery your wife is my mother.

GOBBO   Her name is Margery indeed. I'll be sworn, if
you are Launcelot you are my own flesh and blood.
Lord worshipped might he be, what a beard have
you got! You have got more hair on your chin than
Dobbin my draught horse has on his tail.

LAUNCELOT   It should seem that Dobbin's tail grows
backward. I am sure he had more hair on his tail
than I have on my face when I last saw him.

GOBBO   Lord, how are you changed! How do you and
your master agree? I have brought him a present.
How agree you now?

LAUNCELOT   Well, well; but for my own part, as I
have set up my rest to run away, so I will not rest
till I have run some ground. My master's a very
Jew. Give him a present? Give him a halter! I am
famished in his service; you may tell every finger I
have with my ribs. Father, I am glad you are come.
Give me your present to one Master Bassanio, who
indeed gives rare new liveries. If I serve not him, I
will run as far as God has any ground. O rare
fortune, here comes the man! To him, father, for I
am a Jew if I serve the Jew any longer.

Enter BASSANIO, *with* LEONARDO *and followers*

BASSANIO   You may do so, but let it be so hasted that
supper is ready at the farthest by five of the clock.
See these letters delivered, put the liveries to
making, and desire Gratiano to come straitway to
my lodging.   *Exit one of his men*

LAUNCELOT   To him, father!

GOBBO   God bless your worship!

BASSANIO   Gramercy. Would you aught with me?

GOBBO   Here's my son, sir, a poor boy . . .

LAUNCELOT   Not a poor boy, sir, but the rich Jew's
man that would, sir, as my father shall specify . . .

GOBBO   He has a great infection [affection], sir, as
one would say, to serve . . .

LAUNCELOT   Indeed, the short and the long is, I serve
the Jew, and have a desire, as my father shall
specify . . .

GOBBO   His master and he, saving your worship's
reverence, are scarce kin.

LAUNCELOT   To be brief, the very truth is that the
Jew having done me wrong does cause me, as my
father, being I hope an old man, shall frutify
[certify] unto you . . .

GOBBO   I have here a dish of doves that I would
bestow upon your worship, and my suit is . . .

LAUNCELOT   In very brief, the suit is impertinent
[pertinent] to myself, as your worship shall know
by this honest old man, and though I say it, though
old man, yet poor man, my father . . .

BASSANIO   One speak for both. What would you?

LAUNCELOT   Serve you, sir.

GOBBO   That is the very defect [effect] of the matter,
sir.

BASSANIO
I know you well, you have obtained your suit.
Shylock your master spoke with me this day,
And has preferred you, if it is preferment
To leave a rich Jew's service to become
The follower of so poor a gentleman.

LAUNCELOT   The old proverb is very well parted
between my master Shylock and you, sir. You have
the grace of God, sir, and he has enough.

BASSANIO
　You speak it well. Go, father, with your son;
　Take leave of your old master and inquire
　My lodging out. (*To a Servant*) Give him a livery
　More braided than his fellows'. See it done.
LAUNCELOT　　Father, in. I cannot get a service, no! I
　have never a tongue in my head, well! (*He looks at
　his palm*) If any man in Italy has a fairer table
　which does offer to swear upon a book, I shall have
　good fortune! Go to, here's a simple line of life.
　Here's a small trifle of wives! Alas, fifteen wives is
　nothing; eleven widows and nine maids is a simple
　coming-in for one man. And then to escape
　drowning thrice, and to be in peril of my life with
　the edge of a feather-bed! Here are simple escapes.
　Well, if Fortune is a woman, she's a good wench
　for this business. Father, come. I'll take my leave
　of the Jew in the twinkling.
　　　　　　　　　　Exit Launcelot, with old Gobbo

BASSANIO
　I pray you, good Leonardo, think on this.
　These things being bought and orderly bestowed,
　Return in haste, for I do feast tonight
　My best-esteemed acquaintance. Hie you, go.
LEONARDO
　My best endeavours shall be done herein.

　　　　　　　　　　Enter GRATIANO

GRATIANO
　Where's your master?
LEONARDO　　　　　　　Yonder, sir, he walks.　　*Exit.*
GRATIANO
　Signor Bassanio!

BASSANIO
  Gratiano!
GRATIANO
  I have suit to you.
BASSANIO   You have obtained it.
GRATIANO
  You must not deny me. I must go with you to
    Belmont.
BASSANIO
  Why then you must. But hear you, Gratiano:
  You are too wild, too rude and bold of voice,
  Parts that become you happily enough
  And in such eyes as ours appear not faults;
  But where you are not known, why there they show
  Something too liberal. Pray you take pain
  To allay with some cold drops of modesty
  Your skipping spirit, lest through your wild behavior
  I am misconstrued in the place I go to,
  And lose my hopes.
GRATIANO   Signor Bassanio, hear me:
  If I do not put on a sober habit,
  Talk with respect, and swear but now and then,
  Wear prayer books in my pocket, look demurely,
  Nay more, while grace is saying hood my eyes
  Thus with my hat, and sigh and say amen,
  Use all the observance of civility
  Like one well studied in a sad intent
  To please his grandam—never trust me more.
BASSANIO
  Well, we shall see your bearing.
GRATIANO
  Nay, but I bar tonight. You shall not gauge me
  By what we do tonight.
BASSANIO   No, that were pity.
  I would entreat you rather to put on
  Your boldest suit of mirth, for we have friends

That purpose merriment. But fare you well;
I have some business.

GRATIANO
And I must to Lorenzo and the rest,
But we will visit you at supper-time.   *Exeunt*

SCENE III
Shylock's house.

Enter JESSICA *and* LAUNCELOT *the* CLOWN

JESSICA
I am sorry you will leave my father so.
Our house is hell, and you a merry devil
Did rob it of some taste of tediousness.
But fare you well, there is a ducat for you.
And, Launcelot, soon at supper shall you see
Lorenzo, who is your new master's guest.
Give him this letter; do it secretly.
And farewell; I would not have my father
See me in talk with you.

LAUNCELOT   Adieu! Tears exhibit [inhibit] my tongue.
Most beautiful pagan, most sweet Jew! If a
Christian did not play the knave and beget you, I
am much deceived. But adieu. These foolish drops
do something drown my manly spirit. Adieu!

JESSICA
Farewell, good Launcelot.   *Exit Launcelot*
Alas, what heinous sin is it in me
To be ashamed to be my father's child.
But though I am a daughter to his blood,
I am not to his manners. O Lorenzo,
If you keep a promise, I shall end this strife,
Become a Christian and your loving wife.

SCENE IV
A street.

Enter GRATIANO, LORENZO, SALERIO, *and* SOLANIO

LORENZO
  Nay, we will slink away in supper-time,
  Disguise us at my lodging, and return
  All in an hour.
GRATIANO
  We have not made good preparatiòn.
SALERIO
  We have not spoken yet of torchbearers.
SOLANIO
  'Tis vile, unless it may be quaintly ordered,
  And better in my mind not undertaken.
LORENZO
  'Tis now but four o'clock. We have two hours
  To furnish us.

Enter LAUNCELOT *with a letter*

                      Friend Launcelot, what's the news?
LAUNCELOT   If it shall please you to break up this, it
  shall seem to signify.
LORENZO
  I know the hand. In faith, it is a fair hand,
  And whiter than the paper it wrote on
  Is the fair hand that wrote.
GRATIANO   Love-news, in faith!
LAUNCELOT   By your leave, sir.

LORENZO   Whither go you?

LAUNCELOT   Sure, sir, to bid my old master the Jew
to sup tonight with my new master the Christian.

LORENZO
Hold here, take this (*Gives money*) Tell gentle
Jessica
I will not fail her. Speak it privately. *Exit Launcelot*
Go, gentlemen;
Will you prepare for this masque tonight?
I am provided of a torchbearer.

SALERIO
Ay indeed, I'll be gone about it straight.

SOLANIO
And so will I.

LORENZO   Meet me and Gratiano
At Gratiano's lodging some hoür hence.

SALERIO
It is good we do so.   *Exit with Solanio*

GRATIANO
Was not that letter from fair Jessica?

LORENZO
I must needs tell you all. She has directed
How I shall take her from her father's house,
What gold and jewels she is furnished with,
What page's suit she has in readiness.
If ever the Jew her father comes to heaven,
It will be for his gentle daughter's sake;
And never dare misfortune cross her foot,
Unless she does it under this excuse,
That she is issue to a faithless Jew.
Come, go with me; peruse this as you go.
Fair Jessica shall be my torchbearer.
                        Exit with Gratiano

SCENE V
Before Shylock's house.

Enter SHYLOCK *and* LAUNCELOT, *the Clown*

SHYLOCK
Well, you shall see, your eyes shall be your judge,
The difference of old Shylock and Bassanio. . . .
What, Jessica! You shall not gormandize
As you have done with me . . . What, Jessica! . . .
And sleep, and snore, and rend apparel out . . .
Why, Jessica, I say!

LAUNCELOT   Why, Jessica!

SHYLOCK
Who bids you call? I do not bid you call.

LAUNCELOT   Your worship was wont to tell me I could
do nothing without bidding.

Enter JESSICA

JESSICA
Call you? What is your will?

SHYLOCK
I am bidden forth to supper, Jessica.
There are my keys. But wherefore should I go?
I am not bidden for love, they flatter me,
But yet I'll go in hate to feed upon
The prodigal Christian. Jessica my girl,
Look to my house. I am right loth to go.
There is some ill a-brewing towards my rest,
For I did dream of money bags tonight.

LAUNCELOT   I beseech you, sir, go. My young master
does expect your reproach. [approach]

SHYLOCK   So do I his.

LAUNCELOT   And they have conspired together. I will
not say you shall see a masque, but if you do, then

it was not for nothing that my nose fell a-bleeding
on Black Monday last at six o'clock in the
morning, falling out that year on Ash Wednesday
was four in the afternoon.

SHYLOCK

What, are there masques? Hear you me, Jessica:
Lock up my doors; and when you hear the drum
And the vile squealing of the wry-necked fife,
Clamber not you up to the casements then,
Nor thrust your head into the public street
To gaze on Christian fools with varnished faces.
But stop my house's ears, I mean my casements:
Let not the sound of shallow foppery enter
My sober house. By Jacob's staff I swear
I have no mind of feasting forth tonight,
But I will go. Go you before me, fellow.
Say I will come.

LAUNCELOT   I will go before, sir.
Mistress, look out at window for all this:
    There will come a Christian by
      Will be worth a Jewess' eye.   *Exit*

SHYLOCK

What says that fool of Hagar's offspring, ha?

JESSICA

His words were 'Farewell, mistress', nothing else.

SHYLOCK

The clown is kind enough, but a huge fecder,
Snail-slow in profit, and he sleeps by day
More than the wildcat. Drones hive not with me;
Therefore I part with him, and part with him
To one that I would have him help to waste
His borrowed purse. Well, Jessica, go in.
Perhaps I will return immediately.
Do as I bid you; shut the doors after you.
Fast bind, fast find,
A proverb never stale in thrifty mind.   *Exit*

JESSICA
   Farewell; and if my fortune is not crossed,
   I have a father, you a daughter, lost.   *Exit*

SCENE VI
The same.

Enter the masquers, GRATIANO *and* SALERIO

GRATIANO
   This is the penthouse under which Lorenzo
   Desired us to make stand.
SALERIO   His hour is almost past.
GRATIANO
   And it is marvel he outdwells his hour,
   For lovers ever run before the clock.
SALERIO
   O ten times faster Venus' pigeons fly
   To seal love's bonds new-made than they are wont
   To keep obligèd faith unforfeited!
GRATIANO
   That ever holds. Who rises from a feast
   With that keen appetite that he sits down?
   Where is the horse that does untread again
   His tedious measures with the unbated fire
   That he did pace them first? All things that are
   Are with more spirit chasèd than enjoyed.
   How like a youngster or a prodigal
   The scarfèd bark puts from her native bay,
   Hugged and embracèd by the strumpet wind.
   How like the prodigal does she return,
   With overweathered ribs and ragged sails,
   Lean, rent, and beggared by the strumpet wind.

Enter LORENZO

SALERIO
  Here comes Lorenzo; more of this hereafter.
LORENZO
  Sweet friends, your patience for my long abode.
  Not I but my affairs have made you wait.
  When you shall please to play the thieves for wives,
  I'll watch as long for you then. Approach.
  Here dwells my father Jew. Ho! Who's within?

Enter JESSICA *above, in boy's clothes*

JESSICA
  Who are you? Tell me for more certainty,
  Albeit I'll swear that I do know your tongue.
LORENZO
  Lorenzo, and your love.
JESSICA
  Lorenzo certain, and my love indeed,
  For whom love I so much? And now who knows
  But you, Lorenzo, whether I am yours?
LORENZO
  Heaven and your thoughts are witness that you are.
JESSICA
  Here, catch this casket; it is worth the pains.
  I am glad 'tis night, you do not look upon me,
  For I am much ashamed of my exchange.
  But love is blind, and lovers cannot see
  The pretty follies that themselves commit;
  For if they could, Cupid himself would blush
  To see me thus transformèd to a boy.
LORENZO
  Descend, for you must be my torchbearer.

JESSICA
　　What, must I hold a candle to my shames?
　　They in themselves, good truth, are too too light.
　　Why, 'tis an office of discovery, love,
　　And I should be obscured.
LORENZO   So are you, sweet,
　　Even in the lovely garnish of a boy.
　　But come at once,
　　For the close night does play the runaway,
　　And we are stayed for at Bassanio's feast.
JESSICA
　　I will make fast the doors, and gild myself
　　With some ducats, and be with you straight.
　　　　　　　　　　　　　　　　　　Exit above.

GRATIANO
　　Now by my hood, a gentle and no Jew!
LORENZO
　　Now bless me but I love her heartily!
　　For she is wise, if I can judge of her,
　　And fair she is, if my eyes are true,
　　And true she is, as she has proved herself;
　　And therefore, like herself, wise, fair, and true,
　　Shall she be placèd in my constant soul.

　　　　　　　　　Enter JESSICA *below*

　　What, are you come? On, gentlemen, away!
　　Our masquing mates by this time for us stay.
　　　　　　　　　　　Exit with Jessica and Salerio

　　　　　　　　　Enter ANTONIO

ANTONIO
　　Who's there?
GRATIANO
　　Signor Antonio?

ANTONIO
    Fie, fie, Gratiano! Where are all the rest?
    'Tis nine o'clock; our friends all stay for you.
    No masque tonight. The wind is come about;
    Bassanio instantly will go aboard.
    I have sent twenty out to seek for you.
GRATIANO
    I am glad of it. I desire no more delight
    Than to be under sail and gone tonight.   *Exeunt*

SCENE VII
Portia's house.

Flourish of cornets. Enter PORTIA *with* MOROCCO
and their trains.

PORTIA
    Go, draw aside the curtain and discover
    The several caskets to this noble Prince.
    Now make your choice.
MOROCCO
    This first, of gold, which this inscription bears,
    Who chooses me shall gain what many men desire;
    The second, silver, which this promise carries,
    Who chooses me shall get as much as he deserves;
    This third, dull lead, with warning all as blunt,
    Who chooses me must give and hazard all he has.
    How shall I know if I do choose the right?
PORTIA
    The one of them contains my picture, Prince.
    If you choose that, then I am yours, with it.
MOROCCO
    Some god direct my judgement! Let me see:
    I will survey the inscriptions back again.
    What says this leaden casket?

Who chooses me must give and hazard all he has.
Must give, for what? For lead! Hazard for lead?
This casket threatens; men that hazard all
Do it in hope of fair advantages.
A golden mind stoops not to shows of dross;
I'll neither give nor hazard aught for lead.
What says the silver with her virgin hue?
Who chooses me shall get as much as he deserves.
As much as he deserves? Pause there, Morocco,
And weigh your value with an even hand.
If you are rated by your estimation,
You do deserve enough and yet enough
May not extend so far as to the lady,
And yet to be afraid of my deserving
Were but a weak disabling of myself.
As much as I deserve? Why, that's the lady!
I do in birth deserve her, and in fortunes,
In graces, and in qualities of breeding;
But more than these, in love I do deserve.
What if I strayed no farther, but chose here?
Let's see once more this saying graved in gold:
Who chooses me shall gain what many men desire.
Why that's the lady! All the world desires her;
From the four corners of the earth they come
To kiss this shrine, this mortal breathing saint.
The Hyrcanian deserts and the vasty wilds
Of wide Arabia are as thoroughfares now
For princes to come view fair Portià.
The watery kingdom, whose ambitious head
Spits in the face of heaven, is no bar
To stop the foreign spirits, but they come
As over a brook to see fair Portià.
One of these three contains her heavenly picture.
Is it likely that lead contains her? 'Twere damnation
To think so base a thought; it were too gross

To rib her shroud then in the òbscure grave.
Or shall I think in silver she's immured,
Being ten times undervalued to tried gold?
O sinful thought! Never so rich a gem
Was set in worse than gold. They have in England
A coin that bears the figure of an angel
Stamped in gold—but that is insculped on;
But here an angel in a golden bed
Lies all within. Deliver me the key.
Here do I choose, and thrive as I may!

PORTIA
There, take it, Prince, and if my form lies there,
Then I am yours.

He opens the gold casket

MOROCCO   O hell! What have we here?
A carrion Death, within whose empty eye
There is written scroll. I'll read the writing.
  All that glisters is not gold;
  Often have you heard that told.
  Many a man his life has sold
  But my outside to behold.
  Gilded tombs do worms enfold,
  Had you been as wise as bold,
  Young in limbs, in judgement old,
  Your answer had not been inscrolled.
  Fare you well, your suit is cold.
    Cold indeed, and labour lost.
    Then farewell heat, and welcome frost.
Portia, adieu, I have too grieved a heart
To take a tedious leave. Thus losers part.
                  Exit with his train. Flourish of cornets

PORTIA
A gentle riddance. Draw the curtains, go.
Let all of his complexion choose me so.   *Exeunt*

SCENE VIII
A street.

Enter SALERIO *and* SOLANIO

SALERIO
Why, man, I saw Bassanio under sail;
With him is Gratiano gone along,
And in their ship I am sure Lorenzo is not.
SOLANIO
The villain Jew with outcries raised the Duke,
Who went with him to search Bassanio's ship.
SALERIO
He came too late, the ship was under sail,
But there the Duke was given to understand
That in a gondola were seen together
Lorenzo and his amorous Jessicà.
Besides, Antonio certified the Duke
They were not with Bassanio in his ship.
SOLANIO
I never heard a passion so confused,
So strange, outrageous, and so variable
As the dog Jew did utter in the streets:
'My daughter! O my ducats! O my daughter!
Fled with a Christian! O my Christian ducats!
Justice! The law! My ducats and my daughter!
A sealèd bag, two sealèd bags of ducats,
Of double ducats, stolen from me by my daughter!
And jewels, two stones, two rich and precious
    stones,

Stolen by my daughter! Justice! Find the girl!
She has the stones upon her, and the ducats!'

SALERIO

Why, all the boys in Venice follow him,
Crying his stones, his daughter, and his ducats.

SOLANIO

Let good Antonio look he keeps his day,
Or he shall pay for this.

SALERIO   Indeed, well remembered.
I reasoned with a Frenchman yesterday,
Who told me, in the narrow seas that part
The French and English there miscarrièd
A vessel of our country richly freighted.
I thought upon Antonio when he told me,
And wished in silence that it were not his.

SOLANIO

You were best to tell Antonio what you hear,
Yet do not suddenly, for it may grieve him.

SALERIO

A kinder gentleman treads not the earth.
I saw Bassanio and Antonio part;
Bassanio told him we would make some speed
Of his return. He answered, 'Do not so.
Slubber not business for my sake, Bassanio,
But stay the very ripening of the time.
And for the Jew's bond which he has of me,
Let it not enter in your mind of love.
Be merry, and employ your chiefest thoughts
To courtship and such fair intents of love
As shall conveniently become you there.'
And even there, his eye being big with tears,
Turning his face, he put his hand behind him,
And with affection wondrous sensible
He wrung Bassanio's hand; and so they parted.

SOLANIO

I think he only loves the world for him.

I pray you let us go and find him out,
And quicken his embracèd heaviness
With some delight or other.

SALERIO   Do we so.   *Exeunt*

SCENE IX
Portia's house.

Enter NERISSA *and a Servitor*

NERISSA
Quick, quick, I pray you! Draw the curtain straight.
The Prince of Arragon has taken his oath,
And comes to his election instantly.

Flourish of cornets. Enter ARRAGON, *his train,*
and PORTIA

PORTIA
Behold, there stand the caskets, noble Prince.
If you choose that wherein I am contained,
Straight shall our nuptial rites be solemnized.
But if you fail, without more speech, my lord,
You must be gone from hence immediately.

ARRAGON
I am enjoined by oath to observe three things:
First, never to unfold to anyone
Which casket it was I chose; next, if I fail
Of the right casket, never in my life
To woo a maid in way of marriage;
Lastly,
If I do fail in fortune of my choice,
Immediately to leave you and be gone.

PORTIA

    To these injunctions everyone does swear
    That comes to hazard for my worthless self.

ARRAGON

    And so have I addressed me. Fortune now
    To my heart's hope! Gold, silver, and base lead.
    Who chooses me must give and hazard all he has.
    You shall look fairer ere I give or hazard.
    What says the golden chest? Ha, let me see.
    Who chooses me shall gain what many men desire.
    What many men desire; that 'many' may be meant
    By the fool multitude that choose by show,
    Not learning more than the foolish eye does teach,
    Which pries not to the interior, but like the martlet
    Builds in the weather on the outward wall,
    Even in the force and road of casualty.
    I will not choose what many men desire,
    Because I will not agree with common spirits
    And rank me with the barbarous multitude.
    Why then, to you, you silver treasure house.
    Tell me once more what title you do bear.
    Who chooses me shall get as much as he deserves.
    And well said too, for who shall go about
    To cozen fortune, and be honourable
    Without the stamp of merit? Let none presume
    To wear an undeservèd dignity.
    O that estates, degrees, and offices
    Were not derived corruptly, and that clear honour
    Were purchased by the merit of the wearer!
    How many then should cover that stand bare,
    How many be commanded that command;
    How much low peasantry would then be gleaned
    From the true seed of honour, and how much
      honour

Picked from the chaff and ruin of the times
To be new varnished. Well, but to my choice.
Who chooses me shall get as much as he deserves.
I will assume desert. Give me a key for this,
And instantly unlock my fortunes here.

He opens the silver casket

PORTIA
Too long a pause for that which you find there.
ARRAGON
What's here? The portrait of a blinking idiot
Presenting me a schedule! I will read it.
How much unlike are you to Portià!
How much unlike my hopes and my deservings!
Who chooses me shall have as much as he deserves.
Did I deserve no more than a fool's head?
Is that my prize? Are my deserts no better?
PORTIA
To offend and judge are distinct offices,
And of opposèd natures.
ARRAGON   What is here?
    The fire seven times trièd this;
    Seven times tried that judgement is
    That did never choose amiss.
    Some there are that shadows kiss;
    Such have but a shadow's bliss.
    There are fools alive I wis, [I know]
    Silvered o'er, and so was this.
    Take what wife you will to bed,
    I will ever be your head.
    So be gone; you are sped.
    Still more fool I shall appear
    By the time I linger here.
    With one fool's head I came to woo,
    But I go away with two.

Sweet, adieu. I'll keep my oath,
Patiently to bear my wrath.   *Exit with his train*

PORTIA
Thus has the candle singed the moth.
O these deliberate fools! When they do choose,
They have the wisdom by their wit to lose.

NERISSA
The ancient saying is no heresy:
Hanging and wiving go by destiny.

PORTIA
Come draw the curtain, Nerissa.

Enter Messenger

MESSENGER
Where is my lady?

PORTIA   Here. What would my lord?

MESSENGER
Madam, there is alighted at your gate
A young Venetian, one that comes before
To signify the approaching of his lord,
From whom he brings substantial greetings here:
To wit, besides commends and courteous breath,
Gifts of rich value. Yet I have not seen
So likely an ambassador of love.
A day in April never came so sweet
To show how costly summer was at hand,
As this fore-spurrer comes before his lord.

PORTIA
No more, I pray you, I am half afraid
You will say anon he is some kin to you,
You spend such highday wit in praising him.
Come, come, Nerissa, for I long to see
Quick Cupid's post that comes so mannerly.

NERISSA
Bassanio, Lord, love if your will it be!   *Exeunt*

Act III

SCENE I
A street.

Enter SOLANIO *and* SALERIO

SOLANIO   Now what news on the Rialto?

SALERIO   Why, yet it lives there unchecked that Antonio has a ship of rich lading wrecked on the narrow seas—the Goodwins I think they call the place, a very dangerous flat, and fatal; where the carcasses of many a tall ship lie buried as they say, if my gossip Report is an honest woman of her word.

SOLANIO   I would she were as lying a gossip in that as ever nibbled ginger or made her neighbours believe she wept for the death of a third husband. But it is true, without any slips of prolixity or crossing the plain highway of talk, that the good Antonio, the honest Antonio—O that I had a title good enough to keep his name company . . .

SALERIO   Come, the full stop!

SOLANIO   Ha, what say you? Why the end is, he has lost a ship.

SALERIO   I would it might prove the end of his losses.

SOLANIO   Let me say amen betimes, lest the devil crosses my prayer, for here he comes in the likeness of a Jew.

Enter SHYLOCK

How now, Shylock? What news among the merchants?

SHYLOCK   You knew, none so well, none so well as
you, of my daughter's flight.

SALERIO   That's certain. I for my part knew the tailor
that made the wings she flew with.

SOLANIO   And Shylock for his own part knew the bird
was fledged, and then it is the complexion of them
all to leave the dam.

SHYLOCK   She is damned for it.

SALERIO   That's certain, if the devil may be her judge.

SHYLOCK   My own flesh and blood to rebel!

SOLANIO   Out upon it, old carrion! Rebels it at these
years?

SHYLOCK   I say my daughter is my flesh and blood.

SALERIO   There is more difference between your flesh
and hers than between jet and ivory, more between
your bloods than there is between red wine and
Rhenish. But tell us, do you hear whether Antonio
has had any loss at sea or no?

SHYLOCK   There I have another bad match! A
bankrupt, a prodigal, who dares scarce show his
head on the Rialto, a beggar that used to come so
smug upon the mart! Let him look to his bond. He
was wont to call me usurer. Let him look to his
bond. He was wont to lend money for a Christian
courtesy. Let him look to his bond.

SALERIO   Why, I am sure if he forfeits you will not
take his flesh. What's that good for?

SHYLOCK   To bait fish with. If it will feed nothing
else, it will feed my revenge. He has disgraced me
and hindered me half a million, laughed at my
losses, mocked at my gains, scorned my nation,
thwarted my bargains, cooled my friends, heated
my enemies; and what's his reason? I am a Jew.
Has not a Jew eyes? Has not a Jew hands, organs,
dimensions, senses, affections, passions? Fed with
the same food, hurt with the same weapons,

subject to the same diseases, healed by the same
means, warmed and cooled by the same winter and
summer as a Christian is? If you prick us, do we
not bleed? If you tickle us, do we not laugh? If you
poison us, do we not die? And if you wrong us,
shall we not revenge? If we are like you in the rest,
we will resemble you in that. If a Jew wrongs a
Christian, what is his humility? Revenge. If a
Christian wrongs a Jew, what should his sufferance
be by Christian example? Why, revenge! The
villainy you teach me I will execute, and it shall go
hard but I will better the instruction.

Enter a Man from ANTONIO

MAN   Gentlemen, my master Antonio is at his house
and desires to speak with you both.
SALERIO   We have been up and down to seek him.

Enter TUBAL

SOLANIO   Here comes another of the tribe. A third
cannot be matched, unless the devil himself turns
Jew.

Exeunt Solanio, Salerio, and Man

SHYLOCK   How now, Tubal! What news from Genoa?
Have you found my daughter?
TUBAL   I often came where I did hear of her, but
cannot find her.
SHYLOCK   Why there, there, there, there! A diamond
gone cost me two thousand ducats in Frankfurt!
The curse never fell upon our nation till now; I
never felt it till now. Two thousand ducats in that,

and other precious, precious jewels. I would my
daughter were dead at my foot, and the jewels in
her ear! Would she were hearsed at my foot, and
the ducats in her coffin! No news of them, why
so?—And I know not what's spent in the search.
Why, you loss upon loss! The thief gone with so
much, and so much to find the thief!—And no
satisfaction, no revenge! And no ill luck stirring but
what lights on my shoulders, no sighs but of my
breathing, no tears but of my shedding.

TUBAL   Yes, other men have ill luck too. Antonio, as
I heard in Genoa. . .

SHYLOCK   What, what, what? Ill luck, ill luck?

TUBAL   Has an argosy cast away coming from
Tripoli.

SHYLOCK   I thank God, I thank God! Is it true? Is it
true?

TUBAL   I spoke with some of the sailors that escaped
the wreck.

SHYLOCK   I thank you, good Tubal. Good news, good
news! Ha, ha! Heard in Genoa?

TUBAL   Your daughter spent in Genoa, as I heard, one
night fourscore ducats.

SHYLOCK   You stick a dagger in me. I shall never see
my gold again. Fourscore ducats at a sitting,
fourscore ducats!

TUBAL   There came divers of Antonio's creditors in
my company to Venice that swear he cannot choose
but break.

SHYLOCK   I am very glad of it. I'll plague him; I'll
torture him. I am glad of it.

TUBAL   One of them showed me a ring that he had of
your daughter for a monkey.

SHYLOCK   Out upon her! You torture me, Tubal. It
was my turquoise; I had it of Leah when I was a

bachelor. I would not have given it for a wilderness
of monkeys.

TUBAL   But Antonio is certainly undone.

SHYLOCK   Nay, that's true, that's very true. Go,
Tubal, fee me an officer; bespeak him a fortnight
before. I will have the heart of him if he forfeits,
for were he out of Venice I can make what merchandise I will. Go, Tubal, and meet me at our
synagogue; go, good Tubal; at our synagogue,
Tubal.   *Exeunt*

SCENE II
Portia's house.

Enter BASSANIO, PORTIA, GRATIANO, NERISSA,
and attendants.

PORTIA   I pray you tarry, pause a day or two
Before you hazard, for in choosing wrong
I lose your company. Therefore forbear awhile.
There's something tells me, but it is not love,
I would not lose you; and you know yourself
Hate counsels not in such a quality.
But lest you should not understand me well—
And yet a maiden has no tongue but thought—
I would detain you here some month or two
Before you venture for me. I could teach you
How to choose right, but then I am forsworn.
So will I never be. So may you miss me.
But if you do, you'll make me wish a sin,
That I had been forsworn. But, bless your eyes!
They have overlooked me and divided me;
One half of me is yours, the other half yours,
My own I would say; but if mine then yours,

And so all yours. O these naughty times
Put bars between the owners and their rights.
And so, though yours, not yours. Prove it so,
Let fortune go to hell for it, not I.
I speak too long, but it is to piece the time,
To eke it and to draw it out in length,
To stay you from election.

BASSANIO   Let me choose,
For as I am, I live upon the rack.

PORTIA
Upon the rack, Bassanio? Then confess
What treason there is mingled with your love.

BASSANIO
None but that ugly treason of mistrust
Which makes me fear the enjoying of my love.
There may as well be amity and life
Between snow and fire, as treason and my love.

PORTIA
Ay, but I fear you speak upon the rack,
Where men enforcèd do speak anything.

BASSANIO
Promise me life and I'll confess the truth.

PORTIA
Well then, confess and live.

BASSANIO   Confess and love
Had been the very sum of my confession.
O happy torment, when my torturer
Does teach me answers for deliverance.
But let me to my fortune and the caskets.

PORTIA
Away then, I am locked in one of them;
If you do love me, you will find me out.
Nerissa and the rest, stand all aloof.
Let music sound while he does make his choice,
Then if he loses he makes a swanlike end,

Fading in music. That the comparison
May stand more proper, my eye shall be the stream
And watery deathbed for him. He may win,
And what is music then? Then music is
Even as the flourish when true subjects bow
To a new-crownèd monarch. Such it is
As are those dulcet sounds in break of day
That creep into the dreaming bridegroom's ear
And summon him to marriage. Now he goes,
With no less presence but with much more love
Than young Alcides, when he did redeem
The virgin tribute paid by howling Troy
To the sea monster. I stand for sacrifice;
The rest aloof are the Dardanian wives,
With blearèd visages come forth to view
The issue of the exploit. Go, Hercules;
Live you, I live. With much, much more dismay
I view the fight than you that make the fray.

A song while BASSANIO *comments
on the caskets to himself.*

Tell me where is fancy bred,
Or in the heart, or in the head?
How begot, how nourishèd?
    Reply, reply.
It is engendered in the eyes,
With gazing fed, and fancy dies
In the cradle where it lies.
    Let us all ring fancy's knell.
    I'll begin it—Ding, dong, bell.
ALL   Ding, dong, bell.

BASSANIO

So may the outward shows be least themselves.
The world is ever deceived with ornament.
In law, what plea so tainted and corrupt,
But being seasoned with a gracious voice,
Obscures the show of evil? In religion,
What damnèd error but some sober brow
Will bless it and approve it with a text,
Hiding the grossness with fair ornament?
There is no vice so simple but assumes
Some mark of virtue on its outward parts.
How many cowards whose hearts are all as false
As stairs of sand, wear yet upon their chins
The beards of Hercules and frowning Mars,
Who inward searched, have livers white as milk;
And these assume but valour's ornament
To render them redoubted. Look on beauty,
And you shall see it purchased by the weight,
Which therein works a miracle in nature,
Making them lightest that wear most of it.
So are those crispèd snaky golden locks,
Which make such wanton gambols with the wind
Upon supposèd fairness, often known
To be the dowry of a second head,
The skull that bred them in the sepulchre.
Thus ornament is but the guileful shore
To a most dangerous sea, the beauteous scarf
Veiling an Indian beauty; in a word,
The seeming truth which cunning times put on
To entrap the wisest. Therefore you gaudy gold,
Hard food for Midas, I will none of you;
And none of you, you pale and common drudge

Between man and man. But you, you meager lead
Which rather threaten than do promise aught,
Your paleness moves me more than eloquence,
And here choose I. Joy be the consequence!

PORTIA (*aside*)

How all the other passions fleet to air:
As doubtful thoughts, and rash-embraced despair,
And shuddering fear, and green-eyed jealousy.
O love, be moderate, allay your ecstasy,
In measure rain your joy, scant this excess,
I feel too much your blessing, make it less
For fear I surfeit.

BASSANIO (*opening the leaden casket*)

                         What find I here?
Fair Portia's counterfeit! What demigod
Has come so near creation? Move these eyes?
Or whether, riding on the balls of mine,
Seem they in motion? Here are severed lips
Parted with sugar breath; so sweet a bar
Should sunder such sweet friends. Here in her hairs
The painter plays the spider, and has woven
A golden mesh to entrap the hearts of men
Faster than gnats in cobwebs. But her eyes,
How could he see to do them? Having made one,
I think it should have power to steal both his
And leave itself unfurnished. Yet look how far
The substance of my praise does wrong this shadow
In underprizing it, so far this shadow
Does limp behind the substance. Here's the scroll,
The continent and summary of my fortune:

>   *You that choose not by the view*
>   *Chance as fair, and choose as true.*
>   *Since this fortune falls to you,*
>   *Be content and seek no new.*
>   *If you are well pleased with this*

And hold your fortune for your bliss,
Turn you where your lady is,
And claim her with a loving kiss.
A gentle scroll. Fair lady, by your leave.
I come by note, to give and to receive.
Like one of two contending in a prize,
That thinks he has done well in people's eyes,
Hearing applause and universal shout,
Giddy in spirit, still gazing in a doubt
Whether those peals of praise are his or no.
So, thrice-fair lady, stand I even so,
As doubtful whether what I see is true,
Until confirmed, signed, ratified by you.

PORTIA

You see me, Lord Bassanio, where I stand,
Such as I am. Though for myself alone
I would not be ambitious in my wish
To wish myself much better, yet for you
I would be trebled twenty times myself;
A thousand times more fair, ten thousand times
More rich, that only to stand high in your account,
I might in virtues, beauties, livings, friends,
Exceed account. But the full sum of me
Is sum of something, which to term in gross,
Is an unlessoned girl, unschooled, unpractisèd,
Happy in this, she is not yet so old
But she may learn. Happier than this,
She is not bred so dull but she can learn;
Happiest of all is that her gentle spirit
Commits itself to yours to be directed,
As from her lord, her governor, her king.
Myself and what is mine to you and yours
Are now converted. But now I was the lord
Of this fair mansion, master of my servants,
Queen over myself; and even now, but now,

This house, these servants, and this same myself
Are yours, my lord's. I give them with this ring,
Which when you part from, lose, or give away,
Let it presage the ruin of your love
And be my vantage to exclaim on you.

BASSANIO

Madam, you have bereft me of all words.
Only my blood speaks to you in my veins,
And there is such confusion in my powers
As, after some oration fairly spoken
By a belovèd prince, there does appear
Among the buzzing pleasèd multitude;
Where every something being blent together
Turns to a wild of nothing, save of joy
Expressed and not expressed. But when this ring
Parts from this finger, then parts life from hence,
O then be bold to say Bassanio's dead.

NERISSA

My lord and lady, it is now our time,
That have stood by and seen our wishes prosper,
To cry good joy, good joy, my lord and lady!

GRATIANO

My Lord Bassanio, and my gentle lady,
I wish you all the joy that you can wish,
For I am sure you can wish none from me.
And when your honours mean to solemnize
The bargain of your faith, I do beseech you
Even at that time I may be married too.

BASSANIO

With all my heart, so you can get a wife.

GRATIANO

I thank your lordship, you have got me one.
My eyes, my lord, can look as swift as yours:
You saw the mistress, I beheld the maid.
You loved, I loved; for intermissiòn

No more pertains to me, my lord, than you.
Your fortune stood upon the caskets there,
And so did mine too, as the matter falls.
For wooing here until I sweat again,
And swearing till my very roof was dry
With oaths of love—at last, if promise lasts—
I got a promise of this fair one here
To have her love, provided that your fortune
Achieved her mistress.
PORTIA   Is this true, Nerissa?
NERISSA
Madam, it is, so you stand pleased with it.
BASSANIO
And do you, Gratiano, mean good faith?
GRATIANO
Yes, faith, my lord.
BASSANIO
Our feast shall be much honoured in your marriage.
GRATIANO   We'll play with them, the first boy for a
thousand ducats.
NERISSA   What, and stake down?
GRATIANO   No, we shall never win at that sport, and
stake down.
But who comes here? Lorenzo and his infidel!
What, and my old Venetian friend Salerio!

Enter LORENZO, JESSICA, *and* SALERIO,
a messenger from Venice

BASSANIO
Lorenzo and Salerio, welcome hither,
If now the youth of my new interest here
Has power to bid you welcome. By your leave,
I bid my very friends and countrymen,
Sweet Portia, welcome.

PORTIA   So do I, my lord.
  They are entirely welcome.
LORENZO
  I thank your honour. For my part, my lord,
  My purpose was not to have seen you here,
  But meeting with Salerio by the way,
  He did entreat me past all saying nay
  To come with him along.
SALERIO   I did, my lord,
  And I have reason for it. Signor Antonio
  Commends him to you.

He gives BASSANIO *a letter*

BASSANIO   Ere I open his letter,
  I pray you tell me how my good friend does.
SALERIO
  Not sick, my lord, unless it is in mind,
  Nor well unless in mind. His letter there
  Will show you his estate.

BASSANIO *opens the letter*

GRATIANO
  Nerissa, cheer yon stranger; bid her welcome.
  Your hand, Salerio. What's the news from Venice?
  How does that royal merchant, good Antonio?
  I know he will be glad of our success;
  We are the Jasons, we have won the Fleece.
SALERIO
  I would you had won the fleece that he has lost.
PORTIA
  There are some sharp contènts in yon same paper
  That steal the colour from Bassanio's cheek:
  Some dear friend dead, else nothing in the world

Could turn so much the constitutiòn
Of any constant man. What, worse and worse?
With leave, Bassanio, I am half yourself,
And I must freely have the half of anything
That this same paper brings you.

BASSANIO   O sweet Portia,
Here are a few of the unpleasantest words
That ever blotted paper! Gentle lady,
When I did first impart my love to you,
I freely told you all the wealth I had
Ran in my veins—I was a gentleman—
And then I told you true. And yet, dear lady,
Rating myself at nothing, you shall see
How much I was a braggart. When I told you
My state was nothing, I should then have told you
That I was worse than nothing; for indeed
I have engaged myself to a dear friend,
Engaged my friend to his sheer enemy
To feed my means. Here is a letter, lady,
The paper as the body of my friend,
And every word in it a gaping wound
Issuing life-blood. But is it true, Salerio?
Have all his ventures failed? What, not one hit?
From Tripoli, from Mexico and England,
From Lisbon, Barbary, and India,
And not one vessel escape the dreadful touch
Of merchant-marring rocks?

SALERIO   Not one, my lord.
Besides, it should appear that if he had
The present money to discharge the Jew,
He would not take it. Never did I know
A creature that did bear the shape of man
So keen and greedy to confound a man.
He plies the Duke at morning and at night,
And does impeach the freedom of the state

If they deny him justice. Twenty merchants,
The Duke himself, and the magnificoes
Of greatest sort have all persuaded with him;
But none can drive him from the envious plea
Of forfeiture, of justice, and his bond.

JESSICA

When I was with him, I have heard him swear
To Tubal and to Chus, his countrymen,
That he would rather have Antonio's flesh
Than twenty times the value of the sum
That he did owe him. And I know, my lord,
If law, authority, and power deny not,
It will go hard with poor Antonio.

PORTIA

Is it your dear friend that is thus in trouble?

BASSANIO

The dearest friend to me, the kindest man,
The best-conditioned and unwearied spirit
In doing courtesies; and one in whom
The ancient Roman honour more appears
Than any that draws breath in Italy.

PORTIA

What sum owes he the Jew?

BASSANIO

For me, three thousand ducats.

PORTIA   What, no more?

Pay him six thousand, and deface the bond.
Double six thousand and then treble that,
Before a friend of this description
Shall lose a hair through Bassanio's fault.
First go with me to church and call me wife,
And then away to Venice to your friend!
For never shall you lie by Portia's side
With an unquiet soul. You shall have gold
To pay the petty debt twenty times over.

When it is paid, bring your true friend along.
My maid Nerissa and myself meantime
Will live as maids and widows. Come away,
For you shall hence upon your wedding day.
Bid your friends welcome, show a merry cheer;
Since you are dear bought, I will love you dear.
But let me hear the letter of your friend.

BASSANIO   *Sweet Bassanio, my ships have all
miscarried, my creditors grow cruel, my estate is
very low, my bond to the Jew is forfeit. And since
in paying it, it is impossible I should live, all debts
are cleared between you and me if I might but see
you at my death. Notwithstanding, use your
pleasure. If your love does not persuade you to
come, let not my letter.*

PORTIA
O love, dispatch all business and be gone.

BASSANIO
Since I have your good leave to go away,
I will make haste, but till I come again
No bed shall ever be guilty of my stay,
Nor rest be interposer between us twain.   *Exeunt*

SCENE III
A street.

Enter SHYLOCK, SOLANIO, ANTONIO *and the* Gaoler

SHYLOCK
Gaoler, look to him. Tell not me of mercy.
This is the fool that lent out money gratis.
Gaoler, look to him.

ANTONIO   Hear me yet, good Shylock.

SHYLOCK

I'll have my bond! Speak not against my bond!
I have sworn an oath that I will have my bond.
You called me dog before you had a cause,
But since I am a dog, beware my fangs.
The Duke shall grant me justice. I do wonder,
You nasty gaoler, that you are so foolish
To come abroad with him at his request.

ANTONIO

I pray you hear me speak.

SHYLOCK

I'll have my bond. I will not hear you speak.
I'll have my bond, and therefore speak no more.
I'll not be made a soft and dull-eyed fool,
To shake the head, relent, and sigh, and yield
To Christian intercessors. Follow not.
I'll have no speaking, I will have my bond.   *Exit*

SOLANIO

It is the most impenetrable cur
That ever kept with men.

ANTONIO   Let him alone.

I'll follow him no more with useless prayers.
He seeks my life. His reason well I know:
I oft delivered from his forfeitures
Many that have at times made moan to me.
Therefore he hates me.

SOLANIO   I am sure the Duke

Will never grant this forfeiture to hold.

ANTONIO

The Duke cannot deny the course of law;
For the commodity that strangers have
With us in Venice, if it is denied,
Will much impeach the justice of the state,
Because the trade and profit of the city
Do consist of all nations. Therefore go.

These griefs and losses have so lowered me
That I shall hardly spare a pound of flesh
Tomorrow to my bloody creditor.
Well, Gaoler, on. Pray Bassanio come
To see me pay his debt, and then I care not. *Exeunt*

SCENE IV
Portia's house.

Enter PORTIA, NERISSA, LORENZO, JESSICA,
and BALTHASAR, *a Man of Portia's*

LORENZO
  Madam, although I speak it in your presence,
  You have a noble and a true conception
  Of godlike amity, which appears most strongly
  In bearing thus the absence of your lord.
  But if you knew to whom you show this honour,
  How true a gentleman you send relief,
  How dear a lover of my lord your husband,
  I know you would be prouder of the work
  Than customary bounty can enforce you.
PORTIA
  I never did repent for doing good,
  And shall not now; for in companiòns
  That do converse and waste the time togethcr,
  Whose souls do bear an equal yoke of love,
  There must be needs a like proportiòn
  Of lineaments, of manners, and of spirit.
  Which makes me think that this Antonio,
  Being the bosom lover of my lord,
  Must needs be like my lord. If it is so,
  How little is the cost I have bestowed
  In purchasing the semblance of my soul
  From out the state of hellish cruelty.

This comes too near the praising of myself,
Therefore no more of it. Hear other things:
Lorenzo, I commit into your hands
The husbandry and management of my house
Until my lord's return. For my own part,
I have toward heaven breathed a secret vow
To live in prayer and contemplatiòn,
Only attended by Nerissa here,
Until her husband and my lord's return.
There is a monastery two miles off,
And there we will abide. I do desire you
Not to deny this impositiòn,
Which then my love and some necessity
Now lay upon you.

LORENZO   Madam, with all my heart,
I shall obey you in all fair commands.

PORTIA
My people do already know my mind
And will acknowledge you and Jessica
In place of Lord Bassanio and myself.
So fare you well till we shall meet again.

LORENZO
Fair thoughts and happy hours attend on you!

JESSICA
I wish your ladyship all heart's content.

PORTIA
I thank you for your wish, and am well pleased
To wish it back on you. Fare you well, Jessica.
                              Exeunt Jessica and Lorenzo
Now, Balthasar,
As I have ever found you honest-true,
So let me find you still. Take this same letter,
And use you all the endeavour of a man
In speed to Padua. See you render this

Into my cousin's hand, Doctor Bellario,
And look what notes and garments he does give you.
Bring them, I pray, with all imagined speed
Unto the traject, to the common ferry
Which trades to Venice. Waste no time in words
But get you gone. I shall be there before you.

BALTHASAR

Madam, I go with all convenient speed.

Exit

PORTIA

Come on, Nerissa; I have work in hand
That you yet know not of. We'll see our husbands
Before they think of us.

NERISSA   Shall they see us?

PORTIA

They shall, Nerissa, but in such a habit
That they shall think we are accomplishèd
With that we lack. I'll hold you any wager,
When we are both accoutered like young men,
I'll prove the prettier fellow of the two,
And wear my dagger with the braver grace;
And speak between the change of man and boy
With a reed voice, and turn two mincing steps
Into a manly stride, and speak of frays
Like a fine bragging youth; and tell quaint lies,
How honourable ladies sought my love,
Which I denying, they fell sick and died—
I could not do with it. Then I'll repent,
And wish, for all that, that I had not killed them.
And twenty of these puny lies I'll tell,
That men shall swear I have discontinued school
Above a twelve month. I have within my mind
A thousand raw tricks of these bragging Jacks,
Which I will practise.

NERISSA   Why, shall we turn to men?
PORTIA
  Fie, what a question is that,
  If you were near a lewd interpreter!
  But come, I'll tell you all my whole device
  When I am in my coach, which stays for us
  At the park gate; and therefore haste away,
  For we must measure twenty miles today.   *Exeunt*

SCENE V
A garden.

Enter LAUNCELOT the CLOWN *and* JESSICA

LAUNCELOT   Yes truly, for look you, the sins of the
  father are to be laid upon the children. Therefore, I
  promise you I fear for you. I was always plain with
  you, and so now I speak my agitation [cogitation]
  of the matter. Therefore be of good cheer, for truly I
  think you are damned. There is but one hope in it
  that can do you any good, and that is but a kind of
  bastard hope too.

JESSICA   And what hope is that, I pray you?

LAUNCELOT   Sure, you may partly hope that your
  father begot you not, that you are not the Jew's
  daughter.

JESSICA   That were a king of bastard hope indeed! So
  the sins of my mother should be visited upon me.

LAUNCELOT   Truly then, I fear you are damned both
  by father and mother. Thus when I shun Scylla
  your father, I fall into Charybdis your mother.
  Well, you are gone both ways.

JESSICA   I shall be saved by my husband. He has made
  me a Christian.

LAUNCELOT   Truly, the more to blame he! We were
Christians enough before, even as many as could
well live one by another. This making of Christians
will raise the price of hogs; if we grow all to be
pork-eaters, we shall not shortly have a rasher on
the coals for money.

Enter LORENZO

JESSICA   I'll tell my husband, Launcelot, what you
say. Here he comes.

LORENZO   I shall grow jealous of you shortly,
Launcelot, if you thus get my wife into corners.

JESSICA   Nay, you need not fear us, Lorenzo. Launcelot
and I are out. He tells me flatly there's no mercy
for me in heaven because I am a Jew's daughter;
and he says you are no good member of the
commonwealth, for in converting Jews to
Christians you raise the price of pork.

LORENZO   *(to Launcelot)* I shall answer that better to
the commonwealth than you can the getting up of
the Negro's belly. The Moor is with child by you,
Launcelot.

LAUNCELOT   It is much that the Moor should be more
than reason; but if she is less than an honest
woman, she is indeed more than I took her for.

LORENZO   How every fool can play upon the word! I
think the best grace of wit will shortly turn into
silence, and discourse grow commendable in none
only but parrots. Go in, fellow, bid them prepare
for dinner.

LAUNCELOT   That is done, sir. They have all stomachs.

LORENZO   Goodly Lord, what a wit-snapper are you!
Then bid them prepare dinner.

LAUNCELOT   That is done too, sir. Only 'cover' is the
word.

LORENZO   Will you cover then, sir?

LAUNCELOT   No so, sir, either. I know my duty.

LORENZO   Yet more quarrelling with occasion. Will
you show the whole wealth of your wit in an
instant? I pray you understand a plain man in his
plain meaning: go to your fellows, bid them cover
the table, serve in the meat, and we will come in to
dinner.

LAUNCELOT   For the table, sir, it shall be served in;
for the meat, sir, it shall be covered; for your
coming in to dinner, sir, why let it be as humours
and fancies shall govern.   *Exit Launcelot*

LORENZO
O dear discretion, how his words are suited!
The fool has planted in his memory
An army of good words; and I do know
So many fools that stand in better place,
Garnished like him, that for a tricky word
Defy the matter. How cheer you, Jessica?
And now, good sweet, say your opiniòn,
How do you like the Lord Bassanio's wife?

JESSICA
Past all expressing. It is very meet
The Lord Bassanio live an upright life,
For having such a blessing in his lady,
He finds the joys of heaven here on earth;
And if on earth he does not merit it,
In reason he should never come to heaven.
Why, if two gods should play some heavenly match
And on the wager lay two earthly women,
And Portia one, there must be something else
Pawned with the other, for the poor rude world
Has not her fellow.

LORENZO   Even such a husband
Have you of me as she is for a wife.

JESSICA
  Nay, but ask my opinion too of that!
LORENZO
  I will anon. First let us go to dinner.
JESSICA
  Nay, let me praise you while I have a stomach.
LORENZO
  No, pray you, let it serve for table-talk,
  Then howsoever you speak, among other things
  I shall digest it.
JESSICA   Well, I'll set you forth.   *Exeunt*

Act IV

SCENE I
A court of justice.

Enter the Duke, *the magnificoes,* ANTONIO, BASSANIO,
     SALERIO, *and* GRATIANO *with others*

DUKE
  What, is Antonio here?
ANTONIO
  Ready, so please your grace.
DUKE
  I am sorry for you. You are come to answer
  A stony adversary, an inhuman wretch,
  Incapable of pity, void and empty
  From any dram of mercy.

ANTONIO   I have heard
  Your grace has taken great pains to qualify
  His rigorous course; but since he stands obdùrate,
  And when no lawful means can carry me
  Out of his envy's reach, I do oppose
  My patience to his fury, and am armed
  To suffer with a quietness of spirit
  The very tyranny and rage of his.

DUKE
  Go one, and call the Jew into the court.

SALERIO
  He is ready at the door; he comes, my lord.

                    Enter SHYLOCK

DUKE
  Make room, and let him stand before our face.
  Shylock, the world thinks, and I think so too,
  That you but lead this fashion of your malice
  To the last hour of act; then it is thought
  You will show your mercy and remorse more strange
  Than is your strange apparent cruelty.
  And where you now exact the penalty,
  Which is a pound of this poor merchant's flesh,
  You will not only loose the forfeiture,
  But touched with human gentleness and love,
  Forgive a moiety of the principal;
  Glancing an eye of pity on his losses,
  That have of late so huddled on his back,
  Enough to press a royal merchant down
  And pluck commiseration of his state
  From brassy bosoms and rough hearts of flint,
  From stubborn Turks and Tartars never trained
  To offices of tender courtesy.
  We all expect a gentle answer, Jew.

SHYLOCK

I have informed your grace of what I purpose,
And by our holy Sabbath have I sworn
To have the due and forfeit of my bond.
If you deny it, let the danger light
Upon your charter and your city's freedom!
You'll ask me why I rather choose to have
A weight of carrion flesh than to receive
Three thousand ducats. I'll not answer that,
But say it is my humour. Is it answered?
What if my house is troubled with a rat,
And I am pleased to give ten thousand ducats
To have it poisoned? What, are you answered yet?
Some men there are love not a gaping pig,
Some that are mad if they behold a cat,
And others, when the bagpipe sings in the nose,
Cannot contain their urine. For affection,
Master of passion, sways it to the mood
Of what it likes or loathes. Now for your answer:
As there is no firm reason to be rendered
Why he cannot abide a gaping pig,
Why he a harmless necessary cat,
Why he a woollen bagpipe, but of force
Must yield to such inevitable shame
As to offend, himself being offended.
So can I give no reason, and I will not,
More than a lodged hate and a certain loathing
I bear Antonio, that I follow thus
A losing suit against him. Are you answered?

BASSANIO

This is no answer, you unfeeling man,
To excuse the current of your cruelty.

SHYLOCK

I am not bound to please you with my answers.

BASSANIO

Do all men kill the things they do not love?

SHYLOCK

Hates any man the thing he would not kill?

BASSANIO

Every offence is not a hate at first.

SHYLOCK

What, would you have a serpent sting you twice?

ANTONIO

I pray you, think you question with the Jew.
You may as well go stand upon the beach
And bid the main flood abate its usual height;
You may as well use question with the wolf
Why he has made the ewe bleat for the lamb;
You may as well forbid the mountain pines
To wag their high-tops and to make no noise
When they are fretted with the gusts of heaven.
You may as well do anything most hard
As seek to soften that—than which what's harder?—
His Jewish heart. Therefore I do beseech you
Make no more offers, use no farther means,
But with all brief and plain conveniency
Let me have judgement, and the Jew his will.

BASSANIO

For your three thousand ducats here are six.

SHYLOCK

If every ducat in six thousand ducats
Were in six parts, and every part a ducat,
I would not draw them. I would have my bond.

DUKE

How shall you hope for mercy, rendering none?

SHYLOCK

What judgement shall I dread, doing no wrong?
You have among you many a purchased slave,
Whom like your asses and your dogs and mules
You use in abject and in slavish parts,
Because you bought them. Shall I say to you,

'Let them be free! Marry them to your heirs!
Why sweat they under burdens? Let their beds
Be made as soft as yours, and let their palates
Be seasoned with such viands'? You will answer,
'The slaves are ours.' So do I answer you.
The pound of flesh which I demand of him
Is dearly bought, it is mine, and I will have it.
If you deny me, fie upon your law!
There is no force in the decrees of Venice.
I stand for judgement. Answer; shall I have it?

DUKE

Upon my power I may dismiss this court
Unless Bellario, a learned doctor
Whom I have sent for to determine this,
Comes here today.

SALERIO   My lord, here stays without
A messenger with letters from the doctor,
New come from Padua.

DUKE

Bring us the letters. Call the messenger.

BASSANIO

Good cheer, Antonio! What, man, courage yet!
The Jew shall have my flesh, blood, bones, and all,
Ere you shall lose for me one drop of blood.

ANTONIO

I am a tainted wether of the flock,
Meetest for death. The weakest kind of fruit
Drops earliest to the ground, and so let me.
You cannot better be employed, Bassanio,
Than to live yet, and write my epitaph.

Enter NERISSA *dressed like a lawyer's clerk*

DUKE

Came you from Padua, from Bellario?

NERISSA
From both, my lord. Bellario greets your grace.

She presents a letter

BASSANIO
Why do you whet your knife so earnestly?

SHYLOCK
To cut the forfeiture from that bankrupt there.

GRATIANO
Not on your sole, but on your soul, harsh Jew,
You make your knife keen; but no metal can,
No, not the hangman's axe, bear half the keenness
Of your sharp malice. Can no prayers pierce you?

SHYLOCK
No, none that you have wit enough to make.

GRATIANO
O be you damned, inexorable dog,
And for your life let justice be accused!
You almost make me waver in my faith,
To hold opinion with Pythagoras
That souls of animals infuse themselves
Into the trunks of men. Your currish spirit
Governed a wolf which, hanged for human
    slaughter,
Even from the gallows did his fierce soul flee,
And while you lay in your unhallowed dam,
Infused itself in you; for your desires
Are wolvish, bloody, starved, and ravenous.

SHYLOCK
Till you can rail the seal from off my bond,
You but offend your lungs to speak so loud.
Repair your wit, good youth, or it will fall
To cureless ruin. I stand here for law.

DUKE

This letter from Bellario does commend
A young and learned doctor to our court.
Where is he?

NERISSA   He attends here now hard by
To know your answer whether you'll admit him.

DUKE

With all my heart. Some three or four of you
Go give him courteous conduct to this place.
Meantime the court shall hear Bellario's letter.

NERISSA *Your grace shall understand that at the
receipt of your letter I am very sick; but in the
instant that your messenger came, in loving
visitation was with me a young doctor of Rome.
His name is Balthasar. I acquainted him with the
cause in controversy between the Jew and Antonio
the merchant. We turned over many books
together. He is furnished with my opinion which,
bettered with his own learning, the greatness
whereof I cannot enough commend, comes with
him at my importunity to fill up your grace's
request in my stead. I beseech you let his lack of
years be no impediment to let him lack a reverend
estimation, for I never knew so young a body with
so old a head. I leave him to your gracious
acceptance, whose trial shall better publish his
commendation.*

Enter PORTIA *as* BALTHASAR, *dressed
like a Doctor of Laws*

DUKE

You hear the learned Bellario, what he writes,
And here, I take it, is the doctor come.
Give me your hand. Came you from old Bellario?

PORTIA
   I did, my lord.
DUKE   You are welcome; take your place.
   Are you acquainted with the difference
   That holds this present question in the court?
PORTIA
   I am informed thoroughly of the cause.
   Which is the merchant here? And which the Jew?
DUKE
   Antonio and old Shylock, both stand forth.
PORTIA
   Is your name Shylock?
SHYLOCK   Shylock is my name.
PORTIA
   Of a strange nature is the suit you follow,
   Yet in such rule that the Venetian law
   Cannot impugn you as you do proceed.
   (to Antonio) You stand within his danger, do you
      not?
ANTONIO
   Ay, so he says.
PORTIA   Do you confess the bond?
ANTONIO
   I do.
PORTIA   Then must the Jew be merciful.
SHYLOCK
   On what compulstion must I? Tell me that.
PORTIA
   The quality of mercy is not strained,
   It drops then as the gentle rain from heaven
   Upon the place beneath. It is twice blest,
   It blesses him that gives and him that takes.
   'Tis mightiest in the mightiest, it becomes
   The thronèd monarch better than his crown.
   His sceptre shows the force of temporal power,
   The attribute to awe and majesty,

Wherein does sit the dread and fear of kings.
But mercy is above this sceptred sway,
It is enthronèd in the hearts of kings,
It is an attribute to God himself,
And earthly power does then show likest God's
When mercy seasons justice. Therefore, Jew,
Though justice is your plea, consider this:
That in the course of justice none of us
Should see salvation. We do pray for mercy,
And that same prayer does teach us all to render
The deeds of mercy. I have spoken thus much
To mitigate the justice of your plea,
Which if you follow, this strict court of Venice
Must needs give sentence against the merchant
    there.

SHYLOCK
My deeds upon my head! I crave the law,
The penalty and forfeit of my bond.

PORTIA
Is he not able to discharge the money?

BASSANIO
Yes, here I tender it for him in the court,
Yea, twice the sum. If that will not suffice,
I will be bound to pay it ten times over
On forfeit of my hands, my head, my heart.
If this will not suffice, it must appear
That malice bears down truth. And I beseech you,
Wrest once the law to your authority,
To do a great right, do a little wrong,
And curb this cruel devil of his will.

PORTIA
It must not be. There is no power in Venice
Can alter a decree establishèd.
It will be recorded for a precedent,
And many an error by the same example
Will rush into the state. It cannot be.

SHYLOCK
> A Daniel come to judgement! Yea, a Daniel!
> O wise young judge, how I do honour you!

PORTIA
> I pray you let me look upon the bond.

SHYLOCK
> Here 'tis, most reverend doctor, here it is.

PORTIA
> Shylock, there's thrice your money offered you.

SHYLOCK
> An oath, an oath! I have an oath in heaven;
> Shall I lay perjury upon my soul?
> No, not for Venice!

PORTIA   Why, this bond is forfeit,
> And lawfully by this the Jew may claim
> A pound of flesh, to be by him cut off
> Nearest the merchant's heart. Be merciful,
> Take thrice your money, bid me tear the bond.

SHYLOCK
> When it is paid, according to the tenour.
> It does appear you are a worthy judge,
> You know the law, your exposition
> Has been most sound. I charge you by the law,
> Whereof you are a well-deserving pillar,
> Proceed to judgement. By my soul I swear
> There is no power in the tongue of man
> To alter me. I stay here on my bond.

ANTONIO
> Most heartily I do beseech the court
> To give the judgement.

PORTIA   Why then, thus it is:
> You must prepare your bosom for his knife.

SHYLOCK
> O noble judge! O excellent young man!

PORTIA

For the intent and purpose of the law
Have full relation to the penalty,
Which here appears now due upon the bond.

SHYLOCK

'Tis very true. O wise and upright judge!
How much older are you than your looks!

PORTIA

Therefore lay bare your bosom.

SHYLOCK   Ay, his breast,
So says the bond, does it not, noble judge?
'Nearest his heart', those are the very words.

PORTIA

It is so. Are there balances here to weigh
The flesh?

SHYLOCK   I have them ready.

PORTIA

Have by some surgeon, Shylock, on your charge,
To stop his wounds, lest he does bleed to death.

SHYLOCK

Is it so nominated in the bond?

PORTIA

It is not so expressed, but what of that?
'Twere good you do so much for charity.

SHYLOCK

I cannot find it; it is not in the bond.

PORTIA

You, merchant, have you anything to say?

ANTONIO

But little. I am armed and well prepared.
Give me your hand, Bassanio, fare you well.
Grieve not that I am fallen to this for you,
For herein Fortune shows herself more kind
Than is her custom. It is ever her use

To let the wretched man outlive his wealth
To view with hollow eye and wrinkled brow
An age of poverty; from which lingering penance
Of such misery does she cut me off.
Commend me to your honourable wife,
Tell her the process of Antonio's end,
Say how I loved you, speak me fair in death;
And when the tale is told, bid her be judge
Whether Bassanio had not once a love.
Repent but you that you shall lose your friend,
And he repents not that he pays your debt,
For if the Jew does cut but deep enough,
I'll pay it instantly with all my heart.

BASSANIO

Antonio, I am married to a wife
Who is as dear to me as life itself;
But life itself, my wife, and all the world
Are not with me esteemed above your life.
I would lose all, ay sacrifice them all
Here to this devil, to deliver you.

PORTIA

Your wife would give you little thanks for that
If she were by to hear you make the offer.

GRATIANO

I have a wife whom I protest I love;
I would she were in heaven, so she could
Entreat some power to change this currish Jew.

NERISSA

It is well you offer it behind her back,
The wish would make else an unquiet house.

SHYLOCK

These are the Christian husbands! I have a daughter;
Would any of the stock of Barabbas
Had been her husband, rather than a Christian.
We trifle time. I pray you pursue sentence.

PORTIA

A pound of that same merchant's flesh is yours,
The court awards it, and the law does give it.

SHYLOCK

Most rightful judge!

PORTIA

And you must cut this flesh from off his breast,
The law allows it, and the court awards it.

SHYLOCK

Most learned judge! A sentence! Come, prepare!

PORTIA

Tarry a little, there is something else.
This bond does give you here no jot of blood;
The words expressly are 'a pound of flesh'.
Take then your bond, take you your pound of flesh,
But in the cutting it if you do shed
One drop of Christian blood, your lands and goods
Are by the laws of Venice confiscated
Unto the state of Venice.

GRATIANO

O upright judge! Mark, Jew. O learned judge!

SHYLOCK

Is that the law?

PORTIA   Yourself shall see the act,
For, as you urge justice, be assured
You shall have justice more than you desire.

GRATIANO

O learned judge! Mark, Jew. A learned judge!

SHYLOCK

I take this offer then. Pay the bond thrice
And let the Christian go.

BASSANIO   Here is the money.

PORTIA

Soft!
The Jew shall have all justice. Soft, no haste,
He shall have nothing but the penalty.

GRATIANO

O Jew! An upright judge, a learned judge!

PORTIA

Therefore prepare you to cut off the flesh.
Shed you no blood, nor cut you less nor more
But just a pound of flesh. If you take more
Or less than a just pound, be it but so much
As makes it lighter or heavy in the substance
Or the division of the twentieth part
Of one poor scruple; nay, if the scale does turn
But in the estimation of a hair,
You die, and all your goods are confiscated.

GRATIANO

A second Daniel! A Daniel, Jew!
Now, infidel, I have you on the hip!

PORTIA

Why does the Jew pause? Take your forfeiture.

SHYLOCK

Give me my principal, and let me go.

BASSANIO

I have it ready for you; here it is.

PORTIA

He has refused it in the open court.
He shall have merely justice and his bond.

GRATIANO

A Daniel still say I, a second Daniel!
I thank you, Jew, for teaching me that word.

SHYLOCK

Shall I not have barely my principal?

PORTIA

You shall have nothing but the forfeiture,
To be so taken at your peril, Jew.

SHYLOCK

Why, then the devil give him good of it!
I'll stay no longer question.

PORTIA   Tarry, Jew!
  The law has yet another hold on you.
  It is enacted in the laws of Venice,
  If it is proved against an alien
  That by direct or indirect attempts
  He seeks the life of any citizen,
  The party against whom he does contrive
  Shall seize one half of his goods, the other half
  Comes to the privy coffer of the state.
  And the offender's life lies in the mercy
  Of the Duke only, against all other voice.
  In which predicament I say you stand.
  For it appears by manifest proceeding
  That indirectly, and directly too,
  You have contrived against the very life
  Of the defendant, and you have incurred
  The danger formerly by me rehearsed.
  Down therefore, and beg mercy of the Duke.

GRATIANO
  Beg that you may have leave to hang yourself,
  And yet, your wealth being forfeit to the state,
  You have not left the value of a cord;
  Therefore you must be hanged at the state's charge.

DUKE
  That you shall see the difference of our spirit,
  I pardon you your life before you ask it.
  For half your wealth, it is Antonio's,
  The other half comes to the general state,
  Which humbleness may drive unto a fine.

PORTIA
  Ay, for the state, not for Antonio.

SHYLOCK
  Nay, take my life and all! Pardon not that!
  You take my house when you do take the prop
  That does sustain my house. You take my life
  When you do take the means whereby I live.

PORTIA

What mercy can you render him, Antonio?

GRATIANO

A halter gratis! Nothing else, for God's sake!

ANTONIO

So please my lord the Duke and all the court
To quit the fine for one half of his goods,
I am content, so he will let me have
The other half in use, to render it
Upon his death unto the gentleman
That lately stole his daughter.
Two things provided more: that for this favour
He presently becomes a Christian;
The other, that he does record a gift
Here in the court of all he dies possessed
Unto his son Lorenzo and his daughter.

DUKE

He shall do this, or else I do recant
The pardon that I late pronouncèd here.

PORTIA

Are you contented, Jew? What do you say?

SHYLOCK

I am content.

PORTIA   Clerk, draw a deed of gift.

SHYLOCK

I pray you give me leave to go from hence,
I am not well; send the deed after me,
And I will sign it.

DUKE   Get you gone, but do it.

GRATIANO

In christening shall you have two godfathers.
Had I been judge, you should have had ten more,
To bring you to the gallows, not to the font.

                                    Exit Shylock

DUKE

Sir, I entreat you home with me to dinner.

PORTIA

I humbly do desire your grace of pardon.
I must away this night toward Padua,
And it is meet I instantly set forth.

DUKE

I am sorry that your leisure serves you not.
Antonio, gratify this gentleman,
For in my mind you are much bound to him.

Exit Duke and his train

BASSANIO

Most worthy gentleman, I and my friend
Have by your wisdom been this day acquitted
Of grievous penalties, in lieu whereof
Three thousand ducats due unto the Jew
We freely cope your courteous pains with now.

ANTONIO

And stand indebted, over and above,
In love and service to you evermore.

PORTIA

He is well paid that is well satisfied,
And I delivering you am satisfied,
And therein do account myself well paid;
My mind was never yet more mercenary.
I pray you know me when we meet again,
I wish you well, and so I take my leave.

BASSANIO

Dear sir, of force I must attempt you further.
Take some remembrance of us as a tribute,
Not as fee. Grant me two things, I pray you:
Not to deny me, and to pardon me.

PORTIA

You press me far, and therefore I will yield.
Give me your gloves, I'll wear them for your sake.

BASSANIO *takes off his gloves.*

And for your love I'll take this ring from you.
Do not draw back your hand, I'll take no more,
And you in love shall not deny me this.

BASSANIO

This ring, good sir, alas, it is a trifle!
I will not shame myself to give you this.

PORTIA

I will have nothing else but only this,
And now I think I have a mind to it.

BASSANIO

There's more depends on this than on the value.
The dearest ring in Venice will I give you,
And find it out by proclamatiòn.
Only for this, I pray you pardon me.

PORTIA

I see, sir, you are liberal in offers.
You taught me first to beg, and now it seems
You teach me how a beggar should be answered.

BASSANIO

Good sir, this ring was given me by my wife,
And when she put it on she made me vow
That I should neither sell nor give nor lose it.

PORTIA

That excuse serves many men to save their gifts,
And if your wife is not a mad woman,
And knows how well I have deserved this ring,
She would not hold out enemy for ever
For giving it to me. Well, peace be with you!
                              Exeunt Portia and Nerissa

ANTONIO
    My Lord Bassanio, let him have the ring.
    Let his deservings, and my love with it,
    Be valued against your wife's command in this.
BASSANIO
    Go, Gratiano, run and overtake him,
    Give him the ring and bring him if you can
    Unto Antonio's house. Away, make haste!

Exit Gratiano

    Come, you and I will thither, immediately.
    And in the morning early will we both
    Fly toward Belmont. Come, Antonio.   *Exeunt*

SCENE II
A street.

Enter PORTIA *and* NERISSA, *disguised as before*

PORTIA
    Inquire the Jew's house out, give him this deed,
    And let him sign it. We'll away tonight
    And be a day before our husbands home.
    This deed will be well welcome to Lorenzo.

Enter GRATIANO

GRATIANO
    Fair sir, you are well overtaken.
    My Lord Bassanio upon more advice
    Has sent you here this ring, and does entreat
    Your company at dinner.
PORTIA   That cannot be.
    His ring I do accept most thankfully,
    And so I pray you tell him. Furthermore,
    I pray you show my youth old Shylock's house.

GRATIANO
  That will I do.
NERISSA   Sir, I would speak with you.
  (*aside to Portia*) I'll see if I can get my husband's
    ring,
  Which I did make him swear to keep for ever.
PORTIA   (*aside to Nerissa*)
  You may, I warrant. We shall have old swearing
  That they did give the rings away to men,
  But we'll outface them, and outswear them too.
  Away, make haste. You know where I will tarry.
NERISSA
  Come, good sir, will you show me to this house?
                                            Exeunt

Act V

SCENE I
Before Portia's house.

Enter LORENZO *and* JESSICA

LORENZO
  The moon shines bright. In such a night as this,
  When the sweet wind did gently kiss the trees
  And they did make no noise, in such a night
  Troilus I think mounted the Trojan walls,
  And sighed his soul toward the Grecian tents
  Where Cressida lay that night.

JESSICA   In such a night
   Did Thisbe fearfully overtrip the dew,
   And saw the lion's shadow ere himself,
   And ran dismayed away.

LORENZO   In such a night
   Stood Dido with a willow in her hand
   Upon the wild sea banks, and wafted her love
   To come again to Carthage.

JESSICA   In such a night
   Medea gathered the enchanted herbs
   That did renew old Aeson.

LORENZO   In such a night
   Did Jessica steal from the wealthy Jew,
   And with an unthrifty love did run from Venice
   As far as Belmont.

JESSICA   In such a night
   Did young Lorenzo swear he loved her well,
   Stealing her soul with many vows of faith,
   And never a true one.

LORENZO   In such a night
   Did pretty Jessica, like a little shrew,
   Slander her love, and he forgave it her.

JESSICA
   I would out-night you, did nobody come;
   But hark, I hear the footing of a man.

Enter STEPHANO

LORENZO
   Who comes so fast in silence of the night?

STEPHANO
   A friend.

LORENZO
   A friend? What friend? Your name I pray you, friend.

STEPHANO
   Stephano is my name, and I bring word
   My mistress will before the break of day
   Be here at Belmont. She does stray about
   By holy crosses where she kneels and prays
   For happy wedlock hours.
LORENZO   Who comes with her?
STEPHANO
   None but a holy hermit and her maid.
   I pray you, has my master yet returned?
LORENZO
   He has not, nor have we yet heard from him.
   But go we in, I pray you, Jessica,
   And ceremoniously let us prepare
   Some welcome for the mistress of the house.

Enter LAUNCELOT

LAUNCELOT   Sola, sola! Wo ha ho! Sola, sola!
LORENZO   Who calls?
LAUNCELOT   Sola! Did you see Master Lorenzo?
   Master Lorenzo! Sola, sola!
LORENZO   Leave holloaing, man! Here.
LAUNCELOT   Sola! Where? Where?
LORENZO   Here!
LAUNCELOT   Tell him there's a post come from my
   master, with his horn full of good news. My master
   will be here ere morning.   *Exit*
LORENZO
   Sweet soul, let's in, and there expect their
     coming.
   And yet no matter, why should we go in?
   My friend Stephano, signify, I pray you,
   Within the house, your mistress is at hand,
   And bring your music forth into the air.
                       Exit Stephano

How sweet the moonlight sleeps upon this bank!
Here will we sit and let the sounds of music
Creep in our ears; soft stillness and the night
Become the touches of sweet harmony.
Sit, Jessica. Look how the floor of heaven
Is thick inlaid with patens of bright gold.
There's not the smallest orb which you behold
But in its motion like an angel sings,
Still quiring to the young-eyed cherubins.
Such harmony is in immortal souls,
But while this muddy vesture of decay
Does grossly close it in, we cannot hear it.

Enter Musicians

Come ho, and wake Diana with a hymn,
With sweetest touches pierce your mistress' ear
And draw her home with music.

Music

JESSICA
I am never merry when I hear sweet music.
LORENZO
The reason is your spirits are attentive.
For do but note a wild and wanton herd,
Or race of youthful and unhandled colts
Fetching mad bounds, bellowing and neighing loud,
Which is the hot condition of their blood—
If they but hear perchance a trumpet sound,
Or any air of music touch their ears,
You shall perceive them make a mutual stand,
Their savage eyes turned to a modest gaze
By the sweet power of music. Therefore the poet
Did feign that Orpheus drew trees, stones, and
    floods,

Since naught so stockish, hard, and full of rage
But music for the time does change its nature.
The man that has no music in himself,
And is not moved with concord of sweet sounds,
Is fit for treasons, stratagems, and spoils;
The motions of his spirit are dull as night,
And his affections dark as Erebus.
Let no such man be trusted. Mark the music.

Enter PORTIA *and* NERISSA

PORTIA
That light we see is burning in my hall;
How far that little candle throws its beams!
So shines a good deed in a naughty world.
NERISSA
When the moon shone we did not see the candle.
PORTIA
So does the greater glory dim the less.
A substitute shines brightly as a king
Until a king is by; and then his state
Empties itself, as does an inland brook
Into the main of waters. Music! hark!
NERISSA
It is your music, madam, of the house.
PORTIA
Nothing is good, I see, without compare,
I think it sounds much sweeter than by day.
NERISSA
Silence bestows that virtue on it, madam.
PORTIA
The crow does sing as sweetly as the lark
When neither is attended, and I think
The nightingale, if she should sing by day
When every goose is cackling, would be thought

No better a musician than the wren.
How many things by season seasoned are
To their right praise and true perfectiòn!
Peace!

Music ceases

Ho, the moon sleeps with Endymion,
And would not be awaked.

LORENZO   That is the voice,
Or I am much deceived, of Portià.

PORTIA
He knows me as the blind man knows the cuckoo,
By the bad voice.

LORENZO   Dear lady, welcome home.

PORTIA
We have been praying for our husbands' welfare,
Who speed we hope the better for our words.
Have they returned?

LORENZO   Madam, they are not yet,
But there is come a messenger before
To signify their coming.

PORTIA   Go in, Nerissa,
Give order to my servants that they take
No note at all of our being absent hence,
Nor you, Lorenzo, Jessica, nor you.

A trumpet sounds

LORENZO
Your husband is at hand. I hear his trumpet.
We are no tell-tales, madam; fear you not.

PORTIA
This night it seems is but the daylight sick,
It looks a little paler. It is a day
Such as the day is when the sun is hidden.

Enter BASSANIO, ANTONIO, GRATIANO,
and their followers

BASSANIO
   We should hold day with the Antipodes
   If you would walk in absence of the sun.

PORTIA
   Let me give light, but let me not be light,
   For a light wife does make a heavy husband,
   And never be Bassanio so for me.
   But God sort all! You are welcome home, my lord.

BASSANIO
   I thank you, madam. Give welcome to my friend.
   This is the man, this is Antonio,
   To whom I am so infinitely bound.

PORTIA
   You should in all sense be much bound to him,
   For, as I hear, he was much bound for you.

ANTONIO
   No more than I am well acquitted of.

PORTIA
   Sir, you are very welcome to our house;
   It must appear in other ways than words,
   Therefore I scant this breathing courtesy.

GRATIANO   (*to Nerissa*)
   By yonder moon I swear you do me wrong!
   In faith, I gave it to the judge's clerk.
   Would he were gelded that had it for my part
   Since you do take it, love, so much at heart.

PORTIA
   A quarrel ho, already! What's the matter?

GRATIANO
   About a hoop of gold, a paltry ring
   That she did give me, whose posy was
   For all the world like cutler's poetry
   Upon a knife, 'Love me, and leave me not.'

NERISSA
>What talk you of the posy or the value?
>You swore to me when I did give it you
>That you would wear it till your hour of death,
>And that it should lie with you in your grave.
>Though not for me, yet for your vehement oaths,
>You should have been more careful and have kept it.
>Gave it a judge's clerk! No, God's my judge,
>The clerk will never wear hair on his face that had
>   it!

GRATIANO
>He will then if he lives to be a man.

NERISSA
>Ay, if a woman lives to be a man.

GRATIANO
>Now by this hand, I gave it to a youth,
>A kind of boy, a little stunted boy
>No higher than yourself, the judge's clerk,
>A prating boy that begged it as a fee.
>I could not for my heart deny it him.

PORTIA
>You were to blame—I must be plain with you—
>To part so slightly with your wife's first gift,
>A thing stuck on with oaths upon your finger
>And so riveted with faith unto your flesh.
>I gave my love a ring, and made him swear
>Never to part with it; and here he stands.
>I dare be sworn for him he would not leave it,
>Nor pluck it from his finger for the wealth
>That the world masters. Now in faith, Gratiano,
>You give your wife too unkind a cause of grief.
>If it were me, I should be mad at it.

BASSANIO   *(aside)*
>Why, I were best to cut my left hand off
>And swear I lost the ring defending it.

GRATIANO
>My Lord Bassanio gave his ring away

Unto the judge that begged it, and indeed
Deserved it too. And then the boy, his clerk
That took some pains in writing, he begged mine;
And neither man nor master would take aught
But the two rings.

PORTIA   What ring gave you, my lord?
Not that, I hope, which you received of me?

BASSANIO
If I could add a lie unto a fault,
I would deny it; but you see my finger
Has not the ring upon it, it is gone.

PORTIA
Even so void is your false heart of truth.
By heaven, I will never come in your bed
Until I see the ring!

NERISSA   Nor I in yours
Till I again see mine!

BASSANIO   Sweet Portià,
If you did know to whom I gave the ring,
If you did know for whom I gave the ring,
And would conceive for what I gave the ring,
And how unwillingly I left the ring
When naught would be accepted but the ring,
You would abate the strength of your displeasure.

PORTIA
If you had known the virtue of the ring,
Or half her worthiness that gave the ring,
Or your own honour to contain the ring,
You would not then have parted with the ring.
What man is there so much unreasonable,
If you had pleased to have defended it
With any terms of zeal, wanted the modesty
To urge the thing held as a ceremony?
Nerissa teaches me what to believe,
I'll die for it but some woman had the ring!

BASSANIO

No, by my honour, madam! By my soul
No woman had it, but a civil doctor,
Who did refuse three thousand ducats of me
And begged the ring, which I did then deny him,
And suffered him to go displeased away:
Even he that had held up the very life
Of my dear friend. What should I say, sweet lady?
I was enforced to send it after him.
I was besct with shame and courtesy.
My honour would not let ingratitude
So much besmear it. Pardon me, good lady!
For by these blessèd candles of the night,
Had you been there I think you would have begged
The ring of me to give the worthy doctor.

PORTIA

Let not that doctor ever come near my house.
Since he has got the jewel that I loved,
And that which you did swear to keep for me—
I will become as liberal as you,
I will not deny him anything I have,
No, not my body nor my husband's bed.
Know him I shall, I am well sure of it.
Lie not a night from home; watch me like Argus.
If you do not, if I am left alone,
Now by my honour which is yet my own,
I'll have that doctor for my bedfellow.

NERISSA

And I his clerk. Therefore be well advised
How you do leave me to my own protection.

GRATIANO

Well, do you so. Let not me take him then!
For if I do, I'll mar the young clerk's pen.

ANTONIO

I am the unhappy subject of these quarrels.

PORTIA

Sir, grieve not you, you are welcome
notwithstanding.

BASSANIO

Portia, forgive me this enforcèd wrong,
And in the hearing of these many friends
I swear to you, even by your own fair eyes,
Wherein I see myself . . .

PORTIA   Mark you but that!

In both my eyes he doubly sees himself,
In each eye one. Swear by your double self,
And there's an oath of credit.

BASSANIO   Nay, but hear me.

Pardon this fault, and by my soul I swear
I never more will break an oath with you.

ANTONIO

I once did lend my body for his wealth,
Which but for him that had your husband's ring
Had quite miscarried. I dare be bound again,
My soul upon the forfeit, that your lord
Will never more break faith advisedly.

PORTIA

Then you shall be his surety. Give him this,
And bid him keep it better than the other.

ANTONIO

Here, Lord Bassanio. Swear to keep this ring.

BASSANIO

By heaven, it is the same I gave the doctor!

PORTIA

I had it of him. Pardon me, Bassanio,
For by this ring the doctor lay with me.

NERISSA

And pardon me, my gentle Gratiano,
For that same shrubby boy, the doctor's clerk,
In lieu of this last night did lie with me.

GRATIANO

Why, this is like the mending of highways

In summer, where the ways are fair enough.
What, are we cuckolds ere we have deserved it?
PORTIA

Speak not so grossly. You are all amazed.
Here is a letter, read it at your leisure.
It comes from Padua from Bellario.
There you shall find that Portia was the doctor,
Nerissa there her clerk. Lorenzo here
Shall witness I set forth as soon as you,
And even but now returned, I have not yet
Entered my house. Antonio, you are welcome,
And I have better news in store for you
Than you expect. Unseal this letter soon,
There you shall find three of your argosies
Are richly come to harbour suddenly.
You shall not know by what strange accident
I chanced on this letter.
ANTONIO   I am dumb!
BASSANIO

Were you the doctor and I knew you not?
GRATIANO

Were you the clerk that is to make me cuckold?
NERISSA

Ay, but the clerk that never means to do it,
Unless he lives until he is a man.
BASSANIO

Sweet doctor, you shall be my bedfellow.
When I am absent, then lie with my wife.
ANTONIO

Sweet lady, you have given me life and living,
For here I read for certain that my ships
Are safely come to road.
PORTIA   How now, Lorenzo?
My clerk has some good comforts too for you.
NERISSA

Ay, and I'll give them him without a fee.
There do I give to you and Jessica

From the rich Jew, a special deed of gift,
After his death, of all he dies possessed of.

LORENZO

Fair ladies, you drop manna in the way
Of starvèd people.

PORTIA   It is almost morning,
And yet I am sure you are not satisfied
Of these events at full. Let us go in,
And charge us there on interrogatories,
And we will answer all things faithfully.

GRATIANO

Let it be so. The first interrogatory
That my Nerissa shall be sworn on is
Whether till the next night she had rather stay,
Or go to bed now, being two hours to day.
But were the day come, I should wish it dark
Till I were couching with the doctor's clerk.
Well, while I live I'll fear no other thing
So sore as keeping safe Nerissa's ring.   *Exeunt*

A Midsummer
Night's Dream

INTRODUCTION

A *Midsummer Night's Dream* is the most magical of Shakespeare's early plays, and we now know the occasion for which it was adapted. Sonnet 106, of 1593, tells us that he was thinking of writing a 'summer's story', and was reading Chaucer for it. But the play when finished presents the young lovers coming home not from Midsummer revels, but from celebrating Mayday. The Countess of Southampton, mother of Shakespeare's patron, married as her second husband, Sir Thomas Heneage—as Vice-Chamberlain, second in command to Lord Chamberlain Hunsdon in presenting entertainments at Court. Their marriage took place privately on 2 May 1594, and the young patron's poet-actor-dramatist adapted his play for the occasion. Very appropriately, as in everything he did—tact and courtesy were of his very nature—Duke Theseus and Queen Hippolyta are eldering persons of state, like Sir Thomas Heneage and the Countess.

This wedding provides the framework of the play, which was written, or adapted, for a wedding celebration, as everybody has seen, though not the obvious occasion. The contents of the play are rich and various, deliciously and ingeniously intermingled. We have two pairs of young lovers at cross-purposes, and we have the Fairy King and Queen, Oberon and Titania, quarrelling over a changeling boy. Puck, or Robin Goodfellow, is Oberon's attendant sprite, who administers a love-juice that causes lovers to fall in love with what they first glimpse on waking from their spell. Titania falls ridiculously in love with rough Bottom the weaver, accoutered with an ass's head. After mistaking his man and creating more confusion, Puck at length anoints the right lover to wake up and fall for the proper girl.

They are all astray in the wood outside the city. But so are Bottom the weaver and his fellow craftsmen, 'rude mechanicals', who have taken to the wood to rehearse their play to present for the Duke's wedding. Thus it is that the Fairy Queen is entangled with Bottom. All is magic, and indeed these scenes are magical.

Perhaps we remember best of all Bottom and his fellow tradesmen: Peter Quince the joiner who produces their play, Flute the bellows mender, Snout the tinker, Snug the joiner, Starveling the tailor. They are all straight out of the homely town life of Stratford: they come across to us as real, for all that they are caricatures, after half a millenium, amid all the fantasy, fairy lore and poetry of the rest. Their rehearsals and presentation of their play are excruciatingly funny and never fail in performance still—and they give us the professional actor's comment on the rustic provincial performances he had often seen in his youth in the country. Nevertheless, after their ridiculous performance, the Duke has a kindly word which evidently speaks for Shakespeare: 'the best in this kind are but shadows, and the worst are no worse, if imagination amends them.' And to the amateur players: 'your play needs no excuse. Never excuse—for when the players are all dead, there need none to be blamed.' Here is Shakespeare speaking in his own person.

The fairy lore of *A Midsummer Night's Dream* is no less memorable, and hardly less authentic: it comes straight out of the country legends and beliefs that Shakespeare had so much at heart and that inspired his imagination. As Quiller-Couch writes—a good critic, for he was a creative writer himself: rather than from books Shakespeare 'brought all this fairy-stuff up to London in his own head, packed with nursery legends of his native Warwickshire. When will criticism allow for the enormous drafts made by creative artists such as Shakespeare and Dickens upon their childhood?'

The fairy tale is a primeval, archetypal form of literature that goes right back to the childhood of the race and appeals to the child in us all still. Hence the perennial fascination of *A Midsummer Night's Dream* for all audiences, for young people taking part in it—it is a young people's play—as for all readers. And not for these only: this play has been a fountain source of fairy-tale literature ever after, right up to our time with Kipling's *Puck of Pook's Hill*. It has inspired artists and composers no less: innumerable paintings, drawings, illustrations, and such music as Mendelssohn's delicious suite or Britten's recent opera.

Even the unimaginative, though dedicated, Shakespeare scholar, E.K. Chambers, regarded Puck as the most characteristic creation to remain with us from this play. I agree, though placing Bottom the weaver alongside of him. Country folklore has a continuing creativeness in it, as we see in the New England of Hawthorne and Robert Frost, or in the South of Faulkner, Flannery O'Connor, or Eudora Welty. It is no less living in Shakespeare's evocation of it than in the Elizabethan folksongs of the Appalachians or the hillbilly country folk of Kentucky. Robin Goodfellow is

out of the depths of the English countryside, probably
unrecognised by modern suburbia:

> are not you he
> That frights the maidens of the villagery,
> Skim milk, and sometimes labour in the quern [churn]
> And fruitless make the breathless housewife churn;
> And sometimes make the drink to bear no barm;
> Mislead night-wanderers, laughing at their harm?

When I was a boy in Cornwall we still knew about
Robin Goodfellow: I think it was Shakespeare who fixed
him in the English-speaking tradition as Puck. And we
called being mis-led—losing our way in quite familiar
surroundings—being 'pisky-led', i.e. led by the pixies.

Contemporary references illuminate the circumstances of the play's writing as usual. In 1592 Queen
Elizabeth I made a state visit to Oxford; young
Southampton, a Cambridge man, was among the peers
created M.A. on the occasion. No doubt Shakespeare
was in attendance upon his patron, and this was
recognisably what he registered:

> Where I have come, great clerks have purposèd
> To greet me with premeditated welcomes;
> Where I have seen them shiver and look pale,
> Make periods in the midst of sentences,
> Throttle their practised accent in their fears,
> And in conclusion dumbly have broke off.

Upon occasion this was what happened to frightened
academics when confronting Queen Elizabeth I.

Another reference goes back earlier in the dramatist's
memory, to the famous Entertainments Leicester laid
on for the Queen in 1575 at Kenilworth. All the
countryside of Warwickshire flocked in to the Castle to
view, and perhaps a boy of eleven from nearby Stratford. For here the scene is registered: Cupid aimed

At a fair Vestal, thronèd by the West . . .
But I might see young Cupid's fiery shaft
Quenched in the chaste beams of the watery moon:
And the imperial Votaress passed on
In maiden meditation, fancy-free.

Leicester's famous efforts at Kenilworth were his last attempt to urge, persuade, pressure the Queen to marry him: the tradition was well known, here it is preserved.

Among other contemporary references which anchor the play to 1594, one is particularly interesting:

The thrice three Muses mourning for the death
Of learning, late deceased in beggary.

This refers to the death of Robert Greene, a University wit—and Shakespeare always refers to such politely as the 'learned'—who died in squalor and want in 1592, after indicting his notorious attack on the up-and-coming dramatist on his death-bed.

After being privately presented, the play was produced publicly, probably with a few adaptations, by the Lord Chamberlain's Company, which was founded in this same year, with Shakespeare as a founder-member; his patron, Southampton, having enabled him to purchase a share in it. The text that has come down to us is a good one, and offers few difficulties, except for us moderns in the rustic provincial speech of Bottom and his fellows.

CHARACTERS

THESEUS, Duke of Athens.

HIPPOLYTA, Queen of the Amazons, betrothed to
   Theseus.

LYSANDER } young courtiers *in love w/Hermia*

DEMETRIUS } in love with Hermia. *hates Helena*

HERMIA, in love with Lysander.

HELENA, in love with Demetrius.

EGEUS, Hermia's father.

PHILOSTRATE, Theseus' Master of the Revels.

OBERON, King of the Fairies.

TITANIA, Queen of the Fairies.

PUCK, or Robin Goodfellow.

PEASEBLOSSOM

COBWEB

MOTH   } Fairies, in Titania's service.

MUSTARDSEED

A Fairy

PETER QUINCE, a carpenter.

NICK BOTTOM, a weaver.

FRANCIS FLUTE, a bellows-mender.

TOM SNOUT, a tinker.

SNUG, a joiner.

ROBIN STARVELING, a tailor.

Other Fairies attending on Oberon and Titania.

Lords and Attendants on Theseus and Hippolyta.

Act I

SCENE 1
Athens. The palace of Theseus.

Enter THESEUS, HIPPOLYTA, PHILOSTRATE,
with Attendants.

THE. Now, fair Hippolyta, our nuptial hour
  Draws on apace; four happy days bring in
  Another moon: but O, I think, how slow
  This old moon wanes! She lingers my desires,
  Like to a step-dame or a dowager
  Long withering out a young man's revenue.
HIP. Four days will quickly steep themselves in night;
  Four nights will quickly dream away the time;
  And then the moon, like to a silver bow
  New bent in heaven, shall behold the night
  Of our solemnities.
THE.   Go, Philostrate,
  Stir up the Athenian youth to merriments;
  Awake the pert and nimble spirit of mirth;
  Turn melancholy forth to funerals;
  The pale companion is not for our pomp.
                  [Exit Philostrate.]
  Hippolyta, I wooed you with my sword,
  And won your love doing you injuries;
  But I will wed you in another key,
  With pomp, with triumph, and with revelling.

Enter EGEUS *and his daughter* HERMIA, *and*
LYSANDER *and* DEMETRIUS.

383

EGE.   Happy be Theseus, our renownèd Duke!

THE.   Thanks, good Egeus. What's the news with you?

EGE.   Full of vexation come I, with complaint
Against my child, my daughter Hermia.
Stand forth Demetrius. My noble lord,
This man has my consent to marry her.
Stand forth Lysander. And, my gracious Duke,
This has bewitched the bosom of my child.
You, you, Lysander, you have given her rhymes,
And interchanged love-tokens with my child:
You have by moonlight at her window sung
With faining voice verses of feigning love,
And stolen the impression of her fantasy
With bracelets of your hair, rings, gauds, conceits,
Knacks, trifles, nosegays, sweetmeats—messengers
Of strong prevailment in unhardened youth.
With cunning have you filched my daughter's heart,
Turned her obedience, which is due to me,
To stubborn harshness. And, my gracious Duke,
Be it so she will not here, before your grace,
Consent to marry with Demetrius,
I beg the ancient privilege of Athens.
As she is mine, I may dispose of her;
Which shall be either to this gentleman,
Or to her death, according to our law
Immediately provided in that case.

THE.   What say you, Hermia? Be advised, fair maid.
To you your father should be as a god:
One that composed your beauties, yea, and one
To whom you are but as a form in wax
By him imprinted; and within his power
To leave the figure, or disfigure it.
Demetrius is a worthy gentleman.

HER.   So is Lysander.

THE.   In himself he is;
  But in this kind, wanting your father's voice,
  The other must be held the worthier.
HER. I would my father looked but with my eyes.
THE. Rather your eyes must with his judgement look.
HER. I do entreat your grace to pardon me.
  I know not by what power I am made bold,
  Nor how it may concern my modesty
  In such a presence here to plead my thoughts.
  But I beseech your grace that I may know
  The worst that may befall me in this case,
  If I refuse to wed Demetrius.
THE. Either to die the death, or to abjure
  For ever the society of men.
  Therefore, fair Hermia, question your desires,
  Know of your youth, examine well your blood,
  Whether, if you yield not to your father's choice,
  You can endure the livery of a nun,
  For aye to be in shady cloister mewed,
  To live a barren sister all your life,
  Chanting faint hymns to the cold fruitless moon.
  Thrice blessèd they that master so their blood
  To undergo such maiden pilgrimage;
  But earthlier happy is the rose distilled
  Than that which, withering on the virgin thorn,
  Grows, lives, and dies, in single blessedness.
HER. So will I grow, so live, so die, my lord,
  Ere I will yield my virgin patent up
  Unto his lordship whose unwished yoke
  My soul consents not to give sovereignty.
THE. Take time to pause; and by the next new moon,
  The sealing-day between my love and me
  For everlasting bond of fellowship,
  Upon that day either prepare to die

For disobedience to your father's will,
Or else to wed Demetrius, as he would;
Or on Diana's altar to protest,
For aye, austerity and single life.
DEM.   Relent, sweet Hermia; and Lysander, yield
Your crazèd title to my certain right.
LYS.   You have her father's love, Demetrius:
Let me have Hermia's; do you marry him.
EGE.   Scornful Lysander, true, he has my love;
And what is mine my love shall render him;
And she is mine, and all my right of her
I do estate unto Demetrius.
LYS.   I am, my lord, as well derived as he,
As well possessed; my love is more than his;
My fortunes every way as fairly ranked,
If not with vantage, as Demetrius';
And, which is more than all these boasts can be,
I am beloved of beauteous Hermia.
Why should not I then prosecute my right?
Demetrius, I'll affirm it to his head,
Made love to Nedar's daughter, Helena,
And won her soul: and she, sweet lady, dotes,
Devoutly dotes, dotes in idolatry,
Upon this spotted and inconstant man.
THE.   I must confess that I have heard so much,
And with Demetrius thought to speak thereof;
But, being over-full of self-affairs,
My mind did lose it. But, Demetrius, come,
And come, Egeus; you shall go with me:
I have some private schooling for you both.
For you, fair Hermia, look you arm yourself
To fit your fancies to your father's will;
Or else the law of Athens yields you up—
Which by no means we may extenuate—
To death, or to a vow of single life.

Come, my Hippolyta; what cheer, my love?
Demetrius and Egeus, go along;
I must employ you in some business
About our nuptials, and confer with you
Of something nearly that concerns yourselves.
EGE.   With duty and desire we follow you.
                    Exeunt all but Lysander and Hermia.
LYS.   How now, my love? Why is your cheek so pale?
How chance the roses there do fade so fast?
HER.   Belike for want of rain, which I could well
Provide them from the tempest of my eyes.
LYS.   Ay me! For aught that I could ever read,
Could ever hear by tale or history,
The course of true love never did run smooth;
But either it was different in blood—
HER.   O cross! too high to be enthralled to low.
LYS.   Or else mismatchèd in respect of years—
HER.   O spite! too old to be engaged to young.
LYS.   Or else it stood upon the choice of friends—
HER.   O hell! to choose love by another's eyes.
LYS.   Or, if there were a sympathy in choice,
War, death, or sickness did lay siege to it,
Making it momentary as a sound,
Swift as a shadow, short as any dream,
Brief as the lightning in the darkened night,
That, in a spleen, unfolds both heaven and earth—
And, ere a man has power to say 'Behold!',
The jaws of darkness do devour it up:
So quick bright things come to confusiòn.
HER.   If then true lovers have been ever crossed,
It stands as an edìct in destiny.
Then let us teach our trial patiènce,
Because it is a customary cross,
As due to love as thoughts and dreams and sighs,
Wishes and tears, poor fancy's followers.

LYS.   A good persuasion; therefore hear me, Hermia.
I have a widow aunt, a dowager
Of great revènue, and she has no child—
From Athens is her house remote seven leagues—
And she respects me as her only son.
There, gentle Hermia, may I marry you,
And to that place the sharp Athenian law
Cannot pursue us. If you love me then,
Steal forth your father's house tomorrow night.
And in the wood, a league without the town—
Where I did meet you once with Helena
To do observance to a morn of May—
There will I stay for you.

HER.   My good Lysander,
I swear to you by Cupid's strongest bow,
By his best arrow with the golden head,
By the simplicity of Venus' doves,
By that which knits our souls and prospers loves,
And by that fire which burned the Carthage queen
When the false Trojan under sail was seen.
By all the vows that ever men have broken—
In number more than ever women have spoken—
In that same place you have appointed us,
Tomorrow truly will I meet you thus.

LYS.   Keep promise, love. Look, here comes Helena.

Enter HELENA.

HER.   God speed fair Helena! Whither away?
HEL.   Call you me fair? That fair again unsay!
Demetrius loves your fair: O happy fair!
Your eyes are lode-stars, and your tongue's sweet air
More tuneable than lark to shepherd's ear,
When wheat is green, when hawthorn buds appear.
Sickness is catching; O were features so,

Yours would I catch, fair Hermia, ere I go.
My ear should catch your voice, my eye your eye,
My tongue should catch your tongue's sweet
    melody.
Were the world mine, Demetrius being bated,
    [excepted]
The rest I'd give to be to you translated.
O, teach me how you look, and with what art
You sway the motion of Demetrius' heart.

HER. I frown upon him; yet he loves me still.
HEL. O that your frowns would teach my smiles
    such skill!
HER. I give him curses; yet he gives me love.
HEL. O that my prayers could such affection move!
HER. The more I hate, the more he follows me.
HEL. The more I love, the more he does hate me.
HER. His folly, Helena, is no fault of mine.
HEL. None but your beauty; would that fault were
    mine!
HER. Take comfort: he no more shall see my face;
  Lysander and myself will fly this place.
  Before the time I did Lysander see,
  Seemed Athens as a paradise to me.   *Rhyming*
  O then what graces in my love do dwell, *Couplets*
  That he has turned a heaven unto a hell!
LYS. Helen, to you our minds we will unfold:
  Tomorrow night, when Phoebe does behold
  Her silver visage in the watery glass,
  Decking with liquid pearl the bladed grass—
  A time that lovers' flights do ever conceal—
  Through Athens' gates have we devised to steal.
HER. And in the wood, where often you and I
  Upon faint primrose beds were wont to lie,
  Emptying our bosoms of their counsel sweet,
  There my Lysander and myself shall meet;

And thence from Athens turn away our eyes,
To seek new friends, and stranger companies.
Farewell, sweet playfellow; pray you for us,
And good luck grant you your Demetrius!
Keep word, Lysander; we must starve our sight
From lovers' food, till morrow deep midnight.

Exit Hermia.

LYS.   I will, my Hermia. Helena, adieu;
As you on him, Demetrius dote on you!

Exit Lysander.

HEL.   How happy some o'er other some can be!
Through Athens I am thought as fair as she.
But what of that? Demetrius thinks not so;
He will not know what all but he do know;
And as he errs, doting on Hermia's eyes,
So I, admiring of his qualities.
Things base and vile, holding no quantity,
Love can transpose to form and dignity:
Love looks not with the eyes, but with the mind,
And therefore is winged Cupid painted blind;
Nor has Love's mind of any judgement taste:
Wings, and no eyes, figure unheedy haste.
And therefore is Love said to be a child,
Because in choice he is so oft beguiled.
As waggish boys, in game, themselves forswear,
So the boy Love is perjured everywhere;
For, ere Demetrius looked on Hermia's eyne, [eyes]
He hailed down oaths that he was only mine;
And when this hail some heat from Hermia felt,
So he dissolved and showers of oaths did melt.
I will go tell him of fair Hermia's flight:
Then to the wood will he, tomorrow night,
Pursue her; and for this intelligence
If I have thanks, it is a dear expense.
But herein mean I to enrich my pain,
To have his sight thither and back again.   *Exit.*

SCENE II
A room in Quince's house.

Enter QUINCE, *the Carpenter*, SNUG, *the Joiner*,
BOTTOM, *the Weaver*, FLUTE, *the Bellows-mender*,
SNOUT, *the Tinker; and* STARVELING, *the Tailor.*

QUIN. Is all our company here?

BOT. You were best to call them generally, man by
man, according to the scrip. [script]

QUIN. Here is the scroll of every man's name which
is thought fit through all Athens to play in our
interlude before the Duke and the Duchess, on his
wedding-day at night.

BOT. First, good Peter Quince, say what the play
treats on; then read the names of the actors; and so
grow to a point.

QUIN. Sure, our play is 'The most lamentable
comedy, and most cruel death of Pyramus and
Thisbe'.

BOT. A very good piece of work, I assure you, and a
merry. Now, good Peter Quince, call forth your
actors by the scroll. Masters, spread yourselves.

QUIN. Answer as I call you. Nick Bottom, the weaver?

BOT. Ready. Name what part I am for, and proceed.

QUIN. You, Nick Bottom, are set down for Pyramus.

BOT. What is Pyramus? A lover, or a tyrant?

QUIN. A lover, that kills himself most gallant for love.

BOT. That will ask some tears in the true performing
of it. If I do it, let the audience look to their eyes: I
will move storms, I will condole in some measure.
To the rest—my chief humour is for a tyrant. I could
play Ercles [Hercules] rarely, or a part to tear a cat
in, to make all split.

The raging rocks,
And shivering shocks,

allusion

    Shall break the locks
        Of prison-gates;
    And Phibbus' [Phoebus'] car
    Shall shine from far
    And make and mar
        The foolish fates.
This was lofty. Now name the rest of the players.
This is Ercles' vein, a tyrant's vein: a lover is more
condoling.

QUIN.   Francis Flute, the bellows-mender?

FLU.   Here, Peter Quince.

QUIN.   Flute, you must take Thisbe *figure* on you.

FLU.   What is Thisbe? A wandering knight?

QUIN.   It is the lady that Pyramus must love.

FLU.   Nay, faith, let not me play a woman: I have a
beard coming.

QUIN.   That's all one: you shall play it in a mask; and
you may speak as small as you will.

BOT.   If I may hide my face, let me play Thisbe too.
I'll speak in a monstrous little voice: 'Thisne,
Thisne!'—'Ah, Pyramus, my lover dear! your
Thisbe dear, and lady dear!'

QUIN.   No, no, you must play Pyramus; and Flute,
you Thisbe.

BOT.   Well, proceed.

QUIN.   Robin Starveling, the tailor?

STAR.   Here, Peter Quince.

QUIN.   Robin Starveling, you must play Thisbe's
mother. Tom Snout, the tinker?

SNOUT.   Here, Peter Quince.

QUIN.   You, Pyramus' father; myself, Thisbe's father;
Snug the joiner, you the lion's part. And I hope
here is a play fitted.

SNUG.   Have you the lion's part written? Pray you, if
it be, give it me; for I am slow of study.

QUIN.   You may do it extempore, for it is nothing but
  roaring.
BOT.   Let me play the lion too. I will roar, that I will
  do any man's heart good to hear me. I will roar,
  that I will make the Duke say: 'Let him roar again;
  let him roar again!'
QUIN.   If you should do it too terribly, you would
  fright the Duchess and the ladies, that they would
  shriek; and that were enough to hang us all.
ALL.   That would hang us, every mother's son.
BOT.   I grant you, friends, if you should fright the
  ladies out of their wits, they would have no more
  discretion but to hang us. But I will aggravate my
  voice so, that I will roar you as gently as any
  sucking dove; I will roar you as though any
  nightingale.
QUIN.   You can play no part but Pyramus. For
  Pyramus is a sweet-faced man; a proper man as one
  shall see in a summer's day; a most lovely,
  gentleman-like man. Therefore you must needs
  play Pyramus.
BOT.   Well, I will undertake it. What beard were I
  best to play it in?
QUIN.   Why, what you will.
BOT.   I will discharge it in either your straw-colour
  beard, your orange-tawny beard, your purple-in-
  grain beard, or your French-crown-colour beard,
  your perfect yellow.
QUIN.   Some of your French crowns have no hair at
  all, and then you will play bare-faced. But, masters,
  here are your parts; and I am to entreat you,
  request you, and desire you, to con them by
  tomorrow night; and meet me in the palace wood, a
  mile without the town, by moonlight. There will
  we rehearse, for if we meet in the city, we shall be

dogged with company, and our devices known. In
the meantime I will draw a bill of properties, such
as our play wants. I pray you fail me not.

BOT.   We will meet, and there we may rehearse most
obscenely [seemly] and courageously. Take pains,
be perfect: adieu!

QUIN.   At the Duke's oak we meet.

BOT.   Enough: hold, or you break faith.   *Exeunt.*

Act II

SCENE I
A wood near Athens.

Enter a Fairy *at one door, and* PUCK *at another.*

PUCK.   How now, spirit! Whither wander you?

FAI.   Over hill, over dale,
    Thorough bush, thorough briar,
  Over park, over pale,
    Thorough flood, thorough fire,
  I do wander everywhere,
  Swifter than the moon's sphere;
  And I serve the Fairy Queen,
  To dew her orbs upon the green.
  The cowslips tall her pensioners be,
  In their gold coats spots you see;
  Those are rubies, fairy favours,
  In those freckles live their savours.
  I must go seek some dew-drops here,
  And hang a pearl in every cowslip's ear.

Farewell, you lob of spirits; I'll be gone;
Our Queen and all her elves come here anon.
PUCK.   The King does keep his revels here tonight;
Take heed the Queen comes not within his sight;
For Oberon is passing fell and wrath,
Because that she as her attendant hath [has]
A lovely boy, stolen from an Indian king—
She never had so sweet a changeling;
And jealous Oberon would have the child
Knight of his train, to trace the forests wild.
But she perforce withholds the lovèd boy,
Crowns him with flowers, and makes him all her
    joy.
And now they never meet in grove or green,
By fountain clear, or spangled starlight sheen,
But they do square; that all their elves for fear
Creep into acorn-cups, and hide them there.
FAI.   Either I mistake your shape and making quite,
Or else you are that shrewd and knavish sprite
Called Robin Goodfellow. Are not you he
That frights the maidens of the villagery,
Skim milk, and sometimes labour in the quern,
And fruitless make the breathless housewife churn,
And sometimes make the drink to bear no barm,
Mislead night-wanderers, laughing at their harm?
Those that Hobgoblin call you, and sweet Puck,
You do their work, and they shall have good luck.
Are not you he?
PUCK.   You speak aright;
I am that merry wanderer of the night.
I jest to Oberon, and make him smile
When I a fat and bean-fed horse beguile,
Neighing in likeness of a filly foal.
And sometimes lurk I in a gossip's bowl
In very likeness of a roasted crab,
And when she drinks, against her lips I bob,

And on her withered dewlap pour the ale.
The wisest aunt, telling the saddest tale,
Sometimes for three-foot stool mistakes she me;
Then slip I from her bum, down topples she,
And 'O my' cries, and falls into a cough;
And then the whole choir hold their hips and laugh
And wax more in their mirth, and sneeze, and swear
A merrier hour was never wasted there.
But room, fairy! Here comes Oberon.

FAI.   And here my mistress. Would that he were gone!

Enter OBERON, *the King of Fairies, at one door,
with his* Train; *and* TITANIA, *the Queen, at
another, with hers.*

OBE.   Ill met by moonlight, proud Titania.
TITA.   What, jealous Oberon? Fairies, skip hence;
   I have forsworn his bed and company.
OBE.   Tarry, rash wanton; am not I your lord?
TITA.   Then I must be your lady; but I know
   When you have stolen away from fairy land,
   And in the shape of Corin, sat all day
   Playing on pipes of corn, and versing love
   To amorous Phillida. Why are you here,
   Come from the farthest step of India,
   But that, forsooth, the bouncing Amazon,
   Your buskined mistress and your warrior love,
   To Theseus must be wedded, and you come
   To give their bed joy and prosperity?
OBE.   How can you thus, for shame, Titania,
   Glance at my credit with Hippolyta,
   Knowing I know your love to Theseus?
   Did not you lead him through the glimmering night
   From Perigenia, whom he ravishèd;

And make him with fair Aegles break his faith,
With Ariadne and Antìopa?
TITA.   These are the forgeries of jealousy:
And never, since the middle summer's spring,
Met we on hill, in dale, forest or mead,
By pavèd fountain, or by rushy brook,
Or in the beachèd margin of the sea,
To dance our ringlets to the whistling wind,
But with your brawls you have disturbed our sport.
Therefore the winds, piping to us in vain,
As in revenge have sucked up from the sea
Contagious fogs; which, falling in the land,
Has every pelting river made so proud
That they have overborne their continents.
The ox has therefore stretched his yoke in vain,
The ploughman lost his sweat, and the green corn
Has rotted ere his youth attained a beard.
The fold stands empty in the drownèd field,
And crows are fatted with the murrained flock;
The nine-men's-morris is filled up with mud,
And the quaint mazes in the wanton green
For lack of tread are undistinguishable.
The human mortals want their winter cheer:
No night is now with hymn or carol blest.
Therefore the moon, the governess of floods,
Pale in her anger, washes all the air,
That rheumatic diseases do abound.
And thorough this distemperature we see
The seasons alter: hoary-headed frosts
Fall in the fresh lap of the crimson rose;
And on old Hiems' [Winter's] thin and icy crown,
An odorous chaplet of sweet summer buds
Is, as in mockery, set. The spring, the summer,
The childing autumn, angry winter, change

Their wonted liveries; and the mazèd world,
By their increase, now knows not which is which.
And this same progeny of evils comes
From our debate, from our dissensiòn;
We are their parents and original.

OBE.   Do you amend it then: it lies in you.
Why should Titania cross her Oberon?
I do but beg a little changeling boy
To be my henchman.

TITA.   Set your heart at rest:
The fairy land buys not the child of me.
His mother was a votaress of my order;
And in the spicèd Indian air, by night,
Full often has she gossiped by my side;
And sat with me on Neptune's yellow sands,
Marking embarkèd traders on the flood.
When we have laughed to see the sails conceive
And grow big-bellied with the wanton wind;
Which she, with pretty and with swimming gait
Following—her womb then rich with my young
    squire—
Would imitate, and sail upon the land
To fetch me trifles, and return again
As from a voyage rich with merchandise.
But she, being mortal, of that boy did die;
And for her sake do I rear up her boy;
And for her sake I will not part with him.

OBE.   How long within this wood intend you stay?

TITA.   Perchance till after Theseus' wedding-day.
If you will patiently dance in our round,
And see our moonlight revels, go with us;
If not, shun me, and I will spare your haunts.

OBE.   Give me that boy, and I will go with you.

TITA.   Not for your fairy kingdom. Fairies, away!
We shall chide downright if I longer stay.

                              Exeunt Titania and her Train.

OBE.   Well, go your way; you shall not from this grove
   Till I torment you for this injury.
   My gentle Puck, come hither. You remember
   Since once I sat upon a promontory,
   And heard a mermaid on a dolphin's back
   Uttering such dulcet and harmonious breath
   That the rude sea grew civil at her song
   And certain stars shot madly from their spheres
   To hear the sea-maid's music?
PUCK.   I remember.
OBE.   That very time I saw, but you could not,
   Flying between the cold moon and the earth,
   Cupid all armed. A certain aim he took
   At a fair vestal, thronèd by the west,
   And loosed his love-shaft smartly from his bow
   As it should pierce a hundred thousand hearts.
   But I might see young Cupid's fiery shaft
   Quenched in the chaste beams of the watery moon;
   And the imperial votaress passed on,
   In maiden meditation, fancy-free.
   Yet marked I where the bolt of Cupid fell:
   It fell upon a little western flower,
   Before milk-white, now purple with love's wound:
   And maidens call it 'love-in-idleness'.
   Fetch me that flower; the herb I showed you once.
   The juice of it, on sleeping eyelids laid,
   Will make or man or woman madly dote
   Upon the next live creature that it sees.
   Fetch me this herb, and be you here again
   Ere the leviathan can swim a league.
PUCK.   I'll put a girdle round about the earth
   In forty minutes.
OBE.   Having once this juice,
   I'll watch Titania when she is asleep,
   And drop the liquor of it in her eyes.
   The next thing then she waking looks upon,

Be it on lion, bear, or wolf, or bull,
On meddling monkey, or on busy ape,
She shall pursue it with the soul of love.
And ere I take this charm from off her sight,
As I can take it with another herb,
I'll make her render up her page to me.
But who comes here? I am invisible;
And I will overhear their conference.

Enter DEMETRIUS, HELENA *following him.*

DEM.   I love you not, therefore pursue me not.
Where are Lysander and fair Hermia?
The one I'll slay, the other does slay me.
You told me they were stolen to this wood;
And here am I, and mad within this wood
Because I cannot meet my Hermia.
Hence, get you gone, and follow me no more.
HEL.   You draw me, you hard-hearted adamant—
But yet you draw not iron, for my heart
Is true as steel. Leave you your power to draw,
And I shall have no power to follow you.
DEM.   Do I entice you? Do I speak you fair?
Or rather do I not in plainest truth
Tell you I do not, and I cannot love you?
HEL.   And even for that do I love you the more.
I am your spaniel; and, Demetrius,
The more you beat me, I will fawn on you.
Use me but as your spaniel, spurn me, strike me,
Neglect me, lose me; only give me leave,
Unworthy as I am, to follow you.
What worse place can I beg then in your love—
And yet a place of high respect with me—
Than to be usèd as you use your dog?
DEM.   Tempt not too much the hatred of my spirit;
For I am sick when I do look on you.

HEL.   And I am sick when I look not on you.
DEM.   You do expose your modesty too much
  To leave the city and commit yourself
  Into the hands of one that loves you not:
  To trust the opportunity of night
  And the ill counsel of a desert place
  With the rich worth of your virginity.
HEL.   Your virtue is my privilege: for that
  It is not night when I do see your face,
  Therefore I think I am not in the night.
  Nor does this wood lack worlds of company,
  For you, in my respect, are all the world;
  Then how can it be said I am alone,
  When all the world is here to look on me?
DEM.   I'll run from you and hide me in the brakes,
  And leave you to the mercy of wild beasts.
HEL.   The wildest has not such a heart as you.
  Run when you will; the story shall be changed:
  Apollo flies, and Daphne holds the chase;
  The dove pursues the griffin, the mild hind
  Makes speed to catch the tiger—fruitless speed,
  When cowardice pursues and valour flies!
DEM.   I will not stay your questions; let me go,
  Or if you follow me, do not believe
  But I shall do you mischief in the wood.
HEL.   Ay, in the temple, in the town, the field,
  You do me mischief. Fie, Demetrius!
  Your wrongs do set a scandal on my sex.
  We cannot fight for love, as men may do;
  We should be wooed, and were not made to woo.
                                [Exit Demetrius.]
  I'll follow you, and make a heaven of hell,
  To die upon the hand I love so well.   *Exit.*
OBE.   Fare you well, nymph; ere he does leave this
    grove
  You shall fly him, and he shall seek your love.

Enter PUCK.

Have you the flower there? Welcome, wanderer.
PUCK.   Ay, there it is.
OBE.   I pray you give it me.
I know a bank where the wild thyme blows,
Where oxlips and the nodding violet grows,
Quite over-canopied with luscious woodbine,
With sweet musk-roses, and with eglantine.
There sleeps Titania sometime of the night,
Lulled in these flowers with dances and delight;
And there the snake throws its enamelled skin,
Weed wide enough to wrap a fairy in;
And with the juice of this I'll streak her eyes,
And make her full of hateful fantasies.
Take you some of it, and seek through this grove.
A sweet Athenian lady is in love
With a disdainful youth; anoint his eyes;
But do it when the next thing he espies
May be the lady. You shall know the man
By the Athenian garments he has on.
Effect it with some care, that he may prove
More fond on her than she upon her love:
And look you meet me ere the first cock-crow.
PUCK.   Fear not, my lord, your servant shall do so.
                                             Exeunt.

SCENE II
Another part of the wood.

Enter TITANIA, *Queen of Fairies, with* Attendants.

TITA.   Come, now a roundel and a fairy song;
Then for the third part of a minute, hence:

Some to kill grubs in the musk-rose buds;
Some war with blind bats for their leathern wings,
To make my small elves coats; and some keep back
The clamorous owl, that nightly hoots and wonders
At our quaint spirits. Sing me now asleep;
Then to your offices, and let me rest.

The Fairies sing.

FIRST FAIRY. *You spotted snakes with double tongue,*
    Thorny hedgehogs, be not seen;
    Newts and blind-worms, do no wrong,
    Come not near our fairy queen.
CHORUS. *Philomel, with melody,*
    Sing in our sweet lullaby;
  Lulla, lulla, lullaby; lulla, lulla, lullaby;
    Never harm, nor spell, nor charm,
    Come our lovely lady nigh;
    So goodnight, with lullaby.
FIRST FAIRY. *Weaving spiders, come not here;*
  Hence, you long-legged spinners, hence!
  Beetles black, approach not near;
  Worm nor snail, do no offence.
CHORUS. *Philomel, with melody, &c.* *Titania sleeps.*
SECOND FAIRY. Hence, away! Now all is well;
  One aloof stand sentinel.   [*Exeunt Fairies.*]

Enter OBERON, *and squeezes the juice on*
Titania's eyelids.

OBE. What you see when you do wake,
    Do it for your true love take;
    Love and languish for his sake.
    Be it lynx, or cat, or bear,
    Leopard, boar with bristled hair,

In your eye that shall appear
When you wake, it is your dear.
Wake when some vile thing is near.   [*Exit.*]

Enter LYSANDER *and* HERMIA.

LYS.   Fair love, you faint with wandering in the
    wood,
  And, to speak truth, I have forgotten our way.
  We'll rest us, Hermia, if you think it good,
  And tarry for the comfort of the day.
HER.   Be it so, Lysander: find you out a bed,
  For I upon this bank will rest my head.
LYS.   One turf shall serve as pillow for us both;
  One heart, one bed, two bosoms, and one truth.
HER.   Nay, good Lysander; for my sake, my dear,
  Lie further off yet; do not lie so near.
LYS.   O take the sense, sweet, of my innocence!
  Loves takes the meaning in love's conference.
  I mean that my heart unto yours is knit,
  So that but one heart we can make of it:
  Two bosoms interchainèd with an oath,
  So then, two bosoms and a single truth.
  Then by your side no bed-room me deny;
  For lying so, Hermia, I do not lie.
HER.   Lysander riddles very prettily.
  Now much condemn my manners and my pride,
  If Hermia meant to say Lysander lied!
  But, gentle friend, for love and courtesy,
  Lie further off, in human modesty.
  Such separation as may well be said
  Becomes a virtuous bachelor and a maid,
  So far be distant; and good night, sweet friend:
  Your love ne'er alter till your sweet life end!
LYS.   Amen, amen, to that fair prayer say I;
  And then end life when I end loyalty!
  Here is my bed; sleep give you all his rest.

HER.   With half that wish the wisher's eyes be pressed.
                                          They sleep.

                        Enter PUCK.

PUCK.   Through the forest have I gone;
            But Athenian found I none
            On whose eyes I might approve
            This flower's force in stirring love.
            Night and silence—Who is here?
            Weeds of Athens he does wear:
            This is he my master said
            Despisèd the Athenian maid;
            And here the maiden, sleeping sound,
            On the dank and dirty ground.
            Pretty soul, she durst not lie
            Near this lack-love, this kill-courtesy.
            Churl, upon your eyes I throw
            All the power this charm doth owe [own]:
            When you wake, let love forbid
            Sleep his seat on your eyelid.
            So awake when I am gone;
            For I must now to Oberon.   *Exit.*

            Enter DEMETRIUS *and* HELENA, *running.*

HEL.   Stay, though you kill me, sweet Demetrius!
DEM.   I charge you, hence, and do not haunt me thus.
HEL.   O will you darkling leave me? Do not so.
DEM.   Stay, on your peril; I alone will go.   *Exit.*
HEL.   O, I am out of breath in this fond chase!
    The more my prayer, the lesser is my grace.
    Happy is Hermia, wheresoever she lies,
    For she has blessèd and attractive eyes.
    How came her eyes so bright? Not with salt tears;
    If so, my eyes are oftener washed than hers.
    No, no; I am as ugly as a bear,

For beasts that meet me run away for fear:
Therefore no marvel though Demetrius
Does, as a monster, fly my presence thus.
What wicked and dissembling glass of mine
Made me compare with Hermia's sphery eyne [eyes]?
But who is here? Lysander, on the ground?
Dead, or asleep? I see no blood, no wound.
Lysander, if you live, good sir, awake!

LYS. [*Waking.*] And run through fire I will for your
    sweet sake!
Transparent Helena! Nature shows art,
That through your bosom makes me see your heart.
Where is Demetrius? O how fit a word
Is that vile name to perish on my sword!

HEL. Do not say so, Lysander, say not so.
What though he loves your Hermia? Lord, what
    though?
Yet Hermia ever loves you; then be content.

LYS. Content with Hermia? No. I do repent
The tedious minutes I with her have spent.
Not Hermia, but Helena I love:
Who will not change a raven for a dove?
The will of man is by his reason swayed,
And reason says you are the worthier maid.
Things growing are not ripe until their season:
So I, being young, till now ripe not to reason;
And, touching now the point of human skill,
Reason becomes the marshal to my will,
And leads me to your eyes, where I o'erlook
Love's stories, written in love's richest book.

HEL. Wherefore was I to this keen mockery born?
When at your hands did I deserve this scorn?
Is it not enough, not enough, young man,

That I did never, no, nor ever can
Deserve a sweet look from Demetrius' eye,
But you must flout my insufficiency?
Good truth, you do me wrong, indeed, you do,
In such disdainful manner me to woo.
But fare you well; perforce I must confess
I thought you lord of more true gentleness.
O that a lady, of one man refused,
Should of another therefore be abused!   *Exit.*
LYS.   She sees not Hermia. Hermia, sleep you there,
And never may you come Lysander near!
For, as a surfeit of the sweetest things
The deepest loathing to the stomach brings;
Or as the heresies that men do leave
Are hated most of those they did deceive;
So you, my surfeit and my heresy,
Of all be hated, but the most of me!
And, all my powers, address your love and might
To honour Helen, and to be her knight!   *Exit.*
HER.   [*Starting.*] Help me, Lysander, help me. Do
    your best
To pluck this crawling serpent from my breast!
Ay me, for pity! What a dream was here!
Lysander, look how I do quake with fear.
I thought a serpent ate my heart away,
And you sat smiling at his cruel prey.
Lysander! What, removed? Lysander! lord!
What, out of hearing? Gone? No sound, no word?
Alas, where are you? Speak, and if you hear;
Speak, of all loves! I swoon almost with fear.
No? Then I well perceive you are not nigh.
Either death or you I'll find immediately.   *Exit.*
                    [*Titania remains lying asleep.*]

Act III

SCENE I
The wood.

Titania still lying asleep.

Enter QUINCE, BOTTOM, SNUG, FLUTE, SNOUT,
and STARVELING.

BOT.   Are we all met?

QUIN.   Pat, pat; and here's a marvellous convenient
place for our rehearsal. This green plot shall be our
stage, this hawthorn-brake our tiring-house; and we
will do it in action, as we will do it before the
Duke.

BOT.   Peter Quince!

QUIN.   What say you, bully Bottom?

BOT.   There are things in this comedy of Pyramus and
Thisbe that will never please. First, Pyramus must
draw a sword to kill himself; which the ladies
cannot abide. How answer you that?

SNOUT.   By our Lady, a parlous fear.

STAR.   I believe we must leave the killing out, when
all is done.

BOT.   Not a whit; I have a device to make all well.
Write me a prologue, and let the prologue seem to
say we will do no harm with our swords, and that
Pyramus is not killed indeed. And for the more
better assurance, tell them that I, Pyramus, am not
Pyramus, but Bottom the weaver. This will put
them out of fear.

QUIN. Well, we will have such a prologue; and it
   shall be written in eight and six.
BOT. No, make it two more; let it be written in
   eight and eight.
SNOUT. Will not the ladies be afraid of the lion?
STAR. I fear it, I promise you.
BOT. Masters, you ought to consider with yourself;
   to bring in, God shield us!, a lion among ladies is a
   most dreadful thing; for there is not a more fearful
   wild-fowl than your lion living; and we ought to
   look to it.
SNOUT. Therefore another prologue must tell he is
   not a lion.
BOT. Nay, you must name his name, and half his
   face must be seen through the lion's neck; and he
   himself must speak through, saying thus, or to the
   same effect: 'Ladies,' or 'Fair ladies, I would wish
   you,' or 'I would request you,' or 'I would entreat
   you, not to fear, not to tremble: my life for yours!
   If you think I come hither as a lion, it were pity of
   my life. No, I am no such thing; I am a man, as
   other men are': and there, indeed, let him name his
   name, and tell them plainly he is Snug the joiner.
QUIN. Well, it shall be so. But there are two hard
   things: that is, to bring the moonlight into a
   chamber; for you know, Pyramus and Thisbe meet
   by moonlight.
SNOUT. Does the moon shine that night we play our
   play?
BOT. A calendar, a calendar! Look in the almanac;
   find out moonshine, find out moonshine!
QUIN. Yes, it does shine that night.
BOT. Why, then may you leave a casement of the
   great chamber window, where we play, open; and
   the moon may shine in at the casement.

QUIN.   Ay; or else one must come in with a bush of
   thorns and a lantern, and say he comes to disfigure
   [figure] or to present the person of Moonshine.
   Then there is another thing: we must have a wall
   in the great chamber; for Pyramus and Thisbe, says
   the story, did talk through the chink of a wall.

SNOUT.   You can never bring in a wall. What say you,
   Bottom?

BOT.   Some man or other must present Wall; and
   let him have some plaster, or some loam, or some
   rough-cast about him, to signify wall. And let him
   hold his fingers thus, and through that cranny shall
   Pyramus and Thisbe whisper.

QUIN.   If that may be, then all is well. Come sit
   down, every mother's son, and rehearse your parts.
   Pyramus, you begin: when you have spoken your
   speech, enter into that brake; and so every one
   according to his cue.

Enter PUCK [*behind*].

PUCK.   What hempen homespuns have we swaggering
      here,
   So near the cradle of the Fairy Queen?
   What, a play toward? I'll be an auditor;
   An actor too perhaps, if I see cause.

QUIN.   Speak, Pyramus; Thisbe, stand forth.

BOT.   *Thisbe, the flowers of odious savours sweet—*

QUIN.   'Odorous'! 'odorous'!

BOT.   *Odorous savours sweet;*
   So has your breath, my dearest Thisbe dear.
   But hark, a voice! Stay you but here awhile,
   And by and by I will to you appear.   *Exit.*

PUCK.   A stranger Pyramus than ever played here!

[*Exit.*]

FLU.   Must I speak now?

QUIN.   Ay, sure, must you; for you must understand
he goes but to see a noise that he heard, and is to
come again.

FLU.   *Most radiant Pyramus, most lily-white of hue,*
Of colour like the red rose on triumphant briar,
Most brisky juvenal and, too, most lovely Jew,
As true as truest horse that yet would never
tire;
I'll meet you, Pyramus, at Ninny's tomb.

QUIN.   'Ninus' tomb', man! Why, you must not
speak that yet: that you answer to Pyramus. You
speak all your part at once, cues and all.
Pyramus, enter! Your cue is past; it is 'never tire'.

FLU.   O—*As true as truest horse that yet would never*
tire.

Enter PUCK, *and* BOTTOM *with the ass-head on.*

BOT.   *If I were fair, Thisbe, I were only yours.*

QUIN.   O monstrous! O strange! We are haunted!
Pray, masters! Fly, masters! Help!
Exeunt Quince, Snug, Flute, Snout, and Starveling.

PUCK.   I'll follow you: I'll lead you about a round!
Through bog, through bush, through brake, through
briar;
Sometimes a horse I'll be, sometimes a hound,
A hog, a headless bear, sometimes a fire;
And neigh, and bark, and grunt, and roar, and burn,
Like horse, hound, hog, bear, fire, at every turn. *Exit.*

BOT.   Why do they run away? This is a knavery of them
to make me afraid.

Enter SNOUT.

SNOUT.   O Bottom, you are changed! What do I see on
    you?
BOT.   What do you see? You see an ass-head of your
    own, do you?   [*Exit Snout.*]

Enter QUINCE.

QUIN.   Bless you, Bottom, bless you! You are translated.
                                                        Exit.
BOT.   I see their knavery: this is to make an ass of me,
    to fright me, if they could. But I will not stir from
    this place, do what they can; I will walk up and down
    here, and I will sing, that they shall hear I am not
    afraid.
    [*Sings.*] *The ousel cock, so black of hue,*
            With orange-tawny bill,
        The throstle, with his note so true,
            The wren with little quill—
TITA.   What angel wakes me from my flowery bed?
BOT. [*Sings.*]
            The finch, the sparrow, and the lark,
                The plain-song cuckoo gray,
            Whose note full many a man does mark,
                And dares not answer nay—
    for indeed, who would set his wit to so foolish a
    bird? Who would give a bird the lie, though he cries
    'cuckoo' never so?
TITA.   I pray you, gentle mortal, sing again:
    My ear is much enamoured of your note;
    So is my eye enthrallèd to your shape;
    And your fair virtue's force perforce does move me
    On the first view to say, to swear, I love you.

BOT.   I think, mistress, you should have little reason
for that. And yet, to say the truth, reason and love
keep little company together nowadays. The more
the pity that some honest neighbours will not make
them friends. Nay, I can jest upon occasion.

TITA.   You are as wise as you are beautiful.

BOT.   Not so either; but if I had wit enough to get
out of this wood, I have enough to serve my own
turn.

TITA.   Out of this wood do not desire to go:
You shall remain here, whether you will or no.
I am a spirit of no common rate;
The summer still does tend upon my state;
And I do love you: therefore go with me.
I'll give you fairies to attend on you;
And they shall fetch you jewels from the deep,
And sing, while you on pressed flowers do sleep:
And I will purge your mortal grossness so,
That you shall like an airy spirit go.
Peaseblossom! Cobweb! Moth! and Mustardseed!

Enter four Fairies:
PEASEBLOSSOM, COBWEB, MOTH, *and* MUSTARDSEED.

PEAS.   Ready.
COB.   And I.
MOTH.   And I.
MUS.   And I.
ALL.   Where shall we go?
TITA.   Be kind and courteous to this gentleman;
Hop in his walks, and gambol in his eyes;
Feed him with apricots and blackberries,
With purple grapes, green figs, and mulberries;
The honey-bags steal from the humble-bees,

And for night-tapers crop their waxy thighs,
And light them at the fiery glow-worms' eyes,
To have my love to bed, and to arise;
And pluck the wings from painted butterflies
To fan the moonbeams from his sleeping eyes.
Nod to him, elves, and do him courtesies.

PEAS.   Hail, mortal!

COB.   Hail!

MOTH.   Hail!

MUS.   Hail!

BOT.   I cry your worships mercy, heartily. I beseech
your worship's name?

COB.   Cobweb.

BOT.   I shall desire you of more acquaintance, good
Master Cobweb: if I cut my finger, I shall make
bold with you. Your name, honest gentleman?

PEAS.   Peaseblossom.

BOT.   I pray you, commend me to Mistress Squash,
your mother, and to Master Peascod, your father.
Good Master Peaseblossom, I shall desire you of
more acquaintance too. Your name, I beseech you
sir?

MUS.   Mustardseed.

BOT.   Good Master Mustardseed, I know your
patience well. That same cowardly giant-like ox-
beef has devoured many a gentleman of your house:
I promise you, your kindred has made my eyes
water ere now. I desire you of more acquaintance,
good Master Mustardseed.

TITA.   Come, wait upon him; lead him to my bower.
The moon, it seems, looks with a watery eye,
And when she weeps, weeps every little flower,
Lamenting some enforcèd chastity.
Tie up my love's tongue, bring him silently.

Exeunt.

SCENE II
Another part of the wood.

Enter OBERON, *King of Fairies.*

OBE.   I wonder if Titania is awake;
     Then, what it was that next came in her eye,
     Which she must dote on in extremity.

Enter PUCK.

     Here comes my messenger. How now, mad spirit?
     What night-rule now about this haunted grove?
PUCK.   My mistress with a monster is in love.
     Near to her close and consecrated bower,
     While she was in her dull and sleeping hour,
     A crew of asses, rude mechanicals,
     That work for bread upon Athenian stalls,
     Were met together to rehearse a play
     Intended for great Theseus' nuptial day.
     The shallowest thick-skin of that barren sort,
     Who Pyramus presented in their sport,
     Forsook his scene, and entered in a brake,
     When I did him at this advantage take.
     An ass's nut I fixèd on his head.
     Anon, his Thisbe must be answerèd,
     And forth my mimic comes. When they him spy—
     As wild geese that the creeping fowler eye,
     Or russet-pated choughs, many in sort,
     Rising and cawing at the gun's report,
     Sever themselves, and madly sweep the sky
     So, at his sight, away his fellows fly;
     And at our stamp, here o'er and o'er one falls;
     He murder cries, and help from Athens calls.

Their sense thus weak, lost with their fears thus
    strong,
Made senseless things begin to do them wrong:
For briars and thorns at their apparel snatch;
Some sleeves, some hats, from yielders all things
    catch.
I led them on in this distracted fear,
And left sweet Pyramus translated there;
When in that moment, so it came to pass,
Titania waked, and straightway loved an ass.
OBE.   This falls out better than I could devise.
But have you wetted the Athenian's eyes
With the love-juice, as I did bid you do?
PUCK.   I took him sleeping—that is finished too—
And the Athenian woman by his side,
That when he waked, of force she must be eyed.

Enter DEMETRIUS *and* HERMIA.

OBE.   Stand close: this is the same Athenian.
PUCK.   This is the woman, but not this the man.
                                [They stand apart.]
DEM.   O why rebuke you him that loves you so?
Lay breath so bitter on your bitter foe.
HER.   Now I but chide, but I should use you worse,
For you, I fear, have given me cause to curse.
If you have slain Lysander in his sleep,
Being o'er shoes in blood, plunge in the deep,
And kill me too.
The sun was not so true unto the day
As he to me. Would he have stolen away
From sleeping Hermia? I'll believe as soon
This whole earth may be bored, and that the moon
May through the centre creep, and so displease
Its brother's noon-tide with the Antipodes.

It cannot be but you have murdered him:
So should a murderer look, so dead, so grim.
DEM.   So should the murdered look, and so should I,
Pierced through the heart with your stern cruelty;
Yet you, the murderer, look as bright, as clear,
As yonder Venus in her glimmering sphere.
HER.   What's this to my Lysander? Where is he?
Ah, good Demetrius, will you give him me?
DEM.   I had rather give his carcase to my hounds.
HER.   Out, dog! Out, cur! You drive me past the
   bounds
Of maiden's patience. Have you slain him then?
Henceforth be never numbered among men!
O once tell true; tell true, even for my sake!
Dare you have looked upon him, being awake,
And have you killed him sleeping? O brave touch!
Could not a worm, an adder, do so much?
An adder did it; for with doubler tongue
Than yours, you serpent, never adder stung!
DEM.   You spend your passion on a misprised mood:
I am not guilty of Lysander's blood;
Nor is he dead, for aught that I can tell.
HER.   I pray you tell me then that he is well.
DEM.   And if I could, what should I get therefor?
HER.   A privilege, never to see me more.
And from your hated presence part I so:
See me no more, whether he is dead or no.   *Exit.*
DEM.   There is no following her in this fierce vein;
Here therefore for a while I will remain.
So sorrow's heaviness does heavier grow
For debt that bankrupt sleep does sorrow owe;
Which now in some slight measure it will pay,
If for his tender here I make some stay.   *Lies down and*
                        sleeps. Oberon and Puck come forward.
OBE.   What have you done? You have mistaken quite,

And laid the love-juice on some true love's sight;
Of your mistaking must perforce ensue
Some true love turned, and not a false turned true.

PUCK.   Then fate o'er-rules, that, one man holding truth,
A million fail, confounding oath on oath.

OBE.   About the wood go swifter than the wind,
And Helena of Athens look you find;
All fancy-sick she is, and pale of cheer
With sighs of love, that cost the fresh blood dear.
By some illusion see you bring her here;
I'll charm his eyes for when she does appear.

PUCK.   I go, I go, look how I go!
              Swifter than arrow from the Tartar's bow.

Exit.

OBE.   [*Squeezing the juice on Demetrius' eyelids.*]
              Flower of this purple dye,
              Hit with Cupid's archery,
              Sink in apple of his eye.
              When his love he does espy,
              Let her shine as gloriously
              As the Venus of the sky.
              When you wake, if she is by,
              Beg of her for remedy.

Enter PUCK.

PUCK.   Captain of our fairy band,
              Helena is here at hand;
              And the youth, mistook by me,
              Pleading for a lover's fee.
              Shall we their fond pageant see?
              Lord, what fools these mortals be!

OBE.   Stand aside. The noise they make
              Will cause Demetrius to awake.

PUCK.   Then will two at once woo one:
                That must needs be sport alone;
                And those things do best please me
                That befall preposterously.
                                [*They stand aside.*]

               Enter LYSANDER *and* HELENA.

LYS.   Why should you think that I should woo in scorn?
   Scorn and derision never come in tears.
   Look when I vow, I weep; and vows so born,
   In their nativity all truth appears.
   How can these things in me seem scorn to you,
   Bearing the badge of faith to prove them true?
HEL.   You do advance your cunning more and more.
   When truth kills truth, O devilish-holy fray!
   These vows are Hermia's: will you give her o'er?
   Weigh oath with oath, and you will nothing weigh:
   Your vows to her and me, put in two scales,
   Will even weigh; and both as light as tales.
LYS.   I had no judgement when to her I swore.
HEL.   And none, in my mind, now you give her o'er.
LYS.   Demetrius loves her, and he loves not you.
DEM.   (*Waking.*)O Helen, goddess, nymph, perfect,
     divine!
   To what, my love, shall I compare your eyne
     [eyes]?
   Crystal is muddy. O how ripe in show
   Your lips, those kissing cherries, tempting grow!
   That pure congealèd white, high Taurus' snow,
   Fanned with the eastern wind, turns to a crow
   When you hold up your hand. O let me kiss
   This princess of pure white, this seal of bliss!
HEL.   O spite! O hell! I see you all are bent
   To set against me for your merriment.

If you were civil, and knew courtesy,
You would not do me thus much injury.
Can you not hate me, as I know you do,
But you must join in souls to mock me too?
If you were men, as men you are in show,
You would not use a gentle lady so:
To vow, and swear, and superpraise my parts,
When I am sure you hate me with your hearts.
You both are rivals, and love Hermia;
And now both rivals to mock Helena.
A trim exploit, a manly enterprise,
To conjure tears up in a poor maid's eyes
With your derision! None of noble sort
Would so offend a virgin, and extort
A poor soul's patience, all to make you sport.

LYS.   You are unkind, Demetrius; be not so,
For you love Hermia; this you know I know:
And here, with all good will, with all my heart,
In Hermia's love I yield you up my part;
And yours of Helena to me bequeath,
Whom I do love, and will do till my death.

HEL.   Never did mockers waste more idle breath.

DEM.   Lysander, keep your Hermia; I will none.
If ere I loved her, all that love is gone.
My heart to her but as guest-wise sojourned,
And now to Helen is it home returned,
There to remain.

LYS.   Helen, it is not so.

DEM.   Disparage not the faith you do not know,
Lest to your peril you do buy it dear.
Look where your love comes; yonder is your dear.

Enter HERMIA.

HER. Dark night, that from the eye its function
 takes,
 The ear more quick of apprehension makes;
 Wherein it does impair the seeing sense,
 It pays the hearing double recompense.
 You are not by my eye, Lysander, found;
 My ear, I thank it, brought me to your sound.
 But why unkindly did you leave me so?
LYS. Why should he stay whom love does press to
 go?
HER. What love could press Lysander from my side?
LYS. Lysander's love, that would not let him bide—
 Fair Helena, who more engilds the night
 Than all yon fiery oes and eyes of light.
 Why seek you me? Could not this make you know
 The hate I bare you made me leave you so?
HER. You speak not as you think; it cannot be!
HEL. Lo, she is one of this confederacy!
 Now I perceive they have conjoined all three
 To fashion this false sport in spite of me.
 Injurious Hermia! Most ungrateful maid!
 Have you conspired, have you with these contrived,
 To bait me with this foul derisiòn?
 Is all the counsel that we two have shared,
 The sisters' vows, the hours that we have spent
 When we have chid the hasty-footed time
 For parting us—O, is all forgot?
 All school-days' friendship, childhood innocence?
 We, Hermia, like two artistic gods,
 Have with our needles created both one flower,
 Both on one sampler, sitting on one cushion,
 Both warbling of one song, both in one key,
 As if our hands, our sides, voices and minds,

Had been incorporate. So we grew together,
Like to a double cherry, seeming parted,
But yet an union in partitiòn,
Two lovely berries moulded on one stem;
So, with two seeming bodies, but one heart;
Two of the first, like coats in heraldry,
Due but to one, and crownèd with one crest.
And will you rend our ancient love asunder
To join with men in scorning your poor friend?
It is not friendly, nor is it maidenly;
Our sex, as well as I, may chide you for it,
Though I alone do feel the injury.

HER. I am amazèd at your passionate words:
I scorn you not; it seems that you scorn me.

HEL. Have you not set Lysander, as in scorn,
To follow me, and praise my eyes and face;
And made your other love, Demetrius,
Who even but now did spurn me with his foot,
To call me goddess, nymph, divine and rare,
Precious, celestial? Wherefore speaks he this
To her he hates? And wherefore does Lysander
Deny your love, so rich within his soul,
And tender me, forsooth, affectiòn,
But by your setting on, by your consent?
What though I am not so in grace as you,
So hung upon with love, so fortunate,
But miserable most, to love unloved?
This you should pity rather than despise.

HER. I understand not what you mean by this.

HEL. Ay, do! Persèver: counterfeit sad looks,
Make mouths upon me when I turn my back,
Wink each at other; hold the sweet jest up;
This sport, well carried, shall be chronicled.
If you have any pity, grace, or manners,
You would not make me such an argument.

But fare you well; it is partly my own fault,
Which death, or absence, soon shall remedy.

LYS. Stay, gentle Helena; hear my excuse;
My love, my life, my soul, fair Helena!

HEL. O excellent!

HER. Sweet, do not scorn her so.

DEM. If she cannot entreat, I can compel.

LYS. You can compel no more than she entreat;
Your threats have no more strength than her weak
prayers.
Helen, I love you, by my life I do;
I swear by that which I will lose for you
To prove him false that says I love you not.

DEM. I say I love you more than he can do.

LYS. If you say so, withdraw and prove it too.

DEM. Quick, come!

HER. Lysander, whereto tends all this?

LYS. Away, you Ethiope!

DEM. No, no; he'll
Seem to break loose—[*To Lysander.*] take on as you
would follow,
But yet come not! You are a tame man, go!

LYS. Hang off, you cat, you burr! Vile thing, let
loose,
Or I will shake you from me like a serpent.

HER. Why are you grown so rude? What change is
this,
Sweet love?

LYS. Your love? Out, tawny Tartar, out!
Out, loathed medicine! O hated potion, hence!

HER. Do you not jest?

HEL. Yes, faith, and so do you.

LYS. Demetrius, I will keep my word with you.

DEM. I would I had your bond, for I perceive
A weak bond holds you; I'll not trust your word.

LYS.   What, should I hurt her, strike her, kill her
   dead?
Although I hate her, I'll not harm her so.

HER.   What, can you do me greater harm than hate?
   Hate me? Wherefor? O me! what news, my love?
   Am not I Hermia? Are not you Lysander?
   I am as fair now as I was erewhile.
   Since night you loved me; yet since night you left
     me.
   Why, then you left me—O the gods forbid!—
   In earnest, shall I say?

LYS.   Ay, by my life!
   And never did desire to see you more.
   Therefore, be out of hope, of question, of doubt;
   Be certain, nothing truer; 'tis no jest
   That I do hate you, and love Helena.

HER.   O me! [*To Helena.*] You juggler! You rotten-
   blossom!
   You thief of love! What, have you come by night
   And stolen my love's heart from him?

HEL.   Fine, in faith!
   Have you no modesty, no maiden shame,
   No touch of bashfulness? What, will you tear
   Impatient answers from my gentle tongue?
   Fie, fie, you counterfeit! You puppet, you!

HER.   'Puppet'! Why, so? Ay, that way goes the game!
   Now I perceive that she has made compare
   Between our statures; she has urged her height;
   And with her personage, her tall personage,
   Her height, indeed, she has prevailed with him.
   And are you grown so high in his esteem
   Because I am so dwarfish and so low?
   How low am I, you painted maypole? Speak:
   How low am I? I am not yet so low
   But that my nails can reach unto your eyes.

HEL. I pray you, though you mock me, gentlemen,
   Let her not hurt me. I was never curst;
   I have no gift at all in shrewishness;
   I am a right maid for my cowardice;
   Let her not strike me. You perhaps may think,
   Because she is something lower than myself,
   That I can match her.

HER.   'Lower'? Hark, again!

HEL. Good Hermia, do not be so bitter with me.
   I evermore did love you, Hermia,
   Did ever keep your counsels, never wronged you,
   Save that, in love unto Demetrius,
   I told him of your stealth unto this wood.
   He followed you; for love I followed him;
   But he has driven me hence, and threatened me
   To strike me, spurn me, nay, to kill me too.
   And now, so you will let me quiet go,
   To Athens will I bear my folly back,
   And follow you no further. Let me go:
   You see how simple and how foolish I am.

HER. Why, get you gone! Who is it hinders you?

HEL. A foolish heart that I leave here behind.

HER. What! with Lysander?

HEL.   With Demetrius.

LYS. Be not afraid; she shall not harm you, Helena.

DEM. No sir, she shall not, though you take her
  part.

HEL. O, when she is angry, she is keen and shrewd;
   She was a vixen when she went to school,
   And though she is but little, she is fierce.

HER. 'Little' again? Nothing but 'low' and 'little'?
   Why will you suffer her to flout me thus?
   Let me come to her!

LYS.   Get you gone, you dwarf;
   You minimus, of hindering knot-grass made;
   You bead, you acorn.

DEM.   You are too officious
In her behalf that scorns your services.
Let her alone; speak not of Helena;
Take not her part; for if you do intend
Never so little show of love to her,
You shall pay for it.

LYS.   Now she holds me not:
Now follow, if you dare, to try whose right,
Of yours or mine, is most in Helena.

DEM.   Follow? Nay, I'll go with you, cheek by jowl.
                    Exeunt Lysander and Demetrius.

HER.   You, mistress, all this is because of you.
Nay, go not back.

HEL.   I will not trust you, I,
Nor longer stay in your curst company.
Your hands than mine are quicker for a fray:
My legs are longer though, to run away.   *Exit.*

HER.   I am amazed, and know not what to say.   *Exit.*
                    Oberon and Puck come forward.

OBE.   This is your negligence: ever you mistake,
Or else commit your knaveries wilfully.

PUCK.   Believe me, king of shadows, I mistook.
Did not you tell me I should know the man
By the Athenian garments he had on?
And so far blameless proves my enterprise
That I have anointed an Athenian's eyes.
And so far am I glad it so did sort,
As this their jangling I esteem a sport.

OBE.   You see these lovers seek a place to fight.
Hie therefore, Robin, overcast the night;
The starry sky cover you anon
With drooping fog, as black as Acheron,
And lead these testy rivals so astray
As one come not within another's way.
Like to Lysander sometime frame your tongue,

Then stir Demetrius up with bitter wrong;
And sometime rail you like Demetrius:
And from each other look you lead them thus,
Till o'er their brows death-counterfeiting sleep
With leaden legs and batty wings does creep.
Then crush this herb into Lysander's eye,
Whose liquor has this virtuous property,
To take from thence all error with its might,
And make his eyeballs roll with wonted sight.
When they next wake, all this derisiòn
Shall seem a dream and fruitless visiòn;
And back to Athens shall the lovers wend,
With league whose date till death shall never end.
While I in this affair do you employ,
I'll to my queen, and beg her Indian boy;
And then I will her charmèd eye release
From monster's view, and all things shall be peace.
PUCK.   My fairy lord, this must be done with haste,
For night's swift dragons cut the clouds full fast;
And yonder shines Aurora's harbinger,
At whose approach, ghosts wandering here and
        there
Troop home to churchyards. Damnèd spirits all,
That in cross-ways and floods have burial,
Already to their wormy beds are gone,
For fear lest day should look their shames upon:
They wilfully themselves exiled from light,
And must for aye consort with black-browed night.
OBE.   But we are spirits of another sort:
I with the Morning's love have oft made sport;
And like a forester the groves may tread
Even till the eastern gate, all fiery-red,
Opening on Neptune with fair blessèd beams,
Turns into yellow gold his salt green streams.
But notwithstanding, haste, make no delay;
We may effect this business yet ere day.   [*Exit.*]

PUCK.   Up and down, up and down,
                        I will lead them up and down;
                        I am feared in field and town:
                        Goblin, lead them up and down.
        Here comes one.

                        Enter LYSANDER.

LYS.   Where are you, proud Demetrius? Speak you
    now.
PUCK.   Here, villain, drawn and ready. Where are you?
LYS.   I will be with you straight.
PUCK.   Follow me then
    To plainer ground.
                        [*Exit Lysander, following the voice.*]

                        Enter DEMETRIUS.

DEM.   Lysander, speak again.
    You runaway, you coward, are you fled?
    Speak! In some bush? Where do you hide your head?
PUCK.   You coward, are you bragging to the stars,
    Telling the bushes that you look for wars,
    And will not come? Come, miscreant, come you
        child!
    I'll whip you with a rod; he is defiled
    That draws a sword on you.
DEM.   Yea, are you there?
PUCK.   Follow my voice; we'll try no manhood here.
                                    Exeunt.

                        [*Enter* LYSANDER.]

LYS.   He goes before me, and still dares me on;
    When I come where he calls, then he is gone.

The villain is much lighter-heeled than I:
I followed fast; but faster he did fly,
That fallen am I in dark uneven way,
And here will rest me.   *Lies down.*
                              Come you gentle day:
For if but once you show me your grey light,
I'll find Demetrius, and revenge this spite. [*Sleeps.*]

          Enter PUCK *and* DEMETRIUS.

PUCK.   Ho, ho, ho! Coward, why come you not?
                              They dodge about the stage.
DEM.   Abide me if you dare, for well I know
    You run before me, shifting every place,
    And dare not stand, nor look me in the face.
    Where are you now?
PUCK.   Come hither; I am here.
DEM.   Nay, then, you mock me; you shall buy this
        dear
    If ever I your face by daylight see:
    Now go your way. Faintness constrain now me
    To measure out my length on this cold bed.
                                        [*Lies down.*]
    By day's approach look to be visited.   [*Sleeps.*]

              Enter HELENA.

HEL.   O weary night, O long and tedious night,
    Abate your hours! Shine, comforts, from the east,
    That I may back to Athens by daylight,
    From these that my poor company detest.
    And sleep, that sometimes shuts up sorrow's eye,
    Steal me awhile from my own company.
                              [*Lies down and*] *sleeps.*

PUCK.   Yet but three? Come one more,
                         Two of both kinds make up four.
                         Here she comes, curst and sad:
                         Cupid is a knavish lad
                         Thus to make poor females mad!

                         Enter HERMIA.

HER.   Never so weary, never so in woe,
    Bedabbled with the dew, and torn with briars,
    I can no further crawl, no further go;
    My legs can keep no pace with my desires.
    Here will I rest me till the break of day.
                                        [*Lies down.*]
    Heavens shield Lysander, if they mean a fray!
                                        [*Sleeps.*]
PUCK.   On the ground
                         Sleep sound;
                         I'll apply
                         To your eye,
                         Gentle lover, remedy.
                         [*Squeezes the juice on Lysander's eyelids.*]
                         When you wake,
                         You take
                         True delight
                         In the sight
                         Of your former lady's eye;
                     And the country proverb known,
                     That every man should take his own,
                     In your waking shall be shown:
                         Jack shall have Jill,
                         Nought shall go ill;
    The man shall have his mare again, and all shall be
        well.   [*Exit.*]

Act IV

SCENE I
The wood.

Lysander, Demetrius, Helena, and Hermia, still lying asleep.

Enter TITANIA *and* BOTTOM; PEASEBLOSSOM, COBWEB, MOTH, MUSTARDSEED, *and other* Fairies; OBERON *the King, behind, unseen.*

TITA. Come sit you down upon this flowery bed,
While I your amiable cheeks do coy [caress],
And stick musk-roses in your sleek smooth head,
And kiss your fair large ears, my gentle joy.
BOT. Where's Peaseblossom?
PEAS. Ready.
BOT. Scratch my head, Peaseblossom. Where's Mounsieur Cobweb?
COB. Ready.
BOT. Mounsieur Cobweb, good mounsieur, get you your weapons in your hand, and kill me a red-hipped humble-bee on the top of a thistle; and good mounsieur, bring me the honey-bag. Do not fret yourself too much in the action, mounsieur; and good mounsieur, have a care the honey-bag breaks not. I would be loath to have you overflown with a honey-bag, signior. Where's Mounsieur Mustardseed?
MUS. Ready.

BOT.   Give me your fist, Mounsier Mustardseed. Pray you, leave your courtesy, good mounsieur.

MUS.   What's your will?

BOT.   Nothing, good mounsieur, but to help Cavalier Cobweb to scratch. I must to the barber's, mounsieur, for it seems I am marvellous hairy about the face; and I am such a tender ass, if my hair does but tickle me, I must scratch.

TITA.   What, will you hear some music, my sweet love?

BOT.   I have a reasonable good ear in music. Let's have the tongs and the bones.

TITA.   Or say, sweet love, what you desire to eat?

BOT.   Truly, a peck of provender; I could munch your good dry oats. It seems I have a great desire to a truss of hay: good hay, sweet hay, has no fellow.

TITA.   I have a venturous fairy that shall seek
The squirrel's hoard, and fetch you new nuts.

BOT.   I had rather have a handful or two of dried peas.
But I pray you, let none of your people stir me:
I have an exposition [disposition] of sleep come
      upon me.

TITA.   Sleep you, and I will wind you in my arms.
Fairies, be gone, and be all ways away.
                                            [*Exeunt Fairies.*]
So does the woodbine the sweet honeysuckle
Gently entwist; the female ivy so
Enrings the barky fingers of the elm.
O how I love you! How I dote on you! [*They sleep.*]

Enter PUCK.

OBE.   [*Advancing.*] Welcome, good Robin. See you
      this sweet sight?
Her dotage now I do begin to pity;

For, meeting her of late behind the wood
Seeking sweet favours for this hateful fool,
I did upbraid her and fall out with her.
For she his hairy temples then had rounded
With coronet of fresh and fragrant flowers;
And that same dew, which sometimes on the buds
Was wont to swell like round and orient pearls,
Stood now within the pretty flowerets' eyes
Like tears, that did their own disgrace bewail.
When I had at my pleasure taunted her,
And she in mild terms begged my patiènce,
I then did ask of her her changeling child;
Which straight she gave me, and her fairy sent
To bear him to my bower in fairy land.
And now I have the boy, I will undo
This hateful imperfection of her eyes.
And gentle Puck, take this transformèd scalp
From off the head of this Athenian swain,
That he awaking when the other does
May all to Athens back again repair,
And think no more of this night's accidents
But as the fierce vexation of a dream.
But first I will release the fairy queen.
                    [*Squeezes the juice on her eyelids.*]
               Be as you were wont to be;
               See as you were wont to see:
               Dian's bud o'er Cupid's flower
               Has such force and blessed power.
Now, my Titania, wake you, my sweet queen.

TA. [*Waking.*] My Oberon! What visions have I
    seen!
I thought I was enamoured of an ass.

E. There lies your love.

TA.   How came these things to pass?
O how my eyes do loathe his visage now!

OBE.   Silence awhile. Robin, take off this head.
 Titania, music call; and strike more dead
 Than common sleep of all these five the sense.
TITA.   Music ho, music, such as charms our sleep.
                                              Soft music.
PUCK.   [*Taking the ass-head off Bottom.*] Now when
 you wake with your own fool's eyes peep.
OBE.   Sound, music!   [*Music strikes into a dance.*]
                      Come my queen, take hands with me,
 And rock the ground whereon these sleepers be.
                      [*Oberon and Titania dance.*]
 Now you and I are new in amity,
 And will to-morrow midnight, solemnly,
 Dance in Duke Theseus' house triumphantly,
 And bless it to all fair prosperity.
 There shall the pairs of faithful lovers be
 Wedded, with Theseus, all in jollity.
PUCK.   Fairy king, attend and mark:
                 I do hear the morning lark.
OBE.   Then my queen, in silence sad,
                 Trip we after the night's shade:
                 We the globe can compass soon,
                 Swifter than the wandering moon.
TITA.   Come my lord, and in our flight
                 Tell me how it came this night
                 That I sleeping here was found
                 With these mortals on the ground.
 Exeunt. The four lovers and Bottom still lie asleep.

          To the winding of horns [*within*],
 enter THESEUS, HIPPOLYTA, EGEUS, *and* Train.

THE.   Go one of you, find out the forester;
 For now our observation is performed,
 And since we have the vanguard of the day,

My love shall hear the music of my hounds.
Uncouple in the western valley; let them go;
Dispatch I say, and find the forester.

                       [*Exit an Attendant.*]

We will, fair queen, up to the mountain's top,
And mark the musical confusiòn
Of hounds and echo in conjunctiòn.

HIP.   I was with Hercules and Cadmus once,
When in a wood of Crete they bayed the bear
With hounds of Sparta. Never did I hear
Such gallant chiding; for, besides the groves,
The skies, the fountains, every region near
Seemed all one mutual cry; I never heard
So musical a discord, such sweet thunder.

THE.   My hounds are bred out of the Spartan kind,
So jowelled, so sandy; and their heads are hung
With ears that sweep away the morning dew;
Crook-kneed and dewlapped like Thessalian bulls;
Slow in pursuit, but matched in mouth like bells,
Each under each: a cry more tuneable
Was never hollaed to, nor cheered with horn,
In Crete, in Sparta, nor in Thessaly.
Judge when you hear. But soft, what nymphs are
   these?

EGE.   My lord, this is my daughter here asleep,
And this Lysander; this Demetrius is,
This Helena, old Nedar's Helena.
I wonder of their being here together.

THE.   No doubt they rose up early, to observe
The rite of May; and hearing our intent,
Came here in grace of our solemnity.
But speak, Egeus; is not this the day
That Hermia should give answer of her choice?

EGE.   It is, my lord.

THE.   Go, bid the huntsmen wake them with their
    horns.   *Shout within; winding of horns.*
                    The lovers wake and start up.
  Good-morrow friends. Saint Valentine is past:
  Begin these wood-birds but to couple now?
LYS.   Pardon, my lord.   [*The lovers kneel.*]
THE.   I pray you all, stand up.
  I know you two are rival enemies:
  How comes this gentle concord in the world,
  That hatred is so far from jealousy
  To sleep by hate, and fear no enmity?
LYS.   My lord, I shall reply amazedly,
  Half asleep, half waking; but as yet, I swear,
  I cannot truly say how I came here.
  But as I think—for truly would I speak—
  And now I do bethink me, so it is.
  I came with Hermia hither; our intent
  Was to be gone from Athens, where we might,
  Without the peril of the Athenian law—
EGE.   Enough, enough, my lord; you have enough!
  I beg the law, the law upon his head!
  They would have stolen away, they would,
    Demetrius,
  Thereby to have defeated you and me:
  You of your wife, and me of my consent,
  Of my consent that she should be your wife.
DEM.   My lord, fair Helen told me of their stealth,
  Of this their purpose hither to this wood;
  And I in fury hither followed them,
  Fair Helena in fancy following me.
  But my good lord, I know not by what power—
  But by some power it is—my love to Hermia,
  Melted as the snow, seems to me now
  As the remembrance of an idle toy
  Which in my childhood I did dote upon.

And all the faith, the virtue of my heart,
The object and the pleasure of my eye,
Is only Helena. To her, my lord,
Was I betrothed ere I saw Hermia;
But like a sickness did I loathe this food.
But as in health, come to my natural taste,
Now I do wish it, love it, long for it,
And will for evermore be true to it.

THE.   Fair lovers, you are fortunately met;
Of this discourse we more will hear anon.
Egeus, I will overbear your will;
For in the temple, by and by, with us,
These couples shall eternally be knit.
And, for the morning now is something worn,
Our purposed hunting shall be set aside.
Away, with us, to Athens: three and three,
We'll hold a feast in great solemnity.
Come, Hippolyta.

Exeunt Theseus, Hippolyta, Egeus, and Train.

DEM.   These things seem small and undistinguishable,
Like far-off mountains turned into clouds.

HER.   I think I see these things with parted eye,
When everything seems double.

HEL.   So it seems;
And I have found Demetrius like a jewel,
My own, and not my own.

DEM.   Are you sure
That we are awake? It seems to me
That yet we sleep, we dream. Do not you think
The Duke was here, and bid us follow him?

HER.   Yea, and my father.

HEL.   And Hippolyta.

LYS.   And he did bid us follow to the temple.

DEM.   Why then, we are awake: let's follow him,
And by the way let us recount our dreams. *Exeunt.*

BOT. [*Waking.*] When my cue comes, call me and I
will answer. My next is 'Most fair Pyramus'.
Heigh-ho! Peter Quince? Flute, the bellows-mender?
Snout, the tinker? Starveling? God's my life! Stolen
hence, and left me asleep! I have had a most rare
vision. I have had a dream, past the wit of man to
say what dream it was. Man is but an ass if he goes
about to expound this dream. I thought I was—
there is no man can tell what. I thought I was—and
I thought I had—but man is but a patched fool if he
will offer to say what I thought I had. The eye of
man has not heard, the ear of man has not seen,
man's hand is not able to taste, his tongue to
conceive, nor his heart to report, what my dream
was. I will get Peter Quince to write a ballad of this
dream: it shall be called 'Bottom's Dream', because
it has no bottom; and I will sing it in the latter end
of a play, before the Duke. Peradventure, to make
it the more gracious, I shall sing it at her death.

Exit.

SCENE II
A room in Quince's house.

Enter QUINCE, FLUTE, SNOUT, *and* STARVELING.

QUIN. Have you sent to Bottom's house? Has he
come home yet?
STAR. He cannot be heard of. Out of doubt he is
transported.
FLU. If he comes not, then the play is marred: it goes
not forward, does it?
QUIN. It is not possible. You have not a man in all
Athens able to discharge Pyramus but he.

FLU. No, he has simply the best wit of any handicraft
  man in Athens.

QUIN. Yea, and the best person too; and he is a very
  paramour for a sweet voice.

FLU. You must say paragon. A paramour is, God
  bless us, a thing of naught.

SNUG. Masters, the Duke is coming from the temple,
  and there are two or three lords and ladies more
  married. If our sport had gone forward, we had all
  been men.

FLU. O sweet bully Bottom! Thus has he lost sixpence a day during his life; he could not have
  escaped sixpence a day. If the Duke had not given
  him sixpence a day for playing Pyramus, I'll be
  hanged. He would have deserved it: sixpence a day
  in Pyramus, or nothing.

Enter BOTTOM.

BOT. Where are these lads? Where are these hearts?

QUIN. Bottom! O most courageous day! O most
  happy hour!

BOT. Masters, I am to discourse wonders: but ask
  me not what; for if I tell you, I am not true
  Athenian. I will tell you everything, right as it fell
  out.

QUIN. Let us hear, sweet Bottom.

BOT. Not a word of me. All that I will tell you is,
  that the Duke has dined. Get your apparel together,
  good strings to your beards, new ribbons to your
  pumps; meet presently at the palace; every man
  look over his part: for the short and the long is, our
  play is preferred. In any case, let Thisbe have clean
  linen; and let not him that plays the lion pare his
  nails, for they shall hang out for the lion's claws.

And most dear actors, eat no onions nor garlic, for
we are to utter sweet breath; and I do not doubt but
to hear them say, it is a sweet comedy. No more
words. Away! Go, away!   *Exeunt.*

Act V

SCENE I
The palace of Theseus.

Enter THESEUS, HIPPOLYTA; LORDS *and* Attendants,
among them PHILOSTRATE.

HIP. 'Tis strange, my Theseus, that these lovers
    speak of.
THE.   More strange than true. I never may believe
    These antique fables, nor these fairy toys.
    Lovers and madmen have such seething brains,
    Such shaping fantasies, that apprehend
    More than cool reason ever comprehends.
    The lunatic, the lover, and the poet
    Are of imagination all compact.
    One sees more devils than vast hell can hold;
    That is the madman. The lover, all as frantic,
    Sees Helen's beauty in a brow of Egypt.
    The poet's eye, in a fine frenzy rolling,
    Does glance from heaven to earth, from earth to
        heaven;
    And as imagination bodies forth

Helen of Troy oned oche - brow in Egypt
writer your own r not beautiful

The forms of things unknown, the poet's pen
Turns them to shapes, and gives to airy nothing
A local habitation and a name.
Such tricks has strong imaginatiòn,
That if it would but apprehend some joy,
It comprehends some bringer of that joy:
Or, in the night, imagining some fear,
How easy is a bush supposed a bear!

HIP.   But all the story of the night told over,
And all their minds transfigured so together,
More witnesses than fancy's images,
And grows to something of great constancy;
But howsoever, strange and admirable.

Enter the lovers: LYSANDER, DEMETRIUS, HERMIA,
              and HELENA.

THE.   Here come the lovers, full of joy and mirth.
Joy, gentle friends, joy and fresh days of love
Accompany your hearts!

LYS.   More than to us
Wait in your royal walks, your board, your bed!

THE.   Come now; what masques, what dances shall
   we have,
To wear away this long age of three hours
Between our after-supper and bed-time?
Where is our usual manager of mirth?
What revels are in hand? Is there no play
To ease the anguish of a torturing hour?
Call Philostrate.

PHIL.[*Advancing.*]   Here, mighty Theseus.

THE.   Say, what abridgement have you for this
   evening,
What masque, what music? How shall we beguile
The lazy time, if not with some delight?

PHIL.   There is a brief how many sports are ripe:
          Make choice of which your Highness will see first.
                                        [*Giving a paper.*]

THE.   [*Reads.*] 'The battle with the Centaurs, to be
          sung
          By an Athenian eunuch to the harp'?
          We'll none of that; that have I told my love
          In glory of my kinsman Hercules.
          [*Reads.*] 'The riot of the tipsy Bacchanals,
          Tearing the Thracian singer in their rage'?
          That is an old device, and it was played
          When I from Thebes came last a conqueror.
          [*Reads.*] 'The thrice three Muses mourning for the
          death
          Of learning, late deceased in beggary'?
          That is some satire, keen and critical,
          Not sorting with a nuptial ceremony.
          [*Reads.*] 'A tedious brief scene of young Pyramus
          And his love Thisbe, very tragical mirth'?
          Merry and tragical? Tedious and brief?
          That is hot ice, and wondrous strange snow!
          How shall we find the concord of this discord?

PHIL.   A play there is, my lord, some ten words long,
          Which is as brief as I have known a play;
          But by ten words, my lord, it is too long,
          Which makes it tedious; for in all the play
          There is not one word apt, one player fitted.
          And tragical, my noble lord, it is,
          For Pyramus therein does kill himself;
          Which, when I saw rehearsed, I must confess
          Made my eyes water; but more merry tears
          The passion of loud laughter never shed.

THE.   What are they that do play it?

PHIL.   Hard-handed men that work in Athens here,
   Who never laboured in their minds till now;
   And now have toiled their unbreathed memories
   With this same play, before your nuptiàls.
THE.   And we will hear it.
PHIL.   No, my noble lord,
   It is not for you: I have heard it over,
   And it is nothing, nothing in the world;
   Unless you can find sport in their intents,
   Extremely stretched and conned with cruel pain
   To do you service.
THE.   I will hear that play;
   For never anything can be amiss
   When simpleness and duty tender it.
   Go bring them in; and take your places, ladies.
                      [*Exit Philostrate.*]
HIP.   I love not to see wretchedness o'er-charged,
   And duty in its service perishing.
THE.   Why, gentle sweet, you shall see no such thing.
HIP.   He says they can do nothing in this kind.
THE.   The kinder we, to give them thanks for
   nothing.
   Our sport shall be to take what they mistake:
   And what poor duty cannot do, noble respect
   Takes it in might, not merit.
   Where I have come, great clerks have purposèd
   To greet me with premeditated welcomes;
   Where I have seen them shiver and look pale,
   Make periods in the midst of sentences,
   Throttle their practised accent in their fears,
   And, in conclusion, dumbly have broken off,
   Not paying me a welcome. Trust me, sweet,
   Out of this silence yet I picked a welcome,

And in the modesty of fearful duty
I read as much as from the rattling tongue
Of saucy and audacious eloquence.
Love, therefore, and tongue-tied simplicity
In least speak most, to my capacity.

[*Enter* PHILOSTRATE.]

PHIL.   So please your grace, the Prologue is addressed.
THE.   Let him approach.

Flourish of trumpets.

Enter QUINCE *for the* Prologue.

PRO.   *If we offend, it is with our good will.*
   That you should think, we come not to offend,
   But with good will. To show our simple skill,
   That is the true beginning of our end.
   Consider then, we come but in despite.
   We do not come, as minding to content you,
   Our true intent is. All for your delight,
   We are not here. That you should here repent you,
   The actors are at hand; and by their show,
   You shall know all, that you are like to know.
THE.   This fellow does not mind his points.
LYS.   He has ridden his prologue like a rough colt; he
   knows not the stop. A good moral, my lord: it is
   not enough to speak, but to speak true.
HIP.   Indeed he has played on this prologue like a
   child on a recorder; a sound, but not in
   government..
THE.   His speech was like a tangled chain; nothing
   impaired, but all disordered. Who is next?

Enter, with a Trumpeter before them, BOTTOM *as*
PYRAMUS *and* FLUTE *as* THISBE, *and* SNOUT *as* WALL, *and*
STARVELING *as* MOONSHINE, *and* SNUG *as* LION.

PRO.   *Gentles, perchance you wonder at this show;*
  But wonder on, till truth makes all things plain.
  This man is Pyramus, if you would know;
  This beauteous lady Thisbe is certain.
  This man, with lime and rough-cast, does present
  Wall, that vile wall which did these lovers sunder;
  And through Wall's chink, poor souls, they are
    content
  To whisper. At the which let no man wonder.
  This man, with lantern, dog, and bush of thorn,
  Presents now Moonshine; for, if you will know,
  By moonshine did these lovers think no scorn
  To meet at Ninus' tomb, there, there to woo.
  This grisly beast, which Lion hight by name,
  The trusty Thisbe, coming first by night,
  Did scare away, or rather did affright;
  And as she fled, her mantle she let fall,
  Which Lion vile with bloody mouth did stain.
  Anon comes Pyramus, sweet youth and tall,
  And finds his trusty Thisbe's mantle slain.
  Whereat with blade, with bloody blameful blade,
  He bravely broached his boiling bloody breast;
  And Thisbe, tarrying in mulberry shade,
  His dagger drew, and died. For all the rest,
  Let Lion, Moonshine, Wall, and lovers twain
  At large discourse, while here they do remain.
          Exeunt Prologue, Pyramus, Thisbe, Lion,
                      and Moonshine.

THE.   I wonder if the lion is to speak?

DEM.   No wonder, my lord; one lion may when many
  asses do.

WALL.   *In this same interlude it does befall*
    That I, one Snout by name, present a wall;
    And such a wall as I would have you think
    That had in it a crannied hole, or chink,
    Through which the lovers, Pyramus and Thisbe,
    Did whisper often, very secretly.
    This loam, this rough-cast, and this stone do show
    That I am that same wall; the truth is so:
    And this the cranny is, right and sinister,
    Through which the fearful lovers are to whisper.
THE.   Would you desire lime and hair to speak better?
DEM.   It is the wittiest partition that ever I heard dis-
    course, my lord.

                    Enter PYRAMUS.

THE.   Pyramus draws near the wall; silence!
PYR.   *O grim-looked night! O night with hue so*
       black!
    O night, which ever are when day is not!
    O night, O night, alack, alack, alack,
    I fear my Thisbe's promise is forgot!
    And you, O wall, O sweet, O lovely wall,
    That stand between her father's ground and mine;
    You wall, O wall, O sweet and lovely wall,
    Show me your chink, to blink through with mine
       eyne [eyes].
                        [*Wall stretches out his fingers.*]
    Thanks, courteous wall: Jove shield you well for
       this!
    But what see I? No Thisbe do I see.
    O wicked wall, through whom I see no bliss,
    Cursed by your stones for thus deceiving me!
THE.   The wall, it seems, being sensible, should curse
    again.

PYR.   No, in truth sir, he should not. 'Deceiving me'
is Thisbe's cue: she is to enter now, and I am to
spy her through the wall. You shall see it will fall
pat as I told you: yonder she comes.

Enter THISBE.

THIS.   *O wall, full often have you heard my moans,*
For parting my fair Pyramus and me!
My cherry lips have often kissed your stones,
Your stones with lime and hair knit up in thee.
PYR.   *I see a voice; now will I to the chink,*
To spy and I can hear my Thisbe's face.
Thisbe?
THIS.   *My love you are, my love I think!*
PYR.   *Think what you will, I am your lover's grace;*
And like Limander [Leander] am I trusty still.
THIS.   *And I like Helen, till the Fates me kill.*
PYR.   *Not Shafalus [Cephalus] to Procrus [Procris]*
was so true.
THIS.   *As Shafalus to Procrus, I to you.*
PYR.   *O kiss me through the hole of this vile wall.*
THIS.   *I kiss the wall's hole, not your lips at all.*
PYR.   *Will you at Ninny's tomb meet me*
straightway?
THIS.   *'Come life, come death, I come without delay.*
                    Exeunt Pyramus and Thisbe, severally.
WALL.   *Thus have I, Wall, my part dischargèd so;*
And, being done, thus Wall away does go.
THE.   Now is the mure rased between the two
neighbours.
DEM.   No remedy my lord, when walls are so wilful
to hear without warning.
HIP.   This is the silliest stuff that ever I heard.
THE.   The best in this kind are but shadows; and the
worst are no worse, if imagination amends them.

HIP.   It must be your imagination then, and not theirs.

THE.   If we imagine no worse of them than they of
  themselves, they may pass for excellent men. Here
  come two noble beasts in, a man and a lion.

Enter LION *and* MOONSHINE.

LION.   *You ladies, you whose gentle hearts do fear*
  The smallest monstrous mouse that creeps on floor,
  May now, perchance, both quake and tremble here,
  When lion rough in wildest rage does roar.
  Then know that I as Snug the joiner am
  A lion fierce, nor else no lion's dam;
  For if I should as lion come in strife
  Into this place, 'twere pity on my life.

THE.   A very gentle beast, and of a good conscience.

DEM.   The very best at a beast, my lord, that ever I
  saw.

LYS.   This lion is a very fox for his valour.

THE.   True; and a goose for his discretion.

DEM.   Not so, my lord, for his valour cannot carry his
  discretion; and the fox carries the goose.

THE.   His discretion, I am sure, cannot carry his
  valour; for the goose carries not the fox. It is well:
  leave it to his discretion, and let us listen to the
  moon.

MOON.   *This lantern does the hornèd moon present—*

DEM.   He should have worn the horns on his head.

THE.   He is no crescent, and his horns are invisible
  within the circumference.

MOON.   *This lantern does the hornèd moon present;*
  Myself the Man in the Moon do seem to be.

THE.   This is the greatest error of all the rest; the
  man should be put into the lantern. How is it else
  the Man in the Moon?

DEM.   He dares not come there for the candle; for you
   see it already needs snuffing.
HIP.   I am aweary of this moon. Would he would
   change!
THE.   It appears by his small light of discretion that
   he is in the wane; but yet in courtesy, in all reason,
   we must stay the time.
LYS.   Proceed, Moon.
MOON.   All that I have to say is, to tell you that the
   lantern is the moon; I the Man in the Moon; this
   thorn-bush my thorn-bush; and this dog my dog.
DEM.   Why, all these should be in the lantern, for all
   these are in the moon. But silence: here comes
   Thisbe.

Enter THISBE.

THIS.   *This is old Ninny's tomb. Where is my love?*
LION.   *O—!*   *The Lion roars. Thisbe, dropping*
                                    her mantle, runs off.
DEM.   Well roared, Lion!
THE.   Well run, Thisbe!
HIP.   Well shone, Moon! Truly, the moon shines
   with a good grace.
                     The Lion worries the mantle, and exit.
THE.   Well moused, Lion!
DEM.   And then came Pyramus—
LYS.   And so the lion vanished.

Enter PYRAMUS.

PYR.   *Sweet Moon, I thank you for your sunny*
      beams;
   I thank you, Moon, for shining now so bright;

For by your gracious, golden, glittering gleams,
I trust to take of truest Thisbe sight.
    But stay! O spite!
    But mark, poor knight,
   What dreadful dole is here⸮
    Eyes, do you see⸮
    How can it be⸮
   O dainty duck! O dear!
    Your mantle good,
    What! Stained with blood⸮
  Approach, you Furies fell [fierce].
   O Fates, come, come!
   Cut thread and thrum:
  Quail, crush, conclude, and quell.

THE. This passion, and the death of a dear friend,
 would go near to make a man look sad.

HIP. Bless my heart, but I pity the man.

PYR. O wherefore, Nature, did you lions frame,
 Since lion vile has here deflowered my dear⸮
 Which is—no, no—which was the fairest dame
 That lived, that loved, that liked, that looked with
  cheer.
    Come tears, confound!
    Out sword, and wound
   The pap of Pyramus;
    Ay, that left pap,
    Where heart does hop:
       [Stabs himself.]
   Thus die I, thus, thus, thus!
    Now am I dead,
    Now am I fled;
   My soul is in the sky.
    Tongue, lose your light;
    Moon, take your flight!
     [Exit Moonshine.]
  Now die, die, die, die, die. [Dies.]

DEM.   No die, but an ace for him; for he is but one.

LYS.   Less than an ace, man; for he is dead, he is
nothing.

THE.   With the help of a surgeon he might yet
recover, and prove an ass.

HIP.   How chance Moonshine is gone, before Thisbe
comes back and finds her lover?

THE.   She will find him by starlight.

Enter THISBE.

Here she comes, and her passion ends the play.

HIP.   I think she should not use a long one for such a
Pyramus; I hope she will be brief.

DEM.   A mote will turn the balance, which Pyramus,
which Thisbe, is the better: he for a man, God warrant us: she for a woman, God bless us!

LYS.   She has spied him already with those sweet
eyes.

DEM.   And thus she means, so to say—

THIS: *Asleep, my love?*
                          What, dead, my dove?
                  O Pyramus, arise!
                          Speak, speak! Quite dumb?
                          Dead, dead? A tomb
          Must cover your sweet eyes.
                          These lily lips,
                          This cherry nose,
          These yellow cowslip cheeks,
                          Are gone, are gone!
                          Lovers, make moan;
          His eyes were green as leeks.
                          O Sisters Three,
                          Come, come to me,
          With hands as pale as milk;
                          Lay them in gore,

> *Since you have shore*
> [shorn]
> *With shears his thread of silk.*
> *Tongue, not a word:*
> *Come, trusty sword,*
> *Come, blade, my breast imbrue* [pierce]!
> [*Stabs herself.*]
> *And farewell, friends;*
> *Thus Thisbe ends:*
> *Adieu, adieu, adieu!*   [*Dies.*]

THE. Moonshine and Lion are left to bury the dead.

DEM. Ay, and Wall too.

BOT. [*Starting up.*] No, I assure you; the wall is
down that parted their fathers. [*Flute rises.*] Will it
please you to see the epilogue, or to hear a
Bergomask dance between two of our company?

THE.   No epilogue, I pray you; for your play needs no
excuse. Never excuse; for when the players are all
dead, there need none to be blamed. Indeed, if he
that wrote it had played Pyramus, and hanged
himself in Thisbe's garter, it would have been a
fine tragedy. And so it is, truly, and very notably
discharged. But come, your Bergomask; let your
epilogue alone.

[*Enter* QUINCE, SNUG, SNOUT, *and* STARVELING, *two of
whom dance a Bergamask. Then exeunt
handicraftsmen, including Flute and Bottom.*]

The iron tongue of midnight has told twelve.
Lovers, to bed; 'tis almost fairy time.
I fear we shall outsleep the coming morn
As much as we this night have overwatched.
This palpable-gross play has well beguiled

The heavy gait of night. Sweet friends, to bed.
A fortnight hold we this solemnity
In nightly revels and new jollity.   *Exeunt.*

Enter PUCK.

PUCK.   Now the hungry lion roars,
                      And the wolf howls at the moon;
                      While the heavy ploughman snores,
                      All with weary task fordone.
                      Now the wasted brands do glow,
                      While the screech-owl, screeching
                        loud,
                      Puts the wretch that lies in woe
                      In remembrance of a shroud.
                      Now it is the time of night
                      That the graves, all gaping wide,
                      Every one lets forth his sprite
                      In the church-way paths to glide.
                      And we fairies, that do run
                      By the triple Hecate's team
                      From the presence of the sun,
                      Following darkness like a dream,
                      Now are frolic; not a mouse
                      Shall disturb this hallowed house.
                      I am sent with broom before
                      To sweep the dust behind the door.

Enter OBERON *and* TITANIA *the King and Queen of*
Fairies, with all their Train.

OBE.   Through the house give glimmering
                      light
                      By the dead and drowsy fire;

Every elf and fairy sprite
Hop as light as bird from briar;
And this ditty after me
Sing, and dance it trippingly.

TITA. First rehearse your song by rote,
To each word a warbling note;
Hand in hand, with fairy grace,
Will we sing, and bless this place.

[*Oberon leading, the Fairies sing and dance.*]

OBE. Now, until the break of day,
Through this house each fairy stray.
To the best bride-bed will we,
Which by us shall blessèd be;
And the issue there create
Ever shall be fortunate.
So shall all the couples three
Ever true in loving be;
And the blots of Nature's hand
Shall not in their issue stand:
Never mole, hare-lip, nor scar,
Nor mark prodigious, such as are
Despisèd in nativity,
Shall upon their children be.
With this field-dew consecrate,
Every fairy take his gait,
And each several chamber bless
Through this palace with sweet
     peace;
And the owner of it blest,
Ever shall in safety rest.
Trip away; make no stay;
Meet me all by break of day.

[*Exeunt all but Puck*].

PUCK.   [*To the audience*.] If we shadows have offended,
                    Think but this, and all is mended,
                    That you have but slumbered here
                    While these visions did appear.
                    And this weak and idle theme,
                    No more yielding but a dream,
                    Gentles, do not reprehend:
                    If you pardon, we will mend.
                    And, as I am an honest Puck,
                    If we have unearnèd luck
                    Now to escape the serpent's tongue,
                    We will make amends ere long;
                    Else the Puck a liar call.
                    So, goodnight unto you all.
                    Give me your hands, if we be
                       friends,
                    And Robin shall restore amends.
                                                    [*Exit.*]

                         FINIS

Romeo and Juliet

INTRODUCTION

Many indications make it clear that *Romeo and Juliet* belongs to the period of Shakespeare's Sonnets, and to the latter end of it, 1594. For one thing, three passages of the play are in sonnet-form. There are several echoes from the themes and wording of the Sonnets: that of sworn chastity being such a waste. Of Romeo's first love, Rosaline, who is unresponsive: 'when she dies, with beauty dies her store', and

> in that sparing makes huge waste;
> For beauty, starved with her severity,
> Cuts beauty off from all posterity.

This is followed also by the Dark Lady theme:

> Being black puts us in mind they hide the fair.

We hear again of summers that 'wither in their pride.'

The two-year-long plague of 1592 and 1593, which had such decisive effects in the theatre world and on Shakespeare's career, is not only in the background but is put to use to determine the *dénouement* of this play. It brought about the final disaster. Friar Laurence sent a letter by Friar John to Romeo, telling him of the drug from which Juliet was in a trance in the Capulets' tomb and bidding him back to take her away when she awoke, to Mantua and safety. But Friar John was shut up on account of the plague and could not deliver it,

> Nor get a messenger to bring it you,
> So fearful were they of infectiòn.

What turned Shakespeare's mind at this time to a story of family feud, and to choose a love-story which was placed against that background?

Down at Titchfield his patron, Southampton, was close friends with his Wiltshire neighbours, young Charles and Henry Danvers. The Danvers family of Dauntsey were at bitter feud with the Longs of Wraxall. In an affray at Corsham on 4 October 1594 Southampton's particular friend, Henry Danvers, killed the son and heir of the house of Wraxall. The two brothers then fled; Southampton sheltering them at Titchfield until they could make their get-away across Channel to Henry of Navarre. In the hue-and-cry after them, 'Signor Florio, an Italian', threatened to throw the sheriff on the ferry across the Itchen overboard. Florio, as Southampton's resident Italian tutor, was well known to Shakespeare, who might have got scraps of Italian from him, as well as the reference to Petrarch.

In the play Lady Capulet is vengeful and drives on the charge against Romeo for killing her cousin Tybalt. It may not be relevant, though Shakespeare may have known, what Aubrey tells us about the mother of the Danvers brothers. He says that Lady Danvers was 'an Italian'—he means that she was Italianate, 'of great wit and spirit, but revengeful.' And it is no less interesting that, to obtain her sons' pardon, she married a son of Lord Chamberlain Hunsdon, the Queen's cousin, patron of Shakespeare's Company. These things connect up.

We need not doubt, what many have thought, that there are touches of Marlowe in Mercutio. The love of women was not for Mercutio any more than it had been for Marlowe: he is a devotee of friendship between men. When Romeo is 'stabbed with a white wench's black eye', Mercutio takes to his truckle-bed. And he was just as much of a quarreller, involved in several affrays, as Mercutio, of whom Benvolio says: 'If I were so apt to quarrel as you are, any man should buy the fee-simple [i.e. freehold] of my life for an hour and a quarter.' Marlowe held his life no less cheaply. But it is right that Mercutio is given the finest poetry in the play, the extended passage about Queen Mab and the fairies, which comes straight from Warwickshire folklore:

> She is the fairies' midwife, and she comes
> In shape no bigger than an agate stone
> On the forefinger of an alderman.

Do we need reminding that Shakespeare's father was an alderman at Stratford?

Again Juliet's poetic rhetoric—

> Gallop apace, you fiery-footed steeds,
> Towards Phoebus' lodging—

all very much in Marlowe's rapturous manner, actually echoes a passage from his last play, *Edward II*. Lady Capulet's lament over Juliet, thinking her dead, is an echo from Kyd. They were thrown together in the early theatre, before the decisive event of the formation of the Lord Chamberlain's company in 1594. Almost every work of Shakespeare has a reference to his profession; here, for example,

> We'll have no Cupid hoodwinked [blindfolded]
>   with a scarf,
> Bearing a Tartar's painted bow of lath . . .
> And no without-book prologue, faintly spoken
> After the prompter, for our entrance.

The tragic love story of Romeo and Juliet was well known in various forms in Renaissance Italy, where it was told by the novelists, da Porto and Bandello; popular also in Elizabethan England, where Shakespeare could have read it in prose in Painter's *Palace of Pleasure*. However, Professor Geoffrey Bullough—who agrees with the above dating and the play's relation to the Sonnets period—points out that Shakespeare got all he needed from Arthur Brooke's 'leaden' poem, *The Tragical History of Romeus and Juliet*, with its homely realism and attention to detail. These Shakespeare fastened on to and caught up with his winged imagination. He found the subject 'well laid out and ready for quick dramatisation'— which is what he always sought; but 'the surprising thing is that Shakespeare preserved so much of his source in vitalising its dead stuff.'

Mercutio, for example, in only the first half of the play emerges a three-dimensional character. Even more so the Nurse, who is given an original development all her own—one of the most memorable parts in all Shakespeare, a marvellous opportunity for a great actress: loyalty and devotion, constancy and inconstancy, down to earth, no illusions about men, a bit of a cynic, much of a bawd. The bawdiness of the play, enjoyable as it is, has a double character: there is that of the young bachelors among themselves, and that of the old baggage in the Nurse.

No less humorous are the parts of the serving-men in the Capulets' mansion: from the first Shakespeare had an observant eye for comic effects among the lower orders and rendering their speech. But now we observe his increased familiarity with the way of life in great houses—always open to an actor, but rendered more intimate from acquaintance with Southampton House and Titchfield.

Romeo and Juliet is notable too for the much greater part played by music. A whole scene is given to the musicians engaged by Count Paris for his expected marriage to Juliet; famous Elizabethan songs or tunes occur—'Heart's ease' and 'Fortune, my foe', that haunting refrain. 'When griping grief the heart does wound' was written by Richard Edwards, Master of the Children of the Chapel, who produced their plays. We learn that the part of the Nurse's man, Peter, was played by the comic star of the Company, Will Kemp.

We have a telling description of a charnel house—at Stratford there existed one prominent along the churchway to Holy Trinity. And it is pleasant to be reminded by the glover-alderman's son of 'cheveril', the softest kidskin, of which gloves were made.

CHARACTERS

Chorus

ESCALUS, Prince of Verona

PARIS, a young count, kinsman to the Prince

MONTAGUE Romeos Father

CAPULET Juliet's Father

ROMEO, son to Montague

MERCUTIO, kinsman to the Prince, friend to Romeo

BENVOLIO. nephew to Montague, friend to Romeo

TYBALT, nephew to Lady Capulet

FRIAR LAURENCE } Franciscans
FRIAR JOHN

BALTHASAR, servant to Romeo

ABRAM, servant to Montague

SAMPSON } servants to Capulet
GREGORY

PETER, servant to Juliet's nurse

An old Man of the Capulets

LADY MONTAGUE, wife to Montague

LADY CAPULET, wife to Capulet

JULIET, daughter to Capulet

NURSE to Juliet

An Apothecary

Three Musicians

An Officer

Citizens of Verona, Gentlemen and Gentlewomen of
both houses, Maskers, Torchbearers, Pages,
Guards, Watchmen, Servants, and Attendants

Scene: Verona, Mantua

THE PROLOGUE

Enter Chorus

CHORUS
  Two households, both alike in dignity,
    In fair Verona, where we lay our scene,
  From ancient grudge break to new mutiny,
    Where civil blood makes civil hands unclean.
  From forth the fatal loins of these two foes
    A pair of star-crossed lovers take their life;
  Whose misadventured piteous overthrows
    Do with their death bury their parents' strife.
  The fearful passage of their death-marked love,
    And the continuance of their parents' rage,
  Which, but their children's end, naught could
      remove,
    Is now the two hours' traffic of our stage;
  Which, if you with patient ears attend,
  What here shall miss, our toil shall strive to mend.

                                        Exit

Act I

SCENE I
A street in Verona

Enter SAMPSON *and* GREGORY, *with swords and*
bucklers, of the house of CAPULET.

SAMPSON Gregory, on my word, we'll not carry coals.
GREGORY No, for then we would be colliers.

SAMPSON   I mean, if we are in choler, we'll draw.

GREGORY   Ay, while you live, draw your neck out of
collar.

SAMPSON   I strike quickly, being moved.

GREGORY   But you are not quickly moved to strike.

SAMPSON   A dog of the house of Montague moves me.

GREGORY   To move is to stir, and to be valiant is to
stand. Therefore, if you are moved, you run away.

SAMPSON   A dog of that house shall move me to
stand. I will take the wall of any man or maid of
Montague's.

GREGORY   That shows you a weak slave; for the
weakest goes to the wall.

SAMPSON   'Tis true; and therefore women, being the
weaker vessels, are ever thrust to the wall.
Therefore I will push Montague's men from the
wall and thrust his maids to the wall.

GREGORY   The quarrel is between our masters, and us
their men.

SAMPSON   It is all one. I will show myself a tyrant.
When I have fought with the men, I will be cruel
with the maids—I will cut off their heads.

GREGORY   The heads of the maids?

SAMPSON   Ay, the heads of the maids, or their
maidenheads. Take it in what sense you will.

GREGORY   They must take it in sense that feel it.

SAMPSON   Me they shall feel while I am able to stand;
and 'tis known I am a pretty piece of flesh.

GREGORY   'Tis well you are not fish; if you had, you
had been codfish. Draw your tool! Here come two
of the house of Montagues.

Enter two other Servingmen [ABRAM *and* BALTHASAR].

SAMPSON   My naked weapon is out. Quarrel! I will
back you.

GREGORY   How? Turn your back and run?
SAMPSON   Fear me not.
GREGORY   No, sure. I fear you!
SAMPSON   Let us take the law of our sides; let them
   begin.
GREGORY   I will frown as I pass by, and let them take
   it as they list.
SAMPSON   Nay, as they dare. I will bite my thumb at
   them, which is disgrace to them if they bear it.
ABRAM   Do you bite your thumb at us, sir?
SAMPSON   I do bite my thumb, sir.
ABRAM   Do you bite your thumb at us, sir?
SAMPSON   [aside to Gregory] Is the law of our side if I
   say ay?
GREGORY   [aside to Sampson] No.
SAMPSON   No, sir, I do not bite my thumb at you, sir;
   but I bite my thumb, sir.
GREGORY   Do you quarrel, sir?
ABRAM   Quarrel, sir? No, sir.
SAMPSON   But if you do, sir, I am for you. I serve as
   good a man as you.
ABRAM   No better.
SAMPSON   Well, sir.

Enter BENVOLIO. *nephew matague*

GREGORY   [aside to Sampson] Say 'better.' Here
   comes one of my master's kinsmen.
SAMPSON   Yes, better, sir.
ABRAM   You lie.
SAMPSON   Draw, if you are men. Gregory, remember
   your smashing blow.

They fight.

BENVOLIO   Part, fools!
Put up your swords. You know not what you do.

Enter TYBALT. *nephew to Capulet*

TYBALT
What, are you drawn among these heartless hinds?
Turn you, Benvolio! look upon your death.
BENVOLIO
I do but keep the peace. Put up your sword,
Or manage it to part these men with me.
TYBALT
What, drawn, and talk of peace? I hate the word
As I hate hell, all Montagues, and you.
Have at you, coward!

They fight.
Enter an Officer, *and three or four* Citizens *with clubs or partisans.*

OFFICER   Clubs, bills, and partisans! Strike! beat them
down.
CITIZENS   Down with the Capulets! Down with the
Montagues!   *Town tired of their continuos fighting.*

Enter CAPULET *in his gown, and his* Wife.

CAPULET
What noise is this? Give me my long sword, ho!
LADY CAPULET
A crutch, a crutch! Why call you for a sword?
CAPULET
My sword, I say! Old Montague is come
And flourishes his blade in spite of me.

Enter MONTAGUE *and his* Wife.

MONTAGUE
  You villain Capulet!—Hold me not, let me go.
LADY MONTAGUE
  You shall not stir one foot to seek a foe.

Enter PRINCE ESCALUS, *with his* Train.

PRINCE
  Rebellious subjects, enemies to peace,
    Profaners of this neighbor-stained steel—
    Will they not hear? What, ho! you men, you beasts,
    That quench the fire of your pernicious rage
    With purple fountains issuing from your veins!
    On pain of torture, from those bloody hands
    Throw your mistempered weapons to the ground
    And hear the sentence of your movèd prince.
    Three civil brawls, bred of an airy word
    By you, old Capulet, and Montague,
    Have thrice disturbed the quiet of our streets
    And made Verona's ancient citizens
    Cast by their grave beseeming ornaments
    To wield old weaponry, in hands as old,
    Cankered with peace, to part your cankered hate.
    If ever you disturb our streets again,
    Your lives shall pay the forfeit of the peace.
    For this time all the rest depart away.
    You, Capulet, shall go along with me;
    And, Montague, come you this afternoon,
    To know our farther pleasure in this case,
    To old Freetown, our common judgment place.
    Once more, on pain of death, all men depart.
        Exeunt all but Montague, his Wife, and Benvolio.

MONTAGUE
    Who set this ancient quarrel new abroad?
    Speak, nephew, were you by when it began?
BENVOLIO
    Here were the servants of your adversary
    And yours, close fighting ere I did approach.
    I drew to part them. In the instant came
    The fiery Tybalt, with his sword prepared;
    Which, as he breathed defiance to my ears,
    He swung about his head and cut the winds,
    Which nothing hurt with it, hissed him in scorn.
    While we were interchanging thrusts and blows,
    Came more and more, and fought on part and part,
    Till the Prince came, who parted either part.

LADY MONTAGUE
    O, where is Romeo? Saw you him to-day?
    Right glad I am he was not at this fray.
BENVOLIO
    Madam, an hour before the worshipped sun
    Peered forth the golden window of the East,
    A troubled mind drove me to walk abroad;
    Where, underneath the grove of sycamore
    That westward roots along this city side,
    So early walking did I see your son.
    Towards him I made, but he was wary of me
    And stole into the covert of the wood.
    I, measuring his affections by my own,
    Which then most sought where most might not be
        found,
    Being one too many by my weary self,
    Pursued my humor, not pursuing his,
    And gladly shunned, who gladly fled from me.
MONTAGUE
    Many a morning has he there been seen,
    With tears augmenting the fresh morning's dew,
    Adding to clouds more clouds with his deep sighs.

But all so soon as the all-cheering sun
Should in the farthest East begin to draw
The shady curtains from Aurora's bed,
Away from light steals home my heavy son
And private in his chamber pens himself,
Shuts up his windows, locks fair daylight out,
And makes himself an artificial night.
Black and portentous must this humor prove
Unless good counsel may the cause remove.

BENVOLIO
My noble uncle, do you know the cause?

MONTAGUE
I neither know it nor can learn of him.

BENVOLIO
Have you importuned him by any means?

MONTAGUE
Both by myself and many other friends;
But he, his own affections' counsellor,
Is to himself—I will not say how true—
But to himself so secret and so close,
So far from sounding and discovery,
As is the bud bitten by envious worm
Ere it can spread its sweet leaves to the air
Or dedicate its beauty to the sun.
Could we but learn from whence his sorrows grow,
We would as willingly give cure as know.

Enter ROMEO.

BENVOLIO
See, where he comes. So please you step aside,
I'll know his grievance, or be much denied.

MONTAGUE
I would you were so happy by your stay
To hear the truth. Come, madam, let's away.
Exeunt Montague and Wife.

BENVOLIO
Good morrow, cousin.

ROMEO   Is the day so young?

BENVOLIO
But new struck nine.

ROMEO   Ay, me! sad hours seem long.
Was that my father that went hence so fast?

BENVOLIO
It was. What sadness lengthens Romeo's hours?

ROMEO
Not having that which having makes them short.

BENVOLIO   In love?

ROMEO   Out—

BENVOLIO   Of love?

ROMEO
Out of her favor where I am in love.

BENVOLIO
Alas that love, so gentle in its view,
Should be so tyrannous and rough in proof!

ROMEO
Alas that love, whose view is muffled still,
Should without eyes see pathways to its will!
Where shall we dine? O me! What fray was here?
Yet tell me not, for I have heard it all.
Here's much to do with hate, but more with love.
Why then, O brawling love, O loving hate,
O anything, of nothing first create!
O heavy lightness, serious vanity,
Misshapen chaos of well-seeming forms,
Feather of lead, bright smoke, cold fire, sick health,
Still-waking sleep, that is not what it is!
This love feel I, that feel no love in this.
Do you not laugh?

BENVOLIO   No, cousin, I rather weep.
ROMEO
  Good heart, at what?
BENVOLIO   At your good heart's oppression.
ROMEO
  Why, such is love's transgression.
  Griefs of my own lie heavy in my breast,
  Which you will propagate, to have it prest
  With more of yours. This love that you have shown
  Does add more grief to too much of my own.
  Love is a smoke raised with the fume of sighs;
  Being purged, a fire sparkling in lovers' eyes;
  Being vexed, a sea nourished with lovers' tears.
  What is it else? A madness most discreet,
  A choking gall, and a preserving sweet.
  Farewell, my cousin.
BENVOLIO   Soft! I will go along.
  For if you leave me so, you do me wrong.
ROMEO
  Tut! I have lost myself; I am not here;
  This is not Romeo, he's some other where.
BENVOLIO
  Tell me in sadness, who is that you love?
ROMEO
  What, shall I groan and tell you?
BENVOLIO   Groan? Why, no;
  But sadly tell me who.
ROMEO
  Bid a sick man in sadness make his will.
  Ah, word ill urged to one that is so ill!
  In sadness, cousin, I do love a woman.
BENVOLIO
  I aimed so near when I supposed you loved.

ROMEO

A right good markman. And she's fair I love.

BENVOLIO

A right fair mark, fair cousin, is soonest hit.

ROMEO

Well, in that hit you miss. She'll not be hit
With Cupid's arrow. She has Dian's wit,
And, in strong proof of chastity well armed,
From Love's weak childish bow she lives
     uncharmed.
She will not stay the siege of loving terms,
Nor bide the encounter of assailing eyes,
Nor open her lap to saint-seducing gold.
O, she is rich in beauty; only poor
That, when she dies, with beauty dies her store.

BENVOLIO

Then she has sworn that she will ever live chaste?

ROMEO

She has, and in that sparing makes huge waste;
For beauty, starved with her severity,
Cuts beauty off from all posterity.
She is too fair, too wise, wisely too fair,
To merit bliss by making me despair.
She has forsworn to love, and in that vow
Do I live dead that live to tell it now.

BENVOLIO

Be ruled by me; forget to think of her.

ROMEO

O, teach me how I should forget to think!

BENVOLIO

By giving liberty unto your eyes.
Examine other beauties.

ROMEO   It is the way
To call hers—exquisite— in question more.
These happy masks that kiss fair ladies' brows,

Being black puts us in mind they hide the fair.
He that is struck blind cannot forget
The precious treasure of his eyesight lost.
Show me a mistress that is passing fair,
What does her beauty serve but as a note
Where I may read who passed that passing fair?
Farewell. You can not teach me to forget.

BENVOLIO

I'll pay that doctrine, or else die in debt.   *Exeunt.*

SCENE II
The same.

Enter CAPULET, COUNT PARIS, *and a* Servant.

CAPULET

But Montague is bound as well as I,
In penalty alike; it is not hard, I think,
For men so old as we to keep the peace.

PARIS

Of honorable reckoning are you both,
And pity 'tis you lived at odds so long.
But now, my lord, what say you to my suit?

CAPULET

But saying over what I have said before:
My child is yet a stranger in the world,
She has not seen the change of fourteen years;
Let two more summers wither in their pride
Ere we may think her ripe to be a bride.

PARIS

Younger than she are happy mothers made.

CAPULET

And too soon marred are those so early made.
Earth has swallowed all my hopes but she;

She is the hopeful lady of my earth.
But woo her, gentle Paris, get her heart;
My will to her consent is but a part.
If she agrees within her scope of choice
Lies my consent and fair according voice.
This night I hold an old accustomed feast,
Whereto I have invited many a guest,
Such as I love; and you among the store,
One more, most welcome, makes my number more.
At my poor house look to behold this night
Earth-treading stars that make dark heaven light.
Such comfort as do lusty young men feel
When well-apparelled April on the heel
Of limping Winter treads, even such delight
Among fresh fennel buds shall you this night
Inherit at my house. Hear all, all see,
And like her most whose merit most shall be;
Which, on more view of many, mine, being one,
May stand in number, though in reckoning none.
Come, go with me.

To Servant, *giving him a paper*

                    Go, fellow, trudge about
Through fair Verona; find those persons out
Whose names are written there, and to them say,
My house and welcome on their pleasure stay.
                              Exit with Paris.
SERVANT   Find them out whose names are written
    here? It is written that the shoemaker should
    meddle with his yard and the tailor with his last,
    the fisher with his pencil and the painter with his
    nets; but I am sent to find those persons whose
    names are here written and can never find what

names the writing person has here written. I must
to the learned. In good time!

Enter BENVOLIO *and* ROMEO.

BENVOLIO
Tut, man, one fire burns out another's burning;
   One pain is lessened by another's anguish;
Turn giddy, and be helped by backward turning;
   One desperate grief cures with another's languish.
Take you some new infection to your eye,
And the rank poison of the old will die.
ROMEO
Your plantain leaf is excellent for that.
BENVOLIO
For what, I pray you?
ROMEO   For your broken shin.
BENVOLIO
Why, Romeo, are you mad?
ROMEO
Not mad, but bound more than a madman is;
Shut up in prison, kept without my food,
Whipped and tormented and—Good-even, good
   fellow.
SERVANT   God give good even. I pray, sir, can you
   read?
ROMEO
Ay, my own fortune in my misery.
SERVANT   Perhaps you have learned it without book.
But I pray, can you read anything you see?
ROMEO
Ay, if I know the letters and the language.
SERVANT   You say honestly. Rest you merry.
ROMEO   Stay, fellow; I can read.

He reads the letter.

'Signior Martino and his wife and daughters;
Count Anselmo and his beauteous sisters;
The lady widow of Vitruvio;
Signior Placentio and his lovely nieces;
Mercutio and his brother Valentine;
My uncle Capulet, his wife, and daughters;
My fair niece Rosaline and Livia;
Signior Valentio and his cousin Tybalt;
Lucio and the lively Helena.'
A fair assembly. Whither should they come?
SERVANT   Up.
ROMEO   Whither? To supper?
SERVANT   To our house.
ROMEO   Whose house?
SERVANT   My master's.
ROMEO
Indeed I should have asked you that before.
SERVANT   Now I'll tell you without asking. My
master is the great rich Capulet; and if you are not
of the house of Montagues, I pray come and crush a
cup of wine. Rest you merry.   *Exit.*
BENVOLIO
At this same ancient feast of Capulet's
Sups the fair Rosaline whom you so love;
With all the admirèd beauties of Verona.
Go thither, and with unattainted eye
Compare her face with some that I shall show,
And I will make you think your swan a crow.
ROMEO
When the devout religion of my eye
    Maintains such falsehood, then turn tears to fires;
And these who, often drowned, could never die,
    Transparent heretics, be burnt for liars!
One fairer than my love? The all-seeing sun
    Never saw her match since first the world begun.

BENVOLIO

Tut! you saw her fair, none else being by,
Herself poised with herself in either eye;
But in that crystal scales let there be weighed
Your lady's love against some other maid
That I will show you shining at this feast,
And she shall scant show well that now seems best.

ROMEO

I'll go along, no such sight to be shown,
But to rejoice in splendor of my own.   *Exeunt.*

SCENE III
Verona. Capulet's house.

Enter CAPULET'S Wife, *and* NURSE.

LADY CAPULET

Nurse, where's my daughter? Call her forth to me.

NURSE

Now, by my maidenhead at twelve year old,
I bade her come. What, lamb! what, ladybird!
God forbid, where's this girl? What, Juliet!

Enter JULIET.

JULIET

How now? Who calls?

NURSE   Your mother.

JULIET   Madam, I am here.
What is your will?

LADY CAPULET

This is the matter—Nurse, give leave awhile,
We must talk in secret. Nurse, come back again;
I have remembered, you shall hear our counsel.
You know my daughter's of a pretty age.

NURSE
  Faith, I can tell her age unto an hour.
LADY CAPULET
  She's not fourteen.
NURSE   I'll lay fourteen of my teeth—
  Any yet, to my grief be it spoken, I have but four—
  She's not fourteen. How long is it now
  To Lammastide?
LADY CAPULET   A fortnight and odd days.
NURSE
  Even or odd, of all the days in the year,
  Come Lammas Eve at night shall she be fourteen.
  Susan and she (God rest all Christian souls!)
  Were of an age. Well, Susan is with God;
  She was too good for me. But, as I said,
  On Lammas Eve at night shall she be fourteen;
  That shall she, indeed; I remember it well.
  'Tis since the earthquake now eleven years;
  And she was weaned (I never shall forget it),
  Of all the days of the year, upon that day;
  For I had then laid wormwood to my dug,
  Sitting in the sun under the dovehouse wall.
  My lord and you were then at Mantua.
  Nay, I do bear a brain. But, as I said,
  When it did taste the wormwood on the nipple
  Of my dug and felt it bitter, pretty fool,
  To see it tetchy and fall out with the dug!
  Shake, said the dovehouse! 'Twas no need, I think,
  To bid me trudge.
  And since that time it is eleven years,
  For then she could stand alone; nay, by the rood,
  She could have run and waddled all about;
  For even the day before, she broke her brow;
  And then my husband (God be with his soul!
  He was a merry man) took up the child.

'Yea,' said he, 'do you fall upon your face?
You will fall backward when you have more wit;
Will you not, Jule?' and, by my holy word,
The pretty wretch left crying and said 'Ay.'
To see now how a jest shall come about!
I warrant, if I should live a thousand years,
I never should forget it. 'Will you not, Jule?' said he,
And, pretty fool, it answered and said 'Ay.'

LADY CAPULET

Enough of this. I pray you hold your peace.

NURSE

Yes, madam. Yet I cannot choose but laugh
To think it should leave crying and say 'Ay.'
And yet, I warrant, it had upon its brow
A bump as big as a young cockerel's stone;
A perilous knock; and it cried bitterly.
'Yea,' said my husband, 'fall upon your face?
You will fall backward when you come to age;
Will you not, Jule?' It ceased then and said 'Ay.'

JULIET

And cease you too, I pray you, nurse, say I.

NURSE

Peace, I have done. God mark you to his grace!
You were the prettiest babe that ever I nursed.
If I might live to see you married once,
I have my wish.

LADY CAPULET

Indeed, that 'marry' is the very theme
I came to talk of. Tell me, daughter Juliet,
How stands your disposition to be married?

JULIET

It is an honor that I dream not of.

NURSE

An honor? Were not I your only nurse,
I would say you had sucked wisdom from your teat.

LADY CAPULET
  Well, think of marriage now. Younger than you,
  Here in Verona, ladies of esteem,
  Are made already mothers. By my count,
  I was your mother much upon these years
  That you are now a maid. Thus then in brief:
  The valiant Paris seeks you for his love.

NURSE
  A man, young lady! lady, such a man
  As all the world—why he's a man of wax.

LADY CAPULET
  Verona's summer has not such a flower.

NURSE
  Nay, he's a flower, in faith—a very flower.

LADY CAPULET
  What say you? Can you love the gentleman?
  This night you shall behold him at our feast.
  Read over the volume of young Paris' face,
  And find delight writ there with beauty's pen;
  Examine every married lineament,
  And see how one another lends content;
  And what obscured in this fair volume lies
  Find written in the margin of his eyes.
  This precious book of love, this unbound lover,
  To beautify him only lacks a cover.
  The fish lives in the sea, and 'tis much pride
  For fair without the fair within to hide.
  That book in many's eyes does share the glory,
  That in gold clasps locks in the golden story;
  So shall you share all that he does possess,
  By having him making yourself no less.

NURSE
  No less? Nay, bigger! Women grow by men.

LADY CAPULET
  Speak briefly, can you like of Paris' love?

JULIET
  I'll look to like, if looking liking move;
  But no more deep will I endart my eye
  Than your consent gives strength to make it fly.

Enter Servant

SERVANT   Madam, the guests are come, supper served
  up, you called, my young lady asked for, the nurse
  cursed in the pantry, and everything in extremity. I
  must hence to wait. I beseech you, follow straight.
LADY CAPULET
  We follow you.   *Exit Servant.*
             Juliet, the Count stays.
NURSE
  Go, girl, seek happy nights to happy days.   *Exeunt.*

SCENE IV
Verona. A street.

Enter ROMEO, MERCUTIO, BENVOLIO,
with Maskers; Torchbearers.

ROMEO
  What, shall this speech be spoken for our excuse?
  Or shall we on without apology?
BENVOLIO
  The date is out of such prolixity.
  We'll have no Cupid blindfolded with a scarf,
  Bearing a Tartar's painted bow of lath,
  Scaring the ladies like a crowkeeper;
  And no without-book prologue, faintly spoken
  After the prompter, for our entrance;

But, let them measure us by what they will,
We'll measure them a measure and be gone.

ROMEO

Give me a torch. I am not for this ambling.
Being but heavy, I will bear the light.

MERCUTIO

Nay, gentle Romeo, we must have you dance.

ROMEO

Not I, believe me. You have dancing shoes
With nimble soles; I have a soul of lead
So stakes me to the ground I cannot move.

MERCUTIO

You are a lover. Borrow Cupid's wings
And soar with them above a common bound.

ROMEO

I am too sore enpiercèd with his shaft
To soar with his light feathers; and so bound
I cannot bound a pitch above dull woe.
Under love's heavy burden do I sink.

MERCUTIO

And, to sink in it, should you burden love—
Too great oppression for a tender thing.

ROMEO

Is love a tender thing? It is too rough,
Too rude, too boisterous, and it pricks like thorn.

MERCUTIO

If love is rough with you, be rough with love,
Prick love for pricking, and you beat love down.
Give me a case to put my visage in.
A visor for a visor! [mask] What care I
What curious eye does note deformities?
Here are the beetle brows shall blush for me.

BENVOLIO

Come, knock and enter; and no sooner in
But every man betake him to his legs.

ROMEO

> A torch for me! Let wantons light of heart
> Tickle the senseless rushes with their heels;
> For I am proverbed with a grandsire phrase,
> I'll be a candle-holder and look on;
> The game was never so fair, and I am done.

MERCUTIO

> Quiet as a mouse,—the constable's own word!
> If you are Dun, we'll draw you from the mire[1]
> Of this sir-reverence love, wherein you stick
> Up to the ears. Come, we burn daylight, ho!

ROMEO

> Nay, that is not so.   I mean, sir, in delay

MERCUTIO

> We waste our lights in vain, like lamps by day.
> Take our good meaning, for our judgment sits
> Five times in that ere once in our five wits.

ROMEO

> And we mean well in going to this mask,
> But it is no wit to go.

MERCUTIO   Why, may one ask?

ROMEO

> I dreamt a dream to-night.

MERCUTIO   And so did I.

ROMEO

> Well, what was yours?

MERCUTIO   That dreamers often lie.

ROMEO

> In bed asleep, while they do dream things true.

MERCUTIO

> O, then I see Queen Mab has been with you.
> She is the fairies' midwife, and she comes
> In shape no bigger than an agate stone

---

[1]A contemporary game.

On the forefinger of an alderman,
Drawn with a team of little tiny midgets
Over men's noses as they lie asleep.
Her wagon spokes made of long spiders' legs,
The cover, of the wings of grasshoppers;
Her traces, of the smallest spider web;
Her collars, of the moonshine's watery beams;
Her whip, of cricket's bone; the lash, of film;
Her wagoner, a small grey-coated gnat,
Not half so big as a round little worm
Pricked from the lazy finger of a maid.
Her chariot is an empty hazelnut,
Made by the joiner squirrel or old grub,
Time out of mind the fairies' coachmakers.
And in this state she gallops night by night
Through lovers' brains, and then they dream of love;
O'er courtier's knees, that dream on curtsies
    straight;
O'er lawyers' fingers, who straight dream on fees;
O'er ladies' lips, who straight on kisses dream,
Which oft the angry Mab with blisters plagues,
Because their breaths with sweetmeats tainted are.
Sometimes she gallops over a courtier's nose,
And then dreams he of smelling out a suit;
And sometimes comes she with a tithe-pig's tail
Tickling a parson's nose as he lies asleep,
Then dreams he of another benefice.
Sometimes she drives over a soldier's neck,
And then dreams he of cutting foreign throats,
Of breaches, ambuscadoes, Spanish blades,
Of healths five fathom deep; and then anon
Drums in his ear, at which he starts and wakes,
And being thus frighted, swears a prayer or two,
And sleeps again. This is that very Mab
That plats the manes of horses in the night
And bakes the elflocks in foul sluttish hairs,
Which once untangled much misfortune bodes.

This is the hag, when maids lie on their backs,
That presses them and teaches them to bear,
Making them women of good carriage.
This is she—

ROMEO   Peace, peace, Mercutio, peace!
You talk of nothing.

MERCUTIO   True, I talk of dreams;
Which are the children of an idle brain,
Begotten of nothing but vain fantasy;
Which is as thin of substance as the air,
And more inconstant than the wind, which woos
Even now the frozen bosom of the North
And, being angered, puffs away from thence,
Turning his side to the dew-dropping South.

BENVOLIO
This wind you talk of blows us from ourselves.
Supper is done, and we shall come too late.

ROMEO
I fear, too early; for my mind misgives
Some consequence, yet hanging in the stars,
Shall bitterly begin his fearful date
With this night's revels and expire the term
Of a despised life, closed in my breast,
By some vile forfeit of untimely death.
But he that has the steerage of my course
Direct my sail! On, lusty gentlemen!

BENVOLIO   Strike, drum.

SCENE V

Verona. A hall in Capulet's house.

Enter Musicians, *and* Servingmen.

1. SERVINGMAN   Where's Potpan, that he helps not to
take away? He shift a trencher! he scrape a
trencher!

2. SERVINGMAN   When good manners shall lie all in
one or two men's hands, and they unwashed too,
'tis a foul thing.

1. SERVINGMAN   Away with the joint-stools, remove
the court-cupboard, look to the plate. Good you,
save me a piece of marzipan and, as you love me,
let the porter let in Susan Grindstone and Nell.
[*Exit second Servingman.*] Anthony, and Potpan!

Enter two more Servingmen.

3. SERVINGMAN   Ay, boy, ready.

1. SERVINGMAN   You are looked for and called for,
asked for and sought for, in the great chamber.

4. SERVINGMAN   We cannot be here and there too.
Cheerily, boys! Be brisk awhile, and the longer
liver take all.   *Exeunt third and fourth Servingmen.*

Enter CAPULET, *his* Wife, JULIET, TYBALT, NURSE,
with Guests *and* Maskers.

CAPULET
Welcome, gentlemen! Ladies that have their toes
Unplagued with corns will walk a bout with you.
Ah ha, my mistresses! which of you all
Will now deny to dance? She that makes dainty,
She I'll swear has corns. Am I come near you
      now?
Welcome, gentlemen! I have seen the day
That I have worn a visor and could tell
A whispering tale in a fair lady's ear,
Such as would please. 'Tis gone, 'tis gone, 'tis
      gone!
You are welcome, gentlemen! Come, musicians,
      play.

Music plays, and they dance.

A hall, a hall! give room! and foot it, girls.
More light, you knaves! and turn the tables up,
And quench the fire, the room is grown too hot.
Ah, fellow, this unlooked-for sport comes well.
Nay, sit, nay, sit, good cousin Capulet,
For you and I are past our dancing days.
How long is it now since last yourself and I
Were in a mask?

2. CAPULET   By our Lady, thirty years.

CAPULET

What, man? 'Tis not so much, 'tis not so much;
'Tis since the nuptials of Lucentio,
Come Pentecost as quickly as it will,
Some five-and-twenty years, and then we masked.

2. CAPULET

'Tis more, 'tis more. His son is older, sir;
His son is thirty.

CAPULET   Will you tell me that?

His son was but a ward two years ago.

ROMEO   [*to a Servingman*]

What lady's that, who does enrich the hand
Of yonder knight?

SERVINGMAN   I know not, sir.

ROMEO

O, she does teach the torches to burn bright!
It seems she hangs upon the cheek of night
As a rich jewel in an Ethiop's ear—
Beauty too rich for use, for earth too dear!
So shows a snowy dove trooping with crows
As yonder lady over her fellows shows.
The measure done, I'll watch her place of stand
And, touching her, make blessèd my rude hand.
Did my heart love till now? Forswear it, sight!
For I never saw true beauty till this night.

TYBALT

This, by his voice, should be a Montague.
Fetch me my rapier, boy. What, dares the slave
Come hither, covered with a fancy face,
To sneer and scorn at our solemnity?
Now, by the stock and honor of my kin,
To strike him dead I hold it not a sin.

CAPULET

Why, how now, kinsman? Wherefore storm you so?

TYBALT

Uncle, this is a Montague, our foe;
A villain, that is hither come in spite
To scorn at our solemnity this night.

CAPULET

Young Romeo is it?

TYBALT   'Tis he, that villain Romeo.

CAPULET

Content you, gentle cousin, let him alone.
He bears him like a goodly gentleman,
And, to say truth, Verona brags of him
To be a virtuous and well-governed youth.
I would not for the wealth of all this town
Here in my house do him disparagement.
Therefore be patient, take no note of him.
It is my will, which if you now respect,
Show a fair presence and put off these frowns,
An ill-beseeming semblance for a feast.

TYBALT

It fits when such a villain is a guest.
I'll not endure him.

CAPULET   He shall be endured.
What, goodman boy! I say he shall Go to!
Am I the master here, or you? Go to!
You'll not endure him, God shall mend my soul!
You'll make a mutiny among my guests!
You will set cock-a-hoop, you'll be the man!

TYBALT

Why, uncle, it is a shame.

CAPULET Go to, go to!

You are a saucy boy. Is it so, indeed?
This trick may chance to harm you. I know what.
You must contràry me! Indeed, 'tis time—
Well said, my hearts!—You are a nuisance—go!
Be quiet, or—More light, more light!—For shame!
I'll make you quiet; what!—Cheerily, my hearts!

TYBALT

Patience perforce with willful choler meeting
Makes my flesh tremble in their different greeting.
I will withdraw; but this intrusion shall,
Now seeming sweet, convert to bitterest gall. *Exit.*

ROMEO

If I profane with my unworthiest hand
   This holy shrine, the gentle sin is this;
My lips, two blushing pilgrims, ready stand
   To smooth that rough touch with a tender kiss.

JULIET

Good pilgrim, you do wrong your hand too much,
   Which mannerly devotion shows in this;
For saints have hands that pilgrims' hands do touch,
   And palm to palm is holy palmers' kiss.

ROMEO

Have not saints lips, and holy palmers too?

JULIET

   Ay, pilgrim, lips that they must use in prayer.

ROMEO

O, then, dear saint, let lips do what hands do!
   They pray; grant you, lest faith turns to despair.

JULIET

Saints do not move, though grant for prayers' sake.

ROMEO

Then move not while my prayer's effect I take.
Thus from my lips, by yours my sin is purged.

Kisses her.

JULIET
  Now have my lips the sin that they then took.
ROMEO
  Sin from my lips? O trespass sweetly urged!
    Give me my sin again.

Kisses her.

JULIET   You kiss by the book.
NURSE
  Madam, your mother craves a word with you.
ROMEO
  What is her mother?
NURSE   Sure, bachelor,
  Her mother is the lady of the house,
  And a good lady, and a wise and virtuous.
  I nursed her daughter that you talked with now.
  I tell you, he that can lay hold of her
  Shall have the cash.
ROMEO   Is she a Capulet?
  O dear account! my life is my foe's debt.
BENVOLIO
  Away, be gone; the sport is at the best.
ROMEO
  Ay, so I fear; the more is my unrest.
CAPULET
  Nay, gentlemen, prepare not to be gone;
  We have a trifling foolish banquet towards.
  Is it even so? Why then, I thank you all.
  I thank you, honest gentlemen. Good night.
  More torches here! Come on then, let's to bed.

Ah, fellow, by my faith, it waxes late;
I'll to my rest. *Exeunt all but Juliet and Nurse.*
JULIET
Come hither, nurse. What is yon gentleman?
NURSE
The son and heir of old Tiberio.
JULIET
What's he that now is going out of door?
NURSE
Sure, that, I think, is young Petruchio.
JULIET
What's he that follows there, that would not dance?
NURSE
I know not.
JULIET
Go ask his name.—If he is marrièd,
My grave is like to be my wedding bed.
NURSE
His name is Romeo, and a Montague,
The only son of your great enemy.
JULIET
My only love, sprung from my only hate!
Too early seen unknown, and known too late!
Prodigious birth of love it is to me
That I must love a loathèd enemy.
NURSE
What's this? what's this?
JULIET   A rhyme I learnt even now
Of one I danced with.

One calls within, 'JULIET.'

NURSE   Coming, coming!
Come, let's away; the strangers all are gone.   *Exeunt.*

PROLOGUE

Enter Chorus.

CHORUS
Now old desire does in his deathbed lie,
   And young affection gapes to be his heir;
That fair for which love groaned for and would die,
   With tender Juliet matched, is now not fair.
Now Romeo is beloved and loves again,
   Alike bewitchèd by the charm of looks;
But to his foe supposed he must complain,
   And she steal love's sweet bait from fearful hooks.
Being held a foe, he may not have access
   To breathe such vows as lovers use to swear,
And she as much in love, her means much less
   To meet her new belovèd anywhere;
But passion lends them power, time means, to meet,
Tempering extremities with extreme sweet.   *Exit.*

Act II

SCENE I
Verona. Capulet's orchard.

Enter ROMEO.

ROMEO
Can I go forward when my heart is here?
Turn back, dull earth, and find your centre out.

Enter BENVOLIO *with* MERCUTIO. ROMEO *retires.*

BENVOLIO
Romeo! my cousin Romeo! Romeo!
MERCUTIO   He is wise,
And, on my life, has stolen home to bed.
BENVOLIO
He ran this way and leaped this orchard wall.
Call, good Mercutio.
MERCUTIO   Nay, I'll conjure too.
Romeo! humors! madman! passion! lover!
Appear you in the likeness of a sigh;
Speak but one rhyme, and I am satisfied!
Cry but 'Ay me!' pronounce but 'love' and 'dove';
Speak to my gossip Venus one fair word,
One nickname for her purblind son and heir
Young Abraham Cupid, he that shot so true
When King Cophetua loved the beggar maid!
He hears not, he stirs not, nor does he move;
The ape is dead, and I must conjure him.
I conjure you by Rosaline's bright eyes,
By her high forehead and her scarlet lip,
By her fine foot, straight leg, and quivering thigh,
And the demesnes that there adjacent lie,
That in your likeness you appear to us!
BENVOLIO
But if he hears you, you will anger him.
MERCUTIO
This cannot anger him. It would anger him
To raise a spirit in his mistress' circle
Of some strange nature, letting it there stand
Till she had laid it and conjured it down.
That were some spite; my invocation
Is fair and honest: in his mistress' name,
I conjure only but to raise up him.

BENVOLIO
  Come, he has hid himself among these trees
  To be consorted with the humorous night.   *dark*
  Blind is his love and best befits the dark.

MERCUTIO
  If love is blind, love cannot hit the mark.
  Now will he sit under a medlar tree
  And wish his mistress were that kind of fruit
  As maids call medlars when they laugh alone.
  O, Romeo, that she were, O that she were
  An open et cetera, you a poperin pear![1]
  Romeo, good night. I'll to my trundle-bed;
  This field-bed is too cold for me to sleep.
  Come, shall we go?

BENVOLIO   Go then, for 'tis in vain
  To seek him here that means not to be found.

                                   Exit with Mercutio.

SCENE II
The same

ROMEO *(coming forward)*
  He jests at scars that never felt a wound.

              Enter JULIET *above at a window.*

  But soft! What light through yonder window breaks?
  It is the East, and Juliet is the sun!
  Arise, fair sun, and kill the envious moon,
  Who is already sick and pale with grief
  That you her maid are far more fair than she.
  Be not her maid, since she is envious.
  Her vestal livery is but sick and green,

---

[1]Bawdy pun on Poperinghe (Flanders).

And none but fools do wear it. Cast it off.
It is my lady; O, it is my love!
O that she knew she were!
She speaks, yet she says nothing. What of that?
Her eye discourses; I will answer it.
I am too bold; 'tis not to me she speaks.
Two of the fairest stars in all the heaven,
Having some business, do entreat her eyes
To twinkle in their spheres till they return.
What if her eyes were there, they in her head?
The brightness of her cheek would shame those stars
As daylight does a lamp; her eyes in heaven
Would through the airy region stream so bright
That birds would sing and think it were not night.
See how she leans her cheek upon her hand!
O that I were a glove upon that hand,
That I might touch that cheek!

JULIET   Ay me!
ROMEO   She speaks.
O, speak again, bright angel! for you are
As glorious to this night, being over my head,
As is a wingèd messenger of heaven
Unto the white-upturned wondering eyes
Of mortals that fall back to gaze on him,
When he bestrides the lazy-pacing clouds
And sails upon the bosom of the air.

JULIET
O Romeo, Romeo! wherefore are you, Romeo?
Deny your father and refuse your name;
Or, if you will not, be but sworn my love,
And I'll no longer be a Capulet.

ROMEO [aside]
Shall I hear more, or shall I speak at this?

JULIET
It is but your name that is my enemy.
You are yourself, though not a Montague.
What's Montague? It is nor hand, nor foot,

Nor arm, nor face, nor any other part
Belonging to a man. O, be some other name!
What's in a name? That which we call a rose
By any other name would smell as sweet.
So Romeo would, were he not Romeo called,
Retain that dear perfection which he owns
Without that title. Romeo, doff your name;
And for your name, which is no part of you,
Take all myself.

ROMEO   I take you at your word.
Call me but love, and I'll be new baptized;
Henceforth I never will be Romeo.

JULIET
What man are you that, thus bescreened in night,
So stumble on my counsel?

ROMEO   By a name
I know not how to tell you who I am.
My name, dear saint, is hateful to myself,
Because it is an enemy to you.
Had I it written, I would tear the word.

JULIET
My ears have yet not drunk a hundred words
Of your tongue's uttering, yet I know the sound.
Are you not Romeo, and a Montague?

ROMEO
Neither, fair maid, if either you dislike.

JULIET
How came you hither, tell me, and wherefore?
The orchard walls are high and hard to climb,
And the place death, considering who you are,
In any of my kinsmen find you here.

ROMEO
With love's light wings did I o'erperch these walls;
For stony limits cannot hold love out,
And what love can do, that dares love attempt.
Therefore your kinsmen are no stop to me.

JULIET
  If they do see you, they will murder you.
ROMEO
  Alas, there lies more peril in your eye
  Than twenty of their swords! Look you but sweet,
  And I am proof against their enmity.
JULIET
  I would not for the world they saw you here.
ROMEO
  I have night's cloak to hide me from their eyes;
  If but you love me, let them find me here.
  My life were better ended by their hate
  Than death proroguèd, wanting of your love.
JULIET
  By whose direction found you out this place?
ROMEO
  By love, that first did prompt me to inquire.
  He lent me counsel, and I lent him eyes.
  I am no pilot; yet were you as far
  As that vast shore washed with the farthest sea,
  I should adventure for such merchandise.
JULIET
  You know the mask of night is on my face;
  Else would a maiden blush bepaint my cheek
  For that which you have heard me speak to-night.
  Fain would I dwell on form—fain, fain deny
  What I have spoken; but farewell compliment!
  Do you love me? I know you will say 'Ay';
  And I will take your word. Yet, if you swear,
  You may prove false. At lovers' perjuries,
  They say Jove laughs. O gentle Romeo,
  If you do love, pronounce it faithfully.
  Or if you think I am too quickly won,
  I'll frown, and be perverse, and say you nay,
  If you will woo, but else, not for the world.
  In truth, fair Montague, I am too fond,

And therefore you may think my conduct light;
But trust me, gentleman, I'll prove more true
Than those that have more cunning to be strange.
I should have been more strange, I must confess,
But that you overheard, ere I was aware,
My true-love passion. Therefore pardon me,
And not impute this yielding to light love,
Which the dark night has so discoverèd.

ROMEO
Lady, by yonder blessèd moon I vow,
That tips with silver all these fruit-tree tops—

JULIET
O, swear not by the moon, the inconstant moon,
That monthly changes in her circled orb,
Lest your love proves likewise variable.

ROMEO
What shall I swear by?

JULIET   Do not swear at all;
Or if you will, swear by your gracious self,
Which is the god of my idolatry,
And I will believe you.

ROMEO   If my heart's dear love—

JULIET
Well, do not swear. Although I joy in you,
I have no joy of this contract to-night.
It is too rash, too unadvised, too sudden;
Too like the lightning, which does cease to be
Ere one can say 'It lightens.' Sweet, good night!
This bud of love, by summer's ripening breath,
May prove a beauteous flower when next we meet.
Good night, good night! As sweet repose and rest
Come to your heart as that within my breast!

ROMEO
O, will you leave me so unsatisfied?

JULIET
What satisfaction can you have to-night?

ROMEO
  The exchange of your love's faithful vow for mine.
JULIET
  I gave you mine before you did request it;
  And yet I would it were to give again.
ROMEO
  Would you withdraw it? For what purpose, love?
JULIET
  But to be frank and give it you again.
  And yet I wish but for the thing I have.
  My bounty is as boundless as the sea,
  My love as deep; the more I give to you,
  The more I have, for both are infinite.
  I hear some noise within. Dear love, adieu!

NURSE *calls within.*

  Coming, good nurse! Sweet Montague, be true.
  Stay but a little, I will come again.   *Exit.*
ROMEO
  O blessèd, blessèd night! I am afraid,
  Being in night, all this is but a dream,   (night mirror
  Too flattering-sweet to be substantial.   perhaps?)

Enter JULIET *above.*

JULIET
  Three words, dear Romeo, and good night indeed.
  If your bent of love is honorable,
  Your purpose marriage, send me word tomorrow,
  By one that I'll procure to come to you,
  Where and what time you will perform the rite.
  And all my fortunes at your foot I'll lay
  And follow you my lord throughout the world.
NURSE   [*within*] Madam!

JULIET
    I come, soon.—But if you mean not well,
    I do beseech you —
NURSE   [*within*]
    Madam!
JULIET   By and by I come.—
    To cease your suit and leave me to my grief.
    To-morrow will I send.
ROMEO   So thrive my soul—
JULIET
    A thousand times good night!   *Exit.*
ROMEO
    A thousand times the worse, to want your light!
    Love goes toward love as schoolboys from their
        books;
    But love from love, toward school with heavy looks.

                    Enter JULIET *above again.*

JULIET
    Hist! Romeo, hist! O for a falconer's voice
    To lure this gentle falcon back again!
    Bondage is hoarse and may not speak aloud,
    Else would I tear the cave where Echo lies
    And make her airy tongue more hoarse than mine
    With repetition of 'My Romeo!'
ROMEO
    It is my soul that calls upon my name.
    How silver-sweet sound lovers' tongues by night,
    Like softest music to attending ears!
JULIET
    Romeo!
ROMEO   My sweet?

JULIET   At what o'clock to-morrow
  Shall I send to you?
ROMEO   By the hour of nine.
JULIET
  I will not fail. 'Tis twenty years till then.
  I have forgotten why I did call you back.
ROMEO
  Let me stand here till you remember it.
JULIET
  I shall forget, to have you still stand there,
  Remembering how I love your company.
ROMEO
  And I'll still stay, to have you still forget,
  Forgetting any other home but this.
JULIET
  It is almost morning. I would have you gone—
  And yet no farther than a wanton's bird,
  That lets it hop a little from her hand,
  Like a poor prisoner in his twisted bonds,
  And with a silken thread plucks it back again,
  So loving-jealous of its liberty.
ROMEO
  I would I were your bird.
JULIET   Sweet, so would I.
  Yet I should kill you with much cherishing.
  Good night, good night! Parting is such sweet
sorrow
  That I shall say good night till it is morrow.   *Exit.*
ROMEO
  Sleep dwell upon your eyes, peace in your breast!
  Would I were sleep and peace, so sweet to rest!
  Hence will I to my ghostly father's cell,
  His help to crave and my dear hap to tell.   *Exit.*

SCENE III
Verona. Friar Laurence's cell

Enter FRIAR LAURENCE, *with a basket.*

FRIAR LAURENCE
　The grey-eyed morn smiles on the frowning night,
　Cheering the Eastern clouds with streaks of light;
　And fleckèd darkness like a drunkard reels
　From forth day's path and Titan's fiery wheels.
　Now, ere the sun advances burning eye
　The day to cheer and night's dank dew to dry,
　I must up-fill this osier cage of ours
　With baleful weeds and precious-juicèd flowers.
　The earth that's nature's mother is her tomb.
　What is her burying grave, that is her womb;
　And from her womb children of divers kind
　We sucking on her natural bosom find,
　Many for many virtues excellent,
　None but for some, and yet all different.
　O, so large is the powerful grace that lies
　In plants, herbs, stones, and their true qualities;
　For naught so vile that on the earth does live
　But to the earth some special good does give;
　Nor naught so good but, strained from that fair
　　　use,
　Revolts from true birth, stumbling on abuse.
　Virtue itself turns vice, being misapplied,
　And vice sometimes is by action dignified.

Enter ROMEO.

　Within the infant rind of this weak flower
　Poison has residence, and medicine power;

For this, being smelt, with that part cheers each
    part;
Being tasted, slays all senses with the heart.
Two such opposèd kings encamp them still
In man as well as herbs—grace and rude will;
And where the worse becomes predominant,
Full soon the canker death eats up that plant.

ROMEO
Good morrow, father.

FRIAR LAURENCE   Benedicite!
What early tongue so sweet salutes me now?
Young son, it argues a distempered head
So soon to bid good morrow to your bed.
Care keeps its watch in every old man's eye,
And where care lodges, sleep will never lie;
But where unbruisèd youth with unstuffed brain
Does couch its limbs, there golden sleep does reign.
Therefore your earliness does me assure
You are up-roused with some distemperature;
Or if not so, then here I hit it right—
Our Romeo has not been in bed to-night.

ROMEO
That last is true—the sweeter rest was mine.

FRIAR LAURENCE
God pardon sin! Were you with Rosaline?

ROMEO
With Rosaline, my ghostly father? No.
I have forgotten that name and that name's woe.

FRIAR LAURENCE
That's my good son! But where have you been then?

ROMEO
I'll tell you ere you ask it me again.
I have been feasting with my enemy,
Where on a sudden one has wounded me

That's by me wounded. Both our remedies
Within your help and holy physic lie.
I bear no hatred, blessèd man, for, lo,
My intercession likewise helps my foe.

FRIAR LAURENCE

Be plain, good son, and homely in your drift.
Riddling confession finds but riddling shrift
[absolution].

ROMEO

Then plainly know my heart's dear love is set
On the fair daughter of rich Capulet;
As mine on hers, so hers is set on mine,
And all combined, save what you must combine
By holy marriage. When, and where, and how
We met, we wooed, and made exchange of vow,
I'll tell you as we pass; but this I pray,
That you consent to marry us to-day.

FRIAR LAURENCE

Holy Saint Francis! What a change is here!
Is Rosaline, that you did love so dear,
So soon forsaken? Young men's love then lies
Not truly in their hearts, but in their eyes.
Jesu Maria! What a deal of brine
Has washed your sallow cheeks for Rosaline!
How much salt water thrown away in waste
To season love, that of it does not taste!
The sun not yet your sighs from heaven clears,
Your old groans ring yet in my ancient ears.
Lo, here upon your cheek the stain does sit
Of an old tear that is not washed off yet.
If ever you were yourself, and these woes yours,
You and these woes were all for Rosaline.
And are you changed? Pronounce this sentence then.
Women may fall when there's no strength in men.

ROMEO
  You chid me oft for loving Rosaline.

FRIAR LAURENCE
  For doting, not for loving, pupil mine.

ROMEO
  And bade me bury love.

FRIAR LAURENCE   Not in a grave
  To lay one in, another out to have.

ROMEO
  I pray you chide not. She whom I love now
  Does grace for grace and love for love allow.
  The other did not so.

FRIAR LAURENCE   O, she knew well
  Your love did read by rote, that could not spell.
  But come, young waverer, come go with me.
  In one respect I'll your assistant be;
  For this alliance may so happy prove
  To turn your households' rancor to pure love,

ROMEO
  O, let us hence! I stand on sudden haste.

FRIAR LAURENCE
  Wisely and slow. They stumble that run fast.

                                        Exeunt.

SCENE IV
Verona. A street.

Enter BENVOLIO *and* MERCUTIO.

MERCUTIO
  Where the devil should this Romeo be?
  Came he not home to-night?

BENVOLIO
Not to his father's. I spoke with his man.
MERCUTIO
Why, that same pale hard-hearted wench, that
  Rosaline,
Torments him so that he will sure run mad.
BENVOLIO
Tybalt, the kinsman to old Capulet,
Has sent a letter to his father's house.
MERCUTIO   A challenge, on my life.
BENVOLIO   Romeo will answer it.
MERCUTIO   Any man that can write may answer a
  letter.
BENVOLIO   Nay, he will answer the letter's master,
  how he dares, being dared.
MERCUTIO   Alas, poor Romeo, he is already dead!
  stabbed with a white wench's black eye; run
  through the ear with a love song; the very bulls-eye
  of his heart cleft with the blind bow-boy's butt-
  shaft; and is he a man to encounter Tybalt?
BENVOLIO   Why, what is Tybalt?
MERCUTIO   More than Prince of Cats, I can tell you.
  O, he's the courageous captain of compliments. He
  fights as you sing pricksong—keeps time, distance,
  and proportion; he rests his minim rests, one, two,
  and the third in your bosom! the very butcher of a
  silk button, a duellist, a duellist! a gentleman of
  the very first school, of the first and second
  challenge. Ah, the immortal lunge! the backward
  stroke! the home-thrust!
BENVOLIO   The what?
MERCUTIO   The pox of such grotesque, lisping,
  affecting fantasticoes—these new tuners of accent!
  'By Jesu, a very good blade! a very tall man! a very
  good whore!' Why, is not this a lamentable thing,

good sir, that we should be thus afflicted with
these strange flies, these fashion-mongers, these
pardon-me's, who stand so much on the new form
that they cannot sit at ease on the old bench? O,
their bones, their bones!

Enter ROMEO.

BENVOLIO   Here comes Romeo! here comes Romeo!

MERCUTIO   Without his roe, like a dried herring. O
flesh, flesh, how are you fishified! Now is he for
the numbers that Petrarch flowed in. Laura, to his
lady, was a kitchen wench (sure, she had a better
love to berhyme her), Dido a dowdy, Cleopatra a
gypsy, Helen and Hero bitches and harlots, Thisbe
a grey eye or so, but not to the purpose. Signior
Romeo, bon jour! There's a French salutation to
your French breeches. You gave us the counterfeit
fairly last night.

ROMEO   Good morrow to you both. What counterfeit
did I give you?

MERCUTIO   The slip, sir, the slip. Can you not
imagine?

ROMEO   Pardon, good Mercutio. My business was
great, and in such a case as mine a man may
strain courtesy.

MERCUTIO   That's as much as to say, such a case as
yours constrains a man to bow in the hams.

ROMEO   Meaning, to curtsy.

MERCUTIO   You have most kindly hit it.

ROMEO   A most courteous exposition.

MERCUTIO   Nay, I am the very pink of courtesy.

ROMEO   Pink for flower.

MERCUTIO   Right.

ROMEO   Why, then is my pump well-flowered.

MERCUTIO   Sure, wit, follow me this jest now till you
have worn out your pump, that, when the single
sole of it is worn, the jest may remain, after the
wearing, solely singular.

ROMEO   O single-soled jest, solely singular for the
singleness!

MERCUTIO   Come between us, good Benvolio! My
wits faint.

ROMEO   Switches and spurs, switches and spurs! or
I'll cry a match.

MERCUTIO   Nay, if our wits run the wild-goose chase,
I am done; for you have more of the wild goose in
one of your wits than, I am sure, I have in my
whole five. Was I with you there for the goose?

ROMEO   You were never with me for anything when
you were not there for the goose.

MERCUTIO   I will bite you by the ear for that jest.

ROMEO   Nay, good goose, bite not!

MERCUTIO   Your wit is a very bitter sweeting; it is a
most sharp sauce.

ROMEO   And is it not, then, well served in to a sweet
goose?

MERCUTIO   O, here's a wit of kid-skin, that stretches
from an inch narrow to an ell broad!

ROMEO   I stretch it out for that word 'broad,' which,
added to the goose, proves you far and wide a broad
goose.

MERCUTIO   Why, is not this better now than groaning
for love? Now are you sociable, now are you
Romeo; now are you what you are, by art as well as
by nature. For this drivelling love is like a great
idiot that runs lolling up and down to hide his
bauble in a hole.

BENVOLIO   Stop there, stop there!

MERCUTIO   You desire me to stop in my tale against
   the hair.
BENVOLIO   You would else have made your tale large.
MERCUTIO   O, you are deceived! I would have made it
   short; for I was come to the whole depth of my
   tale, and meant indeed to occupy the argument no
   longer.
ROMEO   Here's goodly gear!

Enter NURSE *and her* Man PETER.

MERCUTIO   A sail, a sail!
BENVOLIO   Two, two! a shirt and a smock.
NURSE   Peter!
PETER   Anon.
NURSE   My fan, Peter.
MERCUTIO   Good Peter, to hide her face; for her fan is
   the fairer face.
NURSE   God give you good morrow, gentlemen.
MERCUTIO   God give you good-even, fair gentlewoman.
NURSE   Is it good-even?
MERCUTIO   'Tis no less, I tell you; for the bawdy hand
   of the dial is now upon the prick of noon.
NURSE   Out upon you! What a man are you!
ROMEO   One, gentlewoman, that God has made for
   himself to mar.
NURSE   By my truth, it is well said. 'For himself to
   mar,' says he? Gentleman, can any of you tell me
   where I may find the young Romeo?
ROMEO   I can tell you; but young Romeo will be older
   when you have found him than he was when you
   sought him. I am the youngest of that name, for
   fault of a worse.
NURSE   You say well.

MERCUTIO   Yea, is the worst well? Very well taken,
   in faith! wisely, wisely.
NURSE   If you are he, sir, I desire some confidence
   [conference] with you.
BENVOLIO   She will endite [invite] him to some supper.
MERCUTIO   A bawd, a bawd, a bawd! So ho!
ROMEO   What have you found?
MERCUTIO   No hare, sir; unless a hare, sir, in a lenten
   pie, that is something stale and hoar ere it be spent.

He walks by them and sings.

> An old hare hoar, [i.e. whore]
> And an old hare hoar,
> Is very good meat in Lent;
> But a hare that is hoar
> Is too much for a score
> When it hoars ere it is spent.

Romeo, will you come to your father's? We'll to
dinner thither.
ROMEO   I will follow you.
MERCUTIO   Farewell, ancient lady. Farewell, [*sings*]
   lady, lady, lady.   *Exeunt Mercutio, Benvolio.*
NURSE   I pray you, sir, what saucy merchant was
   this that was so full of his roguery?
ROMEO   A gentleman, nurse, that loves to hear
   himself talk and will speak more in a minute than
   he will stand to in a month.
NURSE   If he speaks anything against me, I'll take
   him down, if he were lustier than he is, and twenty
   such Jacks; and if I cannot, I'll find those that
   shall. Scurvy knave! I am none of his flirt-girls; I
   am none of his molls. And you must stand by too,
   and suffer every knave to use me at his pleasure!

PETER   I saw no man use you at his pleasure. If I had,
    my weapon should quickly have been out, I
    warrant you. I dare draw as soon as another man, if
    I see occasion in a good quarrel, and the law on my
    side.
NURSE   Now, before God, I am so vexed that every
    part about me quivers. Scurvy knave! Pray you, sir,
    a word; and, as I told you, my young lady bid me
    inquire you out. What she bid me say, I will keep
    to myself; but first let me tell you, if you should
    lead her into a fool's paradise, as they say, it were a
    very gross kind of behavior, as they say; for the
    gentlewoman is young. And therefore, if you should
    deal double with her, truly it were an ill thing to be
    offered to any gentlewoman, and very weak dealing.
ROMEO   Nurse, commend me to your lady and
    mistress. I protest unto you—
NURSE   Good heart, and in faith I will tell her as
    much. Lord, Lord! she will be a joyful woman.
ROMEO   What will you tell her, nurse? You do not
    mark me.
NURSE   I will tell her, sir, that you do protest,
    which, as I take it, is a gentlemanlike offer.
ROMEO
    Bid her devise
    Some means to come to shrift this afternoon;
    And there she shall at Friar Laurence' cell
    Be shrived and married. Here is for your pains.
NURSE   No, truly, sir; not a penny.
ROMEO   Go to! I say you shall.
NURSE   This afternoon, sir? Well, she shall be there.
ROMEO
    And stay, good nurse, behind the abbey wall,
    Within this hour my man shall be with you,

And bring you cords made like a rope ladder,
Which to the high topgallant of my joy
Must be my convoy in the secret night.
Farewell. Be trusty, and I'll quit your pains.
Farewell. Commend me to your mistress.

NURSE
Now God in heaven bless you! Hark you, sir.

ROMEO
What say you, my dear nurse?

NURSE
Is your man secret? Did you never hear say,
Two may keep counsel, putting one away?

ROMEO
I warrant you my man is as true as steel.

NURSE   Well, sir, my mistress is the sweetest lady.
Lord, Lord! when it was a little prating thing—O,
there is a nobleman in town, one Paris, that would
fain lay knife aboard; but she, good soul, had as
soon see a toad, a very toad, as see him. I anger her
sometimes, and tell her that Paris is the properer
man; but I'll warrant you, when I say so, she looks
as pale as any clout in the versal [universal] world.
Do not rosemary and Romeo begin both with a
letter?

ROMEO   Ay, nurse; what of that? Both with an R.

NURSE   Ah, mocker! that's the dog's name. R is for
the—No; I know it begins with some other letter;
and she has the prettiest sententious [sentences] of
it, of you and rosemary, that it would do you good
to hear it.

ROMEO   Commend me to your lady.

NURSE   Ay, a thousand times. *Exit Romeo.* Peter!

PETER   Anon.

NURSE   Peter, take my fan, and go before, and apace.
                                            Exit after Peter

SCENE V
Verona. Capulet's orchard.

Enter JULIET.

JULIET

The clock struck nine when I did send the nurse;
In half an hour she promised to return.
Perchance she cannot meet him. That's not so.
O, she is lame! Love's heralds should be thoughts,
Which ten times faster glide than the sun's beams
Driving back shadows over lowering hills.
Therefore do nimble-pinioned doves draw Love,
And therefore has the wind-swift Cupid wings.
Now is the sun upon the highmost hill
Of this day's journey, and from nine till twelve
Is three long hours; yet she is not come.
Had she affections and warm youthful blood,
She would be as swift in motion as a ball;
My words would hurry her to my sweet love,
And his to me.
But old folks, many feign as they were dead—
Unwieldy, slow, heavy and pale as lead.

Enter NURSE *and* PETER.

O God, she comes! O honey nurse, what news?
Have you met with him? Send your man away.

NURSE

Peter, stay at the gate.   *Exit Peter.*

JULIET

Now, good sweet nurse—O Lord, why look you sad?
Though news are sad, yet tell them merrily;
If good, you shame the music of sweet news
By playing it to me with so sour a face.

NURSE

  I am aweary, give me leave awhile.

  Fie, how my bones ache! What a jaunt have I had!

JULIET

  I would you had my bones, and I your news.

  Nay, come, I pray you speak. Good, good nurse,
    speak.

NURSE

  Jesu, what haste! Can you not stay awhile?

  Do you not see that I am out of breath?

JULIET

  How are you out of breath when you have breath

  To say to me that you are out of breath?

  The excuse that you do make in this delay

  Is longer than the tale you do excuse.

  Are your news good or bad? Answer to that.

  Say either, and I'll stay the circumstance.

  Let me be satisfied, is it good or bad?

NURSE Well, you have made a simple choice; you
know not how to choose a man. Romeo? No, not
he. Though his face is better than any man's, yet
his leg excels all men's; and for a hand and a foot,
and a body, though they be not to be talked on, yet
they are past compare. He is not the flower of
courtesy, but, I'll warrant him, as gentle as a lamb.
Go your ways, wench; serve God. What, have you
dined at home?

JULIET

  No, no. But all this did I know before.

  What says he of our marriage? What of that?

NURSE

  Lord, how my head aches! What a head have I!

  It beats as it would fall in twenty pieces.

  My back on the other side—ah, my back, my back!

  Shame on your heart for sending me about

  To catch my death with jaunting up and down!

JULIET

In faith, I am sorry that you are not well.
Sweet, sweet, sweet nurse, tell me, what says my
   love?

NURSE   Your love says, like an honest gentleman, and
a courteous, and a kind, and a handsome, and I
warrant a virtuous—Where is your mother?

JULIET

Where is my mother? Why, she is within.
Where should she be? How oddly you reply.
'Your love says, like an honest gentleman,
"Where is your mother?" '

NURSE   O God's Lady dear!

Are you so hot? By the Blessed Virgin, I trust.
Is this the poultice for my aching bones?
Henceforward do your messages yourself.

JULIET

Here's such a fuss! Come, what says Romeo?

NURSE

Have you got leave to go to shrift to-day?

JULIET

I have.

NURSE

Then hie you hence to Friar Laurence' cell;
There stays a husband to make you a wife.
Now comes the wanton blood up in your cheeks:
They'll be in scarlet straight at any news.
Hie you to church; I must another way,
To fetch a ladder, by which now your love
Must climb a bird's nest soon when it is dark.
I am the drudge, and toil in your delight;
But you shall bear the burden soon at night.
Go; I'll to dinner; hie you to the cell.

JULIET

Hie to high fortune! Honest nurse, farewell. *Exeunt.*

SCENE VI
Verona. Friar Laurence's Cell

Enter FRIAR LAURENCE *and* ROMEO.

FRIAR LAURENCE
  So smile the heavens upon this holy act
  That after-hours with sorrow chide us not!
ROMEO
  Amen, amen! But come what sorrow can,
  It cannot countervail the exchange of joy
  That one short minute gives me in her sight.
  Do you but close our hands with holy words,
  Then love-devouring death do what he dares,
  It is enough I may but call her mine.
FRIAR LAURENCE
  These violent delights have violent ends
  And in their triumph die, like fire and powder,
  Which, as they kiss, consume. The sweetest honey
  Is loathsome in its own deliciousness
  And in the taste confounds the appetite.
  Therefore love moderately: long love does so;
  Too swift arrives as tardy as too slow.

Enter JULIET.

  Here comes the lady. O, so light a foot
  Will never wear out the everlasting flint.
  A lover may bestride the gossamer
  That idles in the wanton summer air,
  And yet not fall; so light is vanity.
JULIET
  Good even to my ghostly confessor.
FRIAR LAURENCE
  Romeo shall thank you, daughter, for us both.

JULIET
  As much to him, else are his thanks too much.
ROMEO
  Ah, Juliet, if the measure of your joy
  Be heaped like mine, and if your skill be more
  To brighten it, then sweeten with your breath
  This neighbor air, and let rich music's tongue
  Unfold the imagined happiness that both
  Receive in either by this dear encounter.
JULIET
  Thoughts, more rich in matter than in words,
  Brags of its substance, not of ornament.
  They are but beggars that can count their worth;
  But my true love is grown to such excess
  I cannot sum up sum of half my wealth.
FRIAR LAURENCE
  Come, come with me, and we will make short
    work;
  For, by your leaves, you shall not stay alone
  Till Holy Church incorporate two in one.   *Exeunt.*

Act III

SCENE I
Verona. A street.

Enter MERCUTIO, BENVOLIO, *and* Servants.

BENVOLIO
  I pray you, good Mercutio, let's retire.
  The day is hot, the Capulets abroad,

And, if we meet, we shall not escape a brawl,
For now, these hot days, is the mad blood stirring.

MERCUTIO   You are like one of these fellows that,
when he enters the confines of a tavern, claps his
sword upon the table and says 'God send me no
need of you!' and by the operation of the second
cup draws on the drawer, when indeed there is no
need.

BENVOLIO   Am I like such a fellow?

MERCUTIO   Come, come, you are as hot a Jack in
your mood as any in Italy; and as soon moved
to be moody, and as soon moody to be moved.

BENVOLIO   And what to?

MERCUTIO   Nay, if there were two such, we should
have none shortly, for one would kill the other.
You! why, you will quarrel with a man that has a
hair more or a hair less in his beard than you have.
You will quarrel with a man for cracking nuts,
having no other reason but because you have hazel
eyes. What eye but such an eye would spy out such
a quarrel? Your head is as full of quarrels as an egg
is full of meat; and yet your head has been beaten
as addled as an egg for quarrelling. You have
quarrelled with a man for coughing in the street,
because he has wakened your dog that has lain
asleep in the sun. Did you not fall out with a tailor
for wearing his new doublet before Easter? with
another for tying his new shoes with old ribbon?
And yet you will tutor me from quarrelling?

BENVOLIO   If I were so apt to quarrel as you are, any
man should buy the fee simple [freehold] of my life
for an hour and a quarter.

MERCUTIO   The fee simple? O simple!

Enter TYBALT *and others.*

BENVOLIO   By my head, here come the Capulets.
MERCUTIO   By my heel, I care not.
TYBALT
  Follow me close, for I will speak to them.
  Gentlemen, good-even. A word with one of you.
MERCUTIO
  And but one word with one of us?
  Couple it with something; make it a word and a
    blow.
TYBALT   You shall find me apt enough to that, sir,
  if you will give me occasion.
MERCUTIO   Could you not take some occasion without
  giving?
TYBALT   Mercutio, you consort with Romeo.
MERCUTIO   Consort? What, do you make us minstrels?
  If you make minstrels of us, look to hear nothing
  but discords. Here's my fiddlestick; here's that
  shall make you dance. God's wounds, consort!
BENVOLIO
  We talk here in the public haunt of men.
  Either withdraw unto some private place,
  Or reason coldly of your grievances,
  Or else depart. Here all eyes gaze on us.
MERCUTIO
  Men's eyes were made to look, and let them gaze.
  I will not budge for any man's pleasure, I.

Enter ROMEO.

TYBALT
⇥Well, peace be with you, sir. Here comes my man.
MERCUTIO
  But I'll be hanged, sir, if he wears your livery.
  Indeed, go before to field, he'll be your follower!
  Your worship in that sense may call him man.

TYBALT
   Romeo, the love I bear you can afford
   No better term than this: you are a villain.

ROMEO
   Tybalt, the reason that I have to love you
   Does much excuse the appertaining rage
   To such a greeting. Villain am I none.
   Therefore farewell. I see you know me not.

TYBALT
   Boy, this shall not excuse the injuries
   That you have done me; therefore turn and draw.

ROMEO
   I do protest I never injured you,
   But love you better than you can devise
   Till you shall know the reason of my love;
   And so, good Capulet, which name I tender
   As dearly as my own, be satisfied.

MERCUTIO
   O calm, dishonorable, vile submission!
   'At the thrust' then carries it away.

Draws.

   Tybalt, you ratcatcher, will you walk?

TYBALT
   What would you have with me?

MERCUTIO   Good King of Cats, nothing but one of
   your nine lives. That I mean to make bold with,
   and, as you shall use me hereafter, thrash the rest
   of the eight. Will you pluck your sword out of its
   scabbard by the ears? Make haste, lest mine be
   about your ears ere it is out.

TYBALT   I am for you.

Draws.

ROMEO

Gentle Mercutio, put your rapier up.

MERCUTIO   Come, sir, your pass!

They fight.

ROMEO

Draw, Benvolio; beat down their weapons.
Gentlemen, for shame! forbear this outrage!
Tybalt, Mercutio, the Prince expressly has
Forbidden this bandying in Verona streets.
Hold, Tybalt! Good Mercutio!

TYBALT *thrusts* MERCUTIO *in,
and flies with his* Followers.

MERCUTIO   I am hurt.

A plague on both your houses! I am sped.
Has he gone and has nothing?

BENVOLIO   What, are you hurt?

MERCUTIO

Ay, ay, a scratch, a scratch. Sure, 'tis enough.
Where is my page? Go, villain, fetch a surgeon.

Exit Page.

ROMEO

Courage, man. The hurt cannot be much.

MERCUTIO   No, 'tis not so deep as a well, nor so wide
as a church door; but 'tis enough, it will serve. Ask
for me to-morrow, and you shall find me a grave
man. I am peppered, I warrant, for this world. A
plague on both your houses! God's wounds, a dog,
a rat, a mouse, a cat, to scratch a man to death! a
braggart, a rogue, a villain, that fights by the book
of arithmetic! Why the devil came you between us?
I was hurt under your arm.

ROMEO

    I thought all for the best.

MERCUTIO

    Help me into some house, Benvolio,
    Or I shall faint. A plague on both your houses!
    They have made worms' meat of me. I have it,
    And soundly too. Your houses!

                          Exit supported by Benvolio.

ROMEO

    This gentleman, the Prince's near ally,
    My very friend, has got this mortal hurt
    In my behalf—my reputation stained
    With Tybalt's slander—Tybalt, that an hour
    Has been my cousin. O sweet Juliet,
    Your beauty has made me effeminate,
    And in my temper softened valor's steel!

                  Enter BENVOLIO.

BENVOLIO

    O Romeo, Romeo, brave Mercutio is dead!
    That gallant spirit has aspired the clouds,
    Which too untimely here did scorn the earth.

ROMEO

    This day's black fate on more days does depend;
    This but begins the woe others must end.

                  Enter TYBALT.

BENVOLIO

    Here comes the furious Tybalt back again.

ROMEO

    Alive in triumph, and Mercutio slain?
    Away to heaven respective lenity,

And fire-eyed fury be my conduct now!
Now, Tybalt, take the 'villain' back again
That late you gave me; for Mercutio's soul
Is but a little way above our heads,
Staying for yours to keep him company.
Either you or I, or both, must go with him.

TYBALT
You, wretched boy, that did consort him here,
Shall with him hence.

ROMEO   This shall determine that.

They fight. TYBALT *falls.*

BENVOLIO
Romeo, away, be gone!
The citizens are up, and Tybalt slain.
Stand not amazed. The Prince will allot you death
If you are taken. Hence, be gone, away!

ROMEO
O, I am fortune's fool!

BENVOLIO   Why do you stay?   *Exit Romeo.*

Enter Citizens.

CITIZEN
Which way ran he that killed Mercutio?
Tybalt, that murderer, which way ran he?

BENVOLIO
There lies that Tybalt.

CITIZEN   Up, sir, go with me.
I charge you in the Prince's name obey.

Enter PRINCE *attended*, MONTAGUE, CAPULET,
their Wives, *and all.*

PRINCE
  Where are the vile beginners of this fray?

BENVOLIO
  O noble Prince, I can discover all
  The unlucky manage of this fatal brawl.
  There lies the man, slain by young Romeo,
  That slew your kinsman, brave Mercutio.

LADY CAPULET
  Tybalt, my nephew! O my brother's child!
  O Prince! O husband! O, the blood is spilled
  Of my dear kinsman! Prince, as you are true,
  For blood of ours shed blood of Montague.
  O nephew, my nephew!

PRINCE
  Benvolio, who began this bloody fray?

BENVOLIO
  Tybalt, here slain, whom Romeo's hand did slay.
  Romeo, that spoke him fair, bid him bethink
  How slender the quarrel was, and urged with it
  Your high displeasure. All this—utterèd
  With gentle breath, calm look, knees humbly
      bowed—
  Could not take truce with the unruly spleen
  Of Tybalt deaf to peace, but that he tilts
  With piercing steel at bold Mercutio's breast:
  Who, all as hot, turns deadly point to point,
  And, with a martial scorn, with one hand beats
  Cold death aside and with the other sends
  It back to Tybalt, whose dexterity
  Retorts it. Romeo, he cries aloud,
  'Hold, friends! friends, part!' and swifter than his
      tongue,
  His agile arm beats down their fatal points,
  Between them rushes; underneath whose arm

An under-thrust from Tybalt hit the life
Of stout Mercutio, and then Tybalt fled.
But by and by comes back to Romeo,
Who had but newly entertained revenge,
And to it they go like lightning. For, ere I
Could draw to part them, was stout Tybalt slain;
And, as he fell, did Romeo turn and fly.
This is the truth, or let Benvolio die.

LADY CAPULET

He is a kinsman to the Montague;
Affection makes him false, he speaks not true.
Some twenty of them fought in this black strife,
And all those twenty could but kill one life.
I beg for justice, which you, Prince, must give.
Romeo slew Tybalt; Romeo must not live.

PRINCE

Romeo slew him; he slew Mercutio.
Who now the price of his dear blood does owe?

MONTAGUE

Not Romeo, Prince; he was Mercutio's friend;
His fault concludes but what the law should end,
The life of Tybalt.

PRINCE   And for that offense
Immediately we do exile him hence.
I have an interest in your hate's proceeding,
My blood for your rude brawls does lie a-bleeding;
But I will charge you with so strong a fine
That you shall all repent the loss of mine.
I will be deaf to pleading and excuses;
Nor tears nor prayers shall purchase out abuses.
Therefore use none. Let Romeo hence in haste,
Else, when he is found, that hoür is his last.
Bear hence this body, and attend our will.
Mercy but murders, pardoning those that kill.

                                          Exeunt.

SCENE II
Verona. Capulet's orchard.

Enter JULIET *alone.*

JULIET
   Gallop apace, you fiery-footed steeds,
   Towards Phoebus' lodging! Such a wagoner
   As Phaeton would whip you to the west
   And bring in cloudy night immediately.
   Spread your close curtain, love-performing night,
   That runaways' eyes may wink, and Romeo
   Leap to these arms untalked of and unseen.
   Lovers can see to do their amorous rites
   By their own beauties; or, if love is blind,
   It best agrees with night. Come, civil night,
   You sober-suited matron, all in black,
   And teach me how to lose a winning match,
   Played for a pair of stainless maidenhoods.
   Hood my unmanned blood, flushing in my cheeks,
   With your black mantle till strange love grows bold,
   Think true love acted simple modesty.
   Come, night; come, Romeo; come, you day in night;
   For you will lie upon the wings of night
   Whiter than new snow upon a raven's back.
   Come, gentle night; come, loving, black-browed
     night;
   Give me my Romeo; and, when he shall die,
   Take him and cut him out in little stars,
   And he will make the face of heaven so fine
   That all the world will be in love with night,
   And pay no worship to the garish sun.
   O, I have bought the mansion of a love,
   But not possessed it; and though I am sold,

Not yet enjoyed. So tedious is this day
As is the night before some festival
To an impatient child that has new robes
And may not wear them. O here comes my nurse,

Enter NURSE, *with cords.*

And she brings news; and every tongue that speaks
But Romeo's name speaks heavenly eloquence.
Now, nurse, what news? What have you there, the
   cords
That Romeo bid you fetch?
NURSE   Ay, ay, the cords.

Throws them down.

JULIET
Ay me! what news? Why do you wring your hands?
NURSE
Ah, welladay! he's dead, he's dead, he's dead!
We are undone, lady, we are undone!
Alas the day! he's gone, he's killed, he's dead!
JULIET
Can heaven be so envious?
NURSE   Romeo can,
Though heaven cannot. O Romeo, Romeo!
Who ever would have thought it? Romeo!
JULIET
What devil are you that do torment me thus?
This torture should be roared in dismal hell.
Has Romeo slain himself? Say you but 'Ay,'
And that bare vowel 'Ay' shall poison more
Than the death-darting eye of basilisk.
I am not I, if there be such an 'Ay'

Or those eyes' shot that makes the answer 'Ay.'
If he is slain, say 'Ay'; or if not, 'no.'
Brief sounds determine of my weal or woe.

NURSE

I saw the wound, I saw it with my eyes,
(God save the mark!) here on his manly breast.
A piteous corpse, a bloody piteous corpse;
Pale, pale as ashes, all bedaubed in blood,
All in gore-blood. I swoonded at the sight.

JULIET

O, break, my heart! poor bankrupt, break at once!
To prison, eyes; never look on liberty!
Vile earth, to earth resign; end motion here,
And you and Romeo press one heavy bier!

NURSE

O Tybalt, Tybalt, the best friend I had!
O courteous Tybalt! honest gentleman!
That ever I should live to see you dead!

JULIET

What storm is this that blows so contrary?
Is Romeo slaughtered, and is Tybalt dead?
My dearest cousin, and my dearer lord?
Then, dreadful trumpet, sound the general doom!
For who is living, if those two are gone?

NURSE

Tybalt is gone, and Romeo banishèd;
Romeo that killed him, he is banishèd.

JULIET

O God! Did Romeo's hand shed Tybalt's blood?

NURSE

It did, it did! alas the day, it did!

JULIET

O serpent heart, hid with a flowering face!
Did ever dragon keep so fair a cave?

Beautiful tyrant! fiend angelical!
Dove-feathered raven! wolvish-ravening lamb!
Despisèd substance of divinest show!
Just opposite to what you justly seem—
A damnèd saint, an honorable villain!
O nature, what had you to do in hell
When you did bower the spirit of a fiend
In mortal paradise of such sweet flesh?
Was ever book containing such vile matter
So fairly bound? O, that deceit should dwell
In such a gorgeous palace!

NURSE   There's no trust,
No faith, no honesty in men; all perjured,
All forsworn, all naught, all dissemblers.
Ah, where's my man? Give me some aqua vitae
[brandy].
These griefs, these woes, these sorrows make me
old.
Shame come to Romeo!

JULIET   Blistered be your tongue
For such a wish! He was not born to shame.
Upon his brow shame is ashamed to sit;
It is a throne where honor may be crowned
Sole monarch of the universal earth.
O, what a beast was I to chide at him!

NURSE
Will you speak well of him that killed your cousin?

JULIET
Shall I speak ill of him that is my husband?
Ah, poor my lord, what tongue shall smooth your
name
When I, your three-hours wife, have mangled it?
But wherefore, villain, did you kill my cousin?
That villain cousin would have killed my husband.
Back, foolish tears, back to your native spring!

Your tributary drops belong to woe,
Which you, mistaking, offer up to joy.
My husband lives, that Tybalt would have slain;
And Tybalt's dead, that would have slain my
    husband.
All this is comfort; wherefore weep I then?
Some word there was, worse than Tybalt's death,
That murdered me. I would forget it gladly;
But O, it presses to my memory
Like damned guilty deeds to sinners' minds!
'Tybalt is dead, and Romeo—banishèd.'
That 'banishèd,' that one word 'banishèd,'
Has slain ten thousand Tybalts. Tybalt's death
Was woe enough, if it had ended there.
Or, if sour woe delights in fellowship
And needly will be ranked with other griefs,
Why followed not, when she said 'Tybalt's dead,'
Your father, or your mother, nay, or both,
Which normal lamentation might have moved?
But with a rearward following Tybalt's death,
'Romeo is banishèd'—to speak that word
Is father, mother, Tybalt, Romeo, Juliet,
All slain, all dead. 'Romeo is banishèd'—
There is no end, no limit, measure, bound,
In that word's death; no words can that woe sound.
Where are my father and my mother, nurse?

NURSE
Weeping and wailing over Tybalt's corpse.
Will you go to them? I will bring you thither.

JULIET
Wash they his wounds with tears? Mine shall be
    spent,
When theirs are dry, for Romeo's banishment.
Take up those cords. Poor ropes, you are beguiled,
Both you and I, for Romeo is exiled.
He made you for a highway to my bed;

But I, a maid, die maiden-widowèd.
Come, cords; come, nurse. I'll to my wedding bed;
And death, not Romeo, take my maidenhead!

NURSE
Hie to your chamber. I'll find Romeo
To comfort you. I know well where he is.
Hark you, your Romeo will be here at night.
I'll to him; he is hidden at Laurence' cell.

JULIET
O, find him! give this ring to my true knight
And bid him come to take his last farewell.

Exit with Nurse.

SCENE III
Verona. Friar Laurence's Cell.

Enter FRIAR LAURENCE.

FRIAR LAURENCE
Romeo, come forth; come forth, you guilty man.
Affliction is enamored of your parts,
And you are wedded to calamity. It just happens

Enter ROMEO.

ROMEO
Father, what news? What is the Prince's doom?
What sorrow craves acquaintance at my hand
That I yet know not?

FRIAR LAURENCE   Too familiàr
Is my dear son with such sour company.
I bring you tidings of the Prince's doom.

ROMEO
What less than doomsday is the Prince's doom?

FRIAR LAURENCE

A gentler judgment vanished from his lips—
Not body's death, but body's banishment.

ROMEO

Ha, banishment? Be merciful, say 'death';
For exile has more terror in its look,
Much more than death. Do not say 'banishment.'

FRIAR LAURENCE

Hence from Verona are you banishèd.
Be patient, for the world is broad and wide.

ROMEO

There is no world without Verona walls,
But purgatory, torture, hell itself.
Hence banishèd is banished from the world,
And world's exile is death. Then 'banishèd'
Is death mistermed. Calling death 'banishèd,'
You cut my head off with a golden axe
And smile upon the stroke that murders me.

FRIAR LAURENCE

O deadly sin! O rude unthankfulness!
Your fault our law calls death; but the kind Prince,
Taking your part, has rushed aside the law,
And turned that black word 'death' to banishment.
This is dear mercy, and you see it not.

ROMEO

It is torture, and not mercy. Heaven is here,
Where Juliet lives; and every cat and dog
And little mouse, every unworthy thing,
Live here in heaven and may look on her;
But Romeo may not. More validity,
More honorable state, more courtship lives
In carrion flies than Romeo. They may seize
On the white wonder of dear Juliet's hand
And steal immortal blessing from her lips,

Which, even in pure and vestal modesty,
Still blush, as thinking their own kisses sin;
But Romeo may not, he is banishèd.
Flies may do this, but I from this must fly;
They are freemen, but I am banishèd.
And say you yet that exile is not death?
Had you no poison mixed, no sharp-ground knife,
No sudden means of death, though never so mean,
But 'banishèd' to kill me—'banishèd'?
O friar, the damnèd use that word in hell;
Howling attends it! How have you the heart,
Being a divine, a ghostly cònfessor,
A sin-absolver, and my friend professed,
To mangle me with that word 'banishèd'?

FRIAR LAURENCE
You foolish man, hear me a little speak.

ROMEO
O, you will speak again of banishment.

FRIAR LAURENCE
I'll give you armor to keep off that word;
Adversity's sweet milk, philosophy,
To comfort you, though you are banishèd.

ROMEO
Yet 'banishèd'? Hang up philosophy!
Unless philosophy can make a Juliet,
Displant a town, reverse a prince's doom,
It helps not, it prevails not. Talk no more.

FRIAR LAURENCE
O, then I see that madmen have no ears.

ROMEO
How should they, when then wise men have no
    eyes?

FRIAR LAURENCE
Let me dispute with you your prospect now.

ROMEO

You can not speak of that you do not feel.
Were you as young as I, Juliet your love,
An hour but married, Tybalt murderèd,
Doting like me, and like me banishèd,
Then might you speak, then might you tear your
　　hair,
And fall upon the ground, as I do now.
Taking the measure of an unmade grave.

NURSE *knocks.*

FRIAR LAURENCE

Arise; one knocks. Good Romeo, hide yourself.

ROMEO

Not I; unless the breath of heartsick groans
Mist-like infold me from the search of eyes.

Knock.

FRIAR LAURENCE

Hark, how they knock! Who's there? Romeo arise;
You will be taken.—Stay awhile!—Stand up;

Knock.

Run to my study.—By and by!—God's will,
What simpleness is this.—I come, I come!

Knock.

Who knocks so hard? Whence come you? What's
　　your will?

Enter NURSE.

NURSE

Let me come in, and you shall know my errand.
I come from Lady Juliet.

FRIAR LAURENCE   Welcome then.

NURSE

O holy friar, O, tell me, holy friar,
Where is my lady's lord, where's Romeo?

FRIAR LAURENCE

There on the ground, with his own tears made
    drunk.

NURSE

O, he is even in my mistress' case,
Just in her case! O woeful sympathy!
Piteous predicament! Even so lies she,
Blubbering and weeping, weeping and blubbering.
Stand up, stand up! Stand if you are a man.
For Juliet's sake, for her sake, rise and stand!
Why should you fall into so deep an O?

ROMEO   [rises] Nurse—

NURSE

Ah sir! ah sir! Death is the end of all.

ROMEO

Spoke you of Juliet? How is it with her?
Does not she think me an old murderer,
Now I have stained the childhood of our joy
With blood removed but little from her own?
Where is she? and how does she! and what says
My còncealed lady to our cancelled love?

NURSE

O, she says nothing, sir, but weeps and weeps;
And now falls on her bed, and then starts up,
And Tybalt calls; and then on Romeo cries,
And then down falls again.

ROMEO   As if that name,
Shot from the deadly level of a gun,
Did murder her; as that name's cursèd hand

Murdered her kinsman. O, tell me, friar, tell me,
In what vile part of this anatomy
Does my name lodge? Tell me, that I may sack
The hateful mansion.

He draws his dagger

FRIAR LAURENCE   Hold your desperate hand.
Are you a man? Your form cries out you are;
Your tears are womanish, your wild acts denote
The unreasonable fury of a beast.
Unseemly woman in a seeming man!
And ill-beseeming beast in seeming both!
You have amazed me. By my holy order,
I thought your disposition better tempered.
Have you slain Tybalt? Will you slay yourself?
And slay your lady that in your life lives,
By doing damnèd hate upon yourself?
Why rail you on your birth, the heaven and earth?
Since birth and heaven and earth, all three do meet
In you at once; which you at once would lose.
Fie, fie, you shame your shape, your love, your
    sense,
Which, like a usurer, abound in all,
And use none in that true use indeed
Which should bedeck your shape, your love, your
    sense.
Your noble shape is but a form of wax,
Digressing from the valor of a man;
Your dear love sworn but hollow perjury,
Killing that love which you have vowed to cherish.
Your sense, that ornament to shape and love,
Misshapen in the conduct of them both,
Like powder in a skilless soldier's flask,

continue

Is set afire by your own ignorance,
And you dismembererd with your own defense.
What, rouse you, man! Your Juliet is alive,
For whose dear sake you were but lately dead.
There are you happy. Tybalt would kill you,
But you slew Tybalt. There are you happy too.
The law, that threatened death, becomes your friend
And turns it to exile. There are you happy.
A pack of blessings light upon your back;
Happiness courts you in her best array;
But, like a misbehaved and sullen wench,
You pout upon your fortune and your love.
Take heed, take heed, for such die miserable.
Go get you to your love, as was decreed,
Ascend her chamber, hence and comfort her.
But look you stay not till the watch is set,
For then you can not pass to Mantua:
Where you shall live till we can find a time
To blaze your marriage, reconcile your friends,
Beg pardon of the Prince, and call you back
With twenty hundred thousand times more joy
Than you went forth in lamentation.
Go before, nurse. Commend me to your lady,
And bid her hasten all the house to bed,
Which heavy sorrow makes them apt unto.
Romeo is coming.

NURSE

O Lord, I could have stayed here all the night
To hear good counsel. O, what learning is!
My lord, I'll tell my lady you will come.

ROMEO

Do so, and bid my sweet prepare to chide.

NURSE

Here is a ring she bids me give you, sir.
Hie you, make haste, for it grows very late.   *Exit.*

ROMEO
   How well my comfort is revived by this!
FRIAR LAURENCE
   Go hence; good night; and here stands your case:
   Either be gone before the watch is set,
   Or by the break of day disguised from hence.
   Sojourn in Mantua. I'll find out your man,
   And he shall signify from time to time
   Every good hap to you that chances here.
   Give me your hand. 'Tis late. Farewell; good night.
ROMEO
   But that a joy past joy calls out on me,
   It were a grief so brief to part with you.
   Farewell.   *Exeunt.*

SCENE IV
Verona. A hall in Capulet's house.

Enter CAPULET, *his* Wife, *and* PARIS.

CAPULET
   Things have fallen out, sir, so unluckily
   That we have had no time to move our daughter.
   Look you, she loved her kinsman Tybalt dearly,
   And so did I. Well, we were born to die.
   It is very late; she'll not come down to-night.
   I promise you, but for your company,
   I would have been abed an hour ago.
PARIS
   These times of woe afford no times to woo.
   Madam, good night. Commend me to your daughter.

LADY CAPULET

> I will, and know her mind early to-morrow;
> To-night she's mewed up to her heaviness.

CAPULET

> Sir Paris, I will make a desparate tender
> Of my child's love. I think she will be ruled
> In all respects by me; nay more, I doubt it not.
> Wife, go you to her ere you go to bed;
> Acquaint her here of my son Paris' love
> And bid her, mark you me, on Wednesday next—
> But soft! what day is this?

PARIS   Monday, my lord.

CAPULET

> Monday! ha, ha! Well, Wednesday is too soon.
> On Thursday, let it be—on Thursday, tell her,
> She shall be married to this noble earl.
> Will you be ready? Do you like this haste?
> We'll keep no great ado—a friend or two;
> For hark you, Tybalt being slain so late,
> It may be thought we held him carelessly,
> Being our kinsman, if we revel much.
> Therefore we'll have some half a dozen friends,
> And there an end. But what say you to Thursday?

PARIS

> My lord, I would that Thursday were to-morrow.

CAPULET

> Well, get you gone. On Thursday be it then.
> Go you to Juliet ere you go to bed;
> Prepare her, wife, against this wedding day.
> Farewell, my lord.—Light to my chamber, ho!
> Before me, it is so very late that we
> May call it early by and by. Good night.

Exeunt.

SCENE V
Verona. Juliet's chamber

Enter ROMEO *and* JULIET *above.*

JULIET

    Will you be gone? It is not yet near day.
    It was the nightingale, and not the lark,
    That pierced the fearful hollow of your ear.
    Nightly she sings on yon pomegranate tree.
    Believe me, love, it was the nightingale.

ROMEO

    It was the lark, the herald of the morn;
    No nightingale. Look, love, what envious streaks
    Do lace the severing clouds in yonder east.
    Night's candles are burnt out, and jocund day
    Stands tiptoe on the misty mountain tops.
    I must be gone and live, or stay and die.

JULIET

    Yon light is not daylight; I know it, I.
    It is some meteor that the sun exhales
    To be to you this night a torchbearer
    And light you on your way to Mantua.
    Therefore stay yet; you need not to be gone.

ROMEO

    Let me be taken, let me be put to death.
    I am content, so you will have it so.
    I'll say yon grey is not the morning's eye,
    'Tis but the pale reflex of Cynthia's brow;
    And that is not the lark whose notes do beat
    The vaulty heaven so high above our heads.
    I have more care to stay than will to go.
    Come, death, and welcome! Juliet wills it so.
    How is it, my soul? Let's talk; it is not day.

JULIET

  It is, it is! Hie hence, be gone, away!
  It is the lark that sings so out of tune,
  Straining harsh discords and unpleasing sharps.
  Some say the lark makes sweet division;
  This does not so, for she divides us now.
  Some say the lark and loathèd toad change eyes;
  O, now I would they had changed voices too,
  Since arm from arm that voice does us affright,
  Hunting you hence with hunt's-up to the day.
  O, now be gone! More light and light it grows.

ROMEO

  More light and light—more dark and dark our woes.

Enter NURSE

NURSE Madam!
JULIET Nurse?
NURSE

  Your lady mother is coming to your chamber.
  The day is broken; be wary, look about.   *Exit.*
JULIET

  Then, window, let day in, and let life out.
ROMEO

  Farewell, farewell! One kiss, and I'll descend.

He goes down.

JULIET

  Are you gone so, love-lord, ay husband-friend?
  I must hear from you every day in the hour,
  For in a minute there are many days.
  O, by this count I shall be much in years
  Ere I again behold my Romeo!

ROMEO
    Farewell!
    I will omit no opportunity
    That may convey my greetings, love, to you.
JULIET
    O, think you we shall ever meet again?
ROMEO
    I doubt it not; and all these woes shall serve
    For sweet discourses in our times to come.
JULIET
    O God, I have an ill-divining soul!
    I think I see you, now you are so low,
    As one dead in the bottom of a tomb.
    Either my eyesight fails, or you look pale.
ROMEO
    And trust me, love, in my eye so do you.
    Dry sorrow drinks our blood. Adieu, adieu!   *Exit.*
JULIET
    O Fortune, Fortune! all men call you fickle.
    If you are fickle, what do you with him
    That is renowned for faith? Be fickle, Fortune,
    For then I hope you will not keep him long
    But send him back.

                    Enter LADY CAPULET

LADY CAPULET
    Ho, daughter, are you up?
JULIET
    Who is it that calls? It is my lady mother.
    Is she not down so late, or up so early?
    What unaccustomed cause procures her hither?
LADY CAPULET
    Why, how now, Juliet?
JULIET   Madam, I am not well.

LADY CAPULET
  Evermore weeping for your cousin's death?
  What, will you wash him from his grave with tears?
  But if you could, you could not make him live.
  Therefore have done. Some grief shows much of
      love;
  But much of grief shows still some want of sense.
JULIET
  Yet let me weep for such a feeling loss.
LADY CAPULET
  So shall you feel the loss, but not the friend
  Whom you weep for.
JULIET   Feeling so the loss,
  I cannot choose but ever weep the friend.
LADY CAPULET
  Well, girl, you weep not so much for his death
  As that the villain lives who slaughtered him.
JULIET
  What villain, madam?
LADY CAPULET   That same villain Romeo.
JULIET   [aside]
  Villain and he are many miles asunder.—
  God pardon him! I do, with all my heart;
  And yet no man like him does grieve my heart.
LADY CAPULET
  That is because the traitor murderer lives.
JULIET
  Ay, madam, from the reach of these my hands.
  Would none but I might venge my cousin's death!
LADY CAPULET
  We will have vengeance for it, fear you not.
  Then weep no more. I'll send to one in Mantua,
  Where that same banished runagate does live,
  Shall give him such an unaccustomed dram
  That he shall soon keep Tybalt company.
  And then I hope you will be satisfied.

JULIET

Indeed I never shall be satisfied
With Romeo till I behold him—dead—
Is my poor heart so for a kinsman vexed.
Madam, if you could find out but a man
To bear a poison, I would temper it;
That Romeo should, upon receipt thereof,
Soon sleep in quiet. O, how my heart abhors
To hear him named and cannot come to him,
To wreak the love I bore my cousin
Upon his body that has slaughtered him!

LADY CAPULET

Find you the means, and I'll find such a man.
But now I'll tell you joyful tidings, girl.

JULIET

And joy comes well in such a needy time.
What are they, beseech your ladyship?

LADY CAPULET

Well, well, you have a careful father, child;
One who, to put you from your heaviness,
Has sorted out a sudden day of joy
That you expect not, nor did I look out for.

JULIET

Madam, in happy time! What day is that?

LADY CAPULET

Indeed, my child, early next Thursday morn
The gallant, young, and noble gentleman,
The County [Count] Paris, at Saint Peter's Church,
Shall happily make you there a joyful bride.

JULIET

Now by Saint Peter's Church, and Peter too,
He shall not make me there a joyful bride!
I wonder at this haste, that I must wed
Ere he that should be husband comes to woo.
I pray you tell my lord and father, madam,
I will not marry yet; and when I do, I swear

It shall be Romeo, whom you know I hate,
Rather than Paris. These are news indeed!
LADY CAPULET

   Here comes your father. Tell him so yourself,
   And see how he will take it at your hands.

      Enter CAPULET *and* NURSE.

CAPULET

   When the sun sets the earth does drizzle dew,
   But for the sunset of my brother's son
   It rains downright.
   How now? a conduit, girl? What, still in tears?
   Evermore showering? In one little body
   You counterfeit a bark, a sea, a wind:
   For still your eyes, which I may call the sea,
   Do ebb and flow with tears. The bark your body is,
   Sailing in this salt flood; the winds, your sighs,
   Which, raging with your tears and they with them,
   Without a sudden calm will overset
   Your tempest-tossèd body. How now, wife?
   Have you delivered to her our decree?
LADY CAPULET

   Ay, sir; but she will none, she gives you thanks.
   I would the fool were married to her grave!
CAPULET

   Soft! take me with you, take me with you, wife.
   How? Will she none? Does she not give us thanks?
   Is she not proud? Does she not count her blest,
   Unworthy as she is, that we have wrought
   So worthy a gentleman to be her bride?
JULIET

   Not proud you have, but thankful that you have.
   Proud can I never be of what I hate,
   But thankful even for hate that is meant love.

CAPULET

How, how, how, how, chop-logic? What is this?
'Proud'—and 'I thank you'—and 'I thank you not'—
And yet 'not proud'? Mistress minion you,
Thank me no thankings, nor proud me no prouds,
But fettle your fine joints before Thursday next
To go with Paris to Saint Peter's Church,
Or I will drag you on a hurdle thither.
Out, you green-sickness carrion! out, you baggage!
You tallow-face!

LADY CAPULET Fie, fie! what, are you mad?

JULIET

Good father, I beseech you on my knees,
Hear me with patience but to speak a word.

CAPULET

Hang you, young baggage! disobedient wretch!
I tell you what—get you to church on Thursday
Or never after look me in the face.
Speak not, reply not, do not answer me!
My fingers itch. Wife, we scarce thought us blest
That God had lent us but this only child;
But now I see this one is one too much,
And that we have a curse in having her.
Out on her, bitch!

NURSE God in heaven bless her!

You are to blame, my lord, to rate her so.

CAPULET

And why, my Lady Wisdom? Hold your tongue,
Good Prudence. Chatter with your gossips, go!

NURSE

I speak no treason.

CAPULET O, for God's sake!

NURSE

May not one speak?

CAPULET   Peace, you mumbling fool!
  Utter your gravity over a gossip's bowl,
  For here we need it not.
LADY CAPULET   You are too hot.
CAPULET
  God's bread! it makes me mad.
  Day, night, hour; tide, time; work, play;
  Alone, in company; ever my care has been
  To have her matched. And having now provided
  A gentleman of noble parentage,
  Of fair domains, youthful, and nobly trained,
  Stuffed, as they say, with honorable parts,
  Proportioned as one's thought would wish a man—
  And then to have a wretched puling fool,
  A whining mommet, in her fortune's tender,
  To answer 'I'll not wed, I cannot love;
  I am too young, I pray you pardon me'!
  But, if you will not wed, I'll pardon you!
  Graze where you will, you shall not house with me.
  Look to it, think on it; I do not use to jest.
  Thursday is near; lay hand on heart, advise:
  If you are mine, I'll give you to my friend;
  If you are not, hang, beg, starve, die in the streets,
  For, by my soul, I'll never acknowledge you,
  Nor what is mine shall ever do you good.
  Trust to it, bethink you, I'll not be made a fool of.
                                     Exit.
JULIET
  Is there no pity sitting in the clouds
  That sees into the bottom of my grief?
  O sweet my mother, cast me not away!
  Delay this marriage for a month, a week;
  Or if you do not, make the bridal bed
  In that dim monument where Tybalt lies.

LADY CAPULET
  Talk not to me, for I'll not speak a word.
  Do as you will, for I have done with you.   *Exit.*
JULIET
  O God!—O nurse, how shall this be prevented?
  My husband is on earth, my faith in heaven.
  How shall that faith return again to earth
  Unless that husband sends it me from heaven
  By leaving earth? Comfort me, counsel me.
  Alas, that heaven should practise stratagems
  Upon so soft a subject as myself!
  What say you? Have you not a word of joy?
  Some comfort, nurse.
NURSE   Faith, here it is.
  Romeo is banished; and all the world to nothing
  That he dares ever come back to challenge you;
  Or if he does, it needs must be by stealth.
  Then, since the case so stands as now it does,
  I think it best you married with the Count.
  O, he's a lovely gentleman!
  Romeo's a dishclout to him. An eagle, madam,
  Has not so green, so quick, so fair an eye
  As Paris has. Why, bless my very heart,
  I think you are happy in this second match,
  For it excels your first; or if it did not,
  Your first is dead—it is as good he were
  As living here and you no use of him.
JULIET
  Speak you from your heart?
NURSE
  And from my soul too; else curse them both.
JULIET   Amen!
NURSE   What?
JULIET
  Well, you have comforted me marvellous much.
  Go in; and tell my lady I am gone,

Having displeased my father, to Laurence' cell,
To make confession and to be absolved.

NURSE

Sure, I will; and this is wisely done. *Exit.*

JULIET

Ancient damnation! O most wicked fiend!
Is it more sin to wish me thus forsworn,
Or to dispraise my lord with that same tongue
Which she has praised him with above compare
So many thousand times? Go, counsellor!
You and my bosom henceforth shall be twain.
I'll to the friar to know his remedy.
If all else fails, myself have power to die. *Exit.*

Act IV

SCENE I
Verona. Friar Laurence's cell.

Enter FRIAR LAURENCE *and* COUNT PARIS.

FRIAR LAURENCE

On Thursday, sir? The time is very short.

PARIS

My father Capulet will have it so,
And I am nothing slow to slack his haste.

FRIAR LAURENCE

You say you do not know the lady's mind.
Uneven is the course; I like it not.

PARIS

Immoderately she weeps for Tybalt's death,
And therefore have I little talked of love;

For Venus smiles not in a house of tears.
Now, sir, her father counts it dangerous
That she does give her sorrow so much sway,
And in his wisdom hastes our marriage
To stop the inundation of her tears;
Which, too much minded by herself alone,
May be put from her by society.
Now do you know the reason of this haste.

FRIAR LAURENCE   [*aside*]
I would I knew not why it should be slowed.—
Look, sir, here comes the lady toward my cell.

Enter JULIET.

PARIS
Happily met, my lady and my wife!
JULIET
That may be sir, when I may be a wife.
PARIS
That 'may be' must be, love, on Thursday next.
JULIET
What must be shall be.
FRIAR LAURENCE   That's a certain text.
PARIS
Come you to make confession to this father?
JULIET
To answer that, I should confess to you.
PARIS
Do not deny to him that you love me.
JULIET
I will confess to you that I love him.
PARIS
So will you, I am sure, that you love me.
JULIET
If I do so, it will be of more price,
Being spoken behind your back, than to your face.

PARIS

Poor soul, your face is much abused with tears.

JULIET

The tears have got small victory by that,
For it was bad enough before their spite.

PARIS

You wrong it more than tears with that report.

JULIET

That is no slander, sir, which is a truth;
And what I spoke, I spoke it to my face.

PARIS

Your face is mine, and you have slandered it.

JULIET

It may be so, for it is not my own.
Are you at leisure, holy father, now,
Or shall I come to you at evening mass?

FRIAR LAURENCE

My leisure serves me, pensive daughter, now.
My lord, we must entreat the time alone.

PARIS

God shield I should disturb devotion!
Juliet, on Thursday early will I rouse you.
Till then, adieu, and keep this holy kiss.   *Exit.*

JULIET

O, shut the door! and when you have done so,
Come weep with me—past hope, past cure, past
   help!

FRIAR LAURENCE

Ah, Juliet, I already know your grief;
It strains me past the compass of my wits.
I hear you must, and nothing may prorogue it,
On Thursday next be married to this Count.

JULIET

Tell me not, friar, that you heard of this,
Unless you tell me how I may prevent it.
If in your wisdom you can give no help,

Do you but call my resolution wise
And with this knife I'll help it instantly.
God joined my heart and Romeo's, you our hands;
And ere this hand, by you to Romeo's sealed,
Shall be the label to another deed,
Or my true heart with treacherous revolt
Turn to another, this shall slay them both.
Therefore, out of your long-experienced time,
Give me some present counsel. Or, behold,
Between my extremes and me this bloody knife
Shall play the umpire, arbitrating that
Which the commission of your years and art
Could to no issue of true honor bring.
Be not so long to speak. I long to die
If what you speak speaks not of remedy.

FRIAR LAURENCE

Hold, daughter. I do spy a kind of hope,
Which craves as desperate an execution
As that is desperate which we would prevent.
If, rather than to marry the Count Paris,
You have the strength of will to slay yourself,
Then it is likely you will undertake
A thing like death to chide away this shame,
That cope with death himself to escape from it.
And, if you dare, I'll give you remedy.

JULIET

O, bid me leap, rather than marry Paris,
From off the battlements of any tower,
Or walk in thievish ways, or bid me lurk
Where serpents are; chain me with roaring bears,
Or hide me nightly in a charnel house,
O'ercovered quite with dead men's rattling bones,
With reeky shanks and yellow chapless skulls.
Or bid me go into a new-made grave
And hide me with a dead man in his shroud—

Things that, to hear them told, have made me
    tremble—
And I will do it without fear or doubt,
To live an unstained wife to my sweet love.

FRIAR LAURENCE

Hold, then. Go home, be merry, give consent
To marry Paris. Wednesday is to-morrow.
To-morrow night look that you lie alone;
Let not the nurse lie with you in your chamber.
Take you this vial, being then in bed,
And this distilling liquor drink you off.
When presently through all your veins shall run
A cold and drowsy humor; for no pulse
Shall keep its native progress, but surcease.
No warmth, no breath, shall testify you live.
The roses in your lips and cheeks shall fade
To wan ashes, your eyes' windows fall
Like death when it shuts up the day of life.
Each part, deprived of supple government,
Shall, stiff and stark and cold, appear like death;
And in this borrowed likeness of shrunk death
You shall continue for two-and-forty hours,
And then awake as from a pleasant sleep.
Now, when the bridegroom in the morning comes
To rouse you from your bed, there are you dead.
Then, as the manner of our country is,
In your best robes uncovered on the bier
You shall be borne to that same ancient vault
Where all the kindred of the Capulets lie.
In the mean time, before you shall awake,
Shall Romeo by my letters know our drift;
And hither shall he come; and he and I
Will watch your waking, and that very night
Shall Romeo bear you hence to Mantua.
And this shall free you from this present shame,

If no inconstant whim nor womanish fear
Abates your valor in the acting it.

JULIET

Give me, give me! O, tell not me of fear!

FRIAR LAURENCE

Hold! Get you gone, be strong and prosperous
In this resolve. I'll send a friar with speed
To Mantua, with my letters to your lord.

JULIET

Love give me strength! and strength shall help
    afford.
Farewell, dear father.   *Exeunt.*

SCENE II

Verona. A hall in Capulet's house.

Enter CAPULET *and* Wife, NURSE, *and* Servingmen.

CAPULET

So many guests invite as here are written.
                                    Exit a Servingman.
Fellow, go hire me twenty cunning cooks.

SERVINGMAN   You shall have none ill, sir; for I'll try
if they can lick their fingers.

CAPULET

How can you try them so?

SERVINGMAN   Sure, sir, 'tis an ill cook that cannot
lick his own fingers. Therefore he that cannot lick
his fingers goes not with me.

CAPULET   Go, begone.   *Exit Servingman.*
We shall be much unfurnished for this time.
What, is my daughter gone to Friar Laurence?

NURSE   Ay, indeed.

CAPULET
  Well, he may chance to do some good on her.
  A peevish self-willed hussy, sure it is.

Enter JULIET.

NURSE
  See where she comes from shrift with merry look.
CAPULET
  How now, my headstrong? Where have you been
    gadding?
JULIET
  Where I have learnt now to repent the sin
  Of disobedient opposition
  To you and your behests, and am enjoined
  By holy Laurence to fall prostrate here
  To beg your pardon. Pardon, I beseech you!
  Henceforward I am ever ruled by you.
CAPULET
  Send for the Count. Go tell him now of this.
  I'll have this knot knit up to-morrow morning.
JULIET
  I met the youthful lord at Laurence' cell
  And gave him then what seemly love I might,
  Not stepping over the bounds of modesty.
CAPULET
  Why, I am glad of it. This is well. Stand up.
  This is as it should be. Let me see the Count.
  Ay indeed go, I say, and fetch him hither.
  Now, before God, this reverend holy friar,
  All our whole city is much bound to him.
JULIET
  Nurse, will you go with me into my closet
  To help me sort such needful ornaments
  As you think fit to furnish me to-morrow?

LADY CAPULET

No, not till Thursday. There is time enough.

CAPULET

Go, nurse, with her. We'll to church to-morrow.

Exeunt Juliet and Nurse.

LADY CAPULET

We shall be short in our provisiòn.
'Tis now near night.

CAPULET   Tush, I will stir about,
And all things shall be well, I warrant you, wife.
Go you to Juliet, help to deck up her.
I'll not to bed to-night; let me alone.
I'll play the housewife for this once. What, ho!
They are all forth; well, I will walk myself
To the Count Paris, to prepare him
In time to-morrow. My heart is wondrous light,
Since this same wayward girl is so reclaimed.

Exeunt.

SCENE III
Verona. Juliet's Chamber.

Enter JULIET *and* NURSE.

JULIET

Ay, those attires are best; but, gentle nurse,
I pray you leave me to myself to-night;
For I have need of many òrisòns
To move the heavens to smile upon my state,
Which, well you know, is cross and full of sin.

Enter LADY CAPULET.

LADY CAPULET

What, are you busy, ho? Need you my help?

JULIET

  No, madam; we have culled such necessaries
  As are behoveful for our state to-morrow.
  So please you, let me now be left alone,
  And let the nurse this night sit up with you.
  For I am sure you have your hands full all
  In this so sudden business.

LADY CAPULET   Good night.

  Get you to bed, and rest; for you have need.

                  Exeunt Lady Capulet and Nurse.

JULIET

  Farewell! God knows when we shall meet again.
  I have a faint cold fear thrills through my veins
  That almost freezes up the heat of life.
  I'll call them back again to comfort me.
  Nurse!—What should she do here?
  My dismal scene I needs must act alone.
  Come, vial.
  What if this mixture does not work at all?
  Shall I be married then to-morrow morning?
  No, no! This shall forbid it. Lie you there.

               Lays down a dagger.

  What if it is a poison which the friar
  Subtly has ministered to have me dead,
  Lest in this marriage he should be dishonored
  Because he married me before to Romeo?
  I fear it is; and yet I think it should not,
  For he has ever been tried a holy man.
  How if, when I am laid into the tomb,
  I wake before the time that Romeo
  Comes to redeem me? There's a fearful point!
  Shall I not then be stifled in the vault,
  To whose foul mouth no healthsome air breathes in,
  And there die strangled ere my Romeo comes?

Or, if I live, is it not very like
The horrible conception of death and night,
Together with the terror of the place—
As in a vault, an ancient receptacle
Where for this many hundred years the bones
Of all my buried ancestors are packed.
Where bloody Tybalt, yet but green in earth,
Lies festering in his shroud; where, as they say,
At some hours in the night spirits resort—
Alas, alas, is it not likely that I,
So early waking—what with loathsome smells,
And shrieks like mandrakes torn out of the earth,
That living mortals, hearing them, run mad—
O, if I wake, shall I not be distraught,
Environèd with all these hideous fears,
And madly play with my forefathers' joints,
And pluck the mangled Tybalt from his shroud;
And, in this rage, with some great kinsman's bone
As with a club dash out my desperate brains?
O, look! I think I see my cousin's ghost
Seeking out Romeo, that did spit his body
Upon a rapier's point. Stay, Tybalt, stay!
Romeo! Romeo! Romeo! I drink to you.

She falls upon her bed within the curtains.

SCENE IV
Verona. A hall in Capulet's house.

Enter LADY CAPULET *and* NURSE.

LADY CAPULET
   Hold, take these keys and fetch more spices, nurse.

NURSE

They call for dates and quinces in the pastry.

Enter CAPULET.

CAPULET

Come, stir, stir, stir! The second cock has crowed,
The curfew bell has rung, 'tis three o'clock.
Look to the baked meats, good Angelica;
Spare not for cost.

NURSE   Go, you housewife, go,
Get you to bed! Faith, you'll be sick to-morrow
For this night's watching.

CAPULET

No, not a whit. What, I have watched ere now.
All night for lesser cause, and never been sick.

LADY CAPULET

Ay, you have been a mouse-hunt [womaniser] in
    your time;
But I will watch you from such watching now.
                         Exit Lady Capulet and Nurse.

CAPULET

A jealous hood, a jealous hood!

*Enter Servants with
spits and logs and baskets.*

                              Now, fellow,
What is there?

1. SERVANT

Things for the cook, sir; but I know not what.

CAPULET

Make haste, make haste.   *Exit first Servant.*
                    Fellow, fetch drier logs.
Call Peter; he will show you where they are.

2. SERVANT
   I have a head, sir, that will find out logs
   And never trouble Peter for the matter.
CAPULET
   Mass, and well said; a merry bastard, ha!
   You shall be prize blockhead.
                         Exit second Servant, with the others.
                                    God, Father! 'tis day.
   The Count will now be here with music straight,
   For so he said he would.
                Play music.   I hear him near.
   Nurse! Wife! What, ho! What, nurse, I say!

                         Enter NURSE.

   Go waken Juliet; go and trim her up.
   I'll go and chat with Paris. Hie, make haste,
   Make haste! The bridegroom he is come already:
   Make haste, I say.   *Exit.*

SCENE V

NURSE goes to curtains.

NURSE
   Mistress! what, mistress! Juliet! Fast, I warrant her,
      she.
   Why, lamb! why, lady! Fie, you slug-abed.
   Why, love, I say! madam! sweetheart! Why, bride!
   What, not a word? You take your pennyworths now;
   Sleep for a week; for the next night, I warrant,
   The Count Paris has so set up his rest
   That you shall rest but little. God forgive me!
   For sure, and amen. How sound is she asleep!

I needs must wake her. Madam, madam, madam!
Ay, let the Count now take you in your bed;
He'll fright you up, in faith. Will it not be?

Draws aside the curtains.

What, dressed, and in your clothes, and down again?
I must needs wake you. Lady! lady! lady!
Alas, alas! Help, help! my lady's dead!
O welladay that ever I was born!
Some aqua vitae, ho! My lord! my lady!

Enter LADY CAPULET.

LADY CAPULET
  What noise is here?
NURSE   O lamentable day!
LADY CAPULET
  What is the matter?
NURSE   Look, look! O heavy day!
LADY CAPULET
  O me, O me! My child, my only life!
  Revive, look up, or I will die with you!
  Help, help! Call help.

Enter CAPULET.

CAPULET
  For shame, bring Juliet forth; her lord is come.
NURSE
  She's dead, deceased; she's dead, alas the day!
LADY CAPULET
  Alas the day, she's dead, she's dead, she's dead!
CAPULET
  Ha! let me see her. Out alas! she's cold,
  Her blood is settled, and her joints are stiff;

Life and these lips have long been separated.
Death lies on her like an untimely frost
Upon the sweetest flower of all the field.

NURSE

O lamentable day!

LADY CAPULET   O woeful time!

CAPULET

Death, that has taken her hence to make me wail,
Ties up my tongue and will not let me speak.

Enter FRIAR LAURENCE *and*
the COUNT PARIS, *with* Musicians

FRIAR

Come, is the bride ready to go to church?

CAPULET

Ready to go, but never to return.
O son, the night before your wedding day
Has Death lain with your wife. There she lies,
Flowër as she was, deflowered by him.
Death is my son-in-law, Death is my heir;
My daughter he has wedded. I will die
And leave him all. Life, living, all is Death's.

PARIS

Have I thought long to see this morning's face,
And does it give me such a sight as this?

LADY CAPULET

Accursed, unhappy, wretched, hateful day!
Most miserable hour that ever time saw
In lasting labor of its pilgrimage!
But one, poor one, one poor and loving child,
But one thing to rejoice and solace in,
And cruel Death has catched it from my sight.

NURSE

    O woe! O woeful, woeful, woeful day!
    Most lamentable day, most woeful day
    That ever ever I did yet behold!
    O day, O day, O day! O hateful day!
    Never was seen so black a day as this.
    O woeful day! O woeful day!

PARIS

    Beguiled, divorced, wronged, spited, slain!
    Most detestable Death, by you beguiled,
    By cruel cruel you quite overthrown.
    O love! O life! not life, but love in death!

CAPULET

    Despised, distressed, hated, martyred, killed!
    Uncomfortable time, why came you now
    To murder, murder our solemnity?
    O child, O child! my soul, and not my child!
    Dead are you—alas, my child is dead,
    And with my child my joys are buried!

FRIAR

    Peace, ho, for shame! Confusion's cure lives not
    In these confusions. Heaven and yourself
    Had part in this fair maid—now heaven has all,
    And all the better is it for the maid.
    Your part in her you could not keep from death,
    But heaven keeps his part in eternal life.
    The most you sought was her promotion,
    For 'twas your heaven she should be advanced;
    And weep you now, seeing she is advanced
    Above the clouds, as high as heaven itself?
    O, in this love, you love your child so ill
    That you run mad, seeing that she is well.
    She's not well married that lives married long,
    But she's best married that dies married young.

Dry up your tears and stick your rosemary
On this fair corpse, and, as the custom is,
In all her best array bear her to church.
For though our nature bids us all lament,
Yet nature's tears are reason's merriment.

CAPULET

All things that we ordainèd festival
Turn from their office to black funeral—
Our instruments to melancholy bells,
Our wedding cheer to a sad burial feast;
Our solemn hymns to sullen dirges change;
Our bridal flowers serve for a buried corpse;
And all things change them to the contrary.

FRIAR

Sir, go you in; and, madam, go with him;
And go, Sir Paris. Every one prepare
To follow this fair corpse unto her grave.
The heavens do lower upon you for some ill;
Move them no more by crossing their high will.

Exeunt shutting the curtains.
The Nurse and Musicians remain.

1. MUSICIAN

Faith, we may put up our pipes and be gone.

NURSE

Honest good fellows, ah, put up, put up!
For well you know this is a pitiful case.   *Exit.*

1. MUSICIAN

Ay, by my word, the case may be amended.

Enter PETER.

PETER   Musicians, O, musicians, 'Heart's ease,'
'Heart's ease'! O, if you will have me live, play
'Heart's ease.'

1. MUSICIAN   Why, 'Heart's ease'?

PETER   O, musicians, because my heart itself plays 'My heart is full of woe.' O, play me some merry dump to comfort me.

1. MUSICIAN   Not a dump we! 'Tis no time to play now.

PETER   You will not then?

1. MUSICIAN   No.

PETER   I will then give it you soundly.

1. MUSICIAN   What will you give us?

PETER   No money, on my faith, but the jest. I will give you the minstrel.

1. MUSICIAN   Then will I give you the serving-creature.

PETER   Then will I lay the serving-creature's dagger on your pate. I will carry no crotchets. I'll re you, I'll fa you. Do you note me?

1. MUSICIAN   If you re us and fa us, you note us.

2. MUSICIAN   Pray you put up your dagger, and put out your wit.

PETER   Then have at you with my wit! I will beat you with an iron wit, and put up my iron dagger. Answer me like men.

> 'When griping grief the heart does wound,
>   And doleful dumps the mind oppress,
> Then music with her silver sound'—

Why 'silver sound'? Why 'music with her silver sound'? What say you, Simon Catling?

1. MUSICIAN   Sure, sir, because silver has a sweet sound.

PETER   Pretty! What say you, Hugh Rebeck?

2. MUSICIAN   I say 'silver sound' because musicians sound for silver.

PETER   Pretty too! What say you, James Soundpost?

3. MUSICIAN   Faith, I know not what to say.

PETER   O, I cry you mercy! you are the singer. I will say for you. It is 'music with her silver sound'

because musicians have no gold for sounding.
   'Then music with her silver sound
      With speedy help does lend redress.'   *Exit.*
1. MUSICIAN   What a pestilent knave is this same!
2. MUSICIAN   Hang him, Jack! Come we'll in here,
   tarry for the mourners, and stay dinner.   *Exeunt.*

Act V

SCENE I
Mantua, A street.

Enter ROMEO.

ROMEO
   If I may trust the flattering truth of sleep,
   My dreams presage some joyful news at hand.
   My bosom's lord sits lightly in its throne,
   And all this day an unaccustomed spirit
   Lifts me above the ground with cheerful thoughts.
   I dreamt my lady came and found me dead—
   Strange dream that gives a dead man leave to think!—
   And breathed such life with kisses in my lips
   That I revived and was an emperor.
   Ah me! how sweet is love itself possessed,
   When but love's shadows are so rich in joy!

Enter BALTHASAR.

   News from Verona! How now, Balthasar?
   Do you not bring me letters from the friar?

How does my lady? Is my father well?
How fares my Juliet? That I ask again,
For nothing can be ill if she is well.

BALTHASAR

Then she is well, and nothing can be ill.
Her body sleeps in Capel's monument,
And her immortal part with angels lives.
I saw her laid low in her kindred's vault
And presently took post to tell it you.
O, pardon me for bringing these ill news,
Since you did leave it for my office, sir.

ROMEO

Is it even so? Then I defy you, stars!
You know my lodging. Get me ink and paper
And hire posthorses. I will hence to-night.

BALTHASAR

I do beseech you, sir, have patiènce.
Your looks are pale and wild and so import
Some misadventure.

ROMEO   Tush, you are deceived.
Leave me and do the thing I bid you do.
Have you no letters to me from the friar?

BALTHASAR

No, my good lord.

ROMEO   No matter. Get you gone
And hire those horses. I'll be with you straight.

                                        Exit Balthasar.

Well, Juliet, I will lie with you to-night.
Let's see for means. O mischief, you are swift
To enter in the thoughts of desperate men!
I do remember an apothecary,
And hereabouts he dwells; whom late I noted
In tattered weeds, with overhanging brows,
Culling of simples. Meagre were his looks,
Sharp misery had worn him to the bones;
And in his needy shop a tortoise hung,

An alligator stuffed, and other skins
Of ill-shaped fishes. And about his shelves
A beggarly account of empty boxes,
Green earthen pots, bladders, and musty seeds,
Remnants of packthread, and old cakes of roses
Were thinly scattered, to make up a show.
Noting this penury, to myself I said,
'But if a man did need a poison now
Whose sale is present death in Mantua,
Here lives a starving wretch would sell it him.'
O, this same thought did but forerun my need,
And this same needy man must sell it me.
As I remember, this should be the house.
Being holiday, the beggar's shop is shut.
What, ho! apothecary!

Enter APOTHECARY.

APOTHECARY   Who calls so loud?
ROMEO
   Come hither, man. I see that you are poor.
   Hold, there are forty ducats. Let me have
   A dram of poison, such soon-speeding gear
   As will disperse itself through all the veins
   That the life-weary taker may fall dead;
   And that the trunk may be discharged of breath
   As violently as hasty powder fired
   Does hurry from the fatal cannon's womb.
APOTHECARY
   Such mortal drugs I have; but Mantua's law
   Is death to any he that utters them.
ROMEO
   Are you so bare and full of wretchedness
   And fear to die? Famine is in your cheeks,
   Need and oppression starve out of your eyes,
   Contempt and beggary hang upon your back.

The world is not your friend, nor the world's law;
The world affords no law to make you rich;
Then be not poor, but break it and take this.

APOTHECARY
My poverty but not my will consents.

ROMEO
I pay your poverty and not your will.

APOTHECARY
Put this in any liquid thing you will
And drink it off, and if you had the strength
Of twenty men, it would dispatch you straight.

ROMEO
There is your gold—worse poison to men's souls,
Doing more murder in this loathsome world,
Than these poor compounds that you may not sell.
I sell you poison; you have sold me none.
Farewell. Buy food and get yourself in flesh.
Come, cordial and not poison, go with me
To Juliet's grave; for there must I use thee. *Exeunt.*

SCENE II
Verona. Friar Laurence's cell.

Enter FRIAR JOHN.

FRIAR JOHN
Holy Franciscan friar, brother, ho!

Enter FRIAR LAURENCE.

FRIAR LAURENCE
This same should be the voice of Friar John.
Welcome from Mantua. What says Romeo?
Or, if his mind is written, give me his letter.

FRIAR JOHN
  Going to find a barefoot brother out,
  One of our order, to associate me
  Here in this city visiting the sick,
  And finding him, the searchers of the town—
  Suspecting that we both were in a house
  Where the infectious pestilence did reign—
  Sealed up the doors, and would not let us forth,
  So that my speed to Mantua there was stayed.

FRIAR LAURENCE
  Who bore my letter, then, to Romeo?

FRIAR JOHN
  I could not send it—here it is again—
  Nor get a messenger to bring it you,
  So fearful were they of infection.

FRIAR LAURENCE
  Unhappy fortune! By my brotherhood,
  The letter was not trivial, but full of charge,
  Of dear import; and the neglecting of it
  May do much danger. Friar John, go hence,
  Get me an iron crow and bring it straight
  Unto my cell.

FRIAR JOHN   Brother, I'll go and bring it you.   *Exit.*

FRIAR LAURENCE
  Now must I to the monument alone.
  Within this three hours will fair Juliet wake.
  She will reproach me much that Romeo
  Has had no notice of these accidents;
  But I will write again to Mantua,
  And keep her at my cell till Romeo comes—
  Poor living corpse, closed in a dead man's tomb!
                                                    Exit.

SCENE III
Verona. A churchyard.

Enter PARIS *and his* Page.

PARIS
Give me your torch, boy. Hence, and stand aloof.
Yet put it out, for I would not be seen.
Under yon yew tree lay you all along,
Holding your ear close to the hollow ground.
So shall no foot upon the churchyard tread—
Being loose, unfirm, with digging up of graves—
But you shall hear it. Whistle then to me,
As signal that you hear something approach.
Give me those flowers. Do as I bid you, go.
PAGE   [*aside*]
I am almost afraid to stand alone
Here in the churchyard; yet I will
    adventure.   *Retires.*
PARIS
Sweet flower, with flowers your bridal bed I strew—
    O woe! your canopy is dust and stones—
Which with sweet water nightly I will dew;
    Or, wanting that, with tears distilled by moans.
The obsequies that I for you will keep
Nightly shall be to strew your grave and weep.

Page *whistles*

The boy gives warning something does approach.
What cursèd foot wanders this way to-night
To cross my obsequies and true love's rite?
What, with a torch? Muffle me, night, awhile.
                                                 Retires.

Enter ROMEO *and* BALTHASAR.

ROMEO
    Give me that mattock and the wrenching iron.
    Hold, take this letter. Early in the morning
    See you deliver it to my lord and father.
    Give me the light. Upon your life I charge you,
    Whatever you hear or see, stand all aloof
    And do not interrupt me in my course.
    Why I descend into this bed of death
    Is partly to behold my lady's face,
    But chiefly to take thence from her dead finger
    A precious ring—a ring that I must use
    In dear employment. Therefore hence, be gone.
    But if you, curious, do return to pry
    In what I farther shall intend to do,
    By heaven, I will tear you joint by joint
    And strew this hungry churchyard with your limbs.
    The time and my intents are savage-wild,
    More fierce and more inexorable far
    Than empty tigers or the roaring sea.
BALTHASAR
    I will be gone, sir, and not trouble you.
ROMEO
    So shall you show me friendship. Take you that.
    Live, and be prosperous; and farewell, good fellow.
BALTHASAR   [*aside*]
    For all this same, I'll hide me hereabout.
    His looks I fear, and his intents I doubt.
ROMEO   *Retires.*
    You detestable maw, you womb of death,
    Gorged with the dearest morsel of earth,
    Thus I enforce your rotten jaws to open,
    And in despite I'll cram you with more food.

ROMEO *opens the tomb.*

PARIS

This is that banished haughty Montague
That murdered my love's cousin—with which grief
It is supposed the fair creature died—
And here is come to do some villainous shame
To the dead bodies. I will apprehend him.
Stop your unhallowed toil, vile Montague!
Can vengeance be pursued further than death?
Condemned villain, I do apprehend you.
Obey and go with me; for you must die.

ROMEO

I must indeed; and therefore came I hither.
Good gentle youth, tempt not a desperate man.
Fly hence and leave me. Think upon these gone;
Let them affright you. I beseech you, youth,
Put not another sin upon my head
By urging me to fury. O, be gone!
By heaven, I love you better than myself.
For I come hither armed against myself.
Stay not, be gone. Live, and hereafter say
A madman's mercy bid you run away.

PARIS

I do defy your conjuration
And apprehend you for a felon here.

ROMEO

Will you provoke me? Then have at you, boy!

They fight.

PAGE

O Lord, they fight! I will go call the watch.

Exit. Paris falls.

PARIS

   O, I am slain. If you are merciful,
   Open the tomb, lay me with Juliet.

                          Dies.

ROMEO

   In faith, I will. Let me peruse this face.
   Mercutio's kinsman, the noble Count Paris!
   What said my man when my betossèd soul
   Did not attend to him as we rode? I think
   He told me Paris should have married Juliet.
   Said he not so? or did I dream it so?
   Or am I mad, hearing him talk of Juliet,
   To think it was so? O, give me your hand,
   One writ with me in sour misfortune's book!
   I'll bury you in a triumphant grave.
   A grave? O, no, a lantern, slaughtered youth,
   For here lies Juliet, and her beauty makes
   This vault a feasting presence full of light.
   Death, lie you there, by a dead man interred.

            Lays Paris in the tomb.

   How oft when men are at the point of death
   Have they been merry! which their keepers call
   A lightning before death. O, how may I
   Call this a lightning? O my love! my wife!
   Death, that has sucked the honey of your breath,
   Has had no power yet upon your beauty.
   You are not conquered. Beauty's ensign yet
   Is crimson in your lips and in your cheeks,
   And death's pale flag is not advancèd there.
   Tybalt, lie you there in your bloody sheet?
   O, what more favor can I do to you
   Than with that hand that cut your youth in twain
   To sunder his that was your enemy?

Forgive me, cousin! Ah, dear Juliet,
Why are you yet so fair? Shall I believe
That unsubstantial Death is amorous,
And that the lean abhorrèd monster keeps
You here in dark to be his paramour?
For fear of that I ever will stay with you
And never from this palace of dim night
Depart again. Here, here will I remain
With worms that are your chambermaids. O, here
Will I set up my everlasting rest
And shake the yoke of inauspicious stars
From this world-wearied flesh. Eyes, look your last!
Arms, take your last embrace! and, lips, O you
The doors of breath, seal with a righteous kiss
A dateless bargain to engrossing death!
Come, bitter potion; come, unsavory guide!
You desperate pilot, now at once run on
The dashing rocks your seasick weary bark!
Here's to my love! [*Drinks.*] O true apothecary!
Your drugs are quick. Thus with a kiss I die.

Falls.
Enter FRIAR LAURENCE, *with lantern, crow, and spade.*

FRIAR LAURENCE
Saint Francis be my speed! how oft to-night
Have my old feet stumbled at graves! Who's there?
BALTHASAR
Here's one, a friend, and one that knows you well.
FRIAR LAURENCE
Bliss be upon you! Tell me, good friend,
What torch is yon that vainly lends its light
To grubs and eyeless skulls? As I discern,
It burns in the Capulets' monument.

BALTHASAR
  It does, holy sir; and there's my master,
  One that you love.

FRIAR LAURENCE   Who is it?

BALTHASAR   Romeo.

FRIAR LAURENCE
  How long has he been there?

BALTHASAR   Full half an hour.

FRIAR LAURENCE
  Go with me to the vault.

BALTHASAR   I dare not, sir.
  My master knows not but I am gone hence,
  And fearfully did menace me with death
  If I did stay to look on his intents.

FRIAR LAURENCE
  Stay then; I'll go alone. Fear comes upon me.
  O, much I fear some ill unlucky thing.

BALTHASAR
  As I did sleep under this yew tree here,
  I dreamt my master and another fought,
  And that my master slew him.

FRIAR LAURENCE   Romeo!
  Alas, alas, what blood is this which stains
  The stony entrance of this sepulchre?
  What mean these masterless and gory swords
  To lie discolored by this place of peace?

Enters the tomb.

  Romeo! O, pale! Who else? What, Paris too?
  And steeped in blood? Ah, what an unkind hour
  Is guilty of this lamentable chance!
  The lady stirs.

JULIET rises.

JULIET

   O comfortable friar! where is my lord?
   I do remember well where I should be,
   And there I am. Where is my Romeo?

FRIAR LAURENCE

   I hear some noise. Lady, come from that nest
   Of death, contagion, and unnatural sleep.
   A greater power than we can contradict
   Has thwarted our intents. Come, come away.
   Your husband in your bosom there lies dead;
   And Paris too. Come, I'll dispose of you
   Among a sisterhood of holy nuns.
   Stay not to question, for the watch is coming.
   Come, go, good Juliet. I dare no longer stay.

JULIET

   Go, get you hence, for I will not away.   *Exit Friar*
   What's here! A cup, closed in my true love's hand?
   Poison, I see, has been his timeless end.
   O churl! drunk all, and left no friendly drop
   To help me after? I will kiss your lips.
   Haply some poison yet does hang on them
   To make me die with a restorative.

Kisses him.

   Your lips are warm!

CHIEF WATCHMAN   [*within*] Lead, boy. Which way?

JULIET

   Yea, noise? Then I'll be brief. O happy dagger!

Snatches ROMEO'S *dagger.*

This is your sheath; there rust, and let me die.

She stabs herself and falls.
Enter PARIS'S Boy *and* Watch.

BOY

   This is the place. There, where the torch does burn.

CHIEF WATCHMAN

   The ground is bloody. Search about the churchyard.
   Go, some of you; whoever you find attach.

                  Exeunt some of the Watch.

   Pitiful sight! here lies the Count slain;
   And Juliet bleeding, warm, and newly dead,
   Who here has lain this two days burièd.
   Go, tell the Prince; run to the Capulets;
   Raise up the Montagues; some others search.

                  Exeunt others of the Watch.

   We see the ground whereon these woes do lie,
   But the true ground of all these piteous woes
   We cannot without circumstance descry.

      Enter some of the Watch, *with* BALTHASAR.

2. WATCHMAN

   Here's Romeo's man. We found him in the
     churchyard.

CHIEF WATCHMAN

   Hold him in safety till the Prince comes hither.

      Enter FRIAR LAURENCE *and another* Watchman.

3. WATCHMAN

   Here is a friar that trembles, sighs, and weeps.
   We took this mattock and this spade from him
   As he was coming from this churchyard side.

CHIEF WATCHMAN

   A great suspicion! Stay the friar too.

         Enter the PRINCE *and* Attendants.

PRINCE

 What misadventure is so early up,
 That calls our person from our morning rest?

Enter CAPULET *and his* Wife.

CAPULET

 What should it be, that is so shrieked abroad?

LADY CAPULET

 O the people in the street cry 'Romeo,'
 Some 'Juliet,' and some 'Paris'; and all run,
 With open outcry, toward our monument.

PRINCE

 What fear is this which startles in your ears?

CHIEF WATCHMAN

 Sovereign, here lies Count Paris shortly slain;
 And Romeo dead; and Juliet, dead before,
 Warm and new killed.

PRINCE

 Search, seek, and know how this foul murder comes.

CHIEF WATCHMAN

 Here is a friar, and slaughtered Romeo's man,
 With instruments upon them fit to open
 These dead men's tombs.

CAPULET

 O heavens! O wife, look how our daughter bleeds!
 This dagger has mistaken, for, lo, his house
 Is empty on the back of Montague,
 And it missheathèd in my daughter's bosom!

LADY CAPULET

 O me! this sight of death is as a bell
 That warns my old age to a sepulchre.

Enter MONTAGUE.

PRINCE

Come, Montague; for you are early up
To see your son and heir more early down.

MONTAGUE

Alas, my liege, my wife is dead to-night!
Grief of my son's exile has stopped her breath.
What further woe conspires against my age?

PRINCE

Look, and you shall see.

MONTAGUE

O you untaught! what manners is in this,
To press before your father to a grave?

PRINCE

Seal up the mouth of outrage for a while,
Till we can clear these ambiguities
And know their spring, their head, their true
    descent;
And then will I be general of your woes
And lead you even to death. Meantime forbear,
And let mischance be slave to patìence.
Bring forth the parties of suspiciòn.

FRIAR LAURENCE

I am the greatest, able to do least,
Yet most suspected, as the time and place
Do make against me, of this direful murder.
And here I stand, both to impeach and purge
Myself condemnèd and myself excused.

PRINCE

Then say at once what you do know in this.

FRIAR LAURENCE

I will be brief, for my short date of breath
Is not so long as is a tedious tale.
Romeo, there dead, was husband to that Juliet;
And she, there dead, that Romeo's faithful wife.
I married them; and their stolen marriage day

Was Tybalt's doomsday, whose untimely death
Banished the new-made bridegroom from this city.
For whom, and not for Tybalt, Juliet pined.
You, to remove that siege of grief from her,
Betrothed and would have married her perforce
To Count Paris. Then comes she to me
And with wild looks bid me devise some means
To rid her from this second marriàge,
Or in my cell there would she kill herself.
Then gave I her—so tutored by my art—
A sleeping potion; which so took effect
As I intended, for it wrought on her
The form of death. Meantime I wrote to Romeo
That he should hither come on this dire night
To help to take her from her borrowed grave,
Being the time the potion's force should cease.
But he who bore my letter, Friar John,
Was stayed by accident, and yesternight
Returned my letter back. Then all alone
At the prefixèd hoür of her waking
Came I to take her from her kindred's vault;
Meaning to keep her closely at my cell
Till I conveniently could send to Romeo.
But when I came, some minute ere the time
Of her awakening, here untimely lay
The noble Paris and true Romeo dead.
She wakes; and I entreated her come forth
And bear this work of heaven with patiènce.
But then a noise did scare me from the tomb,
And she, too desperate, would not go with me,
But, as it seems, did violence on herself.
All this I know, and to the marriàge
Her nurse is privy; and if aught in this
Miscarried by my fault, let my old life
Be sacrificed, some hour before its time,
Unto the rigor of severest law.

PRINCE

We ever have known you for a holy man.
Where's Romeo's man? What can he say in this?

BALTHASAR

I brought my master news of Juliet's death;
And then in post he came from Mantua
To this same place, to this same monument.
This letter he early bid me give his father,
And threatened me with death, going in the vault,
If I departed not and left him there.

PRINCE

Give me the letter. I will look on it.
Where is the Count's page that raised the watch?
Fellow, what made your master in this place?

PAGE

He came with flowers to strew his lady's grave;
And bid me stand aloof, and so I did.
Anon comes one with light to open the tomb;
And by and by my master drew on him;
And then I ran away to call the watch.

PRINCE

This letter does make good the friar's words,
Their course of love, the tidings of her death;
And here he writes that he did buy a poison
Of a poor apothecary, and therewith it
Came to this vault to die, and lie with Juliet.
Where are these enemies? Capulet, Montague,
See what a scourge is laid upon your hate,
That heaven finds means to kill your joys with love.
And I, for winking at your discords too,
Have lost a brace of kinsmen. All are punished.

CAPULET

O brother Montague, give me your hand
This is my daughter's jointure, for no more
Can I demand.

MONTAGUE   But I can give you more;
  For I will raise her statue in pure gold,
  That while Verona by that name is known,
  There shall no figure at such rate be set
  As that of true and faithful Juliet.
CAPULET
  As rich shall Romeo's by his lady's lie—
  Poor sacrifices of our enmity!
PRINCE
  A glooming peace this morning with it brings.
    The sun for sorrow will not show its head.
  Go hence, to have more talk of these sad things;
    Some shall be pardoned, and some punishèd;
  For never was a story of more woe
  Than this of Juliet and her Romeo.   *Exeunt.*

The Tempest

INTRODUCTION

T*he Tempest*, of 1611, is Shakespeare's penulti-
mate play, with the atmosphere of farewell in it,
as in *Henry VIII*, last of all. Yet it was placed first
when the First Folio was published in 1623, and still
appears first, absurdly, in most editions of the Works.
This is apt to put people wrong, especially in previous
centuries, when they were uncertain of the chronology
of the Plays. How could one hope to estimate Beethoven's
work aright, if one thought that the last Quartets came
first? In the 18th century, as Dr. Johnson tells us,
people did 'know not the exact date of this or the other
plays', and therefore 'cannot tell how our author might
have changed his practice or opinions.' More than this,
it is impossible to appreciate the development of
Shakespeare's mind, the expansion of his art, or the
manner and circumstances of its flowering in response
to both his own experience and his experience of his
time, without a reliable chronology of his work. This is
where an Elizabethan historian comes in, is indeed
indispensable.

The Tempest was performed before James I at
Whitehall, on Hallowmas night, 1 November 1611.
Only two years before, in 1609 the Second Charter of
the Virginia Company had been issued—a national
venture to which hundreds of people subscribed, from

the Archbishop of Canterbury and the Earls of Southampton and Pembroke downwards, to give a solid foundation to the first English colony in America, based upon Jamestown. And Shakespeare had a number of acquaintances in the Virginia Company. But that year the flagship of the fleet going out there, the *Sea Venture*, met with a tornado off Bermuda—'the still-vexed Bermoothes'—ran in on the rocks a wreck, and yet not a life lost.

We shall see all through this modern, yet historically minded, edition how closely Shakespeare responded to the challenge of topical circumstances, from Normandy in 1591, onwards. His box-office sense would indicate that anyway. Now, in the last years of his career, with the war ended and the door to settlement in North America open—for which partly it had been fought—the country was full of interest in the overseas voyages. In consequence Shakespeare's last plays, from *Pericles* (1608) onwards, are full of sea-voyages, wrecks, partings and renewals.

An account of the island wreck was published in 1610: Jourdan's *A Discovery of the Bermudas, otherwise called the Isle of Devils*. But Shakespeare had a closer source of information in the manuscript letter sent back to Blackfriars by William Strachey, Secretary to Virginia. Strachey was closely associated with Blackfriars—as Shakespeare had been from the early days when his Stratford fellow, Richard Field, printed his long poems there, and now from 1608 more than ever as part-owner of the theatre within. The play follows Strachey's account of the tornado, down to the St. Elmo's fire-ball running down the rigging, the break-up of the ship, and yet no one lost.

To contemporaries the uninhabited island was enchanted, vexed not only by storms but by spirits. And the dominant theme of the play is magic, that of Prospero and Ariel, their charms and incantations, while Caliban the only indigenous inhabitant had had a witch for a mother. Here was another strong appeal for contemporaries, with 'Dr.' Forman now much to the fore, and Dr. Dee familiar in the background.

Caliban is the most original creation in the play, entirely of Shakespeare's making, the obvious product of his reading and reflecting on the voyages, notably—but not only—Hakluyt. He looked into Eden's History of Travel, whence he got the name Setebos; and he made use of friend Florio's translation of Montaigne's essay on cannibals for a very different exposure of primitive communism. Dr. Johnson saw, rightly, that he was a 'diligent reader.'

Caliban's speeches clearly reflect Hariot's descriptions in his *Brief and True Report of the New-found-land of Virginia*. Recognisably in—

When you came first

You stroke me and made much of me; would give me
Water with berries in it; and teach me how
To name the bigger light, and how the less
That burn by day and night.

Hariot had astonished the Indians by showing them the sun and moon through his rudimentary telescope.

And then I loved you,

And showed you all the qualities of the isle,
The fresh springs, brine pits, barren place and fertile.

This is as it had been on Roanoke in 1585–6. But it is the rascally Stephano and Trinculo, realistic enough as they are, not Prospero the exiled Duke with his magic power, who get the poor savage drunk—a portent in its way of what was to happen to the Indians from fire-water in the progress of colonisation.

Progress? We see that William Shakespeare had no illusions about primitive man, the state of nature, and all the nonsense about primeval innocence and communism. He puts these ideas into the mouth of a councillor, as it might be of the Leftist Greater London Council today:

> In the commonwealth I would by contraries
> Execute all things; for no kind of traffic
> Would I admit; no name of magistrate;
> Letters should not be known—

we remember Jack Cade's hatred of letters and book-learning, from the earliest play—

> riches and poverty,
> And use of service, none; contract, succession,
> Bourn, bound of land, tilth, vineyard, none;
> No use of metal, corn, or wine, or oil;
> No occupation; all men idle, all.

The women were all to be innocent and pure—no disease: very unlike contemporary life.

> All things in common Nature should produce
> Without sweat or endeavour: treason, felony,
> Sword, pike, knife, gun, or need of any engine,
> Would I not have . . .

To this a questioner asks:

> No marrying among his subjects?

The reply is no doubt William Shakespeare's:

> None, man, all idle: whores and knaves.

This is much like what happened in early days in Virginia, according to Captain John Smith: instead of planting, the colonists played bowls or dug for gold—then starved. And Shakespeare took the reports of gold-digging up into *Timon of Athens*.[1]

---

[1] cf my *The Elizabethans and America*, 192.

Magic was much in the air at this time, with a king too on the throne who was an expert in demonology—and this must have been something new for the audience at Blackfriars, always on the alert for anything new. Caliban thinks Prospero's power is in his books:

> First, to possess his books: for without them
> He's but a sot, as I am, and has not
> One spirit in his command . . .
> Burn but his books.

Prospero is properly mysterious, as a kind of *magus*. Nor is it unlikely that that other magus had himself in mind in his farewell to his art:

> I'll break my staff,
> Bury it certain fathoms in the earth,
> And deeper than did ever plummet sound
> I'll drown my book.

It certainly sounds a personal note of renunciation. *Henry VIII* may have been called for some special occasion—otherwise there is a remarkable, if understandable, silence from the gentleman of Stratford.

One would think that the play was written in the country, not only from the more elaborate stage directions, as if for someone else to produce in London. But also from the marvellous evocations of countryside:

> You elves of hills, brooks, standing lakes, and
>   groves . . .
>   You demi-puppets that
> By moonshine do the green, sour ringlets make,
> Whereof the ewe not bites; and you whose pastime
> Is to make midnight mushrooms, that rejoice
> To hear the solemn curfew . . .

How much this countryman loved the English countryside, and with what close observation! Here, for example, we have the image 'as fast as mill-wheels strike', or tears running down 'like winter's drops from eaves of reeds', i.e. rush-roofed cottages.

How unlike Marlowe! And yet Marlowe is present in mind at the end, as at the beginning. In the magical song, 'Come unto these yellow sands', the phrase 'the wild waves whist' is Marlowe's—after all those years, and all that had happened in between. The phrase 'full fathom five' goes back to *Romeo and Juliet*. It is as if Shakespeare, with infallible sense of propriety, were rounding things up. So too with the Epilogue:

> Now my charms are all o'erthrown,
> And what strength I have's my own.

Then, in the way he had all along sought favour with the audience, unlike Ben Jonson:

> Gentle breath of yours my sails
> Must fill, or else my project fails—
> Which was to please.

Ben was not pleased. He said of his own work, 'if there is never a servant monster [i.e. Caliban] in the fair, who can help it? Nor a nest of antics [buffoons]. He is loth to make Nature afraid in his plays, like those that beget *Tales* [i.e. Winter's Tales], *Tempests*, and such-like drolleries.' The drolleries were more popular than his works and moreover, more enduring. The intellectuals of the time, wrong as usual, thought more highly of Ben Jonson. Shakespeare, even at the end of his career, certainly found something new—as had been his wont all along—in this fairy tale of the enchanted island.

CHARACTERS

ALONSO, King of Naples
SEBASTIAN, his brother
PROSPERO, the rightful Duke of Milan
ANTONIO, his brother, the usurping Duke of Milan
FERDINAND, son of the King of Naples
GONZALO, an honest old councillor
ADRIAN   } lords
FRANCISCO }
CALIBAN, a primitive slave
TRINCULO, a jester
STEPHANO, a butler
Master of a ship, Boatswain, Mariners
MIRANDA, daughter of Prospero
ARIEL, a spirit
IRIS, CERES, JUNO, Nymphs, and Reapers, characters
  in the masque, played by Ariel and Spirits

Act I

SCENE I
A ship at sea.

Thunder and lightning. Enter a Shipmaster and a Boatswain.

MASTER Boatswain!

BOATSWAIN Here, Master. What cheer?

MASTER Good. Speak to the mariners. Fall to it, sharp, or we run ourselves aground. Bestir, bestir! *Exit*

Enter Mariners

BOATSWAIN Heigh, my hearts! Cheerily, cheerily, my hearts! Quick, quick! Take in the topsail! Attend to the Master's whistle!—Blow till you burst your wind, if room enough.

Enter ALONSO, SEBASTIAN, ANTONIO, FERDINAND, GONZALO, *and others.*

ALONSO Good Boatswain, have care. Where's the Master? Act like men.

BOATSWAIN I pray now, keep below.

ANTONIO Where is the Master, Boatswain?

BOATSWAIN Do you not hear him? You mar our labour. Keep your cabins! You do assist the storm.

GONZALO Nay, good, be patient.

BOATSWAIN When the sea is. Hence! What care these roarers for the name of king? To cabin! Silence! Trouble us not.

GONZALO   Good, yet remember whom you have
  aboard.
BOATSWAIN   None that I more love than myself.
  ↝You are a councillor. If you can command these
  elements to silence, and work the peace of the
  present, we will not hand a rope more. Use your
  authority. If you cannot, give thanks you have lived
  so long, and make yourself ready in your cabin for
  the mischance of the hour, if it so happens.—
  Cheerily, good hearts!—Out of our way, I say!   *Exit*
GONZALO   I have great comfort from this fellow. I
  think he has no drowning-mark upon him: his
  complexion is perfect gallows. Stand fast, good
  Fate, to his hanging. Make the rope of his destiny
  our cable, for our own is little advantage. If he is
  not born to be hanged, our case is miserable.
                     Exeunt Gonzalo and the other nobles

                     Enter BOATSWAIN

BOATSWAIN   Down with the topmast! Quick! Lower,
  lower! Bring her to try with main-course.

                     A cry within

A plague upon this howling! They are louder than
the weather, or our office.

          Enter SEBASTIAN, ANTONIO, GONZALO

Yet again? What do you here? Shall we give over
and drown? Have you a mind to sink?
SEBASTIAN   A pox on your throat, you bawling,
  blasphemous, uncharitable dog!
BOATSWAIN   Work you, then.

ANTONIO   Hang, cur, hang, you insolent noisemaker!
  We are less afraid to be drowned than you are.
GONZALO   I'll warrant him for drowning, though the
  ship is no stronger than a nutshell and as leaky as
  an unstanched wench.
BOATSWAIN   Lay her a-hold, a-hold! Set her two
  courses! Off to sea again! Lay her off!

Enter Mariners wet

MARINERS   All lost! To prayers, to prayers! All lost!
                                                      Exeunt
BOATSWAIN   What, must our mouths be cold?
GONZALO
  The King and Prince at prayers, let us assist them,
  For our case is as theirs.
SEBASTIAN   I am out of patience.
ANTONIO
  We are merely cheated of our lives by drunkards.
  This wide-chapped rascal—would you might lie
    drowning
  The washing of ten tides!
GONZALO   He will be hanged yet,
  Though every drop of water swears against it,
  And gapes at widest to glut him.
    A confused noise within: 'Mercy on us!'—'We
    split, we split!'—'Farewell, my wife and
    children!'—'Farewell, brother!'—'We split, we
    split, we split!'   *Exit Boatswain*
ANTONIO   Let us all sink with the King.
SEBASTIAN   Let us take leave of him.
                                          Exit, with Antonio
GONZALO   Now would I give a thousand furlongs of sea
  for an acre of barren ground. Long heath, brown
  furze, anything. The wills above be done, but I
  would rather die a dry death.   *Exit*

SCENE II
Before PROSPERO'S cell.

Enter PROSPERO *and* MIRANDA

MIRANDA
  If by your art, my dearest father, you have
  Put the wild waters in this roar, allay them.
  The sky it seems would pour down stinking pitch,
  But that the sea, mounting to the heaven's cheek,
  Dashes the fire out. O, I have suffered
  With those that I saw suffer! A brave vessel,
  Which had, no doubt, some noble creature in her,
  Dashed all to pieces. O, the cry did knock
  Against my very heart! Poor souls, they perished.
  Had I been any god of power, I would
  Have sunk the sea within the earth, before
  It should the good ship so have swallowed and
  The freighting souls within her.
PROSPERO   Be collected.
  No more amazement. Tell your piteous heart
  There's no harm done.
MIRANDA   O, woe the day!
PROSPERO   No harm.
  I have done nothing but in care of you,
  Of you, my dear one, you my daughter, who
  Are ignorant of what you are, naught knowing
  Of whence I am, nor that I am even better
  Than Prospero, master of a full poor cell,
  And your no greater father.
MIRANDA   More to know
  Did never meddle with my thoughts.
PROSPERO   It is time
  I should inform you farther. Lend your hand,
  And pluck my magic garment from me.—So,

Lie there, my art.—Wipe you your eyes. Have
    comfort.
The direful spectacle of the wreck, which touched
The very virtue of compassion in you,
I have with such provision in my art
So safely ordered, that there is no soul—
No, not so much perdition as a hair
Befallen any creature in the vessel
Which you heard cry, which you saw sink. Sit
    down.
For you must now know farther.

MIRANDA   You have often
    Begun to tell me what I am, but stopped,
    And left me to a fruitless inquisition,
    Concluding, 'Stay: not yet.'

PROSPERO   The hour is now come.
    The very minute bids you open your ear.
    Obey, and be attentive. Can you remember
    A time before we came unto this cell?
    I do not think you can, for then you were not
    Out three years old.

MIRANDA   Certainly, sir, I can.

PROSPERO
    By what? By any other house or person?
    Of any thing the image tells me, that
    Has kept with your remembrance.

MIRANDA   It is far off,
    And rather like a dream than an assurance
    That my remembrance warrants. Had I not
    Four or five women once that tended me?

PROSPERO
    You had, and more, Miranda. But how is it
    That this lives in your mind? What see you else
    In the dark backward and abyss of time?
    If you remember aught ere you came here,
    How you came here you may.

MIRANDA   But that I do not.

PROSPERO

Twelve year since, Miranda, twelve year since,
Your father was the Duke of Milan and
A prince of power.

MIRANDA   Sir, are not you my father?

PROSPERO

Your mother was a piece of virtue, and
She said you were my daughter; and your father
Was Duke of Milan; and his only heir
And princess, no worse issued.

MIRANDA   O the heavens!
What foul play had we, that we came from thence?
Or blessed was it we did?

PROSPERO   Both, both, my girl.
By foul play, as you say, were we heaved thence,
But blessedly helped hither.

MIRANDA   O, my heart bleeds
To think of the grief that I have turned you to,
Now out of my remembrance! Please you, farther.

PROSPERO

My brother and your uncle, called Antonio—
I pray you mark me, that a brother should
Be so perfidious!—he, whom next yourself
Of all the world I loved, and to him put
The manage of my state. And at that time
Through all the signories it was the first;
And Prospero the prime duke, being so reputed
In dignity, and for the liberal arts
Without a parallel. Those being all my study,
The government I cast upon my brother,
And to my state grew stranger, being transported
And rapt in secret studies. Your false uncle—
Do you attend me?

MIRANDA   Sir, most heedfully.

PROSPERO
Being once perfected how to grant suits,
How to deny them, whom to advance, and whom
To check for over-topping, new created
The creatures that were mine, I say, or changed them,
Or else new formed them. Having both the key
Of officer and office, set all hearts in the state
To what tune pleased his ear, that now he was
The ivy which had hidden my princely trunk,
And sucked my verdure out of it. You attend not!

MIRANDA
O, good sir, I do.

PROSPERO
                                        I pray you, mark me.
I, thus neglecting worldly ends, all dedicated
To closeness and the bettering of my mind
With that which—but by being so retired,
O'er-prized all popular rate—in my false brother
Awaked an evil nature. And my trust,
Like a good parent, did beget of him
A falsehood in its contrary, as great
As my trust was, which had indeed no limit,
A confidence boundless. He being thus lorded,
Not only with what my revenue yielded,
But what my power might else exact, like one
Who having unto truth, by telling of it,
Made such a sinner of his memory
To credit his own lie—he did believe
He was indeed the Duke, by substitution
And executing the outward face of royalty,
With all prerogative. Hence his ambition growing—
Do you hear?

MIRANDA   Your tale, sir, would cure deafness.

PROSPERO
To have no screen between this part he played
And him he played it for, he needs will be

Absolute Milan. Me, poor man, my library
Was dukedom large enough. Of temporal royalties
He thinks me now incapable, confederates—
So dry he was for sway—with the King of Naples
To give him annual tribute, do him homage,
Subject his coronet to his crown, and bend
The dukedom yet unbowed—alas, poor Milan—
To most ignoble stooping.

MIRANDA   O the heavens!

PROSPERO

Mark his condition and the event; then tell me
If this might be a brother.

MIRANDA   I should sin

To think but nobly of my grandmother.
Good wombs have borne bad sons.

PROSPERO   Now the condition.

This King of Naples, being an enemy
To me inveterate, hearkens to my brother's suit,
Which was, that he—in lieu of the premises
Of homage and I know not how much tribute—
Should presently extirpate me and mine
Out of the dukedom, and confer fair Milan,
With all the honours, on my brother. Whereon,
A treacherous army levied, one midnight
Fated to the purpose, did Antonio open
The gates of Milan; and, in the dead of darkness,
The ministers for the purpose hurried thence
Me and your crying self.

MIRANDA   Alas, for pity.

I, not remembering how I cried out then,
Will cry it over again. It is a hint
That wrings my eyes to it.

PROSPERO   Hear a little further,

And then I'll bring you to the present business
Which now is upon us; without which, this story
Were most impertinent.

MIRANDA   Wherefore did they not
That hour destroy us?
PROSPERO   Well demanded, wench.
My tale provokes that question. Dear, they durst not,
So dear the love my people bore me; nor set
A mark so bloody on the business, but
With colours fairer painted their foul ends.
In short, they hurried us aboard a bark,
Bore us some leagues to sea, where they prepared
A rotten carcass of a butt, not rigged,
Nor tackle, sail, nor mast. The very rats
Instinctively have quit it. There they hoist us,
To cry to the sea that roared to us, to sigh
To the winds, whose pity sighing back again
Did us but loving wrong.
MIRANDA   Alas, what trouble
Was I then to you!
PROSPERO   O, a cherubin
You were that did preserve me. You did smile,
Infusèd with a fortitude from heaven,
When I have decked the sea with drops full salt,
Under my burden groaned: which raised in me
An undergoing stomach, to bear up
Against what should ensue.
MIRANDA   How came we ashore?
PROSPERO
By Providence divine.
Some food we had, and some fresh water, that
A noble Neapolitan, Gonzalo,
Out of his charity—who being then appointed
Master of this design—did give us; with
Rich garments, linens, stuffs, and necessaries
Which since have helped much. So, of his gentleness,
Knowing I loved my books, he furnished me
From my own library with volumes that
I prize above my dukedom.

MIRANDA   Would I might
  But ever see that man!
PROSPERO   Now I arise.
  Sit still, and hear the last of our sea-sorrow.
  Here in this island we arrived, and here
  Have I, your schoolmaster, made you more profit
  Than other princesses can, that have more time
  For vainer hours, and tutors not so careful.
MIRANDA
  Heaven thank you for it! Now, I pray you, sir,
  For still 'tis beating in my mind, your reason
  For raising this sea-storm?
PROSPERO   Know thus far forth.
  By accident most strange, bountiful Fortune,
  Now my dear lady, has my enemies
  Brought to this shore. And by my prescience
  I find my zenith does depend upon
  A most auspicious star, whose influence
  If now I court not, but omit, my fortunes
  Will ever after droop. Here cease more questions.
  You are inclined to sleep. It is a good dullness,
  And give it way. I know you can not choose.

                    MIRANDA *sleeps*

  Come away, servant, come! I am ready now.
  Approach, my Ariel! Come!

                    Enter ARIEL

ARIEL
  All hail, great master! Grave sir, hail! I come
  To answer your best pleasure, be it to fly,
  To swim, to dive into the fire, to ride
  On the curled clouds. To your strong bidding task
  Ariel and all his quality.

PROSPERO   Have you, spirit,
   Performed to point the tempest that I bade you?
ARIEL
   To every article.
   I boarded the King's ship. Now on the beak,
   Now in the waist, the deck, in every cabin
   I flamed amazement. Sometimes I'd divide,
   And burn in many places. On the topmast,
   The yards, and bowsprit would I flame distinctly,
   Then meet and join Jove's lightnings, the precursors
   Of the dreadful thunderclaps, more momentary
   And sight-outrunning were not. The fire and cracks
   Of sulphurous roaring the most mighty Neptune
   Seem to besiege, and make his bold waves tremble,
   Yes, his dread trident shake.
PROSPERO   My brave spirit!
   Who was so firm, so constant, that this tumult
   Would not infect his reason?
ARIEL   Not a soul
   But felt a fever of the mad, and played
   Some tricks of desperation. All but mariners
   Plunged in the foaming brine, and quit the vessel,
   Then all afire with me. The King's son Ferdinand,
   With hair up-staring—then like reeds, not hair—
   Was the first man that leaped; cried, 'Hell is empty,
   And all the devils are here!'
PROSPERO   Why, that's my spirit!
   But was not this nigh shore?
ARIEL   Close by, my master.
PROSPERO
   But are they, Ariel, safe?
ARIEL   Not a hair perished.
   On their sustaining garments not a blemish,
   But fresher than before; and as you bade me,
   In troops I have dispersed them about the isle.
   The King's son have I landed by himself,

Whom I left cooling the air with sighs
In an odd angle of the isle, and sitting,
His arms in this sad knot.

PROSPERO   Of the King's ship,
The mariners, say how you have disposed,
And all the rest of the fleet?

ARIEL   Safely in harbour
Is the King's ship, in the deep nook where once
You called me up at midnight to fetch dew
From the ever-vexed Bermudas, there she's hid;
The mariners all under hatches stowed,
Who, with a charm joined to their suffered labour,
I have left asleep. And for the rest of the fleet,
Which I dispersed, they all have met again,
And are upon the Mediterranean flood
Bound sadly home for Naples,
Supposing that they saw the King's ship wrecked,
And his great person perish.

PROSPERO   Ariel, your charge
Exactly is performed, but there's more work.
What is the time of the day?

ARIEL   Past the mid-season.

PROSPERO
At least two glasses. The time between six and now
Must by us be spent most preciously.

ARIEL
Is there more toil? Since you do give me pains,
Let me remember you what you have promised,
Which is not yet performed me.

PROSPERO   How now? Moody?
What is it you can demand?

ARIEL   My liberty

PROSPERO
Before the time is out? No more.

ARIEL   I pray,
   Remember I have done you worthy service,
   Told you no lies, made you no mistakings, served
   Without grudge or grumblings. You did promise
   To abate me a full year.
PROSPERO   Do you forget
   From what a torment I did free you?
ARIEL   No.
PROSPERO
   You do; and think it much to tread the ooze
   Of the salt deep,
   To run upon the sharp wind of the north,
   To do me business in the veins of the earth
   When it is baked with frost.
ARIEL   I do not, sir.
PROSPERO
   You lie, malignant thing! Have you forgotten
   The foul witch Sycorax, who with age and envy
   Was grown into a hoop? Have you forgotten her?
ARIEL
   No, sir.
PROSPERO
      You have. Where was she born? Speak! Tell me!
ARIEL
   Sir, in Algiers.
PROSPERO   O, was she so! I must
   Once a month recount what you have been,
   Which you forget. This damned witch Sycorax,
   For mischiefs manifold, and sorceries terrible
   To enter human hearing, from Algiers,
   You know, was banished. For one thing she did
   They would not take her life. Is not this true?
ARIEL
   Ay, sir.

PROSPERO

   This blue-eyed hag was hither brought with child,
   And here was left by the sailors. You, my slave,
   As you report yourself, was then her servant.
   Because you were a spirit too delicate
   To act her earthy and abhorred commands,
   Refusing her behests, she did confine you,
   By help of her more potent ministers,
   And in her most unmitigable rage,
   Into a cloven pine. Within which rift
   Imprisoned, you did painfully remain
   A dozen years; within which space she died,
   And left you there, where you did vent your groans
   As fast as millwheels strike. Then was this island—
   Save for the son that she did litter here,
   A freckled whelp, hag-born—not honoured with
   A human shape.

ARIEL   Yes, Caliban her son.

PROSPERO

   Dull thing, I say so! He, that Caliban
   Whom now I keep in service. You best know
   What torment I did find you in. Your groans
   Did make wolves howl, and penetrate the breasts
   Of ever-angry bears. It was a torment
   To lay upon the damned, which Sycorax
   Could not again undo. It was my art,
   When I arrived and heard you, that made gape
   The pine, and let you out.

ARIEL   I thank you, master.

PROSPERO

   If you more murmur, I will rend an oak,
   And peg you in its knotty entrails, till
   You have howled away twelve winters.

ARIEL   Pardon, master.

   I will be correspondent to command,
   And do my spriting gently.

PROSPERO   Do so, and after two days
    I will discharge you.
ARIEL   That's my noble master!
    What shall I do? Say what! What shall I do?
PROSPERO
    Go make yourself like a nymph of the sea.
    Be subject to no sight but yours and mine, invisible
    To every eyeball else. Go take this shape,
    And hither come in it. Go! Hence with diligence!

                                        Exit Ariel

    Awake, dear heart, awake! You have slept well.
    Awake!
MIRANDA   The strangeness of your story put
    Heaviness in me.
PROSPERO   Shake it off. Come on;
    We'll visit Caliban, my slave, who never
    Yields us kind answer.
MIRANDA   It is a villain, sir,
    I do not love to look on.
PROSPERO   But, as it is,
    We cannot miss him. He does make our fire,
    Fetch in our wood, and serves in offices
    That profit us. What, ho! Slave! Caliban!
    You earth, you, speak!
CALIBAN (*within*)   There's wood enough within.
PROSPERO
    Come forth, I say! There's other business for you.
    Come, you tortoise! When?

            Enter ARIEL *like a water-nymph*

    Fine apparition! My quaint Ariel,
    Hark in your ear.
ARIEL   My lord, it shall be done.   *Exit*
PROSPERO
    You poisonous slave, got by the devil himself
    Upon your wicked dam, come forth!

Enter CALIBAN

CALIBAN
As wicked dew as ever my mother brushed
With raven's feather from unwholesome fen
Drop on you both. A south-west blow on you
And blister you all over.
PROSPERO
For this, be sure, tonight you shall have cramps,
Side-stitches that shall pen your breath up. Hedge-
hogs
Shall, for that vast of night that they may work,
All exercise on you. You shall be pinched
As thick as honey-comb, each pinch more stinging
Than bees that made them.
CALIBAN   I must eat my dinner.
This island's mine, by Sycorax my mother,
Which you take from me. When you came first,
You stroke me, and made much of me, would give
me
Water with berries in it, and teach me how
To name the bigger light, and how the less,
That burn by day and night. And then I loved you,
And showed you all the qualities of the isle,
The fresh springs, brine-pits, barren place and
fertile.
Cursèd be I that did so! All the charms
Of Sycorax—toads, beetles, bats light on you!
For I am all the subjects that you have,
Who first was my own king; and here you sty me
In this hard rock, while you do keep from me
The rest of the island.
PROSPERO   You most lying slave,
Whom stripes may move, not kindness! I have used
you,

Filth as you are, with human care, and lodged you
In my own cell, till you did seek to violate
The honour of my child.

CALIBAN

O ho, O ho! Would it had been done!
You did prevent me. I had peopled else
This isle with Calibans.

MIRANDA   Abhorrèd slave,
Which any print of goodness will not take,
Being capable of all ill! I pitied you,
Took pains to make you speak, taught you each
    hour
One thing or other. When you did not, savage,
Know your own meaning, but would gabble like
A thing most brutish, I endowed your purposes
With words that made them known. But your vile
    race,
Though you did learn, had that in it which good
    natures
Could not abide to be with. Therefore were you
Deservedly confined into this rock, who had
Deserved more than a prison.

CALIBAN

You taught me language, and my profit on it
Is, I know how to curse. The red plague rid you
For teaching me your language!

PROSPERO   Hag seed, hence!
Fetch us in fuel—and be quick, you're best,
To answer other business. Shrug you, malice?
If you neglect, or do unwillingly
What I command, I'll rack you with old cramps,
Fill all your bones with aches and make you roar,
That beasts shall tremble at your din.

CALIBAN   No, pray you!
(aside) I must obey. His art is of such power,

It would control my dam's god Setebos,
And make a vassal of him.

PROSPERO   So, slave. Hence!   *Exit Caliban*

Enter FERDINAND; *and* ARIEL, *invisible,*
playing and singing

ARIEL   *Song*
  Come unto these yellow sands,
   And then take hands.
  Curtsied when you have and kissed,
   The wild waves whist.
  Foot it featly here and there;
  And, sweet sprites, the burden bear.
   Hark, hark!
 (*Burden, dispersedly*) Bow-wow!
   The watch-dogs bark.
 (*Burden, dispersedly*) Bow-wow!
   Hark, hark! I hear
  The strain of strutting chanticleer
   Cry cock-a-diddle-dow!

FERDINAND
 Where should this music be? In the air or the earth?
 It sounds no more; and sure it waits upon
 Some god of the island. Sitting on a bank,
 Weeping again the King my father's wreck,
 This music crept by me upon the waters,
 Allaying both their fury and my passion
 With its sweet air. Thence I have followed it,
 Or it has drawn me, rather. But it is gone.
 No, it begins again.

ARIEL   *Song*
  Full fathom five your father lies,
   Of his bones are coral made;
  Those are pearls that were his eyes;

     Nothing of him that does fade,
    But does suffer a sea-change
    Into something rich and strange.
    Sea-nymphs hourly ring his knell:
(*Burden*) Ding-dong.
    Hark! Now I hear them—Ding-dong bell.

FERDINAND
  The ditty does remember my drowned father.
  This is no mortal business, nor any sound
  That the earth owns. I hear it now above me.

PROSPERO
  The fringèd curtains of your eye advance,
  And say what you see yonder.

MIRANDA   What? A spirit?
  Lord, how it looks about! Believe me, sir,
  It carries a brave form. But it is a spirit.

PROSPERO
  No, wench. It eats and sleeps and has such senses
  As we have, such. This gallant whom you see
  Was in the wreck; and, though he's somewhat stained
  With grief, that's beauty's canker, you might call
    him
  A goodly person. He has lost his fellows,
  And strays about to find them.

MIRANDA   I might call him
  A thing divine, for nothing natural
  I ever saw so noble.

PROSPERO (*aside*)   It goes on, I see,
  As my soul prompts it.—Spirit, fine spirit, I'll free
    you
  Within two days for this!

FERDINAND   Most sure, the goddess
  On whom these airs attend! Grant that my prayer
  May know if you remain upon this island,
  And that you will some good instruction give

How I may bear me here. My prime request,
Which I do last pronounce, is—O you wonder!—
If you are maid or no?

MIRANDA   No wonder, sir,
But certainly a maid.

FERDINAND   My language? Heavens!
I am the best of them that speak this speech,
Were I but where it is spoken.

PROSPERO   How? The best?
What were you if the King of Naples heard you?

FERDINAND
A single thing, as I am now, that wonders
To hear you speak of Naples. He does hear me,
And that he does, I weep. Myself am Naples,
Who with my eyes, never since at ebb, beheld
The King my father wrecked.

MIRANDA   Alas, for mercy!

FERDINAND
Yes, faith, and all his lords, the Duke of Milan
And his brave son being two.

PROSPERO (aside)   The Duke of Milan
And his still braver daughter could control you,
If now it were fit to do it. At the first sight
They have changed eyes. Delicate Ariel,
I'll set you free for this.—A word, good sir.
I fear you have done yourself some wrong. A word!

MIRANDA
Why speaks my father so ungently? This
Is the third man that ever I saw; the first
That ever I sighed for. Pity move my father
To be inclined my way.

FERDINAND   O, if a virgin,
And your affection not gone forth, I'll make you
The Queen of Naples.

PROSPERO   Soft, sir! One word more.
  (aside) They are both in either's powers. But this
    swift business
  I must uneasy make, lest too light winning
  Makes the prize light.—One word more! I charge
    you
  That you attend me. You do here usurp
  The name you own not, and have put yourself
  Upon this island as a spy, to win it
  From me, the lord of it.
FERDINAND   No, as I am a man!
MIRANDA
  There's nothing ill can dwell in such a temple.
  If the ill spirit has so fair a house,
  Good things will strive to dwell with it.
PROSPERO   Follow me.
  (to Miranda) Speak not you for him. He's a traitor.—
    Come!
  I'll manacle your neck and feet together.
  Sea-water shall you drink; your food shall be
  The fresh-brook mussels, withered roots, and husks
  Wherein the acorn cradled. Follow!
FERDINAND   No!
  I will resist such entertainment till
  My enemy has more power.

  He draws, and is charmed from moving

MIRANDA   O dear father,
  Make not too rash a trial of him, for
  He's noble, and not fearful.
PROSPERO   What, I say,
  My foot my tutor?—Put your sword up, traitor,

Who make a show, but dare not strike, your
   conscience
Is so possessed with guilt. Come from your ward!
For I can here disarm you with this stick,
And make your weapon drop.

MIRANDA   Beseech you, father!

PROSPERO

Hence! Hang not on my garments.

MIRANDA   Sir, have pity.

I'll be his surety.

PROSPERO   Silence! One word more
Shall make me chide you, if not hate you. What,
An advocate for an impostor? Hush!
You think there are no more such shapes as he,
Having seen but him and Caliban. Foolish wench!
To the most of men this is a Caliban,
And they to him are angels.

MIRANDA   My affections

Are then most humble. I have no ambition
To see a goodlier man.

PROSPERO   Come on, obey!
Your nerves are in their infancy again,
And have no vigour in them.

FERDINAND   So they are.

My spirits, as in a dream, are all bound up.
My father's loss, the weakness which I feel,
The wreck of all my friends, and this man's threats
To whom I am subdued, are but light to me,
Might I but through my prison once a day
Behold this maid. All corners else of the earth
Let liberty make use of. Space enough
Have I in such a prison.

PROSPERO (*aside*)   It works. (*to Ferdinand*) Come on.—
You have done well, fine Ariel! (*to Ferdinand*)
   Follow me. (*to Ariel*)
Hark what you else shall do me.

MIRANDA   Be of comfort.
  My father's of a better nature, sir,
  Than he appears by speech. This is unwonted
  Which now came from him.
PROSPERO *(to Ariel)*   You shall be as free
  As mountain winds; but then exactly do
  All points of my command.
ARIEL   To the syllable.
PROSPERO
  Come, follow! *(to Miranda)* Speak not for him.
                             Exeunt

Act II

SCENE I
Another part of the island.

Enter ALONSO, SEBASTIAN, ANTONIO, GONZALO,
ADRIAN, FRANCISCO, *and others*

GONZALO
  Beseech you, sir, be merry. You have cause—
  So have we all—of joy; for our escape
  Is much beyond our loss. Our hint of woe
  Is common. Every day, some sailor's wife,
  The masters of some merchant, and the merchant,
  Have just our theme of woe. But for the miracle,
  I mean our preservation, few in millions
  Can speak like us. Then wisely, good sir, weigh
  Our sorrow with our comfort.

ALONSO   Pray you, peace.

SEBASTIAN   *(aside to Antonio)* He receives comfort
like cold porridge.

ANTONIO   *(aside to Sebastian)* The visitor will not
give him over so.

SEBASTIAN   *(aside to Antonio)* Look, he's winding up
the watch of his wit. By and by it will strike.

GONZALO   Sir—

SEBASTIAN   One: tell.

GONZALO
When every grief is entertained, what's offered
Comes to the entertainer—

SEBASTIAN   A dollar.

GONZALO   Dolour comes to him indeed. You have
spoken truer than you purposed.

SEBASTIAN   You have taken it wiselier than I meant
you should.

GONZALO   *(to Alonso)* Therefore, my lord—

ANTONIO   Fie, what a spendthrift is he of his tongue!

ALONSO   I pray you, spare.

GONZALO   Well, I have done. But yet—

SEBASTIAN   He will be talking.

ANTONIO   Which, of he or Adrian, for a good wager,
first begins to crow?

SEBASTIAN   The old cock.

ANTONIO   The cockerel.

SEBASTIAN   Done. The wager?

ANTONIO   A laughter.

SEBASTIAN   A match.

ADRIAN   Though this island seems to be desert—

ANTONIO   Ha, ha, ha!

SEBASTIAN   So, you're paid.

ADRIAN   Uninhabitable, and almost inaccessible—

SEBASTIAN   Yet—

ADRIAN   Yet—

ANTONIO   He could not miss it.

ADRIAN   It must needs be of subtle, tender, and
delicate temperance.

ANTONIO   Temperance was a delicate wench.

SEBASTIAN   Ay, and a subtle, as he most learnedly
delivered.

ADRIAN   The air breathes upon us here most sweetly.

SEBASTIAN   As if it had lungs, and rotten ones.

ANTONIO   Or, as though perfumed by a fen.

GONZALO   Here is everything advantageous to life.

ANTONIO   True, save means to live.

SEBASTIAN   Of that there's none, or little.

GONZALO   How lush and lusty the grass looks! How
green!

ANTONIO   The ground, indeed, is tawny.

SEBASTIAN   With an eye of green in it.

ANTONIO   He misses not much.

SEBASTIAN   No. He does but mistake the truth totally.

GONZALO   But the rarity of it is—which is indeed
almost beyond credit—

SEBASTIAN   As many vouched rarities are.

GONZALO   That our garments being, as they were,
drenched in the sea hold, notwithstanding, their
freshness and glosses; being rather new-dyed than
stained with salt water.

ANTONIO   If but one of his pockets could speak, would
it not say he lies?

SEBASTIAN   Ay, or very falsely pocket up his report.

GONZALO   It seems our garments are now as fresh as
when we put them on first in Africa, at the
marriage of the King's fair daughter Claribel to the
King of Tunis.

SEBASTIAN   It was a sweet marriage, and we prosper
well in our return.

ADRIAN   Tunis was never graced before with such a
paragon to their queen.

GONZALO   Not since widow Dido's time.

ANTONIO Widow? A pox on that! How came that
widow in? Widow Dido!

SEBASTIAN What if he had said 'widower Aeneas' too?
Good Lord, how you take it!

ADRIAN 'Widow Dido', said you? You make me
study of that. She was of Carthage, not of Tunis.

GONZALO This Tunis, sir, was Carthage.

ADRIAN Carthage?

GONZALO I assure you, Carthage.

ANTONIO His word is more than the miraculous harp.

SEBASTIAN He has raised the wall, and houses too.

ANTONIO What impossible matter will he make easy
next?

SEBASTIAN I think he will carry this island home in
his pocket and give it his son for an apple.

ANTONIO And sowing the kernels of it in the sea,
bring forth more islands.

GONZALO Ay.

ANTONIO Why, in good time.

GONZALO (to Alonso) Sir, we were talking, that our
garments seem now as fresh as when we were at
Tunis at the marriage of your daughter, who is now
Queen.

ANTONIO And the rarest that ever came there.

SEBASTIAN Except, I beseech you, widow Dido.

ANTONIO O, widow Dido? Ay, widow Dido.

GONZALO Is not, sir, my doublet as fresh as the first
day I wore it? I mean, in a sort.

ANTONIO That 'sort' was well fished for.

GONZALO When I wore it at your daughter's
marriage.

ALONSO
You cram these words into my ears against
The stomach of my sense. Would I had never
Married my daughter there! For, coming thence,

My son is lost and, in my rate, she too,
Who is so far from Italy removed
I never again shall see her. O you my heir
Of Naples and of Milan, what strange fish
Has made his meal on you?

FRANCISCO   Sir, he may live.
I saw him beat the surges under him,
And ride upon their backs. He trod the water,
Whose enmity he flung aside, and breasted
The surge most swollen that met him. His bold head
Above the contentious waves he kept, and oared
Himself with his good arms in lusty stroke
To the shore, that o'er his wave-worn basis bowed,
As stooping to relieve him. I do not doubt
He came alive to land.

ALONSO   No, no, he's gone.

SEBASTIAN
Sir, you may thank yourself for this great loss,
That would not bless our Europe with your
    daughter,
But rather loose her to an African,
Where she, at least, is banished from your eye,
Who has cause to wet the grief of it.

ALONSO   Pray, peace.

SEBASTIAN
You were kneeled to and importuned otherwise
By all of us; and the fair soul herself
Weighed between loathness and obedience at
Which end of the beam should bow. We have lost
    your son,
I fear, for ever. Milan and Naples have
More widows in them of this business' making
Than we bring men to comfort them.
The fault's your own.

ALONSO   So is the dearest of the loss.

GONZALO
  My lord Sebastian,
  The truth you speak does lack some gentleness,
  And time to speak it in. You rub the sore,
  When you should bring the plaster.
SEBASTIAN   Very well.
ANTONIO   And most surgically.
GONZALO   (*to Alonso*)
  It is foul weather in us all, good sir,
  When you are cloudy.
SEBASTIAN   (*aside to Antonio*)
                        Foul weather?
ANTONIO   (*aside to Sebastian*)   Very foul.
GONZALO
  Had I plantation of this isle, my lord—
ANTONIO   (*aside to Sebastian*)
  He'd sow it with nettle-seed.
SEBASTIAN   (*aside to Antonio*) Or docks, or mallows.
GONZALO
  And were the king of it, what would I do?
SEBASTIAN   (*aside to Antonio*) Escape being drunk, for
  want of wine.
GONZALO
  In the commonwealth I would by contraries
  Execute all things. For no kind of traffic
  Would I admit, no name of magistrate.
  Letters should not be known. Riches, poverty,
  And use of service, none. Contract, succession,
  Boundaries of land, tilth, vineyard, none.
  No use of metal, corn, or wine, or oil.
  No occupation: all men idle, all,
  And women too, but innocent and pure.
  No sovereignty—
SEBASTIAN   (*aside to Antonio*) Yet he would be king of
  it.

ANTONIO   *(aside to Sebastian)* The latter end of his
  commonwealth forgets the beginning.
GONZALO
  All things in common nature should produce
  Without sweat or endeavour. Treason, felony,
  Sword, pike, knife, gun, or need of any engine
  Would I not have. But nature should bring forth
  Of its own kind all plenty, all abundance,
  To feed my innocent people.
SEBASTIAN   *(aside to Antonio)* No marrying among his
  subjects?
ANTONIO   *(aside to Sebastian)* None, man, all idle—
  whores and knaves.
GONZALO
  I would with such perfection govern, sir,
  To excel the Golden Age.
SEBASTIAN   'Save his majesty!
ANTONIO
  Long live Gonzalo!
GONZALO   And—do you mark me, sir?
ALONSO
  Pray, no more. You do talk nothing to me.
GONZALO   I do well believe your highness, and did it
  to minister occasion to these gentlemen, who are of
  such sensible and nimble lungs that they always
  use to laugh at nothing.
ANTONIO   It was you we laughed at.
GONZALO   Who, in this kind of merry fooling, am
  nothing to you; so you may continue, and laugh at
  nothing still.
ANTONIO   What a blow was there given!
SEBASTIAN   If it had not fallen flat-long.
GONZALO   You are gentlemen of brave mettle. You
  would lift the moon out of her sphere, if she would
  continue in it five weeks without changing.

Enter ARIEL, *playing solemn music*

SEBASTIAN   We would so, and then go a-bat-fowling.
ANTONIO   Nay, good my lord, be not angry.
GONZALO   No, I warrant you, I will not adventure my
discretion so weakly. Will you laugh me asleep, for
I am very heavy?
ANTONIO   Go sleep, and hear us.

All sleep except ALONSO, SEBASTIAN, *and* ANTONIO

ALONSO
What, all so soon asleep? I wish my eyes
Would, with themselves, shut up my thoughts. I
find
They are inclined to do so.
SEBASTIAN   Please you, sir,
Do not omit the heavy offer of it.
It seldom visits sorrow; when it does,
It is a comforter.
ANTONIO   We two, my lord,
Will guard your person while you take your rest,
And watch your safety.
ALONSO   Thank you. Wondrous heavy.
                                    Alonso sleeps. Exit Ariel
SEBASTIAN
What a strange drowsiness possesses them!
ANTONIO
It is the quality of the climate.
SEBASTIAN   Why
Does it not then that our eyelids sink? I find
Not myself disposed to sleep.
ANTONIO
Nor I. My spirits are nimble.
They fell together all, as by consent.

They dropped, as by a thunderstroke. What might,
Worthy Sebastian?—O, what might?—No more!
And yet I think I see it in your face,
What you should be. The occasion speaks you, and
My strong imagination sees a crown
Dropping upon your head.

SEBASTIAN   What, are you waking?

ANTONIO
Do you not hear me speak?

SEBASTIAN   I do, and surely
It is a sleepy language, and you speak
Out of your sleep. What is it you did say?
This is a strange repose, to be asleep
With eyes wide open; standing, speaking, moving,
And yet so fast asleep.

ANTONIO   Noble Sebastian,
You let your fortune sleep—die, rather; wink
While you are waking.

SEBASTIAN   You do snore distinctly.
There's meaning in your snores.

ANTONIO
I am more serious than my custom. You
Must be so too, if heed me; which to do
Trebles you over.

SEBASTIAN   Well, I am standing water.

ANTONIO
I'll teach you how to flow.

SEBASTIAN   Do so. To ebb
Hereditary sloth instructs me.

ANTONIO   O,
If you but knew how you the purpose cherish
While thus you mock it! How, in stripping it,
You more invest it! Ebbing men, indeed,
Most often do so near the bottom run
By their own fear, or sloth.

SEBASTIAN   Pray you, say on.
   The setting of your eye and cheek proclaim
   A matter from you; and a birth, indeed,
   Which pains you much to yield.
ANTONIO   Thus, sir:
   Although this lord of weak remembrance, this,
   Who shall be of as little memory
   When he is earthed, has here almost persuaded—
   For he's a spirit of persuasion, only
   Professes to persuade—the King his son's alive,
   'Tis as impossible that he's undrowned
   As he that sleeps here swims.
SEBASTIAN   I have no hope
   That he's undrowned.
ANTONIO   O, out of that no hope
   What great hope have you! No hope that way is
   Another way so high a hope that even
   Ambition cannot pierce a wink beyond,
   But doubt discovery there. Will you grant with me
   That Ferdinand is drowned?
SEBASTIAN   He's gone.
ANTONIO   Then, tell me,
   Who's the next heir of Naples?
SEBASTIAN   Claribel.
ANTONIO
   She that is Queen of Tunis; she that dwells
   Ten leagues beyond man's life. She that from Naples
   Can have no note, unless the sun were post—
   The Man in the Moon's too slow—till newborn
     chins
   Be rough and razorable. She that from whom
   We all were sea-swallowed, though some cast again
   And, by that destiny, to perform an act
   Whereof what's past is prologue, what to come,
   In yours and my discharge.

SEBASTIAN   What stuff is this?
  How say you?
  'Tis true my brother's daughter is Queen of Tunis,
  So is she heir of Naples, between which regions
  There is some space.
ANTONIO   A space whose every cubit
  Seems to cry out, 'How shall that Claribel
  Measure us back to Naples? Keep in Tunis,
  And let Sebastian wake.' Say this were death
  That now has seized them, why, they were no worse
  Than now they are. There are that can rule Naples
  As well as he that sleeps; lords that can prate
  As amply and unnecessarily
  As this Gonzalo. I myself could make
  A chough of as deep chat. O, that you bore
  The mind that I do! What a sleep were this
  For your advancement! Do you understand me?
SEBASTIAN
  I think I do.
ANTONIO   And how does your content
  Tender your own good fortune?
SEBASTIAN   I remember
  You did supplant your brother Prospero.
ANTONIO   True.
  And look how well my garments sit upon me,
  Much better than before. My brother's servants
  Were then my fellows. Now they are my men.
SEBASTIAN
  But, for your conscience?
ANTONIO
  Ay, sir, where lies that? If it were a corn,
  It would put me to my slipper; but I feel not
  This deity in my bosom. Twenty consciences
  That stand between me and Milan, candied be they,
  And melt ere they molest. Here lies your brother,

No better than the earth he lies upon,
If he were that which now he's like—that's dead—
Whom I with this obedient steel, three inches of it,
Can lay to bed for ever. While you, doing thus,
To the perpetual wink for aye might put
This ancient morsel, this Sir Prudence, who
Should not upbraid our course. For all the rest,
They'll take suggestion as a cat laps milk.
They'll tell the clock to any business that
We say befits the hour.

SEBASTIAN   Your case, dear friend,
Shall be my precedent. As you got Milan,
I'll come by Naples. Draw your sword. One stroke
Shall free you from the tribute which you pay,
And I the King shall love you.

ANTONIO   Draw together.
And when I rear my hand, do you the like,
To aim it on Gonzalo.

SEBASTIAN   O, but one word.

Enter ARIEL *with music and song*

ARIEL
My master through his art foresees the danger
That you, his friend, are in, and sends me forth—
For else his project dies—to keep them living.

Sings in GONZALO'S *ear*

While you here do snoring lie,
Open-eyed conspiracy
    His time does take.
If of life you keep a care,
Shake off slumber, and beware.
    Awake, awake!

ANTONIO
　Then let us both be sudden.
GONZALO　　*(awakes)*　　　　　　　Now, good angels
　Preserve the King!

　　　　　　　　The others awake

ALONSO
　Why, how now?—Ho, awake!—Why are you drawn?
　Wherefore this ghastly looking?
GONZALO　　　　　　　　　　　　What's the matter?
SEBASTIAN
　While we stood here securing your repose,
　Even now, we heard a hollow burst of bellowing
　Like bulls, or rather lions. Did it not awake you?
　It struck my ear most terribly.
ALONSO　　　　　　　　　　　　　I heard nothing.
ANTONIO
　O, it was a din to fright a monster's ear,
　To make an earthquake! Sure it was the roar
　Of a whole herd of lions.
ALONSO　　　　　　　　　　Heard you this, Gonzalo?
GONZALO
　Upon my honour, sir, I heard a humming,
　And that a strange one too, which did awake me.
　I shaked you, sir, and cried. As my eyes opened,
　I saw their weapons drawn. There was a noise,
　That's verily. 'Tis best we stand upon our guard,
　Or that we quit this place. Let's draw our weapons.
ALONSO
　Lead off this ground and let's make further search
　For my poor son.
GONZALO　　　　　Heavens keep him from these beasts!
　For he is sure in the island.
ALONSO　　　　　　　　Lead away.

ARIEL
Prospero my lord shall know what I have done.
So, King, go safely on to seek your son.   *Exeunt*

SCENE II
Another part of the island.

Enter CALIBAN *with a burden of wood. Thunder.*

CALIBAN
All the infections that the sun sucks up
From bogs, fens, flats, on Prospero fall; make him
By inches a disease! His spirits hear me,
And yet I needs must curse. But they'll nor pinch,
Fright me with hedgehogs, pitch me in the mire,
Nor lead me, like a firebrand, in the dark
Out of my way, unless he bids them. But
For every trifle are they set upon me;
Sometimes like apes, that mow and chatter at me,
And after bite me; then like hedgehogs, which
Lie tumbling in my barefoot way, and mount
Their pricks at my footfall. Sometimes am I
All wound with adders, who with cloven tongues
Do hiss me into madness.

Enter TRINCULO

                                        Lo, now, lo!
Here comes a spirit of his, and to torment me
For bringing wood in slowly. I'll fall flat.
Perchance he will not mind me.
TRINCULO   Here's neither bush nor shrub, to bear off
any weather at all, and another storm brewing. I
hear it sing in the wind. Yon same black cloud, yon

huge one, looks like a foul barrel that would shed
its liquor. If it should thunder as it did before, I
know not where to hide my head. Yon same cloud
cannot choose but fall by pailfuls. What have we
here? A man or a fish? Dead or alive? A fish! He
smells like a fish; a very ancient and fishlike smell;
a kind of not-of-the-newest salt-hake. A strange
fish! Were I in England now, as once I was, and had
but this fish painted, not a holiday fool there but
would give a piece of silver. There would this
monster make a man. Any strange beast there
makes a man. When they will not give a penny to
relieve a lame beggar, they will lay out ten to see a
dead Indian. Legged like a man! And his fins like
arms! Warm, on my faith! I do now let loose my
opinion, hold it no longer. This is no fish, but an
islander that has lately suffered by a thunderbolt.

Thunder

Alas, the storm is come again. My best way is to
creep under his cloak. There is no shelter
hereabout. Misery acquaints a man with strange
bed-fellows. I will here shroud till the dregs of the
storm are past.

Enter STEPHANO, *singing, a bottle in his hand.*

STEPHANO
  I shall no more to sea, to sea,
   Here shall I die ashore.
This is a very scurvy tune to sing at a man's funeral.
Well, here's my comfort.

He drinks and then sings

The master, the swabber, the boatswain, and I,
  The gunner and his mate,
Loved Mall, Meg, and Marian, and Margery,
  But none of us cared for Kate.
  For she had a tongue with a tang,
  Would cry to a sailor, 'Go hang!'
She loved not the savour of tar nor of pitch,
Yet a tailor might scratch her where'ere she did
  itch.
  Then to sea boys, and let her go hang!
This is a scurvy tune too. But here's my comfort.

He drinks

CALIBAN   Do not torment me! O!

STEPHANO   What's the matter? Have we devils here?
  Do you put tricks upon us with savages and men of
  the Indies, ha? I have not escaped drowning to be
  afraid now of your four legs. For it has been said,
  'As proper a man as ever went on four legs cannot
  make him give ground'; and it shall be said so
  again, while Stephano breathes at his nostrils.

CALIBAN   The spirit torments me! O!

STEPHANO   This is some monster of the isle with four
  legs, and who has got, as I take it, an ague. Where
  the devil should he learn our language? I will give
  him some relief, if it is but for that. If I can recover
  him, and keep him tame, and get to Naples with
  him, he's a present for any emperor that ever trod
  on calves' leather.

CALIBAN   Do not torment me, pray. I'll bring my
  wood home faster.

STEPHANO   He's in his fit now, and does not talk after
  the wisest. He shall taste of my bottle. If he has
  never drunk wine before, it will go near to remove
  his fit. If I can recover him, and keep him tame, I

will not take too much for him. He shall pay for
him that has him, and that soundly.

CALIBAN You do me yet but little hurt. You will soon.
I know it by your trembling. Now Prosper works
upon you.

STEPHANO Come on your ways. Open your mouth.
Here is that which will give language to you, cat.
Open your mouth. This will shake your shaking, I
can tell you, and that soundly. (*He gives Caliban
wine*) You cannot tell who's your friend. Open your
chaps again.

TRINCULO I should know that voice. It should be—
but he is drowned, and these are devils. O, defend
me!

STEPHANO Four legs and two voices—a most delicate
monster. His forward voice now is to speak well of
his friend. His backward voice is to utter foul
speeches and to detract. If all the wine in my bottle
will recover him, I will help his ague. Come!
(*Caliban drinks*) Amen! I will pour some in your
other mouth.

TRINCULO Stephano!

STEPHANO Does your other mouth call me? Mercy,
mercy! This is a devil, and no monster. I will leave
him; I have no long spoon.

TRINCULO Stephano! If you are Stephano, touch me
and speak to me; for I am Trinculo—be not afraid—
your good friend Trinculo.

STEPHANO If you are Trinculo, come forth. I'll pull
you by the lesser legs. If any are Trinculo's legs,
these are they. You are very Trinculo indeed! How
came you to be the seat of this mooncalf? Can he
vent Trinculos?

TRINCULO I took him to be killed with a
thunderstroke. But are you not drowned, Stephano?
I hope now you are not drowned. Is the storm

overblown? I hid me under the dead mooncalf's
cloak for fear of the storm. And are you living,
Stephano? O Stephano, two Neapolitans escaped?

STEPHANO   Pray, do not turn me about. My stomach
is not constant.

CALIBAN   *(aside)*
These are fine things, if they are not sprites.
That's a brave god, and bears celestial liquor.
I will kneel to him.

STEPHANO   How did you escape? How came you
hither? Swear by this bottle how you came hither. I
escaped upon a butt of sack, which the sailors
heaved overboard, by this bottle, which I made of
the bark of a tree, and my own hands, since I was
cast ashore.

CALIBAN   I'll swear upon that bottle to be your true
subject, for the liquor is not earthly.

STEPHANO   Here! Swear, then, how you escaped.

TRINCULO   Swam ashore, man, like a duck. I can
swim like a duck, I'll be sworn.

STEPHANO   Here, kiss the book. *(He gives him wine)*
Though you can swim like a duck, you are made
like a goose.

TRINCULO   O Stephano, got any more of this?

STEPHANO   The whole butt, man. My cellar is in a
rock by the seaside, where my wine is hid. How
now, mooncalf? How does your ague?

CALIBAN   Have you not dropped from heaven?

STEPHANO   Out of the moon, I do assure you. I was
the Man in the Moon when time was.

CALIBAN   I have seen you in her, and I do adore you.
My mistress showed me you, and your dog, and
your bush.

STEPHANO   Come, swear to that. Kiss the book. I will
furnish it soon with new contents. Swear! (CALIBAN
drinks)

TRINCULO   By this good light, this is a very shallow
  monster! I afraid of him? A very weak monster! The
  Man in the Moon? A most poor credulous
  monster!—Well drawn, monster, in good faith!
CALIBAN   I'll show you every fertile inch of the
  island, and I will kiss your foot. I pray you, be my
  god.
TRINCULO   By this light, a most perfidious and
  drunken monster! When his god's asleep, he'll rob
  his bottle.
CALIBAN   I'll kiss your foot. I'll swear myself your
  subject.
STEPHANO   Come on then. Down, and swear!
TRINCULO   I shall laugh myself to death at this puppy-
  headed monster. A most scurvy monster! I could
  find in my heart to beat him—
STEPHANO   Come, kiss.
TRINCULO   But that the poor monster's in drink. An
  abominable monster!
CALIBAN
  I'll show you the best springs. I'll pluck you berries.
  I'll fish for you, and get you wood enough.
  A plague upon the tyrant that I serve!
  I'll bear him no more sticks, but follow you,
  You wondrous man.
TRINCULO   A most ridiculous monster, to make a
  wonder of a poor drunkard!
CALIBAN
  I pray you, let me bring you where apples grow;
  And I with my long nails will dig you pig-nuts,
  Show you a jay's nest, and instruct you how
  To snare the nimble marmoset. I'll bring you
  To clustering filberts, and sometimes I'll get you
  Young mussels from the rock. Will you go with me?
STEPHANO   I pray now, lead the way without any
  more talking.—Trinculo, the King and all our

company else being drowned, we will inherit here.
Here, bear my bottle. Fellow Trinculo, we'll fill
him by and by again.

CALIBAN *sings drunkenly*

CALIBAN   Farewell, master! Farewell, farewell!
TRINCULO   A howling monster! A drunken monster!
CALIBAN
    No more dams I'll make for fish,
      Nor fetch in firing
    At requiring,
    Nor scrape trenchering, nor wash dish.
      Ban, Ban, Ca-Caliban
      Has a new master—get a new man!
Freedom, high-day! High-day, freedom! Freedom,
high-day, freedom!
STEPHANO   O brave monster! Lead the way.   *Exeunt*

Act III

SCENE I
Before PROSPERO'S cell.

Enter FERDINAND, *bearing a log*

FERDINAND
    There are some sports are painful, and their labour
    Delight in them sets off. Some kinds of baseness
    Are nobly undergone, and most poor matters
    Point to rich ends. This my mean task

Would be as heavy to me as odious, but
The mistress whom I serve quickens what's dead,
And makes my labours pleasures. O, she is
Ten times more gentle than her father's crabbed,
And he's composed of harshness. I must remove
Some thousands of these logs and pile them up,
Upon a sore injunction. My sweet mistress
Weeps when she sees me work, and says such
     baseness
Had never like executor. I forget;
But these sweet thoughts do even refresh my
     labours,
Most busy, lest when I do it.

Enter MIRANDA, *and* PROSPERO *at a distance, unseen*

MIRANDA   Alas, now pray you
  Work not so hard. I would the lightning had
  Burnt up those logs that you are enjoined to pile!
  Pray, set it down and rest you. When this burns,
  It will weep for having wearied you. My father
  Is hard at study. Pray now, rest yourself.
  He's safe for these three hours.
FERDINAND   O most dear mistress,
  The sun will set before I shall discharge
  What I must strive to do
MIRANDA   If you'll sit down,
  I'll bear your logs the while. Pray, give me that.
  I'll carry it to the pile.
FERDINAND   No, precious creature.
  I had rather crack my sinews, break my back,
  Than you should such dishonour undergo,
  While I sit lazy by.
MIRANDA   It would become me
  As well as it does you; and I should do it

With much more ease; for my good will is to it,
And yours it is against.

PROSPERO (aside)   Poor worm, you are infected.
This visitation shows it.

MIRANDA   You look wearily.

FERDINAND
No, noble mistress, it is fresh morning with me
When you are by at night. I do beseech you,
Chiefly that I might set it in my prayers,
What is your name?

MIRANDA   Miranda. O my father,
I have broken your behest to say so!

FERDINAND   Admired Miranda!
Indeed, the top of admiration, worth
What is dearest to the world. Full many a lady
I have eyed with best regard, and many a time
The harmony of their tongues has into bondage
Brought my too diligent ear. For several virtues
Have I liked several women; never any
With so full soul but some defect in her
Did quarrel with the noblest grace she owned,
And put it to defeat. But you, O you,
So perfect and so peerless, are created
Of every creature's best.

MIRANDA   I do not know
One of my sex; no woman's face remember,
Save, from my glass, my own. Nor have I seen
More that I may call men than you, good friend,
And my dear father. How features are abroad
I am skill-less of; but, by my chastity,
The jewel in my dower, I would not wish
Any companion in the world but you.
Nor can imagination form a shape,
Besides yourself, to like of. But I prattle
Something too wildly, and my father's precepts
I therein do forget.

FERDINAND   I am, in my condition,
  A prince, Miranda; I do think, a king—
  I would not so—and would no more endure
  This wooden slavery than to suffer
  The flesh-fly blow my mouth. Hear my soul speak.
  The very instant that I saw you did
  My heart fly to your service, there resides
  To make me slave to it; and for your sake
  Am I this patient log-man.
MIRANDA   Do you love me?
FERDINAND
  O heaven, O earth, bear witness to this sound,
  And crown what I profess with kind event,
  If I speak true! If hollowly, invert
  What best is boded me to mischief! I,
  Beyond all limit of what else in the world,
  Do love, prize, honour you.
MIRANDA   I am a fool
  To weep at what I am glad of.
PROSPERO   *(aside)*   Fair encounter
  Of two most rare affections. Heavens rain grace
  On that which breeds between them.
FERDINAND   Wherefore weep you?
MIRANDA
  At my unworthiness, that dares not offer
  What I desire to give, and much less take
  What I shall die to want. But this is trifling;
  And all the more it seeks to hide itself,
  The bigger bulk it shows. Hence, bashful cunning!
  And prompt me, plain and holy innocence.
  I am your wife, if you will marry me.
  If not, I'll die your maid. To be your fellow
  You may deny me, but I'll be your servant
  Whether you will or no.
FERDINAND   My mistress, dearest,
  And I thus humble ever.

MIRANDA   My husband, then?
FERDINAND
  Ay, with a heart as willing
  As bondage ever of freedom. Here's my hand.
MIRANDA
  And mine, with my heart in it; and now farewell
  Till half an hour hence.
FERDINAND   A thousand, thousand!
  Exeunt Ferdinand and Miranda in different directions.
PROSPERO
  So glad of this as they I cannot be,
  Who are surprised with all, but my rejoicing
  At nothing can be more. I'll to my book,
  For yet ere suppertime must I perform
  Much business appertaining.   *Exit*

SCENE II
Another part of the island.

Enter CALIBAN, STEPHANO, *and* TRINCULO

STEPHANO   Tell not me! When the butt is out we will
  drink water; not a drop before. Therefore, bear up
  and board them. Servant monster, drink to me.
TRINCULO   Servant monster? The folly of this island!
  They say there are but five upon this isle. We are
  three of them. If the other two be brained like us,
  the state totters.
STEPHANO   Drink, servant monster, when I bid you.
  Your eyes are almost set in your head.
TRINCULO   Where should they be set else? He were a
  brave monster indeed if they were set in his tail.
STEPHANO   My man-monster has drowned his tongue
  in sack. For my part, the sea cannot drown me. I
  swam, ere I could recover the shore, five and thirty

leagues off and on. By this light, you shall be my
lieutenant, monster, or my bearer.

TRINCULO   Your lieutenant, if you like; he's no
bearer.

STEPHANO   We'll not run, Monsieur Monster.

TRINCULO   Nor walk either; but you'll lie like dogs,
and yet say nothing either.

STEPHANO   Mooncalf, speak once in your life, if you
are a good mooncalf.

CALIBAN
How does your honour? Let me lick your shoe.
I'll not serve him: he is not valiant.

TRINCULO   You lie, most ignorant monster! I am a
body to jostle a constable. Why, you debauched
fish, you, was there ever a man a coward that has
drunk so much sack as I today? Will you tell a
monstrous lie, being but half a fish and half a
monster?

CALIBAN   Lo, how he mocks me! Will you let him,
my lord?

TRINCULO   'Lord' says he? That a monster should be
such a natural!

CALIBAN   Lo, lo, again! Bite him to death, I beg.

STEPHANO   Trinculo, keep a good tongue in your head.
If you prove a mutineer—the next tree! The poor
monster's my subject, and he shall not suffer
indignity.

CALIBAN   I thank my noble lord. Will you be pleased
to hearken once again to the suit I made to you?

STEPHANO   Sure, will I. Kneel, and repeat it. I will
stand, and so shall Trinculo.

Enter ARIEL, *invisible*

CALIBAN   As I told you before, I am subject to a tyrant,
a sorcerer, that by his cunning has cheated me of
the island.

ARIEL   You lie.

CALIBAN   (*to Trinculo*)
>   You lie, you jesting monkey, you.
>   I would my valiant master would destroy you!
>   I do not lie.

STEPHANO   Trinculo, if you trouble him any more in
   his tale, by this hand, I will supplant some of your
   teeth.

TRINCULO   Why, I said nothing.

STEPHANO   Mum, then, and no more. Proceed!

CALIBAN
>   I say, by sorcery he got this isle;
>   From mc he got it. If your greatness will
>   Revenge it on him—for I know you dare,
>   But this one thing dares not—

STEPHANO   That's most certain.

CALIBAN
>   You shall be lord of it, and I'll serve you.

STEPHANO   How now shall this be compassed? Can
   you bring me to the party?

CALIBAN
>   Yes, yes, my lord, I'll yield him you asleep,
>   Where you may knock a nail into his head.

ARIEL   You lie, you can not.

CALIBAN
>   What a pied ninny is this! You scurvy fool!
>   I do beseech your greatness give him blows,
>   And take his bottle from him. When that's gone,
>   He shall drink naught but brine, for I'll not show
>   him
>   Where the quick freshets are.

STEPHANO   Trinculo, run into no further danger.
   Interrupt the monster one word further and, by this
   hand, I'll turn my mercy out of doors, and make a
   stockfish of you.

TRINCULO   Why, what did I? I did nothing. I'll go
   farther off.

STEPHANO   Did you not say he lied?
ARIEL   You lie.
STEPHANO   Do I so? Take you that!

He strikes TRINCULO

As you like this, give me the lie another time.
TRINCULO   I did not give the lie. Out of your wits,
and hearing too? A pox on your bottle! This can
sack and drinking do. A murrain on your monster,
and the devil take your fingers!
CALIBAN   Ha, ha, ha!
STEPHANO   Now forward with your tale.—Pray, stand
further off.
CALIBAN

Beat him enough. After a little time,
I'll beat him too.
STEPHANO   Stand farther.—Come, proceed.
CALIBAN

Why, as I told you, 'tis a custom with him
In the afternoon to sleep. There you may brain him,
Having first seized his books; or with a log
Batter his skull, or paunch him with a stake,
Or cut his windpipe with your knife. Remember
First to possess his books, for without them
He's but a sot, as I am, and has not
One spirit to command. They all do hate him
As rootedly as I. Burn but his books.
He has brave utensils, for so he calls them,
Which, when he has a house, he will deck with.
And that most deeply to consider is
The beauty of his daughter. He himself
Calls her a nonpareil. I never saw a woman
But only Sycorax my dam and her;
But she as far surpasses Sycorax
As greatest does least.

STEPHANO   Is it so brave a lass?

CALIBAN

   Ay, lord. She will become your bed, I warrant,

   And bring you forth brave brood.

STEPHANO   Monster, I will kill this man. His

   daughter and I will be King and Queen—save our

   graces!—and Trinculo and yourself shall be

   viceroys. Do you like the plot, Trinculo?

TRINCULO   Excellent.

STEPHANO   Give me your hand. I am sorry I beat you;

   but while you live, keep a good tongue in your head.

CALIBAN

   Within this half hour will he be asleep.

   Will you destroy him then?

STEPHANO   Ay, on my honour.

ARIEL   This will I tell my master.

CALIBAN

   You make me merry. I am full of pleasure.

   Let us be jocund! Will you troll the catch

   You taught me but while-ere?

STEPHANO   At your request, monster, I will do

   reason, any reason. Come on, Trinculo, let us sing.

Sings

> *Flout 'em and scout 'em,*
> *And scout 'em and flout 'em!*
> *Thought is free.*

CALIBAN   That's not the tune.

ARIEL *plays the tune on a drum and pipe.*

STEPHANO   What is this same?

TRINCULO   This is the tune of our catch, played by

   the picture of Nobody.

STEPHANO   If you are a man, show yourself in your
  likeness. If you are a devil, take it as you like.

TRINCULO   O, forgive me my sins!

STEPHANO   He that dies pays all debts. I defy you.
  Mercy upon us!

CALIBAN   Are you afraid?

STEPHANO   No, monster, not I.

CALIBAN

  Be not afraid; the isle is full of noises,
  Sounds, and sweet airs, that give delight and hurt
    not.
  Sometimes a thousand twangling instruments
  Will hum about my ears; and sometimes voices
  That, if I then had waked after long sleep,
  Will make me sleep again. And then, in dreaming,
  The clouds I thought would open, and show riches
  Ready to drop upon me, that when I waked
  I cried to dream again.

STEPHANO   This will prove a brave kingdom to me,
  where I shall have my music for nothing.

CALIBAN   When Prospero is destroyed.

STEPHANO   That shall be by and by. I remember the
  story.

TRINCULO   The sound is going away. Let's follow it,
  and after do our work.

STEPHANO   Lead, monster; we'll follow. I would I
  could see this drummer. He lays it on.

TRINCULO   Will you come?—I'll follow, Stephano.

                                              Exeunt

SCENE III
Another part of the island.

Enter ALONSO, SEBASTIAN, ANTONIO, GONZALO, ADRIAN,
        FRANCISCO, *and others*

GONZALO
  By our lady, I can go no further, sir.
  My old bones ache. Here's a maze trod indeed,
  Through forthrights and meanders! By your patience,
  I needs must rest me.
ALONSO
                    Old lord, I cannot blame you,
  Who am myself attacked with weariness
  To the dulling of my spirits. Sit down and rest.
  Even here I will put off my hope, and keep it
  No longer for my flatterer. He is drowned
  Whom thus we stray to find, and the sea mocks
  Our frustrate search on land. Well, let him go.
ANTONIO   *(aside to Sebastian)*
  I am right glad that he's so out of hope.
  Do not, for one repulse, forgo the purpose
  That you resolve to effect.
SEBASTIAN   *(aside to Antonio)*
                                    The next advantage
  Will we take thoroughly.
ANTONIO   Let it be tonight;
  For, now they are oppressed with travel, they
  Will not, and cannot, use such vigilance
  As when they are fresh.
SEBASTIAN   *(aside to Antonio)*
                              I say tonight. No more.

  Solemn and strange music; and PROSPERO *on the
    top, invisible. Enter several strange shapes,
  bringing in a banquet; and dance about it with
  gentle actions of salutations; and, inviting the
        King, etc., to eat, they depart*

ALONSO
  What harmony is this? My good friends, hark!

GONZALO   Marvellous sweet music!

ALONSO
  Give us kind keepers, heavens! What were these?

SEBASTIAN
  A living drollery. Now I will believe
  That there are unicorns; that in Arabia
  There is one tree, the phoenix' throne, one phoenix
  At this hour reigning there.

ANTONIO   I'll believe both;
  And what docs else want credit, come to me
  And I'll be sworn 'tis true. Travellers never did lie,
  Though fools at home condemn them.

GONZALO   If in Naples
  I should report this now, would they believe me?
  If I should say I saw such islanders?—
  For certain, these are people of the island—
  Who, though they are of monstrous shape, yet
    note,
  Their manners are more gentle, kind, than of
  Our human generation you shall find
  Many, nay, almost any.

PROSPERO   *(aside)*   Honest lord,
  You have said well, for some of you there present
  Are worse than devils.

ALONSO   I cannot too much muse
  Such shapes, such gesture, and such sound,
    expressing,
  Although they want the use of tongue, a kind
  Of excellent dumb discourse.

PROSPERO   *(aside)*   Praise in departing.

FRANCISCO
  They vanished strangely.

SEBASTIAN   No matter, since
  They have left their viands behind, for we have
    stomachs.
  Will it please you taste of what is here?

ALONSO   Not I.
GONZALO
   Faith, sir, you need not fear. When we were boys,
   Who would believe that there were mountaineers
   Dewlapped like bulls, whose throats had hanging at
     them
   Wallets of flesh? Or that there were such men
   Whose heads stood in their breasts? Which now we
     find
   Each putter-out of five for one will bring us
   Good warrant of.
ALONSO   I will stand to and feed,
   Although my last—no matter, since I feel
   The best is past. Brother, my lord the Duke,
   Stand to, and do as we.

    Thunder and lightning. Enter ARIEL, *like a harpy,*
   claps his wings upon the table, and, with a quaint
        device, the banquet vanishes.

ARIEL
   You are three men of sin, whom destiny—
   That has to instrument this lower world
   And what is in it—the never-surfeited sea
   Has caused to belch up you, and on this island
   Where man does not inhabit, you among men
   Being most unfit to live. I have made you mad;
   And even with suchlike valour men hang and drown
   Their proper selves.

  ALONSO, SEBASTIAN, *and the others draw their swords*

                You fools! I and my fellows
   Are ministers of Fate. The elements,
   Of whom your swords are tempered, may as well

Wound the loud winds, or with bemocked-at stabs
Kill the ever closing waters, as diminish
One feather in my plume. My fellow ministers
Are like invulnerable. If you could hurt,
Your swords are now too massy for your strengths,
And will not be uplifted. But remember—
For that's my business to you—that you three
From Milan did supplant good Prospero,
Exposed unto the sea, which has requit it,
Him and his innocent child. For which foul deed
The powers, delaying, not forgetting, have
Incensed the seas and shores, yea, all the creatures
Against your peace. You of your son, Alonso,
They have bereft; and do pronounce by me
Lingering perdition—worse than any death
Can be at once—shall step by step attend
You and your ways. Whose wraths to guard you
    from,
Which here, in this most desolate isle, else falls
Upon your heads, is nothing but heart's sorrow,
And a clear life ensuing.

*He vanishes in thunder. Then, to soft music,
enter the shapes again, and dance with mocks
and mows, carrying out the table.*

PROSPERO
Bravely the figure of this harpy have you
Performed, my Ariel: a grace it had, devouring.
Of my instruction have you nothing abated
In what you had to say. So, with good life
And observation strange, my meaner ministers
Their several kinds have done. My high charms
    work,
And these, my enemies, are all knit up

In their distractions. They now are in my power;
And in these fits I leave them while I visit
Young Ferdinand, whom they suppose is drowned,
And his and my loved darling. *Exit*

GONZALO

In the name of something holy, sir, why stand you
In this strange stare?

ALONSO

O, it is monstrous, monstrous!
I thought the billows spoke, and told me of it;
The winds did sing it to me; and the thunder,
That deep and dreadful organ-pipe, pronounced
The name of Prospero: it did bass my trespass.
Therefore my son in the ooze is bedded, and
I'll seek him deeper than ever plummet sounded,
And with him there lie mudded. *Exit*

SEBASTIAN But one fiend at a time,
I'll fight their legions over.

ANTONIO I'll be your second.
Exeunt Antonio and Sebastian

GONZALO

All three of them are desperate. Their great guilt,
Like poison given to work a great time after,
Now begins to bite the spirits. I do beseech you,
That are of suppler joints, follow them swiftly,
And hinder them from what this craziness
May now provoke them to.

ADRIAN Follow, I pray you.
Exeunt

Act IV

SCENE I
Before PROSPERO'S cell.

Enter PROSPERO, FERDINAND, *and* MIRANDA

PROSPERO

If I have too austerely punished you,
Your compensation makes amends, for I
Have given you here a third of my own life,
Or that for which I live; who once again
I tender to your hand. All your vexations
Were but my trials of your love, and you
Have strangely stood the test. Here, before heaven,
I ratify this my rich gift. O Ferdinand,
Do not smile at me that I boast hereof,
For you shall find she will outstrip all praise,
And make it halt behind her.

FERDINAND   I do believe it
Against an oracle.

PROSPERO

Then, as my gift, and your own acquisition
Worthily purchased, take my daughter; but
If you do break her virgin-knot before
All sanctimonious ceremonies may
With full and holy rite be ministered,
No sweet aspersion shall the heavens let fall
To make this contract grow. But barren hate,
Sour-eyed disdain and discord shall bestrew
The union of your bed with weeds so loathly

That you shall hate it both. Therefore take heed,
As Hymen's lamps shall light you.

FERDINAND   As I hope
For quiet days, fair issue, and long life,
With such love as it is now, the murkiest den,
The most opportune place, the strongest suggestion
Our worser genius can, shall never melt
My honour into lust, to take away
The edge of that day's celebration
When I shall think that Phoebus' steeds are
    foundered
Or Night kept chained below.

PROSPERO   Fairly spoken.
Sit then and talk with her: she is your own.
What, Ariel! My industrious servant, Ariel!

Enter ARIEL

ARIEL
What would my potent master? Here I am.

PROSPERO
You and your meaner fellows your last service
Did worthily perform, and I must use you
In such another trick. Go bring the rabble,
Over whom I give you power, to this place.
Incite them to quick motion, for I must
Bestow upon the eyes of this young couple
Some vanity of my art. It is my promise,
And they expect it from me.

ARIEL   Immediately?

PROSPERO
Ay, with a twink.

ARIEL
    Before you can say, 'Come' and 'Go',
    And breathe twice, and cry, 'So, So',

Each one, tripping on his toe,
Will be here with mop and mow.
Do you love me, master? No?

PROSPERO
Dearly, my delicate Ariel. Do not approach
Till you do hear me call.

ARIEL   Well, I conceive.   *Exit*

PROSPERO
Look you be true. Do not give dalliance
Too much the rein. The strongest oaths are straw
To the fire in the blood. Be more abstemious,
Or else, good night your vow.

FERDINAND   I warrant you, sir,
The white cold virgin snow upon my heart
Abates the ardour of my liver.

PROSPERO   Well.
Now come, my Ariel! Bring a corollary,
Rather than want a spirit. Appear, and pertly.
No tongue! All eyes! Be silent.

Soft music. Enter IRIS

IRIS
Ceres, most bounteous lady, your rich leas
Of wheat, rye, barley, vetches, oats, and pease;
Your turfy mountains, where live nibbling sheep,
And flat meads thatched with forage them to
     keep;
Your banks with undercut and frillèd brims,
Which spongy April at behest betrims,
To make cold nymphs chaste crowns; and your
     broom-groves,
Whose shadow the dismissèd bachelor loves,
Being lass-lorn: your poll-clipt vineyard,
And your sea-marge, sterile and rocky-hard,

Where you yourself do air—the queen of the sky,
Whose watery arch and messenger am I,
Bids you leave these, and with her sovereign grace,
Here on this grass-plot, in this very place,
To come and sport. Her peacocks fly amain.

JUNO *descends*

Approach, rich Ceres, her to entertain.

Enter CERES

CERES
Hail, many-coloured messenger, that ne'er
Do disobey the wife of Jupiter;
Who, with your saffron wings, upon my flowers
Diffuse the honey-drops, refreshing showers;
And with each end of your blue bow do crown
My bosky acres and my unshrubbed down,
Rich scarf to my proud earth. Why has your queen
Summoned me hither to this short-grassed green?
IRIS
A contract of true love to celebrate,
And some donation freely to estate
On the blest lovers.
                            Tell me, heavenly bow,
CERES
If Venus or her son, as you do know,
Does now attend the queen? Since they did plot
The means that husky Dis my daughter got,
Her and her blind boy's scandalled company
I have forsworn.
IRIS   Of her society
Be not afraid. I met her deity

Cutting the clouds towards Paphos, and her son
Dove-drawn with her. Here thought they to have
    done
Some wanton charm upon this man and maid,
Whose vows are, that no bed-right shall be paid
Till Hymen's torch be lighted: but in vain.
Mars's hot minion is returned again;
Her waspish-headed son has broken his arrows,
Swears he will shoot no more, but play with
    sparrows,
And be a boy right out.
CERES   Highest queen of state,
Great Juno comes; I know her by her gait.
JUNO
How does my bounteous sister? Go with me
To bless this twain, that they may prosperous be,
And honoured in their issue.

                    They sing

JUNO

    Honour, riches, marriage-blessing,
    Long continuance, and increasing,
    Hourly joys be still upon you!
    Juno sings her blessings on you.
CERES

    Earth's increase, harvest plenty,
    Barns and garners never empty,
    Vines with clustering bunches growing,
    Plants with goodly burden bowing;
    Spring come to you at the farthest
    In the very end of harvest.
    Scarcity and want shall shun you,
    Ceres' blessing so is on you.

FERDINAND
    This is a most majestic vision, and
    Harmonious charmingly. May I be bold
    To think these spirits?
PROSPERO   Spirits, which by my art
    I have from their confines called to enact
    My present fancies.
FERDINAND   Let me live here ever!
    So rare a wondered father and a wise
    Makes this place Paradise.

JUNO *and* CERES *whisper, and send* IRIS *on employment.*

PROSPERO   Sweet, now, silence!
    Juno and Ceres whisper seriously.
    There's something else to do. Hush and be mute,
    Or else our spell is marred.
IRIS
    You nymphs, called Naiads, of the winding brooks,
    With your sedged crowns and ever-harmless looks,
    Leave your crisp channels, and on this green land
    Answer your summons; Juno does command.
    Come temperate nymphs, and help to celebrate
    A contract of true love. Be not too late.

Enter certain Nymphs

    You sunburned sicklemen, of August weary,
    Come hither from the furrow, and be merry.
    Make holiday; your rye-straw hats put on,
    And these fresh nymphs encounter every one
    In country footing.

Enter Reapers, *properly habited. They join with
the* Nymphs *in a graceful dance, towards the end
whereof,* PROSPERO *starts suddenly and speaks; after*

which, to a strange, hollow, and confused noise,
they heavily vanish.

PROSPERO   *(aside)*
  I had forgotten that foul conspiracy
  Of the beast Caliban and his confederates
  Against my life. The minute of their plot
  Is almost come.—Well done! Avoid! No more!—
FERDINAND
  This is strange. Your father's in some passion
  That works him strongly.
MIRANDA   Never till this day
  Saw I him touched with anger so distempered.
PROSPERO
  You do look, my son, in a movèd sort,
  As if you were dismayed. Be cheerful, sir.
  Our revels now are ended. These our actors,
  As I foretold you, were all spirits, and
  Are melted into air, into thin air;
  And, like the baseless fabric of this vision,
  The cloud-capped towers, the gorgeous palaces,
  The solemn temples, the great globe itself,
  Yea, all that it inherits, shall dissolve,
  And, like this insubstantial pageant faded,
  Leave not a rack behind. We are such stuff
  As dreams are made on; and our little life
  Is rounded with a sleep. Sir, I am vext.
  Bear with my weakness; my old brain is troubled.
  Be not disturbed with my infirmity.
  If you be pleased, retire into my cell
  And there repose. A turn or two I'll walk,
  To still my beating mind.
FERDINAND *and* MIRANDA   We wish your peace.
                       Exeunt Ferdinand and Miranda

PROSPERO
  Come with a thought. I thank you, Ariel. Come!

Enter ARIEL

ARIEL
  Your thoughts I cleave to. What's your pleasure?
PROSPERO   Spirit,
  We must prepare to meet with Caliban.
ARIEL
  Ay, my commander. When I presented Ceres,
  I thought to have told you of it, but I feared
  Lest I might anger you.
PROSPERO
  Say again, where did you leave these varlets?
ARIEL
  I told you, sir, they were red-hot with drinking.
  So full of valour that they smote the air
  For breathing in their faces, beat the ground
  For kissing of their feet; yet always bending
  Towards their project. Then I beat my drum,
  At which, like unbacked colts, they pricked their
      ears,
  Advanced their eyelids, lifted up their noses
  As they smelt music. So I charmed their ears
  That calf-like they my lowing followed, through
  Toothed briars, sharp furzes, pricking gorse, and
      thorns,
  Which entered their frail shins. At last I left them
  In the filthy mantled pool beyond your cell,
  There dancing up to the chins, that the foul lake
  O'erstunk their feet.
PROSPERO   This was well done, my bird!
  Your shape invisible retain you still.
  The trumpery in my house, go bring it hither,
  Decoy to catch these thieves.
ARIEL   I go, I go!
                                            Exit

PROSPERO
　A devil, a born devil, on whose nature
　Nurture can never stick; on whom my pains,
　Humanely taken, all, all lost, quite lost.
　And as with age his body uglier grows,
　So his mind cankers. I will plague them all
　Even to roaring.

　　　Enter ARIEL, *loaded with glistering apparel, etc.*

　　　　Come, hang them on this line.

　　Enter CALIBAN, STEPHANO, *and* TRINCULO, *all wet*

CALIBAN
　Pray you, tread softly, that the blind mole may not
　Hear a foot fall. We now are near his cell.
STEPHANO　Monster, your fairy, which you say is a
　harmless fairy, has done little better than played
　the Jack with us.
TRINCULO　Monster, I do smell all horse-piss, at which
　my nose is in great indignation.
STEPHANO　So is mine. Do you hear, monster? If I
　should take a displeasure against you, look you—
TRINCULO　You were but a lost monster.
CALIBAN
　Good my lord, give me your favour still.
　Be patient, for the prize I'll bring you to
　Shall hoodwink this mischance. Therefore, speak
　　softly.
　All is hushed as midnight yet.
TRINCULO　Ay, but to lose our bottles in the pool—
STEPHANO　There is not only disgrace and dishonour
　in that, monster, but an infinite loss.
TRINCULO　That's more to me than my wetting. Yet
　this is your harmless fairy, monster.

STEPHANO   I will fetch off my bottle, though I am
over ears for my labour.

CALIBAN
Pray you, my king, be quiet. See you here,
This is the mouth of the cell. No noise, and enter.
Do that good mischief which may make this island
Your own for ever, and I, your Caliban,
For aye your foot-licker.

STEPHANO   Give me your hand. I do begin to have
bloody thoughts.

TRINCULO   O King Stephano! O peer! O worthy
Stephano, look what a wardrobe here is for you!

CALIBAN
Let it alone, you fool! It is but trash.

TRINCULO   O ho, monster! We know what belongs to
a frippery. O King Stephano!

STEPHANO   Put off that gown, Trinculo. By this hand,
I'll have that gown!

TRINCULO   Your grace shall have it.

CALIBAN
The dropsy drown this fool! What do you mean
To dote thus on such luggage? Let it alone,
And do the murder first. If he awakes,
From toe to crown he'll fill our skins with pinches,
Make us strange stuff.

STEPHANO   Be you quiet, monster. Mistress line, is
not this my jerkin? Now is the jerkin under the
line. Now, jerkin, you are like to lose your hair and
prove a bald jerkin.

TRINCULO   Do, do! We steal by line and level, if it
likes your grace.

STEPHANO   I thank you for that jest. Here's a garment
for it. Wit shall not go unrewarded while I am king
of this country. 'Steal by line and level' is an
excellent pass of wit. There's another garment for
it.

TRINCULO   Monster, come put some lime upon your
  fingers, and away with the rest.
CALIBAN
  I will have none of it. We shall lose our time,
  And all be turned to barnacles, or to apes
  With foreheads villainous low.
STEPHANO   Monster, lay to your fingers. Help to bear
  this away where my hogshead of wine is, or I'll
  turn you out of my kingdom. Go to, carry this!
TRINCULO   And this.
STEPHANO   Ay, and this.

  A noise of hunters heard. Enter divers Spirits *in
  shape of dogs and hounds, hunting them about,*
  PROSPERO *and* ARIEL *setting them on.*

PROSPERO   Hey, Mountain, hey!
ARIEL   Silver! There it goes, Silver!
PROSPERO   Fury, Fury! There, Tyrant, there! Hark,
  hark!

  CALIBAN, STEPHANO, *and* TRINCULO *are driven out.*

  Go, charge my goblins that they grind their joints
  With dry convulsions, shorten up their sinews
  With agèd cramps, and more pinch-spotted make
      them
  Than leopard or mountain-cat.
ARIEL   Hark, they roar!
PROSPERO
  Let them be hunted soundly. At this hour
  Lie at my mercy all my enemies.
  Shortly shall all my labours end, and you
  Shall have the air at freedom. For a little
  Follow, and do me service.   *Exeunt*

Act V

SCENE I
Before PROSPERO'S cell.

Enter PROSPERO, *in his magic robes, and* ARIEL

PROSPERO
　Now does my project gather to a head.
　My charms crack not, my spirits obey, and time
　Goes upright with its carriage. How's the day?
ARIEL
　On the sixth hour, at which time, my lord,
　You said our work should cease.
PROSPERO　　　　　　　　　　　　　　I did say so,
　When first I raised the tempest. Say, my spirit,
　How fare the King and his followers?
ARIEL　　　　　　　　　　　　　　Confined together
　In the same fashion as you gave in charge,
　Just as you left them—all prisoners, sir,
　In the line-grove which weather-fends your cell.
　They cannot budge till your release. The King,
　His brother, and yours, abide all three distracted,
　And the remainder mourning over them,
　Brimful of sorrow and dismay. But chiefly,
　Him that you termed, sir, the good old lord
　　　Gonzalo,
　His tears run down his beard like winter's drops
　From eaves of reeds. Your charm so strongly works
　　　them
　That if you now beheld them your affections
　Would become tender.
PROSPERO　　　　　　　　　　　Do you think so, spirit?

664

ARIEL
  Mine would, sir, were I human.
PROSPERO   And mine shall.
  Have you, which are but air, a touch, a feeling
  Of their afflictions, and shall not myself,
  One of their kind, that relish all as sharply,
  Passion as they, be kindlier moved than you are?
  Though with their high wrongs I am struck to the
    quick,
  Yet with my nobler reason against my fury
  Do I take part. The rarer action is
  In virtue than in vengeance. They being penitent,
  The sole drift of my purpose does extend
  Not a frown further. Go release them, Ariel.
  My charms I'll break, their senses I'll restore,
  And they shall be themselves.
ARIEL   I'll fetch them, sir.
                                        Exit

PROSPERO
  You elves of hills, brooks, standing lakes, and
    groves,
  And you that on the sands with printless foot
  Do chase the ebbing Neptune, and do fly him
  When he comes back; you demi-puppets that
  By moonshine do the green, sour ringlets make,
  Whereof the ewe not bites; and you whose pastime
  Is to make midnight mushrooms, that rejoice
  To hear the solemn curfew, by whose aid—
  Weak masters though you are—I have bedimmed
  The noontide sun, called forth the mutinous winds,
  Between the green sea and the azured vault
  Set roaring war; to the dread rattling thunder
  Have I given fire, and rifted Jove's stout oak
  With his own bolt; the strong-based promontory
  Have I made shake, and by the spurs plucked up
  The pine and cedar; graves at my command

Have wakened their sleepers, opened, let them forth
By my so potent art. But this rough magic
I here abjure, and when I have required
Some heavenly music—which even now I do—
To work my end upon their senses that
This airy charm is for, I'll break my staff,
Bury it certain fathoms in the earth,
And deeper than did ever plummet sound
I'll drown my book.

Solemn music
Here enters ARIEL *before; then* ALONSO *with a*
frantic gesture, attended by GONZALO: SEBASTIAN
and ANTONIO *in like manner, attended by*
ADRIAN *and* FRANCISCO. *They all enter the circle*
which PROSPERO *had made, and there stand*
charmed; which PROSPERO *observing, speaks.*

A solemn air, and the best comforter
To an unsettled fancy, cure your brains,
Now useless, boiled within your skull. There stand,
For you are spell-stopped.
Holy Gonzalo, honourable man,
My eyes, even sociable to the show of yours,
Let fall fellowly drops. The charm dissolves apace,
And as the morning steals upon the night,
Melting the darkness, so their rising senses
Begin to chase the ignorant fumes that mantle
Their clearer reason. O good Gonzalo,
My true preserver, and a loyal sir
To him you follow, I will pay your graces
Home both in word and deed. Most cruelly
Did you, Alonso, use me and my daughter.
Your brother was a furtherer in the act.
You are pinched for it now, Sebastian. Flesh and
   blood,

You, brother mine, that entertained ambition,
Expelled remorse and nature, who, with
    Sebastian—
Whose inward pinches therefore are most strong—
Would here have killed your king, I do forgive you,
Unnatural though you are. Their understanding
Begins to swell, and the approaching tide
Will shortly fill the reasonable shore
That now lies foul and muddy. Not one of them
That yet looks on me, or would know me. Ariel,
Fetch me the hat and rapier in my cell.
I will unclothe me, and myself present
As I was sometime Milan. Quickly, spirit!
You shall ere long be free.

> ARIEL *sings and helps to attire him.*

ARIEL

> *Where the bee sucks, there suck I,*
> *In a cowslip's bell I lie;*
> *There I couch when owls do cry.*
> *On the bat's back I do fly*
> *After summer merrily.*
> *Merrily, merrily shall I live now,*
> *Under the blossom that hangs on the bough.*

PROSPERO

Why, that's my dainty Ariel! I shall miss you,
But yet you shall have freedom—so, so, so.
To the King's ship, invisible as you are!
There shall you find the mariners asleep
Under the hatches. The Master and the Boatswain
Being awake, enforce them to this place,
Immediately, I pray.

ARIEL

I drink the air before me, and return
Ere ever your pulse twice beats.   *Exit*

GONZALO

  All torment, trouble, wonder, and amazement
  Inhabit here. Some heavenly power guide us
  Out of this fearful country!

PROSPERO   Behold, sir King,

  The wronged Duke of Milan, Prospero.
  For more assurance that a living prince
  Does now speak to you, I embrace your body,
  And to you and your company I bid
  A hearty welcome.

ALONSO   Whether you are he or no,

  Or some enchanted trifle to abuse me,
  As late I have been, I not know. Your pulse
  Beats as of flesh and blood; and, since I saw you,
  The affliction of my mind amends, with which
  I fear a madness held me. This must crave—
  If this should be at all—a most strange story.
  Your dukedom I resign, and do entreat
  You pardon me my wrongs. But how should
    Prospero
  Be living, and be here?

PROSPERO   First, noble friend,

  Let me embrace your age, whose honour cannot
  Be measured or confined.

GONZALO   Whether this is

  Or is not, I'll not swear.

PROSPERO   You do yet taste

  Some subtleties of the isle, that will not let you
  Believe things certain. Welcome, my friends all!
  (aside to SEBASTIAN and ANTONIO)
  But you, my brace of lords, were I so minded,
  I here could pluck his highness' frown upon you,
  And justify you traitors. At this time
  I will tell no tales.

SEBASTIAN   (aside) The devil speaks in him.

PROSPERO   No.
  For you, most wicked sir, whom to call brother
  Would even infect my mouth, I do forgive
  Your rankest fault—all of them; and require
  My dukedom of you, which perforce, I know,
  You must restore.
ALONSO   If you are Prospero,
  Give us particulars of your preservation;
  How you have met us here, whom three hours since
  Were wrecked upon this shore; where I have lost—
  How sharp the point of this remembrance is!—
  My dear son Ferdinand.
PROSPERO   I am sad for it, sir.
ALONSO
  Irreparable is the loss, and patiènce
  Says it is past her cure.
PROSPERO   I rather think
  You have not sought her help, of whose soft grace
  For the like loss, I have her sovereign aid,
  And rest myself content.
ALONSO   You the like loss?
PROSPERO
  As great to me, as late, and supportable
  To make the dear loss, have I means much weaker
  Than you may call to comfort you, for I
  Have lost my daughter.
ALONSO   A daughter?
  O heavens, that they were living both in Naples,
  The King and Queen there! That they were, I wish
  Myself were mudded in that oozy bed
  Where my son lies. When did you lose your
    daughter?
PROSPERO
  In this last tempest. I perceive these lords
  At this encounter do so much wonder

That they devour their reason, and scarce think
Their eyes do offices of truth, their words
Are natural breath. But, howsoever you have
Been jostled from your senses, know for certain
That I am Prospero, and that very Duke
Who was thrust forth of Milan, who most strangely
Upon this shore, where you were wrecked, was
   landed
To be the lord of it. No more yet of this,
For it is a chronicle of day by day,
Not a relation for a breakfast, nor
Befitting this first meeting. Welcome, sir.
This cell's my court. Here have I few attendants,
And subjects none abroad. Pray you, look in.
My dukedom since you have given me again,
I will requite you with as good a thing,
At least bring forth a wonder to content you,
As much as me my dukedom.

Here PROSPERO *discovers* FERDINAND *and* MIRANDA,
playing at chess.

MIRANDA
  Sweet lord, you play me false.
FERDINAND   No, my dearest love,
  I would not for the world.
MIRANDA
  Yes, for a score of kingdoms you should wrangle,
  And I would call it fair play.
ALONSO   If this proves
  A vision of the island, one dear son
  Shall I twice lose.
SEBASTIAN   A most high miracle.
FERDINAND
  Though the seas threaten, they are merciful.
  I have cursed them without cause.

He comes forward, and kneels.

ALONSO   Now all the blessings
  Of a glad father compass you about!
  Arise, and say how you came here.
MIRANDA   O, wonder!
  How many goodly creatures are there here!
  How beauteous mankind is! O brave new world,
  That has such people in it!
PROSPERO   It is new to you.
ALONSO
  What is this maid with whom you were at play?
  Your eldest acquaintance cannot be three hours.
  Is she the goddess that has severed us,
  And brought us thus together?
FERDINAND   Sir, she is mortal;
  But by immortal Providence, she's mine.
  I chose her when I could not ask my father
  For his advice, nor thought I had one. She
  Is daughter to this famous Duke of Milan,
  Of whom so often I have heard renown,
  But never saw before; of whom I have
  Received a second life; and second father
  This lady makes him to me.
ALONSO   I am hers.
  But, O, how oddly will it sound that I
  Must ask my child forgiveness!
PROSPERO   There, sir, stop.
  Let us not burden our remembrances with
  A heaviness that's gone.
GONZALO   I have inly wept,
  Or should have spoken ere this. Look down, you
      gods,
  And on this couple drop a blessèd crown!
  For it is you that have chalked forth the way
  Which brought us hither.

ALONSO   I say amen, Gonzalo.
GONZALO

Was Milan thrust from Milan that his issue
Should become kings of Naples? O, rejoice
Beyond a common joy, and set it down
With gold on lasting pillars. In one voyage
Did Claribel her husband find at Tunis,
And Ferdinand her brother found a wife
Where he himself was lost; Prospero his dukedom
In a poor isle, and all of us ourselves
When no man was his own.
ALONSO   (to Ferdinand and Miranda)

                                    Give me your hands.
Let grief and sorrow still embrace his heart
That does not wish you joy.
GONZALO   Be it so! Amen.

Enter ARIEL, *with the* Master *and* Boatswain
amazedly following.

O look sir, look sir, here is more of us!
I prophesied, if a gallows were on land,
This fellow could not drown. Now, blasphemy,
That swear grace overboard, not an oath on shore?
Have you no mouth by land? What is the news?
BOATSWAIN

The best news is that we have safely found
Our King and company; the next, our ship—
Which, but three glasses since, we gave out split—
Is tight and ready, bravely rigged, as when
We first put out to sea.
ARIEL   (aside to Prospero) Sir, all this service
Have I done since I went.
PROSPERO   (aside to Ariel) My tricksy spirit!

ALONSO
    These are not natural events. They strengthen
    From strange to stranger. Say, how came you hither?
BOATSWAIN
    If I did think, sir, I were well awake,
    I'd strive to tell you. We were dead of sleep
    And—how we know not—all clapped under hatches;
    Where, but even now, with strange and several
      noises
    Of roaring, shrieking, howling, jingling chains,
    And more diversity of sounds, all horrible,
    We were awaked; straightway at liberty.
    Where we, in all our trim, freshly beheld
    Our royal, good, and gallant ship, our Master
    Capering to eye her. On a trice, so please you,
    Even in a dream, were we divided from them,
    And were brought moping hither.
ARIEL   *(aside to Prospero)*   Was it well done?
PROSPERO   *(aside to Ariel)*
    Bravely, my diligence. You shall be free.
ALONSO
    This is as strange a maze as ever men trod,
    And there is in this business more than nature
    Was ever conduct of. Some oracle
    Must rectify our knowledge.
PROSPERO   Sir, my lord,
    Do not infest your mind with beating on
    The strangeness of this business. At picked leisure—
    Which shall be shortly—single I'll resolve you,
    Which to you shall seem probable, of every
    These happened accidents. Till when, be cheerful,
    And think of each thing well. *(aside to Ariel)* Come
      hither, spirit.
    Set Caliban and his companion free.

Untie the spell.   *Exit Ariel*
                How fares my gracious sir?
There are yet missing of your company
Some few odd lads that you remember not.

Enter ARIEL, *driving in* CALIBAN, STEPHANO, *and*
    TRINCULO *in their stolen apparel.*

STEPHANO   Every man shift for all the rest, and let no
  man take care for himself, for all is but fortune.
  Coragio, bully-monster, coragio!
TRINCULO   If these are true spies which I wear in my
  head, here's a goodly sight!
CALIBAN
  O Setebos, these are brave spirits indeed!
  How fine my master is! I am afraid
  He will chastise me.
SEBASTIAN   Ha, ha!
  What things are these, my lord Antonio?
  Will money buy them?
ANTONIO   Very like. One of them
  Is a plain fish, and no doubt marketable.
PROSPERO
  Mark but the badges of these men, my lords,
  Then say if they are true. This misshapen knave,
  His mother was a witch, and one so strong
  That could control the moon, make flows and ebbs,
  And deal in her command without her power.
  These three have robbed me, and this demi-devil—
  For he's a bastard one—had plotted with them
  To take my life. Two of these fellows you
  Must know and own. This thing of darkness I
  Acknowledge mine.
CALIBAN   I shall be pinched to death.
ALONSO
  Is not this Stephano, my drunken butler?

SEBASTIAN

He is drunk now. Where had he wine?

ALONSO

And Trinculo is reeling ripe. Where should they
Find this grand liquor that has gilded them?
How came you in this pickle?

TRINCULO   I have been in such a pickle since I saw
you last that I fear me will never out of my bones.
I shall not fear fly-blowing.

SEBASTIAN   Why, how now, Stephano?

STEPHANO   O, touch me not! I am not Stephano, but
a cramp!

PROSPERO   You would be king of the isle, fellow?

STEPHANO   I should have been a sore one, then.

ALONSO

This is a strange thing as ever I looked on.

PROSPERO

He is as disproportioned in his manners
As in his shape.—Go, fellow, to my cell.
Take with you your companions. As you look
To have my pardon, trim it handsomely.

CALIBAN

Ay, that I will; and I'll be wise hereafter,
And seek for grace. What a thrice double ass
Was I to take this drunkard for a god,
And worship this dull fool!

PROSPERO   Go to. Away!

ALONSO

Hence, and bestow your luggage where you found it.

SEBASTIAN

Or stole it, rather.

                    Exeunt Caliban, Stephano, and Trinculo

PROSPERO

Sir, I invite your highness and your train
To my poor cell, where you shall take your rest
For this one night; which, part of it, I'll waste

With such discourse as, I not doubt, shall make it
Go quick away—the story of my life,
And the particular accidents gone by
Since I came to this isle. And in the morn,
I'll bring you to your ship, and so to Naples,
Where I have hope to see the nuptials
Of these our dear-belovèd solemnized;
And thence retire me to my Milan, where
Every third thought shall be my grave.

ALONSO   I long
To hear the story of your life, which must
Take the ear strangely.

PROSPERO   I'll deliver all,
And promise you calm seas, auspicious gales,
And sail so expeditious, that shall catch
Your royal fleet far off.—My Ariel, chick,
That is your charge. Then to the elements
Be free, and fare you well.—Please you, draw near.

Exeunt

EPILOGUE

Spoken by PROSPERO

Now my charms are all o'erthrown,
And what strength I have's my own,
Which is most faint. Now 'tis true
I must be here confined by you,
Or sent to Naples. Let me not,
Since I have my dukedom got
And pardoned the deceiver, dwell
In this bare island by your spell;
But release me from my bands
With the help of your good hands.

Gentle breath of yours my sails
Must fill, or else my project fails,
Which was to please. Now I want
Spirits to enforce, art to enchant;
And my ending is despair,
Unless I be relieved by prayer,
Which pierces so, that it assaults
Mercy itself, and frees all faults.
As you from crimes would pardoned be,
Let your indulgence set mc frce.   *Exit*

Mariner Typographers Inc.